Praise for *The Power and the Money*

"*The Power and the Money* invites readers to 'follow the money' on a fascinating journey through a century and a half of American history. Filled with larger-than-life personalities, startling vignettes, and brilliant insights, Tevi Troy's tour de force demonstrates that politics and business can make not only strange bed-fellows and marriages of convenience but also, occasionally, relationships built on mutual respect."

—Christopher Cox, former SEC Chair and author of
Woodrow Wilson: The Light Withdrawn

"For 150 years, ever since the United States became an industrial power, its elected presidents have alternately battled or begged assistance of moguls and entrepreneurs who have become unofficial collaborators in managing the economy. From Rockefeller and Morgan to Zuckerberg and Musk, Tevi Troy introduces a Hollywood-worthy cast of power players, all part of a historical rethink as ambitious as it is original."

—Richard Norton Smith, presidential historian and author of
many books, including *An Ordinary Man: The Surprising Life
and Historic Presidency of Gerald R. Ford*

"I had the pleasure of working with Tevi Troy and have seen firsthand his deep knowledge of the inner workings of government. In *The Power and the Money*, Tevi combines his expertise in government with his training as a historian—from the University of Texas, of course—to provide readers with a terrific glimpse into our nation's success. He shows how the relationship between presidents and CEOs has shaped and continues to shape our nation even today. Tevi does this all with fascinating stories and great insights. *The Power and the Money* is an impressive achievement, and a must read."

—Margaret Spellings, former Secretary of Education and
President, Bipartisan Policy Center

"Government. Business. Two independent entities? In his insightful book, Dr. Tevi Troy compellingly argues that these two spheres are not only interconnected but have also profoundly shaped the United States together. Those connections have steadily strengthened while also becoming increasingly intricate. If you seek to grasp the nuances of those dynamics and the pivotal figures who have molded them, *The Power and the Money* is an indispensable primer."

—Dr. Noam Wasserman, Dean, Yeshiva University's
Sy Syms School of Business and bestselling author of
The Founder's Dilemmas and *Life Is a Startup*

THE
POWER
AND THE
MONEY

THE POWER AND THE MONEY

THE EPIC CLASHES BETWEEN COMMANDERS IN CHIEF AND TITANS OF INDUSTRY

TEVI TROY

REGNERY
HISTORY

Regnery History books may be purchased in bulk at special discounts for sales promotion, corporate gifts, fund-raising, or educational purposes. Special editions can also be created to specifications. For details, contact the Special Sales Department, Regnery History, 307 West 36th Street, 11th Floor, New York, NY 10018 or info@skyhorsepublishing.com.

Regnery® is an imprint of Skyhorse Publishing, Inc.®, a Delaware corporation.

Visit our website at www.regnery.com.

Please follow our publisher Tony Lyons on Instagram @tonylyonsisuncertain.

10 9 8 7 6 5 4 3 2

Library of Congress Cataloging-in-Publication Data is available on file.

Cover design by John Caruso
Cover image courtesy of Lincoln Financial Foundation Collection

Print ISBN: 978-1-68451-540-0
eBook ISBN: 978-1-5107-8174-0

Printed in the United States of America

To Matt Robinson, terrific editor and true friend

"[T]he chief business of the American people is business."

—Calvin Coolidge

"No business which depends for existence on paying less than living wages to its workers has any right to continue in this country."

—Franklin D. Roosevelt

"My father always told me that all businessmen were sons of bitches, but I never believed it until now."

—John F. Kennedy

"Government's view of the economy could be summed up in a few short phrases: If it moves, tax it. If it keeps moving, regulate it. And if it stops moving, subsidize it."

—Ronald Reagan

CONTENTS

INTRODUCTION

P residents come and go. They serve four years, sometimes eight. But CEOs—Chief Executive Officers of large corporations—in contrast, can potentially reign for decades. Given their long tenures, they can interact with multiple presidents, necessitating models of engagement for coping with the most powerful person in the land. Those models have become increasingly important over the past century as America has shifted from a mostly laissez-faire free market economy to one in which government is increasingly enmeshed in corporate behavior and decisions. Today, government rules oversee what businesses they acquire; whom they can hire; how they run their workplace; how much they pay in taxes; what environmental regulations apply to them; what kind of subsidies they (or their rivals) get; and whether they can sell their products abroad—or at all. This list only scratches the surface. If a large company wants to survive and thrive, it must have a strategy for dealing with an increasingly powerful and interventionist federal government.

All these rules do not mean that corporations are hurting. Far from it. The 2022 aggregate sales for the Fortune 500 were $41 trillion, more than a third of the world's total GDP. In addition, the whole tangle of rules and regulations can benefit corporations, which can afford to pay for compliance costs for rules, that flummox small and upcoming businesses. The current regulatory regime means that corporations can make large profits while government gets to direct their behavior. For the rest of us, this partnership costs us money in the form of higher prices, and restricts our freedom of choice, in the form of limitations on behavior and a limited ability to form or patronize new and competing entities.

While the government entanglement with big business is profitable for corporations, it also brings challenges that carry definite risks. Increasing federal requirements mean that CEOs face a concomitant increase in the need to engage with Washington's cultural, financial, and political realities. A CEO or a corporation that alienates the Washington establishment can be subjected to a painful variety of regulatory impositions that can potentially pose existential threats to companies in the form of banned products or outlawed business practices.

CEOs need to make sure this does not happen to them or their shareholders. Given their dependence on, and vulnerability to Washington, CEOs have their corporations spend an estimated $3 billion annually lobbying Washington to shape regulations and legislation in ways that are more favorable to them.[1]

These lobbying efforts are necessary, but not necessarily determinative. An analysis by the consulting firm Baron Public Affairs found that companies with competing interests usually fight one another to a draw in terms of lobbying resources thrown at a particular problem. In this environment, the engagement of the CEO can be a tiebreaker. A CEO who has a good relationship with the president and political establishment can get the company a hearing that it might not get in other ways. A celebrity CEO can also get messages out via the media in ways that a more diffident CEO is unable or unwilling to do, as a message coming from a CEO will usually get more traction than standard communiques from corporate press shops.[2]

These messages can shape the political environment in which policymakers operate. Politicians, especially presidents, are subject to the whims of the voters. As a result, Democrats and Republicans come and go as dictated by a political calendar and shifting ideological winds. Corporations have longer time horizons, so they try benefiting from the party in power, yet work with the other side of the aisle for when the political pendulum swings back. This can be tricky. As Paul Weaver notes in *The Suicidal Corporation*, "Companies and trade associations never know who their allies and enemies will be in the future. That is why business likes to go along with those in power and hates to oppose them."[3]

Another important dynamic is that not all CEOs are equal. They have different skills, interests, and weaknesses. Richard Pepler at HBO is a believer in the

"permanent campaign," seeking out every opportunity to shape the public dialogue in ways that are helpful to his company, and to make sure the company is
well positioned with policymakers in the event of a crisis. Other CEOs, whose
names most of us will never know, prefer to focus on business operations and
profit and loss—making sure that the nuts and bolts of internal systems work and
that the company gets its product out in an efficient and timely way. Some CEOs,
like Apple's Tim Cook, get their start as operational managers but then realize the
necessity of engaging with Washington and, in Cook's case, realize that they are
quite good at it.[4]

Sometimes the gravity of the business or political challenges demand that
CEOs must go straight to the top in their lobbying efforts. That means, of course,
the president of the United States. In this, they bring with them some important
advantages. Unlike presidents, CEOs are not term limited, and a long-serving
CEO can therefore have relationships with many presidents. Lee Iacocca, for
example, knew ten different presidents in his career as a leader at two auto companies and in his retirement role of all-around post-CEO celebrity. Looking at
his relationships with multiple presidents can help guide today's leaders on which
strategies might work for engaging Washington.

At the same time, a look at the history of CEO-presidential engagement can
shed light on the seeming hostility between elected officials and corporations.
This examination can help put the current period of bipartisan hostility towards
corporations in context and judge whether we are living through an anomalous
period or a challenging reality that will continue into the future.

While it is impossible to answer questions about the future in a definitive way,
this examination of the past can help us learn where the current debates are coming from, and give us a sense of where things are likely to go. To do this, this book
examines the relationships between 18 CEOs and the presidents that each of them
interacted with. In doing so, it looks at friendships and enmities, successes and
failures, and how they originated and evolved. Although the universe of CEOs
who deal with presidents is enormous, the number of CEOs with consequential
interactions with more than one president is more finite. As such, this volume
looks at CEOs from industry-leading corporations who came to know multiple

presidents over their tenures. These 18 CEOs navigated their relationships during ten key periods in American political life. Across this century-and-a-half period, two things happened: the US economy expanded and advanced, from the industrial stocks that dominated the Dow Jones when it was first created, to the high-tech FAANG stocks that move much of the S&P 500 today. Along this march of progress, we saw the emergence of car manufacturing, news media, Hollywood, large banks, and the initial wave of tech companies that launched in the 1970s and 1980s. At the same time, the federal government grew, from a largely laissez-faire entity to the current behemoth that directs corporate behavior in a multitude of ways. Each industry, and each political period, contributed to the different strategies that CEOs deployed to work with presidents to the potential benefit of their companies.[5]

In this period, CEOs had to carefully forge relationships with presidents and key White House aides in order to protect and to promote their companies. John D. Rockefeller and Henry Ford brought economy and society-transforming products to the world. In the process, they built powerful empires, but also found themselves targeted by presidents who saw political opportunity in the CEOs' unpopularity. Henry Luce and Katharine Graham ran powerful media platforms, but they also saw that what they published could anger the presidents they covered. The Warner Brothers and Rupert Murdoch used their power to bolster presidents they liked, although, in Murdoch's case, he also went after presidents he did not like, and the presidents he targeted reciprocated in kind. Lee Iacocca and Lew Wasserman learned that relationships with presidents could help them in their efforts to shape policies beneficial to their companies. Jack Welch and Oprah Winfrey found that their own celebrity made them sought after by presidents. Jamie Dimon and J. P. Morgan may have been criticized for their important roles on Wall Street, but they also helped presidents rescue the economy in challenging times. Mark Zuckerberg and Tim Cook learned from watching others the importance of engaging in Washington, while Steve Jobs and Warren Buffett were able to remain outsiders, largely because they were less dependent on government support in building their companies. Finally, Elon Musk offers a cautionary tale of someone who grew enormously wealthy in part because of federal incentives and contracts, but found that alienating the powers that be could have deleterious effects on his business, and his reputation.

For current and future CEOs, this book can be a guide for how to engage with an increasingly powerful and involved federal government, especially in our era in which both Democrats and Republicans target corporations in their rhetoric and often in their policy prescriptions. For the rest of us, this is a cautionary tale of what happens when the federal government gets too big and too enmeshed in the activities of the producers and innovators in our economy: our costs go up while our freedom diminishes.

CHAPTER 1

THE BLANK SLATE

Presidents: Ulysses S. Grant, Rutherford B. Hayes, Chester A. Arthur, Benjamin Harrison, Grover Cleveland, William McKinley
CEOs: *John D. Rockefeller, JP Morgan*

Today, corporations are subject to a panoply of government impositions in the form of regulations and legislation that shape the way they do business. Everything from taxes to hiring to environmental impact to hours worked is regulated to some degree and plays into business strategies and consideration. This is far different than the situation as it stood in the late nineteenth century, when men like J. P. Morgan and John D. Rockefeller built their monopolies with little federal governmental input. In the era of laissez faire, they had a blank slate on which to carve out their empires. Throughout their ascents, they operated independently and unfettered until, late in life, they found that both popular opinion and a newly empowered president curtailed their freedom of action.

Morgan: From a Domineering Father to Dominating the Economy

Morgan was born first, to a comfortable family in 1837. His father was a driven and successful banker who made sure young J. P. was well educated. Morgan attended school in both New England and in Europe before entering the financial world. The younger Morgan was initially hindered by the impositions of his domineering father, but eventually Morgan emerged as his own person and went on to become an unquestioned titan of American finance.

In his youth, Morgan was sickly and moved around a lot. He went to nine schools in a 13-year period. Morgan was an excellent math student, prompting one of his professors at Germany's University of Göttingen to envision him as a future professor. Instead, he entered the banking world of his father, starting at a New York firm that invested in railroads. Then he worked at his father's company for 10 years before creating his own company in 1871, Drexel, Morgan & Co. Throughout, Morgan continued to analyze the railroads, which were chaotic at the time. Presidential candidate Abraham Lincoln saw this firsthand in 1860, when he visited New York to give his famous Cooper Union address. The four-day trip required four train transfers and two ferries. The system did not make sense. Only two entities had the capacity to bring about the needed changes: Wall Street and the federal government. Thanks to Morgan, Wall Street stepped into the breach first, furthering his lifelong quest to bring order to the railroads, to Wall Street, and to the American economic system.[1]

With his skill in investing, and the promise of the emerging American economic colossus, Morgan would get his chance to rein in the chaos. Morgan was blessed with immense powers of concentration. This meant he could focus on a problem very deeply, but it also led him to shut out others and exhaust himself. In his efforts to tame the economy, he was often an army of one.[2]

Morgan's first interactions with presidents were relatively innocuous. As a Republican and an admirer of Ulysses S. Grant, Morgan and some other financiers raised money to bankroll a house befitting the former president on East 66th Street. Grant would live there for most of his post-presidential life.[3]

Ten years later, Drexel Morgan moved into an impressive New York building of its own, a six-story structure at 23 Wall Street. It was a grand building, nicknamed "the Corner," and was the place from which Morgan exerted his influence. One of his most important deals was with Thomas Edison, inventor of the light bulb. It was a mutually beneficial relationship. Drexel Morgan provided the financing and Edison provided the six hundred light bulbs needed to illuminate the

Corner, which became one of the first buildings in the world that provided its lighting exclusively via electricity. In 1892, Drexel Morgan orchestrated the deal that created General Electric out of the smaller companies of Edison and his main competitor. GE would go on to become one of America's largest and most powerful companies for over a century. The Edison dealings were part of the many ways in which Drexel Morgan used its resources to shape the growing and developing American industrial economy.[4]

John D. Rockefeller and the Powering of America

John D. Rockefeller had a much less comfortable childhood. He was born in Richford, New York, in 1839, the son of a bigamist and con man. Without a dependable father to rely on, the industrious Rockefeller set out at sixteen to find employment to support himself and his family, embarking on one of the most legendary job searches in American history. Rockefeller scoured Cleveland, where the family had settled, looking for a suitable employer, receiving a trial run as a bookkeeper for a small merchant trading operation called Hewitt and Tuttle.

Rockefeller quickly proved himself hardworking and eagle-eyed—traits that made what was supposed to be a temporary job permanent. The ambitious Rockefeller then began an impressive rise in the organization, eventually gaining the confidence to go out on his own. He created a new partnership, Clark and Rockefeller. Rockefeller skipped service in the Civil War by recruiting paid substitutes, even though he was a Republican and an Abe Lincoln man, to whom he granted his first presidential vote. He then got involved in the early stages of the chaotic oil business, on the refining side of things. In 1870, he formed Standard Oil, which soon became one of the most famous and powerful corporations in history.

Oil changed America in almost every conceivable way, beginning in the nineteenth century and continuing into the 20th and 21st centuries. It first illuminated homes and businesses where it replaced whale oil, and then served as the foundation to power America and the world. It enabled the development of vast industries, safer study in the evenings, temperature-controlled environments, and every modern form of transportation. Yet the very development of an oil industry was an uncertain endeavor, as costly questions of discovery, refinement, distribution, and application have befuddled and bankrupted many a talented entrepreneur for more than a century.

As challenging as the oil industry was in its early years, Rockefeller benefited from starting his business at a time when there were few federal restrictions on monopolistic or rapacious business practices. Government was involved in granting contracts, and thus most efforts at political influence had more to do with seeking government largesse than staving off government restrictions. It was in this environment that Rockefeller built his monopoly, using a variety of sharp-elbowed and unsavory tactics to out-compete and force out rivals in an effort to eliminate what he referred to as "ruinous competition." These tactics included colluding with rail companies on special rebates unavailable to others; undercutting competitors and then buying them out; and using spies and agents to help advance his cause.[5]

Although Rockefeller's tactics were clearly unethical, there are a number of points in his defense. First, even his greatest detractor, the muckraking journalist Ida Tarbell, acknowledged that his efforts were not illegal at the time. Second, the oil industry was turbulent, with massive booms and busts. Given the anarchic state of the industry at the time, it might not have survived without his consolidating and standardizing efforts. His competitors suffered, but consumers benefited in the form of cheap and reliable kerosene, which he made standard, hence the name Standard Oil. The industry certainly would not have evolved the way it did without him, which brings us to the third defense: his innovative creation of a system of refineries and distribution that enabled the powering and illumination of America.

To tame the tumultuous ups and downs of the different stages of petroleum production, Rockefeller wanted total control of the oil industry. He sought a world in which "the Standard Oil Company will one day refine all the oil and make all the barrels." He did not quite get there, but he came close. By 1879, Standard Oil held 90% of U.S. refining capacity.[6] This reality set him on a course to collide with the American president.

Rockefeller: Attracting Presidential Attention

Rockefeller built his monopoly in the 1870s, during the presidency of the former Civil War general Ulysses S. Grant. In 1872, Rockefeller initiated the creation of the South Improvement Company, an intentionally vaguely named enterprise that sought to provide railroad price rebates to SIC members for shipping, while at the same time giving SIC members payments for oil shipped by companies not involved in the scheme. The scheme bordered on racketeering and never actually came to fruition. The very real threat of it, though, allowed Rockefeller to buy out understandably frightened competitors, which was likely its purpose to begin with. The Grant administration took notice. Grant issued a public statement on March 30, 1872, saying, "I have noticed the progress of monopolies, and have long been convinced that the National Government would have to interfere and protect the people against them."[7]

Grant had his own troubles, of course, most famously the railroad-pricing scandal called Credit Mobilier. Even though Credit Mobilier also involved questionable railroad pricing, it did not directly involve Rockefeller. Orville Babcock, Grant's private secretary, was indicted in the affair, which both damaged Grant's reputation and limited his ability to address the problem. The scandal did not lead to regulation of the monopolies, but it did help initiate civil service reforms that diminished the sway of the spoils system that governed federal appointments at the time. In addition, Grant was the most prominent of many voices that denounced the emergence of monopolies; over time, those voices would have significant implications for Rockefeller and Standard Oil.[8]

Grant's replacement, Rutherford B. Hayes, had little to do with Rockefeller. In 1877, when Standard Oil was battling the Pennsylvania Railroad over rates and rebates, Pennsylvania executive Tom Scott tried to cut costs on the backs of his workers. The resulting firings and wage cuts led to labor strife, which escalated into a violent and destructive multi-state strike. Multiple governors called in their militias, and President Hayes contributed federal troops. The unrest spread to Cleveland and there was some thought that Rockefeller could be targeted, but he managed to escape unharmed. Overall, it is notable that in the decade from 1870 to 1880, when Rockefeller did the most to establish his monopoly, Grant and

Hayes, the two presidents of that period, were essentially tangential to Rockefeller's considerations.[9]

Even though Hayes as president did not engage directly with Rockefeller, he did not think much of the man. In 1890, when former president Hayes sought to organize a conference on the plight of the nation's African-Americans, *Cleveland Leader* editor John C. Covert recommended that Hayes invite Rockefeller. Hayes recognized that Rockefeller would be helpful to the effort, but hated the man so much that he could not bear to issue the invite himself. He asked conference collaborator Albert K. Smiley to issue it for him instead. Rockefeller did not attend, raising the question of whether a direct (ex-)presidential invite would have made a difference.[10]

Like Hayes, James A. Garfield was from Ohio, but he was initially unfamiliar with Rockefeller. In fact, Garfield had never met him when he was running for president in 1880, even though they were both prominent Ohio Republicans. Garfield did not even know how to spell the tycoon's name. During the presidential campaign, Garfield wondered if Rockefeller could be a source for that which politicians need most, campaign contributions. He sought the advice of Cleveland businessman Amos Townsend, asking him "if Mr. Rockafeller [sic] would be willing to assist?" adding, "Do you know his state of feeling toward me? Is it such that I might safely invite him for consultation and talk freely with him about Indiana and ask his cooperation?"[11]

Townsend knew that Rockefeller had resources and that he did indeed contribute generously to Republican campaigns. But Townsend also recognized that interacting with Rockefeller brought with it political liabilities. Townsend replied to Garfield, "It would not be safe for him to visit you as it would be reported and cut like a knife in Pennsylvania. He is, however, all right and will do what he can." Rockefeller indeed did what he could and contributed to Garfield's campaign, albeit without a direct request from the candidate. Interestingly, Townsend also told Garfield "to keep your hand off paper," showing just how radioactive Rockefeller was beginning to be by that point.[12]

Townsend was right to be wary. In March of 1881, progressive journalist Henry Demarest Lloyd published the first major exposé of the bare-knuckle tactics

Rockefeller and Standard Oil used to build their monopoly. Demarest's "John D. Rockefeller's Standard Oil Trust" appeared in *The Atlantic*, a publication that was helping to create a national consciousness at a time when emerging technologies such as the telegraph, the railroads, and the power printing press were connecting the American public. Ironically, these technologies, as well as the illumination for nighttime reading of Demarest and his fellow writers' works, were powered by Rockefeller's distribution of kerosene. In later years, Rockefeller-provided gasoline would fuel the automobile, which did even more to forge a national sensibility. Rockefeller unwittingly enabled the unifying technologies that made him a national villain and target of politicians on both sides of the aisle.

Demarest's writings, especially his 1894 book, *Wealth Against Commonwealth*, would help make Rockefeller and Standard Oil villains beyond just the circle of competitors and others directly affected by his tactics. Even before Demarest, the savvy Townsend recognized Rockefeller's unpopularity before it would be discovered more broadly, when politicians like Garfield would not even have to ask if interacting with Rockefeller could bring with it vulnerabilities as well as benefits. Townsend's warning to Garfield shows an early instance of the promise and peril of presidential-CEO interactions, dating back almost 150 years.

Rockefeller's lack of personal engagement regarding his critics hindered him in understanding the depth of animosity toward him and prevented him from cultivating defenders. The decision to be so distant from the political process would jeopardize the very empire he was so focused on preserving. This failure contrasted strongly with J. P. Morgan, who would recognize the value of highlighting the strengths of business and the importance of personal involvement in shaping America's political destiny.

Morgan: Coming to the Aid of Presidents

While Rockefeller was at arm's length from presidents, J. P. Morgan was actively admired by them. In 1892, President Benjamin Harrison wrote a letter to businessman and Republican operative Cornelius Bliss, recommending Morgan for a slot on the Silver Conference regarding currency valuations. According to the letter, Harrison knew "Mr. Morgan's very high standing and that no one could better represent the financial world in New York." Harrison did something else as president that would have major implications for Morgan's business interests and for his relationship with future presidents. On July 2, 1890, Harrison signed the Sherman Antitrust Act into law, giving the federal government a powerful tool for controlling monopolistic behavior by businesses, if it chose to do so.[13]

Morgan was also different from Rockefeller in the ways in which he aided a number of American presidents. Grover Cleveland replaced Harrison in 1892, after having lost to him in 1888. Cleveland was a Democrat, but the kind of Democrat Morgan could appreciate. Morgan even voted for Cleveland in 1884, the only time he ever voted for a Democrat for president. Cleveland supported the gold standard, important to Morgan, and was friendly with Morgan's firm. Morgan's positive feeling for Cleveland—and for the U.S. economy as a whole— would come in handy in 1895 with the U.S. still reeling from the recession induced by the Panic of 1893. U.S. gold reserves had sunk to a dangerously low level—$9 million, with $10 million in obligations coming due. Morgan saw that the U.S. was in trouble. On February 7, 1895, he headed to Washington to confer with Cleveland.[14]

Cleveland was wary of the political fallout of meeting with Morgan. He initially refused to see the banker, sending intermediaries to tell him not to come. Morgan was undeterred, telling them, "I have come down to see the president. And I am going to stay here until I see him." Morgan stayed at a hotel near the White House and waited. The next morning, a messenger came to tell him that Cleveland would indeed meet with him at the White House. Facing a devastating financial collapse, Cleveland asked, "What suggestion have you to make, Mr. Morgan?"[15]

Morgan's solution was daring, creative, successful—and, ultimately, profitable. He proposed a syndicate of his creation that would provide the gold and receive government bonds in return. It did not have to go through Congress—and the political process—as it could be done via the president's emergency powers, something confirmed by Attorney General Richard Olney. The scheme worked, and the liquidity crisis was averted. Alas, though, the coordination with Wall Street hurt Cleveland politically and increased public skepticism of bankers. In the wake of the deal, the fiery populist and critic of the gold standard William Jennings

Bryan took over the Democratic Party. Over the next thirteen years, Bryan won the presidential nomination three times, while losing the presidency all three times. As for Cleveland, his conservative approach to governing, including his willingness to work with Morgan, not only got him disavowed by the Democrats at the time, but also by generations of Democrats who followed, despite having a relatively successful presidency.[16]

With Cleveland out of the picture and the threat of Bryan looming, Morgan and his moneyed friends looked to Ohio Governor William McKinley for deliverance. Morgan donated $250,000 to McKinley's 1896 campaign, about $8.4 million in today's dollars. (The budget for the Democrats' entire campaign that year was $400,000.) Morgan's investment was money well spent. Morgan lobbied for, and got, a plank in the Republican platform endorsing the gold standard, and McKinley signed a law in 1900 codifying that standard. Unsurprisingly, Morgan was deeply grieved by the assassination of McKinley in 1900, telling a reporter, "The news is very sad. There is nothing I can say at this time."[17]

In helping a number of U.S. presidents, both with financial contributions and assistance to the U.S. economy, Morgan helped create his own more cooperative model of engagement. His assistance to presidents on both sides of the aisle showed that CEOs do not necessarily have to have partisan alignments to be effective. This model also showed why presidents would often have their own reasons for cultivating CEOs, as a good relationship with CEOs could potentially help presidents in a variety of ways.

Rockefeller as Political Villain

Rockefeller, meanwhile, learned nothing from Morgan's efforts at a moment of national peril. Like something out of Hollywood, he continued down the path of political villain. By the 1880s, politicians of both parties would recognize that associating with the unpopular Rockefeller was dangerous. In 1884, Cleveland, who had represented Standard Oil in private practice, was elected president. That same year, the Ohio legislature elected to the Senate Henry Payne, father of Standard Oil treasurer Oliver Payne. This was in the period in which state legislatures, not the people, sent senators to Washington. Oliver was specifically tasked with a mission of securing positions for friends of Standard Oil in Washington, in line with Rockefeller's shortsighted theory that "I care not who is President, provided I have the 'pull' with his Secretary of the Treasury."[18]

Still, Oliver's selection of his own father for the Senate seemed too much. Coupled with this were serious allegations of election irregularities in the form of direct payments from Standard Oil to Ohio legislators. The Republicans in Ohio investigated the charges and sent their findings to the U.S. Senate, which debated expelling Senator Payne. Grover Cleveland's intimate William C. Whitney, whom Oliver also helped get appointed as Cleveland's Secretary of the Navy, worked within the Cleveland administration to make sure that Cleveland did not back Payne's expulsion. The maneuvering worked, but at a large reputational cost for Rockefeller and Standard Oil. As Rockefeller biographer Silas Hubbard wrote in 1904, "The Payne scandal served more perhaps than any other event of twenty years to concentrate public attention on the Standard Oil and Rockefeller. It raised a storm which has never subsided."[19]

In the 1888 presidential campaign, both Cleveland and Republican Benjamin Harrison were going after "the trusts" in campaign rhetoric. Rockefeller aide John Archbold, who would take over running Standard Oil when Rockefeller retired in 1896, told his boss not to worry about the denunciations. Archbold wrote to his boss, "We do not think that much will come of the talk at Washington regarding Trusts. . . . The demagogues are simply trying to outtalk each other for political effect."[20]

Archbold was wrong. Harrison, who unseated Cleveland in that 1888 election, had spoken out against the trusts while a senator and had argued for a railroad commission that would limit Standard Oil's ability to coerce rebates for itself. As president, Harrison signed the Sherman Antitrust Act on July 2, 1890, making trusts—the organizing principle under which Standard Oil could evade regulation—illegal. The passage of the act showed the political unpopularity of Rockefeller and his fellow monopolists, but its initial policy impact was limited. Standard Oil, even if no longer constituted as a trust as of 1892, would continue to operate for more than two decades before its eventual government-mandated breakup. The passage of the Sherman Antitrust Act and the dissolution of the trust did not end Standard Oil's monopoly; indeed, it managed only to strike a glancing blow.[21]

Even though Standard Oil retained its power after passage of the Sherman Act, it had further secured its villain status and became a regular target of political denunciations. Rockefeller himself, sensing the darkening public mood, began to sleep with a revolver by his bedside. He was by this time fabulously wealthy, earning an estimated $3 million annually in Standard Oil dividends alone, approximately $100 million in today's dollars. But the wealth came coupled with unpopularity, which made it more challenging to find politicians willing to be supportive of him or his company.[22]

Rockefeller's unpopularity made the opportunity presented by a friendly politician so welcome and unexpected. Yet it was the very surprise nature of the opportunity that made the sudden loss of that president—and the equally sudden entry into the White House of a bitter enemy—so painful. In 1896, Rockefeller and Standard Oil actively backed the presidential candidacy of Ohio governor William McKinley, contributing $250,000—just as Morgan had—to McKinley's campaign, with $2,500 of it coming from Rockefeller himself. Rockefeller, himself generally skeptical of politicians, was more expressive about his support of McKinley, saying, "I can see nothing else for us to do, to serve the country and our honor." McKinley's victory was a huge win for Rockefeller, who was in the process of phasing out his official duties as head of Standard Oil.[23]

McKinley's top political adviser was Republican National Committee chair Mark Hanna, famous for his saying, "There are two things that are important in politics. The first is money, and I can't remember what the second one is." Hanna was a high school classmate of Rockefeller's, and popular sentiment held that the Sherman Act would have little potency in a McKinley administration. McKinley was certainly better for Standard Oil, and for business in general, than McKinley's 1896—and 1900—opponent, anti-corporate populist William Jennings Bryan. But even McKinley, with the donations and the closeness to Rockefeller's schoolmate, saw which way the political winds were blowing. In 1898, he signed into law the creation of an Industrial Commission, something that President Cleveland had previously vetoed. Rockefeller, technically no longer running the company, was nevertheless induced to testify before the commission. Little came of it. But President McKinley did do something else that was far worse for Rockefeller, although he could not have known it at the time. In making his selection for his vice president, McKinley unwittingly brought an end to the laissez faire era and helped usher in the progressive era, which would have enormous ramifications for American business. [24]

CHAPTER 2

THE RISE OF THE PROGRESSIVES

Presidents: Theodore Roosevelt, William Howard Taft, Woodrow Wilson
CEOs: Rockefeller, Morgan, Henry Ford

In the early 1900s, American businesses started to recognize the way things were shifting. The era of laissez fair was over, and the federal government was taking a far more careful look at companies, especially when they formed dominating monopolies. While the federal government was not nearly as large or as powerful as it is now, it was big enough—and had sufficient civil authority—that it forced farsighted companies to take notice. Some companies even started to realize that working with government to shape regulations was a more effective strategy than fruitless opposition to seeing them enacted in the first place. The first seeds of the current entanglement, and what came to be known as regulatory capture, emerged in this era. According to Gregory Kolko, "The Progressive Era regulations in fact came to be due to the efforts of businesses rather than workers. The force that drove business to work with the government was the need for stability, predictability, and security."[1]

The major CEOs of this era were still corporate founders, including a "retired" but still active Rockefeller, Morgan, and a powerful upstart who reshaped the transportation system named Henry Ford. They took different approaches to their relationships with presidents, but by the dawn of the progressive era, they all recognized that presidents had become too important and too potent to ignore. This realization was most powerfully brought about by the first president of the Progressive Era, an "accidental" president named Teddy Roosevelt.

A New Sheriff in Town

Theodore "Teddy" Roosevelt had a meteoric rise to the White House. Born to a wealthy New York family in 1858, he wrote his first book—a naval history of the War of 1812—before finishing his studies at Harvard. He joined the New York State Assembly in 1882, but came to prominence as police commissioner of New York in 1895. Six years later, he would be president.

In those six years Roosevelt held a succession of jobs of increasing importance and responsibility. Roosevelt left the commissioner's post to become assistant secretary of the Navy, where he was intimately involved in preparations for the Spanish-American War of 1898. He then left his post to gain great fame as the head of the Rough Riders, celebrated for their charge up San Juan Hill in Cuba. With his newfound popularity, Roosevelt ran for and won the governorship of New York.

In 1900, William McKinley put the popular and reform-minded Roosevelt on the presidential ticket, replacing first-term vice president, Garret Hobart, who had died in 1899. This came at the urging and maneuvering of Standard Oil's Henry Rogers, with the help of Pennsylvania senator Matthew Quay and New York political boss Thomas Platt—and against the wishes of Republican king-maker Mark Hanna. Rogers later said, "We forced Roosevelt's nomination as Vice-President. He was very troublesome as Governor of New York and we wanted him out of the way . . ." It was a miscalculation. Roosevelt, who often employed the rhetoric of a progressive reformer, knew that Standard Oil and other industrialists had maneuvered to get him out of the state house and into the seemingly ineffectual position of vice president. He hated Rockefeller and Standard Oil, and he did not much like J. P. Morgan, either.[2]

Rockefeller: In Roosevelt's Sights

It did not take long before it became clear that Standard Oil and Roosevelt's other enemies had miscalculated in getting the Rough Rider on the presidential ticket. Roosevelt served only nine months as vice president before becoming president on September 14, 1901, when McKinley was assassinated by Polish-American anarchist Leon Czolgosz. For the 42-year-old Roosevelt, it was a stunning ascension: six jobs in six years, culminating in the presidency.

As a New York politician with a reformist sensibility, Roosevelt was certainly aware of Rockefeller and Standard Oil. Rockefeller even donated $1,000 to Roosevelt's failed mayoral campaign of 1886, viewing Roosevelt as less dangerous than the radical economic journalist—and best-selling author—Henry George. Standard Oil executives such as Henry Flagler also backed Roosevelt's 1898 run for governor, although they were disappointed when Governor Roosevelt turned on them, backing both a corporate franchise tax and regulation of factories. A disappointed Flagler said of Roosevelt's pivot, "I have no command of the English language that enables me to express my feelings regarding Mr. Roosevelt."[3]

The initial response within Standard Oil to McKinley's assassination and Roosevelt's ascension was panic. Standard Oil executives worried about what a President Roosevelt might do, and there was also concern that Czosglosz's action may have foreshadowed a wider radical response. Rockefeller doubled the bodyguards around his estate and stayed indoors in case he might have been targeted by assassins as well.[4]

Initially, it was an overreaction. Roosevelt was not as radical at the time, and Czosglosz was not part of a larger anarchist conspiracy. But Roosevelt definitely made things harder for Standard Oil than McKinley or his predecessors had. Roosevelt used his "bully pulpit" to attack industrial "evils," and pushed the creation of a Bureau of Corporations to look into monopolistic corporate practices. As part of that effort, Roosevelt was willing to use Rockefeller as a punching bag, and even to be misleading in the process. While the Bureau of Corporations bill was being considered in Congress, Roosevelt railed against improper lobbying against the bill, citing telegrams sent to six senators opposing Roosevelt's legislation. Roosevelt claimed, inaccurately, that Rockefeller had sent them. The telegrams had indeed been sent, but by John Jr., who was still at the company, and not the retired—and reviled—senior Rockefeller. No matter. Roosevelt called the telegrams "the most brazen attempt in the history of lobbying," and his attack made front-page news. The publicity aided Roosevelt's effort in favor of the bill, which passed in February of 1903. Roosevelt credited the telegram ploy with helping him get the bill passed, and the CEO-as-villain motif had demonstrated its potency.[5]

Even with the bill passed, and despite the occasional presidential potshots, Rockefeller and Standard Oil remained relatively unscathed in Roosevelt's first term. The oil companies were not the Bureau's first targets, and Standard Oil still felt that it could work with Roosevelt, even supporting him for a second term. But other winds were blowing during Roosevelt's first term that would soon intensify the confrontation, with severe implications for Standard Oil, and for Rockefeller.

Miss Tar Barrel: The Media Shapes Perceptions—and Policy

In November of 1902, a fierce and dogged 6-foot-tall reporter named Ida Tarbell began running stories in *McClure's* magazine about Standard Oil. The stories, which detailed Standard Oil's—and Rockefeller's—predatory tactics in building its powerful monopoly, were an immediate sensation. The stories went on for two years and helped build the circulation of *McClure's* to 375,000—the equivalent of over 1.5 million today—making Rockefeller even more hated than he already was. Tarbell's ultimate conclusion was devastating: "Mr. Rockefeller has systematically played with loaded dice, and it is doubtful if there has ever been a time since 1872 when he has run a race with a competitor and started fair." Sentiment against Rockefeller was so negative that the reformist monthly *The Arena* wrote, "There are worse men than John D. Rockefeller. There is probably no one, however, who in the public mind so typifies the grave and startling menace to the social order."[6]

Tarbell's series stung. Standard Oil knew that it would, and tried to curtail it. Tarbell discussed the article with Standard Oil's Henry Rogers at the company's headquarters and he asked, politely but plaintively, "Is there any way we can stop this?" Tarbell's steely response: "No, there is no way on earth in which you can prevent the publication of this story."[7]

Rogers's belated plea revealed a great oversight on Standard Oil's part. While it was ruthless in building itself out both vertically and horizontally, it gave little attention to the press or to managing its reputation with the public. There had been earlier warnings about bad press as a potential problem. In 1888, Standard Oil executive Paul Babcock warned Rockefeller that "this anti-trust fever is a craze, which we should meet in a very dignified way and parry every question with answers which while perfectly truthful are evasive of bottom facts." Rockefeller was uninterested in responding to the press then, and would remain so as long as he was at the company. But his lack of interest in the press showed that he misunderstood the degree to which an increasingly powerful—and national—press could shape perceptions, and with it, government policy.[8]

Even in the midst of the Tarbell onslaught, Rockefeller and Standard Oil remained slow to face the public relations challenge her series created. When a friend of Rockefeller offered to rebut some of Tarbell's arguments, he stopped the friend in his tracks, saying, "Not a word! Not a word about that misguided woman." Later, and somewhat more thoughtfully, Rockefeller noted that he had "thought once of having an answer made to the McClure articles, but you know it has always been the policy of the Standard to keep silent under attack and let our acts speak for themselves." It was an unwise policy. Rockefeller dismissively—and ineffectually—referred to her as "Miss Tar Barrel" as her articles savaged the reputations of both him and the company he had built.[9] Rockefeller's nicknaming could not change the narrative, as things beyond just government policies were changing at the time. America was no longer so clubby, so dominated by elites; the popular media was becoming more aggressive, and a populist sensibility was on the rise.

While Rockefeller was practicing a self-destructive policy of unilateral disarmament, his enemies were taking advantage of the situation. Roosevelt included Tarbell's articles in his vast reading—he read as many as three books a day, even as president—and even sent her a fan letter about the series. This was typical of Roosevelt. He had a long history of reading social criticism, learning from it, and befriending the authors.

Roosevelt's reading and his relationships with authors could directly affect policy. He read Upton Sinclair's harrowing novel *The Jungle*, which described unsafe and unsanitary conditions in the Chicago meatpacking plants. After reading the book, Roosevelt requested a report from Secretary of Agriculture James Wilson on plant conditions, which contributed to the passage of the Meat Inspection Act in 1906.[10]

Roosevelt saw Sinclair and Tarbell as part of a group who would become known as "muckrakers." The term came from Roosevelt's April 14, 1906, speech laying a cornerstone at the House of Representatives. In the speech, Roosevelt called out the value of a "man with a muck rake," a reference to John Bunyan's *Pilgrim's Progress*. According to Roosevelt, the man with the rake "could look no way but downward." These muckrakers could denigrate but could not get beyond their critiques to the place of real solutions. Roosevelt, however, could.[11]

Despite their limitations, Roosevelt found the muckrakers useful in that they highlighted societal problems that Roosevelt wanted to address. *The Jungle* did not alert Roosevelt to the problems of the nation's meatpacking plants. He had discussed them previously, even before Sinclair's book came out. What Sinclair did, however, was bring additional public support—not to mention outrage—that would help Roosevelt achieve his policy goals. [12]

Tarbell's work was similar. Roosevelt was already skeptical of Rockefeller and his fellow industrialists. But in skewering Rockefeller, Tarbell created a political opportunity for Roosevelt. The Tarbell series was another example of Roosevelt's smart use of his prodigious reading to develop new policy ideas and advance his political goals.

Unlike Rockefeller, Roosevelt understood public relations. He would later grumble about Henry Ford's relentless public relations efforts to develop his popular image. Rockefeller had not yet had that insight, and Roosevelt took advantage of it.

Tarbell was a perfect vehicle for Roosevelt. As a native of Titusville, Pennsylvania, whose father's business had been destroyed by Rockefeller, she took her local perspective on Rockefeller's misdeeds and brought them to national attention. Roosevelt was determined to make use of that attention in a second term in the White House.[13]

First, though, Roosevelt had to win that second term. This was not fore-ordained. Mark Hanna, now a senator from Ohio and the head of the Republican National Committee, disliked Roosevelt and had tried to prevent him from joining McKinley's ticket in 1900. When McKinley died, Hanna's famous reaction was "Now we've got that damned cowboy as President!" Hanna hoped to run against Roosevelt in 1904, but got ill and died on February 15th, forestalling the possibility of a serious internal challenge.[14]

Hanna may have died, but his dictum about the importance of money in politics remained—and remains—alive. George Cortelyou, known as the first White House aide, took over the reins at the Republican National Committee and worked to raise funds for Roosevelt's reelection with the assistance of RNC treasurer Cornelius Bliss. Standard Oil, as well as the other industrialists, had warily decided to back Roosevelt, recognizing that he was likely to win. Perhaps they felt that campaign contributions would lessen his ire against them. Rockefeller aide Archbold personally handed Bliss a check for $100,000—over $3 million in current dollars—but wanted to make sure Bliss was under no illusions about its source: "Now, Mr. Bliss, we want to make this contribution, but we do not want to do it without its being known and thoroughly approved of by the powers that be." Bliss took the check, saying, "You need have no apprehension about it whatever."[15]

Bliss's assurances notwithstanding, Archbold was right to be apprehensive. Getting a check from Standard Oil was an issue for Roosevelt, and Democratic politician and newspaper publisher Joseph Pulitzer blasted the Republican campaign for it. In an open letter to Cortelyou in Pulitzer's *New York World*, he called out Cortelyou over campaign contributions and specifically asked how much the Roosevelt campaign had received from the oil trust. Roosevelt, however, was a savvy pol, and he feared a political hit over getting money from Standard Oil. He sent a letter, telegram, and a memo to Cortelyou on October 26, 1904, demanding that he return the money: "I have just been informed that the Standard Oil people have contributed one hundred thousand dollars to our campaign. This may be entirely untrue. But if true I must ask you to direct that the money be returned to them forthwith."[16]

The incident gave Roosevelt an opportunity both to blunt a political attack and to go on offense. He continued, "It is entirely legitimate to accept contributions, no matter how large they are, from individuals and corporations on the terms on which I happen to know that you have accepted them: that is, with the explicit understanding that they were given and received with no thought of any more obligation . . . than is implied by the statement that every man shall receive a square deal, no more and no less. . . ." He followed up by saying, "in view of my past relations with the Standard Oil Company" the donation might be seen "as putting us under an improper obligation." Roosevelt's memo was smart politics. He justified his many other political donations, called out Standard Oil, reminded voters that he had taken action against the company, and even got in a plug for his "Square Deal" campaign slogan. He also followed up with Cortelyou to make sure that the money was returned. Not bad for a $100,000 campaign hit. Roosevelt won the 1904 election with 56 percent of the vote.[17]

As for Rockefeller and Standard Oil, they had made a terrible investment. Not that it mattered, but it's not clear whether the company even got its money back. Attorney General Philander Cox, who had heard Roosevelt dictate the letter to Cortelyou, told him, "Why, Mr. President, the money has been spent. They cannot pay it back—they haven't got it." Roosevelt, who did not care if the truth got in the way of his PR efforts, responded, "Well, the letter will look well on the record, anyhow." The money was unimportant to Standard Oil, of course. Roosevelt had once again scored points off the company and found his political target for his second term. When Roosevelt won the election, Rockefeller sent him a telegram: "I congratulate you most heartily on the grand result of yesterday's election." This personal outreach would not help in the slightest.[18]

Targeting Morgan

Roosevelt did not much like Rockefeller, but he did not like Morgan, either. The dislike was not obvious upon Roosevelt's ascension to the presidency, though. Roosevelt's view on the economy was pragmatic. On the train ride to Washington after he had learned of McKinley's death, Roosevelt told his friend H. H. Kohlsaat, "I don't care a damn about stocks and bonds, but I don't want to see them go down the first day I am President!" Roosevelt also had been wary of, but not hostile to, Morgan. When running for governor of New York in 1898, Roosevelt refused a contribution from Morgan and other top businessmen, telling state party head Thomas Platt that "I cannot accept contributions from the men you mention. Really, I must decline." As the newly elected vice president, however, Roosevelt hosted a dinner for Morgan. When inviting his friend Elihu Root, Roosevelt said, "I hope you can come to my dinner to J. Pierpont Morgan. You see, it represents an effort on my part to become a conservative man in touch with the influential classes and I think I deserve encouragement."[19]

As president, Roosevelt's attitude towards Morgan was less mixed. In 1902, Roosevelt filed suit against the Northern Securities Company, a holding company through which Morgan controlled multiple railroads and pursued a northwestern railroad monopoly. Morgan was both angry about being blindsided by the suit and wanted to work things out without a lawsuit. He met with Roosevelt on February 23 and asked why Roosevelt did not warn him, to which the president replied, "This is just what we did not want to do." Morgan had no more luck with his next request, which was to rectify matters without government action, "If we have done anything wrong, send your man to my man and they can fix it up." Roosevelt was unmoved and his government continued with the suit. After Morgan left, Roosevelt observed that Morgan "could not help regarding me as a big rival operator, who either intended to ruin all his interests or else could be induced to come to an agreement to ruin none." The Roosevelt administration won its case before the Supreme Court and disbanded Northern in 1904.[20]

Yet even as they clashed on one issue, Roosevelt and Morgan coordinated on another. They had shared interests in stopping the 1902 anthracite miners' strike, which severely curtailed America's coal supply. Morgan tried to intercede on Roosevelt's behalf to resolve matters, with limited initial success. Eventually, thanks to pressure from both the president and the financier, the strike was settled via arbitration, which raised the miners' wages but did not recognize any union. Roosevelt thanked Morgan for his efforts, writing, "If it had not been for your going in the matter, I do not see how the strike could have been settled at this time, and the consequences that might have followed . . . are . . . very dreadful to contemplate." Morgan did not respond.[21]

In 1904, Morgan pressed Hanna to challenge Roosevelt for the Republican nomination. Hanna's untimely death forestalled that possibility, and Morgan donated $150,000 to Roosevelt's successful reelection effort. This did not suggest the end of the dislike between the two men, but it did indicate a level of accommodation.[22]

Rockefeller: Second-Term Roosevelt Unbound

With the 1904 election behind Roosevelt, and both Standard Oil and Rockefeller reeling from the Tarbell series, Roosevelt felt liberated to take more aggressive action in his second term. He also felt additional motivation as he was angry at Standard Oil for unsuccessfully opposing his Bureau of Corporations bill. As he later put it, Standard Oil had "antagonized me before my election, when I was getting through the Bureau of Corporations bill, and I then promptly threw down the gauntlet to it."[23]

The newly formed Bureau began by looking more closely at Standard Oil. On May 4, 1906, Roosevelt spoke to Congress and touted a Bureau report on railroad rebates, saying, "The report shows that the Standard Oil Company has benefited enormously up almost to the present moment by secret rates, many of these secret rates being clearly unlawful." Thanks in part to Roosevelt's message and the underlying report, the Hepburn Rate Act, which let the Interstate Commerce Commission regulate railroad shipping rates—and consequently prevent improper rebates—moved forward in Congress. The Act was signed into law on June 29, 1906.[24]

Regulation was followed by prosecution. In June of 1906, Roosevelt had a special nighttime Cabinet meeting to plan the legal case against Standard Oil. Shortly afterwards Attorney General William Moody announced a preliminary investigation against Standard Oil. In September, Roosevelt wrote to Moody, "I do not see how we can refrain from taking action about them [Standard Oil]. I wish the formal report to be ready at the earliest day practicable in October, as I should like to dispose of the matter as soon as possible after my return to

Washington." Standard Oil knew it was in trouble, and Archbold told Rockefeller that "there is no doubt that the special Cabinet meeting, which the President called, and where the action was entirely dominated by him, led to the instituting of the proceedings." Multiple lawsuits followed, with the Bureau of Corporations reports providing indispensable material for the plaintiffs. Government prosecutor Charles Morrison would tell Bureau head Herbert Knox Smith that "the help you have been to us is so great that it can hardly be estimated." The most impactful lawsuit, seeking the dissolution of Standard Oil, was filed months later, on November 18, 1906."[25]

The onslaught of lawsuits had an impact. In August of 1907, U.S. District Court Judge (and future commissioner of baseball) Kennesaw Mountain Landis fined Standard Oil of Indiana $29 million, almost $1 billion in today's dollars. A recalcitrant Rockefeller remarked that Landis would be dead before Standard Oil paid a dime. Landis, it should be said, lived until 1944, outliving Rockefeller and certainly living long enough to see the 1911 breakup of Standard Oil.[26]

Standard Oil knew it was in the crosshairs, but there was little it could do about it. The three elements of the Roosevelt assault—regulation, prosecution, and political attacks—continued. Archbold, who had given the disastrous contribution to Roosevelt's 1904 campaign, whined that, "Darkest Abyssinia never saw anything like the course of treatment we received at the hands of the administration following Mr. Roosevelt's election in 1904." Henry C. Frick expressed similar sentiments in a more cynical way: "We bought the son of a bitch, but he wouldn't stay bought."[27]

The Panic of 1907: Helping Out for the Good of the Country

In 1907, national economic troubles held out the promise of a brief respite for Standard Oil. During October's Panic of 1907, Rockefeller had pledged some of his own personal wealth to help prop up a reeling stock market. Rockefeller was involved in the financial markets as an investor. Morgan, however, was a financial market shaper, and would consequently have a bigger role than Rockefeller in dealing with the financial crisis.

As with Rockefeller, Morgan found Roosevelt's second term challenging. Despite this, Morgan would come to the president's—and the country's—rescue again, just as he had under Grover Cleveland. In many ways, the Panic of 1907 resembled the 2007 collapse a century later: a cascading series of bank disasters threatened to create a series of bankruptcies and send the economy into a tailspin.

Morgan, with his vast knowledge of the markets and the economy, came up with a plan to stave off disaster. The plan entailed U.S. Steel, of which Morgan was a director, purchasing another steel company from Moore & Schley, one of the teetering banks. In 1895, he was able to present a similar plan to a wary Cleveland by stubbornly outwaiting Cleveland's refusal to see him. By 1907, things had changed enormously. It was not presidential wariness but outright enmity that stood in the way of things. Furthermore, there was now a recognition by some that an increasingly powerful federal government could stand in the way of carrying out the plan.

U.S. Steel president Elbert Gary warned Morgan of this eventuality. In discussing the plan, Gary said to Morgan, "Before we go ahead with this, we must consult President Roosevelt." Morgan was initially dismissive, asking, "But what has the president to do with it?" Gary explained that the deal created the very kind of monopoly Roosevelt had long been railing against. Morgan was convinced, and asked, "Can you go at once?" When Gary asked Roosevelt, the president gave a circumlocutory ok, saying, "I do not believe that anyone could justly criticize me for saying that I would not feel like objecting to the purchase under the circumstances."[28]

While Morgan's actions helped steady the economy, they proved a challenge for Roosevelt. Roosevelt had to allow Morgan's intervention for the sake of the economy, but that consent weakened him politically. It also contributed to his decision not to run again in 1908, a decision he would later regret. Morgan came out on top, but it did not make him like Roosevelt any better. Later, when he learned that Roosevelt would be going on safari in Africa, Morgan joked that he hoped the lions would perform their duty.[29]

This model, of bailing out a president in a time of national need, was a recurring one that would be exhibited by other CEOs in the future, including Henry

Ford with his armaments factory, and Jamie Dimon during the 2008 financial crisis. Patriotic CEOs can be helpful to presidents, and the nation, in times of great need, even if, as in the case of Morgan and Roosevelt—or Ford and Franklin Roosevelt—they dislike each other personally.

Rockefeller: Late in Life Civic Mindedness

Rockefeller's efforts in the Panic of 1907 were of less import than Morgan's but they did suggest a late-in-life change in approach. His civic-minded effort to prop up the plummeting stock market stocks coincided with Rockefeller finally recognizing that cultivating good press might be helpful. By this time, he had been retired for a decade and spent his time largely on philanthropy and his daily game of golf. Mark Twain joked about Rockefeller's charitable giving in a *Harper's* essay, and Rockefeller himself kibitzed with reporters, joking that he had been "made into a sort of frightful ogre, to slay which has become a favorite resource of men seeking public favor." He even appeared to show remorse, or at least openness to regulation, saying that "capital and labor are both wild forces which require intelligent legislation to hold them in restriction." In the wake of the crisis, and the revised PR approach, Rockefeller noted that reporters had "spoken very kindly and favorably, and all have shown great appreciation of what we have tried to do to save the ship."[30]

The goodwill did not last. Rockefeller made the mistake of criticizing the Roosevelt administration to a reporter, saying (off the record, not that it mattered when it appeared in print), "The runaway policy of the past administration can have but one result. It means disaster to the country, financial depression, and chaos." The comment angered Roosevelt, who was also annoyed that Rockefeller, whose daily golf game was widely publicized, cited poor health when he begged off coming to the White House for a conversation about Standard Oil. In Roosevelt's telling, Rockefeller would not come because he felt insulted by what the Bureau of Corporations had revealed about Standard Oil's practices. Roosevelt may have been right, but Rockefeller likely understood that Roosevelt would not be averse to using the publicity of a White House meeting with Rockefeller against the aging tycoon.[31]

Roosevelt held his fire for a while, but once 1908, his last year in office, began, he picked up the cudgel once again. Roosevelt gave a special message to Congress in which he described his antitrust crusade as a "campaign against privilege." He railed against Standard Oil for opposing his reforms, and he specifically called out Rockefeller's Standard Oil and E. H. Harriman's Santa Fe Railroad, referring to them as "the most dangerous member of the criminal class—the criminals of great wealth." He also continued to press forward with the lawsuits, telling Attorney General Charles Bonaparte, "If we have a criminal case against these men, I should be very reluctant to surrender it."[32]

Roosevelt: Finding and Undermining a Successor

As 1908 progressed, Roosevelt's thoughts shifted to identifying his successor. Roosevelt wanted his friend and Secretary of War William Howard Taft, but Taft was not the only candidate for the GOP nomination. Ohio senator Joseph Foraker was interested in the job, but Roosevelt did not want Foraker—seen as Wall Street's candidate—in the White House. On January 22, 1907, at the annual Gridiron Dinner, Roosevelt went after Foraker directly. Seated, uncomfortably for both men, at the same table, Roosevelt heard Foraker make a reprehensible racist remark. Seeing an opportunity, Roosevelt asked to speak. He began by attacking the wealthy, and warning that without his reforms, the only alternative would be a takeover by "the mob, the mob, the mob." Then he went after Foraker by name and repeated Foraker's remark, disagreed with it, and threw down his program in disgust. The incident made a splash in the *Washington Post*, and Foraker was damaged, but not destroyed, in the process.[33]

Taft got the nomination, but the Foraker story was not yet over. In September of 1908, newspaper magnate William Randolph Hearst disclosed a letter exchange between Foraker and Archbold revealing direct payments from Standard Oil to Foraker, including a staggering $150,000—$5.4 million in today's dollars—to help pay for the decoration of Foraker's Washington, D.C. mansion. (It turns out that Garfield adviser Amos Townsend was correct to warn Garfield against putting anything regarding Rockefeller or Standard Oil on paper).[34]

Always one to seize a political opportunity. Roosevelt urged Taft to pounce. Roosevelt told Taft to "[make] a fight openly on the ground that you stood in the Republican party and before the people for the triumph over the forces which were typified by the purchase of a United States senator to do the will of the Standard Oil Company." Taft, typically less aggressive than Roosevelt, passed, but won the election nonetheless. As for Foraker, the revelation ended his political career. Being Wall Street's preferred candidate was one thing, but taking direct payments from Standard Oil was another.[35]

The incident revealed differences between Roosevelt and Taft that would have huge implications. Taft gained Standard Oil's—and Rockefeller's—support in 1908, but he did so legitimately, as Rockefeller saw him as more palatable than Bryant. Rockefeller even issued a statement backing Taft, saying, in part, "I will vote for Taft. If for no other reason I support Taft because on comparing him with [William Jennings] Bryan, his chief opponent, I find the balance of fitness and temperament entirely on his side. The election of Mr. Taft, will, I believe, make for law and order and stability in business. He is not a man, I judge, to venture with rash experiments or to impede the return of prosperity by advocating measures subversive of industrial progress."[36]

The Roosevelt White House put out its own statement, claiming that the Taft endorsement was "a perfectly palpable and obvious trick on the part of the Standard Oil people to damage Taft." The incident, and Taft's non-disavowal of the endorsement, irked Roosevelt so much that he even considered breaking his pledge to step down and supplant Taft as his chosen successor.[37]

As the story shows, Taft lacked Roosevelt's PR instincts. Roosevelt was miffed at Taft for allowing himself—and his enormous girth—to be photographed in golf attire, something Roosevelt thought was a huge mistake. As he advised Taft, "I never let friends advertise my tennis, and never let a photograph of me in tennis costume appear."[38]

As president, Taft was personally more friendly to Rockefeller than Roosevelt was. In 1910, Taft and Rockefeller encountered each other at Augusta's Hotel Bon Air. Both men were avid golfers and agreed to hit the links together, only to have a wary Mrs. Taft put a kibosh on it. At another encounter, Rockefeller asked Taft to say hello to his granddaughter, five-year-old Mathilde McCormick. Taft not only greeted her but lifted her high into the air, showing no bad blood between the two men.[39]

The vindictiveness was gone, but the prosecution remained. Taft got to preside over something Roosevelt had wanted but did not attain in his presidency: the demise of Standard Oil. Rockefeller brooded over the pending case and felt the whole effort against the company he built was "vindictive." He may have been right. By 1911, Standard Oil was not even a monopoly anymore. Its market share, once 90 percent, was now 60 percent. Many of its more rapacious market practices had been called out and now prevented by law, and in retrospect, Standard Oil had inarguably provided enormous consumer and industrial benefits. According to antitrust analyst David Koppel, "Before Standard Oil revolutionized oil derivatives by lowering prices and improving quality, the high prices and limited supplies of whale oil and candles, prevented all but the wealthy from being able to work or entertain after dark." Afterwards, Koppel wrote, "Thanks to Standard Oil, families could illuminate their homes for just one cent per hour."[40]

Unfortunately for Standard Oil, Robert Bork's theories on monopolies having utility if they benefit the consumers were decades in the future. At 4:00 p.m. on May 15, 1911, the Supreme Court spoke and ordered the dissolution of Rockefeller's creation, a decade and a half after he stepped back from day-to-day operations. Rockefeller was right about two important things. First, the court had overturned the fine, meaning that even though Judge Landis would live another thirty years, he would never see the company pay that fine. Second, the breakup was not the end of oil profits, far from it.[41]

Rockefeller heard about the Court's decision on the golf course, and initially remained nonchalant. He told his golfing partner, Father J. P. Lennon, that if he had any money, he should do just one thing with it: "Buy Standard Oil." He even sent out a mock obituary to friends, saying, "Dearly beloved, we must obey the Supreme Court. Our splendid, happy family must scatter." Standard Oil of New Jersey finally let Rockefeller retire. The company would break up into thirty-four parts, with investors getting a share of each one. Those parts would become incredibly successful energy companies that we know today: ExxonMobil, Chevron, British Petroleum, among many others. The company had broken up, but big oil was here to stay.[42]

The breakup made Rockefeller even wealthier than he already was. His focus now was on philanthropy, and it showed. The Rockefeller charitable endeavors, including Spelman College—Spelman was his wife's maiden name—a host of medical schools, the Rockefeller Institute, the Rockefeller Foundation, and the University of Chicago, were truly astounding. But they had a twofold purpose beyond just the charitable instinct.

First, Rockefeller, encouraged by his wife, came to see the public relations value of his charitable giving, which was an important part of the improvement in his reputation from the depths of the immediate post-Tarbell period. But there was another benefit as well. The federal income tax was passed by Congress on July 2, 1909, under Taft, and ratified February 3, 1913, during the Wilson administration. The Rockefeller Foundation was not coincidentally founded in 1913 with a $183 million endowment, just at the very time when Rockefeller was facing the prospect of the income tax. Like Henry Ford would do during the Franklin Roosevelt administration, Rockefeller set up a powerful foundation to wield influence and protect his holdings, in direct response to federal government policies.[43]

Coda: Morgan's End

Unsurprisingly, Morgan also had an easier time with Taft than he had with Roosevelt. Taft, while friendlier to Morgan than Roosevelt, was still wary of the financier. He did not pursue Morgan's business interests, as Roosevelt had, but neither did he pursue direct interactions with the unpopular banker. When Taft won the presidency, Morgan telegraphed the new president his "heartfelt congratulations on to-day's splendid results." At the same time, Morgan's London office telegraphed New York, "Hope now we can have peace quiet and good business." They got their wish, for a time. Morgan died on March 31, 1913, shortly after the end of Taft's presidency and just a few weeks into the administration of Woodrow Wilson.[44]

Henry Ford: Automobiles and the Transport of America

No invention changed the landscape and economy of America more than the automobile. Cars gave individual Americans a mobility unimagined in previous generations, and enabled the movement and economic unification of a large nation dominated by regionalism and geographic divides. No one was more instrumental in the rise of the car than Henry Ford. It was Ford who took the internal combustion engine and made it available to the masses. Ford wasn't content with just reshaping American culture and economic life. He also sought to influence America's politics. In this last effort to transform the nation, Ford found that influencing American presidents was more challenging and more elusive than all the manufacturing processes he revolutionized in the production of the automobile.

Ford was born on July 30, 1863, on a farm in Dearborn, Michigan. He was a tinkerer from an early age, and was interested in building a steam car. As a teenager, he built a steam car that ran with a kerosene heater boiler, but realized that the market for such a vehicle was too small, so he kept tinkering, eventually working with an internal combustion engine.[45]

In 1896, Ford built one of the first gas-operated vehicles, calling it the Quadricycle. He managed to meet Thomas Edison at the annual Edison Convention in New York City, and told him about his prototype. Edison was encouraging, telling him, "You have the thing. Keep at it."[46]

Ford would indeed keep at it, starting his first car company, the Detroit Automobile Company, in 1899, and then launching the Ford Motor Company in 1903. He eventually developed the legendary Model T in 1908, the first affordable car for the masses. Sales of the Model T exploded, from 18,000 in 1909 to almost 250,000 in 1913, to over 1 million in 1920. Ford was obsessed with scale and with cost-cutting, and he kept cutting the price as he found savings: the price dropped from $1,000 initially to $355 in 1920 (approximately $5,500 today).[47]

As part of his quest to reduce costs, Ford developed the assembly line, revolutionizing the means of production. Ford's other major innovation was the five-dollars-a-day wage. Two insights led to this massive pay hike for the time. One was that Ford needed reliable workers. He kept shaving minutes off the time it took it to make a car but found that the human factor was slowing him down. Worker absences and departures made it hard to meet his deadlines, so Ford came up with the high wage that would both attract and retain workers. Ford did not make it easy to get that daily five dollars. You had to show up on time and work reliably for six months—generally be a model employee in order to keep getting it. Although workers were expected to maintain a fast, even punishing, pace and regularly work through lunch, five dollars a day was a huge incentive for workers at the time, enough to keep them in those grueling jobs.[48]

The second driver behind Ford's pay hike was that he saw the power of the supply side to create an even bigger market for his cars. Ford had this question in mind back in the 1870s, when he realized there was little potential for a costly steam-powered car in the commercial marketplace. With the five-dollars a day wage, Ford was paying his workers enough to enable them to be his customers as well. Later, when Ford introduced the five-day work week at his factories in 1926, at least part of his thinking was that two days of leisure time would give workers more time to drive cars, and thus more of an incentive to buy them.[49]

These insights reveal Ford to be a kind of reformer, cognizant of the impact his business decisions had on his factories, his workforce, his customer base, and ultimately his business. His ideas would spread, thereby magnifying his impact on American life. In his autobiography, *Henry Ford: My Life and Work*, published in 1922, Ford made it clear that he thought industry should help mold society for the better. As Ford wrote, "The highest use of capital is not to make more money, but to make money do more service for the betterment of life. Unless we in our industries are helping to solve the social problem, we are not doing our principal work. We are not fully serving."[50]

Although Ford was able to shape American society in far-reaching ways with his business decisions, he would find shaping government decisions to be much more difficult. In his memoirs, Ford also revealed a level of skepticism of reformers, of Washington, and of government in general. Regarding reformers he said, quite starkly, "I am not a reformer. I think there's entirely too much attempt at reforming in the world, and that we pay too much attention to reformers." According to Ford, a reformer was "the sort of man who would tear up a whole shirt because the collar button did not fit the buttonhole. It would never occur to him to enlarge the buttonhole."[51]

Ford was even harsher on government, writing that "law never does anything constructive." Ford felt that it was "a waste of time to look to our state capitals, or Washington to do that which law was not designed to do." He also believed that in government, in contrast to business, actions would have an impact opposite their intent: "As long as we look to legislation to cure poverty, or to abolish special privilege, we are going to see poverty spread and special privilege grow." Ultimately, Ford felt that "we may help the government; the government cannot help us."[52]

Ford's Dislike of Washington

No president earned a mention in Ford's memoirs. Nevertheless, Ford knew at least seven of them, and clashed with most of the ones he knew. His skepticism of Washington affected his approach and shaped the results of those interactions. Taft was president when the Model T took off, and he was somewhat of a car enthusiast. He was the first president to attend an auto show, and it was during his presidency that Congress first appropriated funds for the purchase of two White House automobiles to transport the president. Neither was a Ford.[53] But in 1914, as an ex-president, Taft was quite impressed with his visit to the Ford factory in Highland Park, saying, "It's wonderful. Wonderful! I am amazed at the magnitude of the establishment. I can almost hear the wheels buzz, and the machinery hum now."[54]

Things became somewhat more complicated under Taft's successor Woodrow Wilson. In 1914, Wilson met Ford, requesting he come to the White House to discuss the worrisome state of the economy. Ford was bullish about the economy and counseled patience. The meeting would get Ford labelled as "A New Adviser to the President" in the papers.[55] It was an early instance of a president using a business leader for a photo-op, something that would become a tried-and-true tactic of presidents. It would also be far from the last time that Ford would be summoned to the White House during troubling economic times.

Wilson may have wanted Ford's advice as a business tycoon, but Wilson was also enamored with cars. That same year, Wilson attracted national coverage when he purchased a Model T for his summer home.[56] The automobile would play an important role in Wilson's life. Following the death of his first wife, Ellen, the bereaved Wilson spotted an attractive widow, Edith Bolling, around Washington. She was the first woman to get a driver's license in Washington, D.C. They met, and had a whirlwind courtship, riding together in the back seat of a Secret Service-driven car. The two of them would draw the curtain so as to get some backseat privacy.[57] Shortly afterwards, they married.

Although Ford and Wilson had shared interests in the economy, they eventually found themselves taking divergent positions on foreign policy. Ford was a pacifist, and adamantly opposed to war, and to U.S. involvement overseas in general. His pacifism came from a number of sources. As a businessman obsessed with efficiency and wary of government, he felt that war was bad for business and good for the state. In addition, his mother had a brother die in the Civil War, while another brother was injured.

Ford's reading also contributed to this attitude, including the *McGuffey Eclectic Readers*, which he read in his youth. This widely read publication for schoolchildren had run an essay called "Things by Their Right Names." According to the essay, the right name for soldier was "murderer." As an adult, in 1915, Ford told the *Detroit Free Press* that, "I hate war, because war is murder, desolation and destruction, causeless, unjustifiable, cruel and heartless to those of the human race who do not want it, the countless millions, the workers. I hate it none the less for its waste, its uselessness, and the barriers it causes against progress." Ford's adamant anti-war views would put him at odds with multiple presidents. Those views would also lead to the first of many times he would be burned by getting involved in politics.[58]

Booted from the White House

In November of 1915, Ford and a press aide, Louis Lochner, traveled to Washington to see Wilson. The Great War—only later to be labelled World War I—had started in August of 1914, with Germany executing a two-pronged attack on France and Russia. Soon, Europe was embroiled in a war and many Americans wondered if they would be joining the conflict. In May of 1915, a German U-Boat sank the British cruiser the *Lusitania*, killing 1,195 passengers, including 123 Americans. Many Americans, including former president Theodore Roosevelt, were arguing for "prepared-ness," an arms buildup to prepare America—and its citizenry—for war. Wilson had been uninterested, but the sinking of the *Lusitania* had captured his attention. Ford came to Washington to keep Wilson in the anti-war camp.[59]

Ford used his time on the train with Lochner to prepare for meeting the president. He thought the war was a bad idea from the beginning. In his memoirs, he would later write, "I have never been able to discover any honourable [sic] reasons for the beginning of the World War." With Lochner, Ford tested out different talking points to persuade the president, including "men sitting around a table, not men dying in a trench, will finally settle differences." Liking the sound of that one, he told Lochner, "Make a note of that. We'll give it to the boys in the papers when we get to New York."[60]

Wilson was initially welcoming to the visitors. When Ford told Wilson that he looked well, the president explained that he tried to leave work behind when he went home and that he also enjoyed a good joke regularly. Lochner, ever the PR man, jumped in: "Some of them Ford jokes, I hope?" he said. Ford, on cue, shared a joke told about himself: Henry Ford drives by a cemetery and notices a gravedigger preparing an enormous grave. Ford asked whether the grave was for a whole family, but the gravedigger responded that it was for one man, who asked in his will to be buried in a Ford. The reason? A Ford had gotten him out of every hole to date, and he was confident it would pull him out of this one. The joke earned a chuckle from the president.[61]

As this exchange suggests, Ford jokes were a known thing in America in the 1910s, showing what a phenomenon he had become in the short time since the Model T had taken America by storm. The jokes would appear on postcards. One from 1915 read: "A little spark, a little coil, a little gas, a little oil, a piece of tin, 2 inch of board, put 'em together, and you have a Ford."[62] There was even a 1915 book called *Funny Stories About the Ford, Vol. 1*, a title that suggests that there would also be a Volume 2. One of the biggest spreaders of these jokes was Ford himself, so he was glad to have the opportunity to share one with the president.

And the fact that the priggish Wilson laughed, and even shared a joke of his own in response, was a positive development.[63]

Unfortunately for Ford, the joke exchange was the high point of the meeting. After the jokes, Ford turned to business. He asked Wilson to appoint a neutral commission, to be financed by Ford, to try to resolve the war in Europe. Wilson was friendly to Ford but understandably noncommittal. Stymied by Wilson, Ford tried a different approach. He told Wilson that "Tomorrow at ten in New York, representatives of every big newspaper will come to my apartment for a story. I have today chartered a steamship. I offer it to you to send delegates to Europe. If you feel you can't act, I will." All presidents hate threats, especially threats of bad publicity, and Wilson did not take well to the news. According to historians Frank Ernest Hill and Allan Nevins, Wilson had both Ford and Lochner "escorted out of the White House." Upon leaving the White House, a disappointed Ford told Lochner of Wilson, "He's a small man."[64]

Ford may have been an industrial genius, but that did not make him a political expert. The effort backfired. This steamship, officially the "*Oskar II*," would be renamed "The Peace Ship," and the publicity with which Ford threatened Wilson would end up harming Ford far more than Wilson.

Ford and Lochner headed to New York, as promised, and gave a press conference at the Biltmore Hotel on November 24, 1915, describing the mission. He would bring a group of peace advocates to Europe to try to settle matters among the warring powers. Ford had invited many illustrious guests, including former president Taft to join, but most, including Taft, wisely declined the invitation. Ford also made a serious gaffe when he told forty assembled reporters, "We're going to try to get the boys out of the trenches before Christmas. I've chartered a ship, and some of us are going to Europe." In the great tradition of New York newspaper headline writers, the *New York Tribune* seized on this with a headline reading, "GREAT WAR ENDS CHRISTMAS DAY: FORD TO STOP IT." The fighting would go on for another three years, and the U.S. entered the war about seventeen months later, in April of 1917.[65]

Peace Ship Mockery for Ford

The Peace Ship would take off on December 4, 1915, at 2:00 p.m. Ford was a passenger, and he opened himself to more ridicule with a pre-departure message filled with cliches, and sounding reminiscent of the McGuffey essay he had read in his youth: "War is murder"; "The word 'murderer' should be embroidered in red letters across the breast of every soldier"; "I will devote my life to fight this spirit of militarism." The effort did not cost him his life, but it did harm his reputation, and cost him a great deal of money in the process. Press mockery included calling Ford "God's fool" and "a clown," while the *Oskar II* was dubbed "a loon ship." Ford's wife Clara begged him to get off the ship.[66]

Other press outlets weighed in negatively as well. The *Philadelphia Record* wrote that "Henry Ford's millions have gone to his head. The fact that a man can make a cheap automobile is not necessarily a qualification for becoming a world leader and showing all the belligerents how much pleasanter and cheaper peace is than war." The *Louisville Courier* seized on his harassment of Wilson, writing that "it is worse than ineffable folly for pestiferous busybodies in this country like Henry Ford to nag the President to make an ass of himself." The mockery even hit Ford in his own backyard. The *Detroit Saturday Night* called Ford's effort "a humiliation to his city and his country."[67]

Challenging the president's position on foreign policy attracted the ire of other politicians, including a well-known former president whose own missteps had helped get Wilson elected in the first place. In 1912, Roosevelt chose to challenge incumbent President Taft, his hand-picked successor, for the Republican nomination. Failing to win the nomination, Roosevelt then launched a third-party bid under the Bull Moose, or Progressive Party banner, which split the Republican vote and landed Wilson in the White House. Roosevelt dismissed Ford's effort as completely ineffectual, saying that "Mr. Ford's visit abroad will not be mischievous only because it is ridiculous." Demonstrating the bipartisan nature of the mockery, former Democratic presidential candidate Alton B. Parker—who lost to Roosevelt in 1904—derided Ford as "a clown strutting on the stage for a little time."[68]

Ford's peace endeavor, which went on for another fourteen months even after Ford's return to U.S. soil, was a failure on many levels. It did not bring about peace or even accelerate a peace effort. It had gotten him kicked out of the White House by the sitting president. It earned him the derision of the media across the country. It had gotten him attacked by politicians from both parties. And it was financially costly, requiring Ford to put up $500,000 of his own money—$14.5 million in today's dollars. To add insult to injury, Ford contracted the flu on the journey.[69] Most tragic of all, the effort didn't bring peace—or anything close to it.

Despite this litany of headaches, Ford continued to view his effort as the right and noble thing to do. He wrote in his memoir: "I do not regret the attempt. The mere fact that it failed is not, to me, conclusive proof that it was not worth trying. We learn more from our failures than from our successes. What I learned on that trip was worth the time and the money expended." Unlike many business leaders, it also revealed that Ford had a thick skin. He brushed off the press criticism, saying of the media that "the best fertilizer in the world is weeds."[70]

Ford's pacifism even applied to incidents in which the U.S. was protecting its citizens. In June of 1916, Wilson initiated a series of national guard patrols to protect Americans in U.S. border towns and encampments from Francisco "Pancho" Villa's raiders and to capture Villa himself. The raids, an outgrowth of the Mexican Revolution, may have been an attempt by Villa to draw America into the Mexican conflict, but that was not Wilson's interest. Regardless, Ford did not approve, denouncing Wilson's deployment of troops there as "organized murder." Ford's opposition to the border protection initiative earned him more press criticism; the *Chicago Tribune* wrote an article criticizing Ford and denounced him in an editorial as "deluded," "an ignorant idealist," and "an anarchistic enemy of the nation which protects him in his wealth." Ford would sue the *Tribune* for libel, and the resulting trial would prove Ford's ignorance of foreign affairs far more than the editorial's assertion itself had.[71]

Still, Ford's continued pacifism did not seem to damage relations between Wilson and Ford. The two men had shared political interests. Despite his worries about World War I, Ford agreed to endorse Wilson in 1916, largely as a result of Wilson's campaign pledge to keep the U.S. out of the war. Wilson even adopted the slogan, "He Kept Us Out of War," but once reelected, he would break that promise.

In contrast to Ford, Rockefeller supported Wilson in the lead up to World War I. In response to suggestions that he was against Wilson's actions, Rockefeller went to his newfound friends in the press and disabused them of that notion. He issued a statement saying, "We must all stand behind the President regardless of consequences. Party, racial, and religious differences must be sunk into the melting pot of the common cause—harmonious patriotism. A state of war already exists with Germany. German U-boats are sinking ships without regard to cargo, life, nationality, or property values as recklessly as any pirate of the Spanish Main and American vessels are being compelled to arm themselves to stand off this menace." Rockefeller also put his money where his mouth was, contributing over $70 million to the war effort by purchasing liberty loans and contributing to the YMCA, the Red Cross, and Belgian Relief. As a result, Rockefeller once again became a crowd favorite, earning cheers and even having a street named after him in France.[72]

Ford: Running for Office

For Wilson, allying with Ford was beneficial, as Ford was surprisingly popular, even after the Peace Ship debacle. Despite not filing as a candidate, and even saying that "the filing of my name . . . was a joke," Ford managed to win Michigan's 1916 Republican presidential primary and make a strong showing in Nebraska as well. He even won a *St. Louis Times* poll ranking potential Republican presidential candidates. Ford clearly had grassroots support. One North Carolina resident sent a letter to Highland Park saying, "I am just a humble farmer, but my three greatest desires are to vote for Ford, own a Ford, and see Ford elected president by the greatest majority given any man." And a handbill printed in South Dakota read, "No names are greater in the whole universe than George Washington, Abraham Lincoln, and Henry Ford."[73]

The effort to get Ford the GOP nomination, unaided by Ford, would go nowhere. The eventual Republican nominee, Charles Evans Hughes, appeared to be a formidable candidate. A former governor of New York and a Supreme Court justice, Hughes had a reputation as a reformer and was favored to beat Wilson in the 1916 election. Given the challenge, Wilson was receptive to Ford's help. Ford shared his two best political assets with Wilson: his popularity and his wealth. In a meeting with the Democratic National Committee in New York, Ford pledged to provide funding for Wilson's campaign. As part of that effort, Ford spent $58,500 on a pro-Wilson newspaper ad that appeared in five hundred papers, reading, in part, "I am for Wilson and urge my fellow citizens to stand for him." He also gave Wilson his personal blessing, saying, "I spent four hours with him the other day and found him the most humane man, the most sensible man, the most businesslike man withal, I ever encountered." Wilson would win California by less than five thousand votes. Had Wilson lost California, Hughes would have become president. Given Ford's popularity, his endorsement—and his spending—may have proved decisive. Ford's help made Wilson's effort to cultivate Ford worthwhile; CEO prominence and wealth continue to be reasons that presidents seek relationships with CEOs.[74]

As so often happens, Ford found that his closeness to a politician did not shape that politician's views. If anything, it was Wilson who would shape Ford. While Ford did not renounce his pacifism, he did soften his opposition to the war. In February of 1917, the U.S. severed diplomatic relations with Germany. Public sentiment shifted, and Ford's views shifted as well.

On February 3, Ford said, "I will stand with our President, and in the event of a declaration of war will place our factory at the disposal of the United States government and will operate without one cent of profit." The U.S. declared war against Germany two months later, on April 6. Later, when asked about his views, Ford said that his backing of neutrality "had no application, once the United States entered the war. From April 1917 until November 1918, our factory worked practically exclusively for the government."[75]

Ford's foray into politics in this period brought him both perks and costs. From the perks perspective, he got to be close to Wilson, and Wilson even encouraged his political ambitions. Ford joined Wilson for a press conference on June 13, 1918, yet another chance for Ford to get close to Wilson. But this particular interaction ushered in a new form of presidential munificence. Ford left the White House, escorted out more respectfully this time by the president himself, and approached his awaiting car. Entering the vehicle, Ford told his aide Ernest Liebold, "He wants me to run for Senator."[76]

With Wilson's blessing, Ford ran for Senate from Michigan in 1918. It was an open seat, and Ford ran for both the Democratic and Republican nominations. He lost the Republican contest to former Secretary of the Navy Truman Newberry, but won the Democratic nod. Newberry was wealthy, although not as wealthy as Ford. Ford got high-profile endorsements from high-profile people, including Bernard Baruch and William Jennings Bryan, and the Democratic press pushed for Ford despite his lack of knowledge on key policy issues. Yet some who knew Ford better were skeptical of the effort. His friend Thomas Edison, knowing Ford's strengths as well as his liabilities, had warned him against the attempt, saying, "What do you want to do that for? You can't speak. You wouldn't say a damn word. You'd be mum." Edison was right. Once again, Ford faced Newberry, and once again he lost.[77]

Ford's narrow loss revealed something about the negative side of getting involved in politics. His reputation had taken a hit, something that Newberry successfully exploited. By getting involved in politics, Ford attracted critics, most notably Roosevelt, who continued to bash him long after the Peace Ship debacle.[78] Roosevelt did not like Ford's relentless PR efforts, noting that "Henry, like Barnum, has been a great advertiser." But he also did not like Ford's pacifism, nor Ford's efforts to keep his son, Edsel, from serving in the military. According to Roosevelt, "The expenditures on behalf of pacifism by Mr. Ford in connection with the Peace Ship . . . [were] as thoroughly demoralizing to the conscience of the American people as anything that has ever taken place. The failure of Mr. Ford's son to go into the army at this time, and the approval by the father of the son's refusal, represent exactly what might be expected from the moral disintegration inevitably produced by such pacifist propaganda." Newberry, who had served in the Roosevelt administration, also pressed the Edsel issue, and made sure to highlight photos of him with his two sons in uniform.[79]

World War I ended in 1919, and with its conclusion came the end of the Progressive Era. A more pro-business period was coming, and Ford remained in the thick of it. Ford may have lost his Senate race, but he was not done with politics. In 1920, Ford was considered a candidate for president—this time as a Republican—but lost out to Warren G. Harding, the first president of the Roaring Twenties.

CHAPTER 3

THE ROARING TWENTIES

Presidents: Warren G. Harding, Calvin Coolidge, Herbert Hoover
CEOs: *The Warner Brothers, Henry Luce, Rockefeller, Ford*

The 1920s were a good time for businesses and business leaders. This was the decade in which Calvin Coolidge would say, in 1925, "After all, the chief business of the American people is business. They are profoundly concerned with producing, buying, selling, investing and prospering in the world."[1]

Roosevelt and Wilson were no longer on the scene, and the Progressive Era's regulatory ardor had cooled. While the direction of regulatory encroachments on business has gone in the direction of greater government involvement, these things tend to go in waves. The 1920s were a period of recovery from the difficult war and pandemic-laden decade that preceded it. Warren G. Harding famously called for a "return to normalcy" in his 1920 campaign for president. As the "Roaring Twenties" economy boomed, the decade offered new hope for starting innovative business endeavors. It also offered opportunities for those innovators to befriend presidents and even to celebrate them. These friendly engagements demonstrated a new kind of presidential-CEO interaction, genuine relationships based on friendship and mutual benefit. Presidents learned that CEOs could not just be targets, or bail them out in times of crisis, but they could also provide political opportunities.

Interlude: Ford and Antisemitism

Henry Ford was one of the most popular Americans going into the 1920s. According to historian and author Steven Watts, Ford received twice as much publicity as John D. Rockefeller, Junior and Senior, and more publicity than all but four Americans—Wilson, Roosevelt, Charles Evans Hughes, and Bryan—in the period from 1915 to 1920. Those other four had all been presidents or candidates for president. In the twenties, Ford—the man who brought cars to the masses—got more attention than anyone but Calvin Coolidge, who was vice president and president for eight of the decade's ten years. The *New York Times* averaged 145 pieces on Ford annually. *Detroit Saturday Night* diagnosed the nation with a case of Ford-osis, saying, "They gobble the Ford stuff, and never stop to reason whether they like it, or whether it has any real merit in it."[2]

Despite his popularity, Ford was also a mixed bag. In 1918, Liebold, Ford's private secretary, purchased the *Dearborn Independent* and used it as a pro-Ford organ. In 1919, Ford himself purchased the paper and used it to disseminate his own views. These views were not only pacifist, but they were anti-Semitic as well. The paper's antisemitism worsened with the publication of the infamous anti-Semitic forgery, "The Protocols of the Elders of Zion," issued as part of the paper's reprehensible and long-standing series on "the International Jew." Liebold was an antisemite and a factor in the paper's editorial decisions, but Ford himself was a bad actor as well. He was a believer in—and purveyor of—conspiracy theories about Jews, even though he personally associated with Jews, including his architect, Alfred Kahn, and employed thousands of Jews in his factories.

This antisemitism rightly led to widespread condemnations of Ford. It did not make him a pariah, but it definitely harmed his image, both at the time and historically. It also brought about denunciations from multiple presidents. In 1920, former President Taft said in a speech to B'nai B'rith's Anti-Defamation League that, "One of the chief causes of suffering and evil in the world today is race hatred, and any man who stimulates that hatred has much to answer for," adding that, "When he does this by the circulation of unfounded and unjust charges and the arousing of mean and groundless fears, his fault is more to be condemned." Ford's name did not have to be mentioned for everyone to know who Taft meant. The next year, Taft would join outgoing President Wilson, incoming President Harding, and over one hundred other notable "citizens of Gentile extraction and Christian faith" in signing a statement by Ford critic John Webster Spargo called "The Perils of Racial Prejudice."[3]

In addition to the reputational hits, Jews also organized a boycott of Ford products, which hit Ford where it hurt. He had been warned long before, in the run-up to World War I, by his executive-turned-Detroit-mayor and Republican senator James Couzens, that his political views would negatively impact sales. Despite the warning, Ford continued on his destructive path until finally backing away from his antisemitism in the late 1920s. Ford's pacifism and his antisemitism were controversial and earned him significant criticism. Nevertheless, his popularity and the popularity of his automobiles made him a force in U.S. presidential politics in the 1920s, even as his poor public speaking and his antisemitism limited his political potential.[4]

Ford: Hanging Out with Harding, Coolidge, and the Vagabonds

Ford's ownership of the anti-Semitic *Dearborn Independent* was an extracurricular activity that damaged his reputation. But another, less controversial activity generated lots of positive publicity for the auto magnate. In the period from 1915-1924, Ford had formed a camping group with three other famous friends, Thomas Edison, the tire magnate Harvey Firestone, and the naturalist and best-selling author John Burroughs. The four called themselves the Vagabonds, and their trips earned enormous publicity. Harding met up with the Vagabonds in Maryland on the 1921 trip, along with his wife, a secretary, and Secret Service protection. Harding impressed the Vagabonds by contributing to the effort by chopping wood for the campfire. The trip was great publicity for Harding, showing him to be a regular guy, but Ford benefited as well. Employees from Ford Motion Picture Laboratories and Ford Photographic Department accompanied the Vagabonds, and the trips were useful PR for promoting automobile adoption.[5]

The trips were about more than just the publicity. They were a great way for the Vagabonds, especially Ford, to get to know the president. Part of the calculus for Ford was that he had business before the president. Ford was interested in purchasing an Alabama dam and nitrate plant complex called Muscle Shoals. The government had used it for the development of explosives during the war, but with the war over, Ford saw an opportunity to purchase the energy- and fertilizer-generating land at a bargain price. Ford's bid got held up amidst lobbying from competitors in Washington, and he hoped for an opportunity to secure Harding's support for his bid.[6]

It was not to be. Though Harding and the Vagabonds did stay up late talking around the campfire, Harding skillfully dominated the conversation and did not bring up Muscle Shoals. Harding did talk about a "Limitations of Arms" confer-ence and, according to Firestone, "about the trials of being president and the vast amount of unnecessary detail imposed upon the office. . . . He also spoke of the nuisance of a President being forced to seek a second term, and thought that a single term of six years would be far better and leave the President with more time to attend to his duties." One other thing that Harding said that must have sat well with Ford and Firestone was his idea "that it was time to stop attacking business because it was business, and legitimate business ought to be protected and not interfered with." If nothing else, that statement was a win for the businessmen. Yet Harding benefited as well, mostly from newspaper editorials praising his egalitarianism, such as the one in the *Oakland Tribune* writing that "the President chumming with Thomas Edison and Henry Ford in a mountain camp is . . . characteristically American, illuminating a phase of life peculiar to this country. It would be impossible to think of a president of any other land chopping the wood to cook his meal."[7]

Despite the positive press from the camping trip, Harding was a weak and unpopular president. There was even talk of Ford replacing him in 1924, with Ford for President clubs forming and a 1923 Colliers poll having Ford in the lead among all candidates, including the incumbent. Ford himself was even interested, saying privately of Washington, "I'd . . . like to go down there for about six weeks and throw some monkey wrenches into the machinery." But Ford in '24 was not to be. In July of 1923, Harding began having heart problems and contracted pneumonia. On August 2, he died of cardiac arrest. Vice President Coolidge took over, severely curtailing the fledgling Ford for President boomlet. As Ford told reporters later that month, "I hope that President Coolidge will follow closely in the footsteps of his illustrious predecessor, the late President Harding. I know nothing about President Coolidge. I was very intimately acquainted with the late President Harding as it was only two years ago that we were on a similar camping trip to this."[8]

Muscle Shoals was also not to be. In September, Ford and his son Edsel met with the new president seeking his backing for Muscle Shoals in exchange for Ford not running for president. Ford had made progress in the House but the project stalled in the Senate, largely due to the opposition of Nebraska senator George Norris, who objected to Ford getting an $85 million facility for his bid of $5 million.[9]

Ford did consider the possibility that Coolidge's support could break the log-jam. Yet Coolidge was a savvy political operative. He briefly agreed not to oppose the project, but he did not explicitly support it. The apparent deal for Muscle Shoals led to a public outcry. Facing Norris's opposition and public resistance, Ford withdrew his bid. The whole episode was a clear win for Coolidge and a loss for Ford. Ford never got Muscle Shoals, but the land would eventually be converted under the Franklin Roosevelt administration to a famous facility that we now know as the Tennessee Valley Authority.[10]

Despite being on different sides of the Muscle Shoals issue, Coolidge saw the benefit from associating with Ford. In 1924, with Ford no longer running for president, he and the Vagabonds would go to Coolidge's native Vermont on their summer trip. There, they visited Coolidge for an hour. Coolidge gave Ford a century old sugar bucket used in the making of maple syrup. Ford liked the gift enough to say, "I've never received anything since I married Mrs. Ford that I appreciated so much." Coolidge signed it with an inscription, "Made for and used by John Coolidge, one of the original settlers of Plymouth, Vermont. Died 1822. Used also by Calvin Coolidge in sugar lot when he was a boy at home." In return, Ford gave Coolidge a compass of the sort used by the Vagabonds for John, Coolidge's surviving son. They then went to the Plymouth Notch cheese factory, where the Vagabonds sampled Vermont cheese, which later caused them gastro-intestinal distress.[11]

Coolidge got the better part of the exchange. Ford had warm words for Coolidge's upcoming candidacy, saying, "The only issue in this campaign is Calvin Coolidge. There is no other. The people as a whole have implicit confidence in him." Ford added that he backed Coolidge because "he stands for law and order and that is what the country needs. There is too much lawlessness and too much disregard for the things that have made America the greatest nation in the world." In the end, Coolidge got an endorsement from one of the nation's most popular entrepreneurs. Ford and his friends ended up with indigestion.[12]

Henry Luce: Building a New American Medium

The 1920s were a time of the expansion of new forms of media. One of the most innovative CEOs in this regard was *TIME*'s Henry Luce, who pioneered the idea of making the news national rather than regional. Yet Luce, who was the prime intellectual force behind the idea that the twentieth century was quintessentially "The American Century," was not even born in the geographical confines of the United States. Headman Luce was born in Tengchowfu, China, in 1898. His parents were missionaries, and he spoke Mandarin Chinese before he spoke English. At fourteen, he left, alone, for St. Albans in England before moving to the United States to attend the Hotchkiss School in Connecticut. While at Hotchkiss, Luce met Briton "Britt" Haddon, with whom he would go to Yale and with whom he would also initiate his media empire.

Even at Hotchkiss, Luce had grand ambitions. He worked with Hadden on the *Hotchkiss Weekly Record* and wrote poems for *The Lit*, aspiring to serve as its editor. When upperclassman and future Yale instructor Erdman Harris asked him about his plans as editor, Luce told him that he planned to have former president Theodore Roosevelt contribute to the high school magazine. Harris was a little taken aback by this and was further surprised to learn that Luce had already put out feelers to solicit Roosevelt's contribution. This brazenness alerted Erdman that his younger interlocutor was "no ordinary schoolboy."[13]

Roosevelt was a hero to Luce. Luce's missionary father, also a TR fan, used to send Luce pictures of Roosevelt, which the son treasured. Luce would later consider Roosevelt one of the great men of history, and Roosevelt's vision of American primacy would continue to inspire Luce throughout his career.[14]

While at Yale, Luce and Hadden worked on the *Yale Daily News*, which continued to whet their appetite for journalism. Luce's hero Roosevelt died while they worked on the *YDN*, and the paper's front-page celebration of Roosevelt on his passage lauded him as having "a spirit unique among men . . . [like] that which imbued Napoleon. He possessed courage which never flinched . . ." They both were in the prestigious and secretive Skull and Bones, and both received accolades from their classmates upon graduation in 1920. Hadden was deemed "Most Likely to Succeed"; Luce secured "Most Brilliant."[15]

Upon graduation, Luce studied for a year at Oxford, then returned to the U.S. where he, along with Hadden, continued in journalism at the *Baltimore News* for $40 a week. Neither man was impressed with the state of journalism at the time, an assessment that included the *New York Times*.

Luce and Hadden had good reason to be unimpressed. There was no national news at the time, even as the technologies to create that kind of news were emerging. Film had already arrived, and by 1920 former President Roosevelt was the most filmed person on the planet. Radio had also begun to emerge, and presidents were beginning to recognize its potential. Warren Harding was the first president to speak as president over the radio, and supposedly "silent" Cal Coolidge was the first president to speak regularly to the American people over the radio. Coolidge liked the medium and demonstrated as much by saying that "I am very fortunate that I came in with the radio . . . . I have a good radio voice, and now I can get my messages across . . . without acquainting [listeners] with my lack of oratorical ability or without making any rhetorical display in their presence."[16]

When it came to print, though, there was an odd lag. The wire services—the Associated Press began in 1846, and United Press International started in 1907—brought local news to a network of big papers across the country. There were also large papers like the *New York Times* and Robert McCormick's *Chicago Tribune*, but they were more regional powerhouses, without a national voice. Few publications—including *The Literary Digest*, a news aggregator that was Luce's supposed competition—reached or addressed a national audience. It was this gap that Luce and Hadden looked to fill.

After work each day, Luce and Hadden would play around with their idea for a national magazine to be called *Facts*, filled with 200-word summaries of the key issues of the day. The vision, Luce wrote to his girlfriend and later first wife Lila Hotz, was of "articles on politics, books, sport, scandal, science, society . . . [for] . . . the illiterate upper classes, the busy businessman, the tired debutante, to prepare them at least once a week for a table conversation." Hadden and Luce prepared for this effort in their off hours following the 3:00 p.m. end of the day at the *Baltimore News.* Without word processing, they developed a format by "chopping up the *New York Times,* and reorganizing [it] on a weekly basis, and then trying to put these stories together."[17]

Luce and Hadden then took a seven-week leave of absence to consider what a new enterprise might look like. They realized that they would need $100,000 to get started, the equivalent of $1.6 million in today's dollars. It was not an easy sum to raise. The initial thought was to raise $10,000 each from ten friends, but the ten donors did not materialize. They lived cheaply while they worked, renting a low-cost townhouse, before finally securing $86,000—enough to get started—by November of 1922. Their magazine launched at the end of February, with a 28-page black-and-white issue dated March 3, 1923. It was no longer called *Facts*. It was now called *TIME*. And that one magazine would soon expand to three, with *Fortune* coming in 1930, and *Life* in 1936. (*Sports Illustrated* would come later, in 1954.)[18]

As the nation's first and at the time only national news magazine, *TIME* had the potential for an enormous political impact from the start. *TIME* and Luce elevated the office of the presidency, regardless of its occupant, by breathlessly reporting the most minute and non-policy-related presidential actions: birthdays, vacations, walks in the rain. *TIME* had a popular section, "The President's Week," devoted to these presidential activities. In addition, it was *TIME*'s initial inclination to take a respectful view towards the nation's leaders, particularly its presidents. All this makes sense as Luce himself was reportedly interested in the presidency, even checking with a lawyer to see if he was eligible despite his Chinese birth to American parents. He was.[19]

When it came to individual preferences, Luce initially looked to assess the man, not the party. His father, the Reverend Luce, was a strong Republican, and Luce often agreed with his father, but not always. In fact, when *TIME* began and in its early years, Luce had not yet sided with either the Democrats or the Republicans. Given Luce's pro-presidency predisposition, *TIME* described Warren Harding—today consistently ranked among the worst presidents—as "important and successful as the embodiment of the American ideal of humility exalted by homely virtues into the highest eminence." Luce was somewhat disappointed with subsequent presidents Coolidge and Hoover, but each was nevertheless praised in the pages of *TIME*. Coolidge, per *TIME*, had "genuine humility" and "flinty integrity," as well as a "kinship with his people." Herbert Hoover was dubbed "a high-minded, able, industrious, conscientious individual who is devoted to his country, to the art of Government, to children," with "unbounded faith in himself."[20] But that would change with the economic collapse that was coming.

Harry and Jack Warner: Building Another New American Medium

During this same period of national news outlets, another innovation sprang forth: cinema. At the apex of this new sector of the American economy were the Warner brothers, who made movies—and in the process helped create a new form of cultural expression and storytelling. The Warner brothers (numbering four) hailed from a family of twelve. Four of them—Sam, Jack, Harry, and Albert—would define and shape the fledgling movie business. They launched their cinematic efforts in 1903 in New Castle, Pennsylvania. Within a decade and a half, they had moved to Hollywood and started one of the first studios.

Together, they were innovators and visionaries. By the 1920s, Sam Warner saw the promise of talking pictures and championed the production of *The Jazz Singer*, the first talking picture. With Sam's death just a day before the film's premiere in 1927, Harry, born in Poland in 1881, and Jack, born in Canada in 1892, were left in charge of the studio with the hottest new technology in Hollywood, at a time when one hundred million Americans were attending movies weekly. They would use that audience and that technology to become wealthy, to befriend presidents, and to spread their ideas about what America was—to their fellow citizens and to people around the world.[21]

The studio the Warner brothers created reflected their own sensibilities. As immigrants and Jews, they loved America with an outsider's perspective and appreciation, and made films accordingly. While studio products are often interchangeable today, they weren't so then. According to the filmmaker Billy Wilder, "Studios had faces then. They had their own style. They could bring you blindfolded into a movie house and you opened it and looked up and you knew." Warner Brothers exemplified this reality—boldly exploring new film technologies, showing gratitude for the American experiment, and engaging in American politics.[22]

When Hollywood was founded, most studio heads were Republicans. Jack Warner had once hosted President Calvin Coolidge at the studio, and even tried to convince him to run for reelection in 1928. That effort failed, and Coolidge was replaced by Herbert Hoover. Harry Warner was unimpressed with Hoover, though, which left him open to looking elsewhere in the next election.

Ford: Celebrating American Innovation with Hoover

The Hoover administration started with great promise. A trained engineer, Hoover was known as the "Master of Emergencies" for his skillful work helping feed refugees in World War I, heading the U.S. Food Association under Woodrow Wilson, and, with the American Relief Administration, helping Soviet victims of Communist-inflicted famine. As secretary of commerce under Calvin Coolidge, Hoover led the administration's relief efforts in response to the 1927 Mississippi Flood.[23]

Hoover also came from the world of business. In one of Hoover's first acts as president, he had a telephone placed on his desk, the first president to do so. A telephone had been in the White House for fifty years, since the administration of Rutherford B. Hayes, but Hoover was the first to put one in the Oval Office, signaling that his was to be a presidency of action.[24]

In October of 1929, seven months into Hoover's presidency, he travelled to Dearborn, Michigan, to participate in Henry Ford's celebration of the fiftieth anniversary of Edison's invention of the incandescent light bulb. To honor his friend and mentor, Ford had recreated Edison's legendary Menlo Park lab in Greenfield Village, the site of the Edison Memorial Foundation, later renamed the Henry Ford Museum. Ford unveiled the recreated labs on the Golden Jubilee of Edison's achievement. Hoover was the most illustrious of the many invited guests, including John D. Rockefeller, Charles Schwab, and Will Rogers.[25]

At the event, Hoover talked about the impact of Edison's invention on civilization, noting that it spared "the human race from the curse of always cleaning oil lamps, scrubbing up candle drips, and everlastingly carrying one or the other of them about." Then Edison, Ford, Hoover, and Edison's assistant Francis Jehl went into the Menlo Park lab to revisit the legendary moment of invention. Americans across the nation turned off their lights for the occasion, relighting them after Edison and Jehl connected the two wires to light a bulb, just as they had done a half century earlier. The moment was designed to symbolize the light brought on by Edison's great achievement, contrasting it with the darkness that had existed beforehand.[26]

No one knew it at the time, but the nation was about to descend into another form of darkness. Until that point, though, the twenties were a period of peace and prosperity, presided over by three Republican presidents. As such, new government interventions were minimal, and CEOs could generally operate without having to engage in defensive operations to protect their businesses from being targeted by American presidents. But CEOs were also gaining influence, in the form of new platforms: be it the national news disseminated by Luce; the movies produced by the Warners; or Ford, via the newspaper he ran and his general popularity that got him mentioned regularly in the news. For presidents, these platforms served as opportunities to leverage to their political advantage. For CEOs, their platforms became a beneficence they could bestow on presidents to whom they were favorably inclined.

CHAPTER 4

THE GREAT DEPRESSION

Presidents: Hoover, Franklin Delano Roosevelt
CEOs: The Warner Brothers, Ford, Rockefeller, Henry Luce

On Black Thursday, October 24, 1929, the stock market crashed. Market drops continued into the next week with Black Monday and Black Tuesday. This was the first public signal of the Great Depression that would roil America for the next decade. The American people would respond to the collapse by electing a new leader, one who would challenge American businesses like never before. Some business leaders would celebrate him, others would loathe him, but they would all have to deal with the changes and interventions he brought about. Before that, though, the embattled incumbent would try to deal with the economic disaster in the making.

Ford and Rockefeller: Looking to Help Hoover

With the economy cratering, Herbert Hoover needed help. One month after the triumphal Menlo Park celebration of Edison's innovation, Hoover invited business leaders to the White House for advice, a confidence boost, and a photo op. Henry Ford answered the White House invitation, along with General Motors head Alfred P. Sloan, chemical magnate Pierre DuPont, and chair of the Radio Corporation of America Owen D. Young.[1]

The meeting with Hoover went on for three hours. Hoover was planning to issue a statement afterwards, so the other leaders said "no comment" to the members of the press begging for some details on what had taken place.

Ford, typically, had a different approach. He had his secretary hand members of the press a typed statement criticizing the stock market for its "promise of quick profits in speculation." Nevertheless, he also expressed optimism that things would return to normal following the reversion to more appropriate valuations. Then he added that the solution to the problem was lower priced goods and higher wages, the very innovations he had brought via the Model T and the five dollars day, which was by that point up to six dollars a day.[2]

After a quick lunch break, Ford returned to meet with Hoover a second time. After this second consultation, Ford announced that he would be raising wages at Ford Motor Company within ten days. This idea had not been agreed to at the first meeting and indeed was contrary to Hoover's released statement saying that the assembled leaders did not believe that wages should be increased. Ford's statement was bold, but it also irked the other leaders who had not agreed to any such wage increase.[3]

Ford lived up to his word. On December 1, 1929, he announced that he would increase wages from six dollars a day to seven dollars a day. The announcement was a sensation, just as the five dollars a day declaration had been in January of 1914.

Rockefeller tried to help the economy as well. He and Charles Schwab, along with Ford, tried to prop up the stock market after the October crash. They invested heavily in the market, seeking bargain prices, and briefly succeeded in stabilizing markets. Rockefeller was bullish, or at least philosophical, on the economy, and said, "These are days when many are discouraged. In the 93 years of my life, depressions have come and gone. Prosperity has always returned and will again." But Rockefeller and his wealthy friends could not stave off the inevitable, as the structural shocks to the economy were too great for individual interventions or top-down positivity to help. Hoover was soundly beaten in the 1932 election, and the onset of the Great Depression would have political implications for a number of CEOs as well. For Rockefeller, Hoover's defeat and the ascension of Franklin Roosevelt would plant the seeds for his family's redemption. For movie moguls Harry and Jack Warner, it would bring a treasured friend to the White House. But for Ford and *TIME* magazine founder Henry Luce, it would bring to power a bitter enemy and create two of the biggest enmities ever between an American president and some of our nation's most iconic CEOs.[4]

The Warners: A Growing Friendship with Roosevelt

Before the 1932 Democratic Convention, Harry Warner invited his brother Jack to a mysterious meeting in New York. To get him there, Harry told his brother, "There's going to be a meeting, Jack. It's so secret I won't even talk about it on the phone. I want you here for it." The meeting was for supporters of Franklin Roosevelt. At the meeting, the assessment was frank—and dire: "The country is in chaos. There is revolution in the air, and we need a change." Harry then told Jack, "If Governor Roosevelt is nominated, we want you to help out on the West Coast campaign." Jack was not yet sure about Roosevelt, but he agreed to help, telling Harry and his colleagues, "I'm your man." This was a bold step that would alienate the predominantly Republican studio heads of the time, such as MGM's Louis B. Mayer.[5]

Not long after, Jack met Franklin Roosevelt on a train to Los Angeles and was impressed, finding him "vital and enormously magnetic." The men became friends. Jack headed the film chapter of "Roosevelt for President," raising money and organizing events for Roosevelt, including a star-studded one with Charlie Chaplin, Clark Gable, Will Rogers, Laurel and Hardy, and Boris Karloff.[6]

After Roosevelt's election, Warner and a trainload of Hollywood stars went to Washington for Roosevelt's inauguration. Jack had dinner at the White House and stayed overnight in the Lincoln bedroom. Roosevelt laughed at Warner's jokes and plied Warner for information about the movie business.[7]

As president, Roosevelt continued to find ways to use the Warners. Jack became Los Angeles chairman for the National Recovery Act, an unpopular law among many businessmen, but not with the Warners. Roosevelt offered Jack a job overseas, causing Jack to joke later that, "I might have been the first Jewish ambassador to Ireland!" He demurred, though, saying, "I'm very flattered Mr. President. But I think I can do better for your foreign relations with a good picture about America now and then." This offhand comment would lead to a close collaboration with the Warners and the White House on message-oriented films to help advance the Roosevelt administration's political and policy goals.[8]

The Warners supported FDR on film in a variety of ways. They put images of Roosevelt himself in their movies, beginning with 1933's *Footlight Parade*.

Roosevelt was depicted in film more than any other president. Not all of these were Warner films, but many were, including 1942's *Yankee Doodle Dandy*. In addition, Warner, more than other studios, started the trend, producing films about social issues and current events, often in a way that was complementary—and complimentary—to the efforts of the Roosevelt administration. According to Harry, these films were made to show "the world as it is." Accordingly, an estimated twenty percent of Warner films in this period came from ideas rooted in newspaper headlines.[9]

Warner films of this period were also patriotic, and often portrayed great moments in American history. Films like *Give Me Liberty* (1936), *Teddy the Rough Rider* (1937), *The Declaration of Independence* (1938), *The Bill of Rights* (1939), and *The Monroe Doctrine* (1939) presented America in the best possible light. Patriotic themes were important and would continue into the 1940s as the Warners' support for Roosevelt would extend to the war effort as well.

After Roosevelt's presidency, the Warners continued to interact with other presidents. After Harry died in 1958, Jack was vacationing in the Riviera and told his guests, "Look at this. It's a letter of condolence from President Eisenhower. Ain't that something?" With Harry gone, Jack tacked back to his Republican roots, backing Richard Nixon in 1960. After Nixon's defeat, Jack tried to befriend Jack Kennedy, using his old trick of the propaganda film. Warner produced *PT-109*, a critically panned but marginally profitable film glorifying Kennedy's service in the Pacific. Kennedy personally approved of the selection of the actor Cliff Robertson to play Kennedy and attended a screening of the film in Washington. None of the postwar relationships would approach the mutually beneficial friendship Jack Warner had with Franklin Roosevelt. It was hard to recapture that magic.[10]

Yet as positive as the relationship between FDR and the Warners was, there were other CEOs who progressed down a different track with our longest-serving president. And those stories show how an opportunity for a relationship can come and go quickly—and then descend into bitterness as powerful men clash. Such was the case with both Henry Luce and Henry Ford.

Luce and FDR: Growing Enmity

Henry Luce and his empire began looking less kindly at President Hoover as the Depression worsened. In 1932, a *Fortune* essay ripped into Hoover's Great Depression claim that "no one has starved," by putting the infelicitous phrase in the title of the piece, and adding the harsh but accurate subtitle, "Which isn't true." Sometimes his magazines went a little too far. The anti-big business *Fortune* ran an article in which it claimed that banker Bernard Baruch called former President Hoover "old cheese face." Baruch had not done so, and Luce was forced to run a retraction.[11]

Hoover tested the limits of Luce's pro-presidency disposition. Franklin Delano Roosevelt's administration would end it. This change would have both implications and lessons for how presidents and chief executives would interact going forward. Luce was no dyed-in-the-wool Republican. He had supported the Democrat Al Smith—an early *TIME* subscriber—over Hoover in 1928, donating one hundred dollars to Smith's campaign, but he did back Hoover for reelection in 1932. Luce would continue to back Republicans from that point on, not supporting another Democrat for president until Lyndon Johnson in 1964. Luce tried to shade *TIME*'s coverage in favor of Hoover, but to little avail, as most of the members of the editorial team—not to mention most of the country—were in Roosevelt's camp.

Even though Luce supported Hoover, he did not hate Roosevelt. Yet. That would come later. Initially there were reasons to expect that Luce might even like Roosevelt, who was *TIME*'s Man of the Year in both 1932 and 1934. First, there was the understandable disappointment with Hoover's poor performance as president. The Great Depression may not have been bad for the rapidly growing *TIME* empire—net profits went from $3,860 in 1928 to $2.2 million in 1935, with circulation surpassing 400,000—but it was decidedly bad for America. Between 1929 and 1932, net farm income dropped from $6 billion to $2 billion; residential construction went down by 82 percent; and national income dropped from $87.4 billion to $41.7 billion. As for the stock market, the Dow plummeted from 294 in the spring of 1930 to 41 in July of 1932. Luce and the rest of America had ample reason to seek a change from Hoover's leadership. Upon Roosevelt's election, Luce even said, "This country will feel better and that's fine."[12]

In addition to Luce's recognition of the need for a change, there was also the fact that he and Roosevelt shared some significant similarities in their backgrounds. Both men went to elite prep schools—Luce to Hotchkiss and Roosevelt to Groton. Both attended top Ivy League colleges—Roosevelt to Harvard and Luce to Yale. Although Luce's father was a Republican, and Roosevelt's a Democrat, Roosevelt obviously also had prominent Republicans among his relatives, most notably former president Theodore, whom Luce revered.

In addition to their similar backgrounds and shared experiences, Luce and FDR had a mutual friend in Archibald MacLeish. MacLeish was a prominent poet and playwright who spent much of the 1920s with the American literary crowd in Paris. He too had gone to Hotchkiss and Yale, where the younger Luce looked up to him. When MacLeish returned to the U.S., he joined Luce's staff at *Fortune*, and helped make *Fortune* "probably the most interesting magazine in the United States," according to the late historian Alan Brinkley. While there, he talked up Roosevelt to Luce, and encouraged a meeting between the two men.[13]

The meeting took place in early 1933, after Roosevelt's inauguration. MacLeish, assigned to write a *Fortune* profile of FDR, tagged along. Luce was impressed with what he saw, and even said of FDR after the meeting, "What a man! What a man!" As was typical of things in Luce's world, positive impressions led to positive coverage, and both *TIME* and *Fortune* gave Roosevelt favorable notices through 1933. *TIME* also gave Roosevelt early credit for a "careful and cautious start," and praised Roosevelt appointees like Labor Secretary Frances Perkins—the first female cabinet secretary—brain truster and Columbia Law professor Raymond Moley, and Interior Secretary Harold Ickes.[14]

TIME's initially positive coverage soon began to wane in the face of FDR's other personnel and policy choices. Luce was not a New Dealer by nature, but he was patient until Roosevelt gave official recognition to the Soviet Union. Luce was a staunch anti-communist—anti-communism would be one of the defining and unchanging characteristics of Luce's worldview—and recognition was an unforgivable sin in Luce's eyes. Roosevelt, for his part, was a careful reader of reporter Walter Duranty's ongoing whitewashing of the murderous Soviet regime in the *New York Times*, which likely colored Roosevelt's views in favor of the USSR.[15]

A longtime skeptic of the *New York Times*, Luce was not as easily fooled. Recognition of Soviet Russia also opened Luce's eyes to Roosevelt's other transgressions—and the New Deal was replete with enough capricious actions to make any self-made American businessman blanch. Luce did not like the regulations and the taxes that he believed would have a damaging effect on growth and competitiveness. He also saw dangers in Roosevelt's rhetoric and what he considered to be Roosevelt's demagogic tendencies.

Luce used his platforms to express his growing dissatisfaction. In 1935, knowing MacLeish's affection for the president, Luce made MacLeish write an anti-Roosevelt feature in *Fortune*. In the piece, called "The Case Against Roosevelt," *Fortune* hit both of Luce's major objections to the New Deal: the specifics of its policies as well as what it portended in terms of the expansion of both Roosevelt's power and the power of the presidency. The article criticized the New Deal's "feel of the human interferer" and its "personal character" targeted against big business. More pointedly, the piece claimed that Roosevelt "has opened a door through which a dictator could easily pass," which became a recurrent accusation from Luce's empire. While New Deal policies could potentially hurt his business, his complaints were from a national perspective, rather than from a desire to help his company per se, in contrast to many other politically involved CEOs.[16]

In 1936, Luce further showed his displeasure with Roosevelt by seeking to have Roosevelt defeated in his bid for reelection. At this point, it was not a foregone conclusion that Luce would be backing the Republican over the Democrat, even if his unhappiness with Roosevelt was becoming increasingly apparent. That year, *TIME* wrote of Roosevelt that he "has so bitterly aroused the enmity of a whole class. . . . Regardless of party and regardless of region, today, with few exceptions, members of the so-called Upper Class frankly hate Franklin Roosevelt." This may not have been true of everyone in the "so-called Upper Class," but it was certainly true of Luce.[17]

To defeat Roosevelt, though, Luce needed a candidate. He thought he discovered one in Kansas Republican governor Alf Landon. Luce personally traveled to Topeka to see Landon and found him impressive. Landon received the cover treatment in *TIME*, complete with what was known as "the Breakfast Technique."

This was a standard *TIME* maneuver for profiles, especially positive ones, in which one paragraph would be devoted to the subject's preferred morning intake. For Landon, the relevant paragraph read, "At 7:20 he was down to a breakfast of orange juice, fruit, scrambled eggs and kidneys, toast and coffee . . . husky, broad-shouldered Governor Landon . . . a wide smile crinkling his plain, friendly face. 'Top o' the mornin' to you all.'"[18]

The Breakfast Technique had multiple purposes. First, it was supposed to endear the subject to the audience, humanizing him by showing how he handled his morning routine. But it had another purpose as well, to show *TIME*'s audience how plugged in *TIME* was, how its reporters shared something as private and intimate as the morning meal with the world's movers and shakers. And, of course, assuming that the subject liked the profile, Breakfast Technique and all, it could endear *TIME* and its reporters to the subject, making *TIME* all the more likely to get access, quotes, and scoops in the future. And it was memorable. As former *TIME* writer Lance Morrow wrote eight decades later in 2022, "No reader ever forgot the kidneys."[19]

In recent years, the Breakfast Technique has fallen out of favor with the rise of social media and reality television. But in the 1930s, it was cutting edge. Theodore White, an ex-*TIME* reporter, relied on it heavily for his popular *The Making of the President* books in the 1960s and 1970s. After a while, though, White recognized that it had become a bit of a cliché. As he told the author of *Boys on the Bus*, Timothy Crouse, about candidate reporting in 1972, "All of us are observing him, taking notes like mad, getting all the little details. Which I think I invented as a method of reporting and which I now sincerely regret." In sum, White thought, "Who gives a f— if the guy had milk and Total for breakfast?"[20]

In 1936, despite the Breakfast Technique's popularity as a journalistic trope, it was not enough to lift Landon. Luce soon recognized that Landon was out of his depth, and he backed off from his support as the election neared. *TIME* informed its readers about campaign mistakes by the Landon team, speeches before empty halls, and booing crowds. It also praised Roosevelt's "masterpiece" reelection effort.[21]

Luce's bet-hedging on Landon revealed a pragmatic side to his political efforts. Sure, he hated Roosevelt, but he also had a magazine to sell, and Roosevelt was a popular politician. Furthermore, Roosevelt was president, and Luce both wanted to have influence and did not want to antagonize a chief executive who had no compunction about targeting business. This hard reality explains why the magazine might lambast Roosevelt's policies, while FDR the man was always prominently and positively featured in the "The President's Week" section. Luce hoped the Democrats would lose Congress in the 1934 midterm elections, but he made FDR "Man of the Year" after his party won. It is also why Luce maintained the lines of communication with the White House. After a 1939 speech in which Luce praised Roosevelt, the two had lunch in the White House on May 10, 1939. Unfortunately, however, the lunch did not go well because FDR kept calling Luce "Henry" instead of his preferred nickname, which was "Harry."[22]

For the most part, these pleasantries, awkward as they were, were the exception. Luce regularly criticized Roosevelt in print and in his speeches, including a 1937 speech that accused Roosevelt of basing "his political popularity on the implication that business is antisocial, unpatriotic, vulgar, and corruptive." But the speeches and the coverage were unable to dislodge FDR from office. Luce strongly backed Roosevelt opponent Wendell Willkie in the 1940 election, giving him foreign policy advice. (Luce was so involved that he was rumored to be Secretary of State in a potential Willkie administration.) Once again, his efforts were to no avail. As powerful as Luce was, he ultimately had little impact on Roosevelt's ability to get reelected three times.[23]

Part of the problem for Luce may have been that while he was personally anti-Roosevelt, his team was not. MacLeish was only one of multiple liberals in the Luce operation, including MacLeish, the critic Dwight MacDonald, the editor Ralph Ingersoll, and *Let Us Now Praise Famous Men* author James Agee. *Fortune*, in particular, was anti-business and pro-Roosevelt in the early 1930s. In this, Luce often found himself at odds with his own employees. Roosevelt, he could do little about. His own team he could address.

By 1935, Luce's patience with the liberals at *Fortune* had begun to run out, and he sought to "get *Fortune* a little bit straightened out ideologically." He started to get rid of the leftist writers, aiming to get a more amenable team on board. In 1937, Luce made his changes more official, pursuing what he called a "Respectus" in which "*Fortune* can be either a great Communist magazine or a great Capitalist magazine." Going forward, *Fortune* would "have a platform with two planks," a "free and fearless journalism of inquiry," and one with "a bias in favor of private enterprise" and against "State-control." As Luce put it, "*Fortune* views with alarm the weakness in private capitalism which invokes collectivism; and points with pride to those merits in private capitalism which argue against collectivism." Getting *Fortune* back on a pro-business path was the main goal of the Respectus, but having another organ with which to hit Roosevelt was another benefit as well.[24]

Roosevelt was of course aware of Luce's antipathy. Roosevelt was also willing to hit back in ways that may not be appropriate for a chief executive, but that foreshadowed some of the ways in which future presidents would push back against media executives whose organs criticized them. Roosevelt would complain directly to Luce about both the substance and the style of *TIME*'s criticism. After Roosevelt's successful reelection, he wrote but did not send Luce a lengthy missive complaining about *TIME*'s "deliberate falsehoods," declaring that "I hate to see an educated group of people doing things to their country which their very education, in the better sense of the word, should keep them from doing." Instead, Roosevelt had aide Lowell Mellett send Luce a shorter note airing some of the White House's grievances. Luce sent back a response that did not impress Roosevelt, who called it a "slippery reply." On another occasion, Roosevelt referred to *TIME* as "a serious detriment to the future of successful democracy in the United States," a statement that seemed to vindicate Luce's complaints about Roosevelt's demagoguery.[25]

Ford and FDR: Angry Exchanges

Franklin Roosevelt disliked Henry Ford. In 1932, even before becoming president, Roosevelt denounced Ford at a campaign speech in Pittsburgh. In an October 19 "Address on the Federal Budget," Roosevelt accused "the Republican campaign management and people like Henry Ford and General Atterbury of the Pennsylvania Railroad" of being "guilty of spreading the gospel of fear." Despite these attacks, Roosevelt expressed confidence in the American people, who would not "be fooled by shifting the boast of the full dinner pail made in 1928, to the threat of the continued empty dinner pail in 1932."[26]

Roosevelt continued to criticize Ford as president, too. He saw Ford as a convenient political punching bag, and one likely to rile up his audiences. Ford was wary of Roosevelt from the beginning. When Ford listened to Roosevelt's inaugural address with other Ford executives, he silently shook his head in disapproval.[27]

Ford's problem with Roosevelt was less personal than policy-based. Ford had even sent Roosevelt a letter expressing his "deep respect" for Roosevelt "personally and as President." In addition, Ford believed that Roosevelt had "an earnest and religious desire to do everything possible to ease the situation of this country . . . " Yet Ford opposed the New Deal and what Roosevelt was trying to do on many levels. In the same letter, Ford criticized Roosevelt's plan for the National Industrial Recovery Act, calling it a "complicated and impractical plan." Yet Ford was still careful to separate Roosevelt the person from his policies, making what he called a "sharp distinction . . . between the President and the NIRA."[28]

Upon seeing the letter, Charles Edison, an administration ally and the son of Ford's old friend the inventor, tried to smooth things out. He drafted a letter with the assistance of Roosevelt's secretary Marvin McIntyre, reminding Ford that Roosevelt "is, after all, the President of the United States." He added that Roosevelt's view of Ford was "a very friendly one. I noted no note of antagonism, beyond his statement made with a smile that 'If Henry will quit being a dam [sic] fool about this matter and call me on the telephone I would be glad to talk with him.'" Roosevelt himself edited and signed off on the letter, but no call from Ford was forthcoming. Edison sighed, "As a Clearing House, I guess I'm something of a flop."[29]

Roosevelt continued with his policies and Ford continued with his opposition. Early in the administration, Roosevelt passed the National Industrial Recovery Act, which, among other things, created the National Recovery Administration. The NRA created a code of conduct for the auto industry, compliance with which would earn participants a "Blue Eagle" symbol, which they could display on storefronts or on packaging. Elements of the code included prices, work hours, wages, and working conditions across industries. Ford balked. When told that failure to comply would mean Ford facilities could not display the Blue Eagle, Ford was recalcitrant, saying, "Hell, that Roosevelt buzzard! I wouldn't put it on the car!"[30]

A heavy-handed Roosevelt emissary stepped in to get Ford on board. Roosevelt had put the energetic and insistent General Hugh Johnson in charge of the NRA, and of NRA compliance. Johnson was the designer of the "Roosevelt Buzzards" as well as the creepy NRA slogan, "We Do Our Part." He went to visit Ford secretly not long after NIRA passed. The meeting lasted two hours. *Dearborn Independent* editor William Cameron observed that Ford "listened to him longer than any man I've ever known him to listen to." Still, Ford was unmoved, telling Johnson, "Well, General, you're making it awful hard for a young man to start in this country." The secret mission and private talk had been a failure.[31]

On September 5, Ford made it official. He refused to sign the NRA compliance form, angering Johnson. At a press conference, Johnson went after Ford directly, saying, "I think maybe the American people will crack down on him when the Blue Eagle is on other cars and he does not have one." Ford remained unmoved. Johnson followed up his rhetorical and possibly quasi-fascistic threat with government action: he declared that the federal government would boycott Ford products, a new step in government efforts to get companies to heel. He also threatened to refer Ford to the Department of Justice if he found that Ford was not complying with the law's wage and hour requirements.[32]

Ford Motor Company issued an official statement hitting back. It accused Johnson, not unfairly, of "assuming the airs of a dictator." Then, in a jab at the NRA code of conduct, the statement called for "a code of fair publicity for Mr. Johnson's interviews." Another statement, equally hard-hitting, to Luce's *TIME*, read, "Signing a code is not in the law. Flying the Blue Eagle is not in the law. Johnson's daily expression of opinion is not in the law." Sending it to *TIME* was no accident, as Luce was also no fan of Roosevelt or the New Deal.[33]

The Johnson efforts did not end the attempts to bring Ford and Roosevelt together. Senator James Couzens, the former Ford executive and now Republican senator who had warned Ford that involvement in politics could damage his business interests, told Ford that Roosevelt wanted to meet him. In inviting Ford to the White House on November 7, 1933, Roosevelt referred to Ford as "an old friend whom I used to know in my Navy days." Ford once again rebuffed the entreaty, using the questionable excuse that he feared it would be seen as an attempt to get the government to purchase his vehicles.[34]

Another aborted attempt at a meeting took place in 1934. Ford telegraphed surprisingly gracious birthday greetings to Roosevelt on January 30, 1934, saying, "We all admire the directness with which you are attacking the nation's problems," Ford wrote, "and we are all the grateful beneficiaries of your immeasurable services in maintaining a courageous spirit amongst all the people." Roosevelt responded with a relatively open-ended invitation for Ford to visit with him. Nothing came of that, but in October of 1934, Roosevelt tried again, inviting Henry and Edsel to the White House to discuss the relocation of city residents to rural locales in a "country communities" initiative. This time things stalled on the White House side, as Mrs. Roosevelt was wary of the politics of having the industrialist Ford at the White House. She told Steve Early, Roosevelt's press secretary, "It would be a 'stupid political mistake' to have them here, invited by you." In her view, "Ford did more than any other man to wreck NRA; to have him here would be to encourage NRA opposition and discourage the friends of NRA."[35]

The Roosevelts did issue an invitation, but after the midterm elections and not for the White House. The Roosevelts invited the Fords to visit Warm Springs, Georgia, the "Little White House" vacation home, where Roosevelt went annually to soothe his polio-ravaged body in the naturally heated waters. Ford once again begged off, claiming that his wife was in ill health, but Edsel attended, along with his wife Eleanor, on November 24, 1934. Edsel's visit would be the start of an effort to moderate the father's hostility to the administration with a softer approach from the son.[36]

Ultimately, Ford won the NRA battle, as the Supreme Court struck down the NIRA on May 25, 1935. But winning the NRA battle did little to lessen Ford's dislike of the president. In 1938, Ford went to *TIME* again, criticizing Roosevelt directly this time, and not through a company statement. In Roosevelt, Ford said,

Americans had "a leader who is putting something over on them, and they deserve it."[37]

Off the record, Ford said even worse things about Roosevelt. When asked by his barber Joseph Zaroski if he was going to listen to one of FDR's famous Fireside Chat radio addresses, Ford responded with "some language you don't hear in church." He also said privately that "Roosevelt was too much of a sissy" for the competitive world of business and industry. Ford believed false stories that Roosevelt was Jewish which, coupled with Ford's anti-Semitism compounded his dislike of the man. For fun, Ford would tell Roosevelt jokes, just like he used to tell Ford jokes. In one, two boys save Roosevelt from drowning. When Roosevelt offered to reward the boys, one asked for and received a job for his unemployed father. The other one, however, was inconsolable, telling the president that "If I tell my father who I pulled out of the water, he'll kill me!" As Ford labor advisor Harry Bennett summed it up, "Mr. Ford hated Roosevelt."[38]

Unsurprisingly, when 1936 came around, Ford, like Luce, did not want to see Roosevelt reelected. Louisiana's Governor Huey Long, a staunch Roosevelt critic, inquired if Edsel might run against Roosevelt, but neither the younger nor the older Ford was interested in that happening. Instead of Edsel, Ford backed Roosevelt's opponent, saying, "I am for [Alf] Landon. I haven't voted for 20 years, but I am going to vote this time." According to Ford, a Roosevelt victory would mean that workingmen "will be put still further under the control of international financiers.... Anyone who thinks that the real inside finances are opposed to the New Deal doesn't know what is going on."[39]

Despite Ford's opposition, Roosevelt was reelected easily. Ford would finally meet Roosevelt as president during Roosevelt's second term, in April of 1938. The meeting came at Roosevelt's telegraphed invitation, but at a time when both men had been weakened by external events. Ford was experiencing both labor strife and a downturn in automobile sales. Roosevelt's plan to "pack the court"—to increase the number of justices on the Supreme Court in response to judicial defeats such as the voiding of the NIRA—had run aground as well, and the economy was still doing poorly. This backdrop may have been what encouraged

FDR to invite the man whom the *New York Times* described as one of the New Deal's "severest critics," and for Ford to finally accept.[40]

In the run-up to the meeting, Ford was typically cheeky, saying, "I am going to give the President a chance to look at somebody who doesn't want anything." This line would be parodied by *New York Sun* columnist Harry I. Phillips, who previewed the meeting with satirical dialogue. In the exchange, Phillips has Roosevelt and Ford bantering back and forth like Borscht Belt comedians:

> **President:** You're like all industrialists; you criticize without making any helpful suggestions. Why don't you tell me what I ought to do?
> **Henry:** How do I know you'd listen?
> **President:** I listen to everybody.
> **Henry:** That's the trouble![41]

As for what Ford planned to say in the actual meeting, Ford said, "I shall not give any advice. I am just going to renew an old acquaintanceship of years' standing. I first met President Roosevelt when he was Assistant Secretary of the Navy. We built ships together." Of course, he followed the statement with some advice, offering that "only a back-to-the-farm movement will save the country."[42]

As Ford came to Washington via train, along with Edsel and aide William Cameron, he once again downplayed the substantive aspects of the widely anticipated meeting. As he told reporters, "You know I never have anything to say. I'm just going down to Washington to see the President." Roosevelt was welcoming, saying, "Oh, Mr. Ford, I'm so glad to see you," and adding, "My mother was so pleased to know that you were coming. She said, 'Franklin, I'm so glad that you're going to see Mr. Ford because Mr. Ford is not only a great man, he's a good man.'"[43]

Ford was his typically terse self in the two-hour meeting. When it ended, he offered, "You know, Mr. President, before you leave this job, you're not going to have many friends, and then I'll be your friend." He did not say anything to reporters on the way out, nor had he said anything on the way in. Ford went next to the newspaper publishers' banquet at New York's Waldorf Astoria hotel, where he decided against giving a scheduled speech, recalling Edison's old observation about Ford's incompetence in front of a crowd. Privately, though, he remained his anti-Roosevelt self, telling Ford employee Walter G. Nelson, "Mrs. Roosevelt was a wonderful woman, but that man was a rascal!" As for FDR, he was his typical unflappable self. When reporters asked for his read-out of the meeting with Ford, he said that he "was interested to see what the press said about it."[44]

Coda: The End of Rockefeller

Roosevelt was the last president of John D. Rockefeller's long life. While FDR was a cousin of Rockefeller's nemesis Theodore Roosevelt, FDR himself was not a Rockefeller enemy. There was no point, since by the onset of the second Roosevelt administration, Rockefeller was three decades into a life of golfing and philanthropy. The Roosevelt administration would even coordinate with Rockefeller's son, John D. Rockefeller Jr. When FDR's designated corporate basher, Interior Secretary Harold Ickes, wanted the cooperation of a recalcitrant oil executive, he would often ask for the help of John Jr., who knew Ickes through Rockefeller's generous donations to the national parks. John Jr. would call the executives at Ickes's behest, and they would usually fall in line as a result.[45]

Rockefeller himself could have benefitted from his son's approach. Throughout most of his time in the business, Rockefeller and Standard Oil had too often been on the defensive in its dealings with both the federal government and the press. A more proactive approach earlier on, in which the company had tried to articulate the benefits it and the industry as a whole had brought to consumers and the public, might have made a difference in how the story played out. Instead, Standard Oil learned a painful lesson, that once public trust is lost it can be very difficult to recover, even over the course of generations. By failing to engage with presidents and the press for decades, Rockefeller made a fundamental error, and it cost his company, and his industry, dearly.

There is an interesting postscript to the story. The second Roosevelt presidency helped launch the career of Rockefeller's grandson, Nelson, who served in this second Roosevelt administration as coordinator of Inter-American Affairs and later assistant secretary of state for American Republic Affairs. Nelson would become governor of New York and later vice president, both positions held by Rockefeller family nemesis Theodore Roosevelt. Nelson sought the presidency three times, but he never quite made it.

Over the course of a long career, Rockefeller's tactics and dominance of the oil industry earned him a lot of enemies. His unpopularity made him the target of multiple presidents. Given the small size of the federal regulatory state at the time he built his monopoly, Rockefeller's major government concerns were initially regarding Congress, and his personal interactions with presidents were fewer than we would see from comparably powerful twentieth and twenty-first century CEOs. Nevertheless, Rockefeller and his agents certainly worked hard to protect the company and its interests from Congress, with significant success for a while. Over time, though, he and his empire became increasingly vulnerable to presidential attention as well. Even though his biggest defeat, the court-mandated breakup of Standard Oil in 1911, came over a dozen years after he had retired from heading the company, Rockefeller still felt it acutely and could not even bear to mention it in three years of conversations with his official biographer.[46]

Rockefeller entered the oil industry at a time of few rules for appropriate business behavior. He and his lieutenants essentially wrote the rules and created the industry that is still with us today—Chevron, ExxonMobil, Marathon, and BP are all offshoots of the original Standard Oil. He unwisely thought that he could ignore his rising unpopularity and the federal attention that came with it. Later, he came around to the recognition that public relations and stronger ties to presidents could provide benefits, and potentially forestall challenges. In doing so, Rockefeller led to the creation of the playbook for future president and CEO relations, as we continue to see the echoes of Rockefeller in many subsequent presidential-CEO interactions.

CHAPTER 5

CORPORATIONS AND THE GREAT WAR

President: Franklin Delano Roosevelt
CEOs: The Warner Brothers, Luce, Ford

Ford and World War II: Arming His Enemy against America's Enemy

As the 1930s came to a close, the storm clouds of war were gathering ominously. In this period, Henry Ford's pacifist views once again put him at odds with a president trying to manage a complex world situation. Like President Wilson before him, Roosevelt made an appearance of neutrality while recognizing that the U.S. would have to get involved and would be opposing Germany. This time, the situation was further complicated by Ford's antisemitism, his advanced age, Adolf Hitler's admiration for Ford, and the existence of an important Ford plant in Cologne, Germany.

Ford had apologized for his antisemitism and had stopped running anti-Semitic articles in the *Dearborn Independent* in 1927. But his anti-Semitic reputation stuck with him: Ford earned the dubious distinction of being the only American mentioned in Adolf Hitler's *Mein Kampf.*

Hitler had also told a *Chicago Tribune* reporter in 1924 that "We look to Heinrich Ford as the leader of the growing Fascist movement in America. . . . We have just had his anti-Jewish articles translated and published. The book is being circulated in millions throughout Germany." As dictator, Hitler's admiration for Ford remained high. He professed to be a fan of Fordism, *Volksmotorisierung*, he called it, and implemented a version of it as his economic policy. In 1938, four months after German troops took over Austria in the *Anschluss*, German officials bestowed upon Ford the Grand Cross of the German Eagle on Ford's 75th birthday. Ford was surprised, but he nevertheless accepted the award. These developments linked Ford, not always accurately, with the Nazi regime.[1]

Hitler's attempted cultivation of Ford had a larger purpose. Ford had a factory in Germany that was important both for industrial production as well as for importing key war materiel. Ford AG, the German division of Ford, changed its name to Ford-Werke AG to make it more German, and it continued to help with Nazi industrial production. In a dictatorship like Germany, there was not much Ford could do about it, and in any event, they had removed Edsel and other Anglo directors from the Ford-Werke AG board. But Ford's record of antisemitism, the praise from Hitler, and his acceptance of the award all made for a bad look for Ford.[2]

Eddie Cantor, the Jewish entertainer, denounced Ford, saying, "I question the Americanism of Henry Ford for accepting a citation from the biggest gangster in the world. . . . Whose side is Mr. Ford on?" Ford issued a statement in response to the criticism, declaring "no sympathy on my part with Nazism. . . . Those who have known me for many years realize that anything that breeds hate is repulsive to me." The statement would have been more convincing without Ford's early history of antisemitism.[3]

Edsel Ford was both more pro-Roosevelt and more farsighted about where things were going. He signed a contract to produce Rolls-Royce Merlin aircraft engines for both the Americans and the British. Ford went along with it, until he didn't. Initially, he drew the line at helping the British, telling Roosevelt's head of industrial production, "I won't make motors for the British government. For the American government, yes; for the British government, no." William Knudsen, a former auto executive—and former Ford employee—whom Roosevelt put in charge of industrial production, tried to change Ford's mind. As part of this effort, Knudsen made the mistake of saying, "We have your word that you would make them. I told the President your decisions, and he was very happy about it." Ford was enraged at hearing Roosevelt's name mentioned and said, "We won't build the engine at all. Withdraw the whole order." The incident was terribly embarrassing to Edsel. When Treasury Secretary Henry Morgenthau heard about it, he said, "I guess Edsel isn't old enough yet to have a view of his own." Edsel was in his late forties at the time.[4]

Edsel, however, did not give up. He continued negotiating with U.S. defense officials, and he continued to work on convincing his father. Eventually, it was a Roosevelt-hating argument that helped sway Ford, the prospect that the Roosevelt administration could take over an uncooperative company. This was not an idle threat. Ford's anti-unionism had alienated Roosevelt, Mrs. Ford—who had threatened to leave him over his hardline stance—and large swaths of the American people. When Ford's name was mentioned at a 1940 campaign rally at Madison Square Garden, loud booing from the crowd made the building shake. Roosevelt aide and designated Republican-basher Harold L. Ickes attacked Ford's "big business fascism," much like his son Harold M. Ickes would serve as an attack dog for the Clinton administration decades later. The specter of a government takeover was a real one.[5]

External events beyond Ford's increasing unpopularity in multiple quarters played a role as well. In January of 1940, Ford said of Ford Motor Company that "During this crisis our organization wants to do everything possible to help America and the President." He boasted that Ford factories had the capacity to build a thousand planes daily, albeit, he added, "they are to be for defense only." Hitler's increased militarism, including a German bombing of a Ford plant in England, softened his views of England. In early 1941, he said, "We have to get in 100% and help the British out. They have to win."[6]

By 1942, following the Japanese attack on Pearl Harbor and the declaration of war against Nazi Germany, Ford was all in. The Ford bomber production facility in Willow Run, Michigan, which was built in 1941, became the most storied factory of World War II. It employed over 35,000 people and produced approximately half of the 18,000 B-24 Liberators that Ford made. It was a joint project with the U.S. government, which contributed $200 million to the effort. The 975-acre factory was designed by Ford's Jewish architect and frequent collaborator, Alfred Kahn.[7]

In September of 1942, Roosevelt came to visit Willow Run. Ford was unhappy about the visit, and unhappy that Roosevelt came two hours late. When Roosevelt did arrive, Ford employees had to search for their boss to bring him to the president. On the tour, which also included Edsel and Willow Run manager Charles Sorensen, the wiry Ford was jammed into the back seat of a car, a bulletproof Ford Phaeton, between Roosevelt and Mrs. Roosevelt. Edsel and Sorensen sat in jump seats across from them. Sorensen recalled that when he or Edsel caught Ford's eye, the old man "would glare at us furiously." The cheers Roosevelt received from Ford employees as he toured the facility did not improve Ford's mood.[8]

Ford may have been miserable, but Roosevelt was enjoying himself. It was his first-ever visit to an airplane factory, and he and Eleanor enjoyed asking Sorensen questions and pointing out the sights to one another. Roosevelt was particularly excited at one famous landmark, saying, "And so this is the city line!" Ford had built the plant in an L shape, to conform to county lines and keep the entirety of the plant in Republican-voting territory. Roosevelt had won national election three straight times, but thanks to Ford's machinations, the area around Willow Run had not voted for him. Roosevelt, himself a staunch partisan, took Ford's petty shot at him bemusedly. They ended the visit with a twenty-minute talk among Roosevelt, Edsel, and Ford that unfortunately was lost to history, although Edsel did give Roosevelt a scale model of a B-24 Liberator. It appears to be the last time Ford and Roosevelt ever saw each other.[9]

It probably was not Roosevelt's intent, but the visit from the president did Ford some good. Because of Willow Run's productivity and some puffery from *TIME*, Ford began to be seen as an American asset in the area of war production. In March of 1942, six months before the visit, *TIME* called Ford a "fighting pacifist" and credited him with participating in the "miracle of war production." According to *TIME*, Ford's "America Firstness" had been "bombed away at Pearl Harbor" and that "Henry Ford is more like most Americans than most Americans realize." *TIME* was on to something. In 1943, in the aftermath of the Ford visit, a poll showed that Americans saw Henry Ford as the Detroit industrialist who had committed the most to the war effort.[10]

Coda: Ford's Legacy

The three men in the Willow Run meeting did not last much longer on the American or the world stage. Edsel would die far too young in 1943, and Roosevelt died in April of 1945. Later that year, when Ford saw footage from the concentration camps for the first time, he ran from the room in horror. Not long afterwards, he had a debilitating stroke from which he never fully recovered.[11]

When Ford died in 1947, a host of corporate and political leaders praised him, including Roosevelt's replacement, President Harry Truman. The praise came despite Ford's record of antisemitism, his hatred of Roosevelt, and his opposition to the New Deal. Truman had met Ford in the early 1940s, when he was still a senator from Missouri, but he recounted the meeting in a press conference he gave as president in 1951. In his comments, Truman noted that he had asked Ford about his pacifism, and that Ford had been "very certain that things would come out of the tremendous effort which ourselves and our allies had put forth that would be of great benefit to civilization." Ford's assessment, Truman noted, "has been absolutely true."[12]

In telling this story, Truman revealed that he had been the last of seven presidents to cross paths with Ford. Ford helped reshape American life with his cars, his industrial policies, and his wages, but he also created a new model for dealing with presidents. His cranky attitude and idiosyncratic ideas complicated matters for his interactions, but his dealings with various presidents, from the Peace Ship effort, to the Vagabond trips, to the visits with a president he disliked in Franklin Roosevelt, elevated even Ford's considerable public profile.

Ford claimed not to want anything from presidents. This was not quite true. Even when he did not want anything tangible, he seemed to like the enhanced public profile that at least some of his presidential interactions brought him. And, as he learned to his chagrin, as government became more and more powerful, especially under FDR, Ford increasingly wanted what government and presidents were no longer willing to give: to be left alone.

The Warners: Supporting America at War through Film

Harry and Jack Warner helped the Roosevelt administration in its fight against fascism the best way they knew how: by producing propaganda films in advance of and during World War II. Even the legendary Warner Brothers cartoons of the 1940s had a relentlessly anti-Nazi take, introducing generations of younger Americans to the evils of Hitler's regime. Part of their effort stemmed from their support for Roosevelt, but an equally large part was a result of the Warners' hatred of the Nazis. As Harry said of their propaganda efforts, "You may correctly charge me with being anti-Nazi. But no one can charge me with being anti-American."[13]

One of the Warners' chief allies in their propaganda efforts was a future president. Ronald Reagan made thirty movies for Warner between 1937 and 1942, and eleven of them fit into the propaganda film category, promoting preparedness, U.S. government bonds, the military, or the plight of the British against the Nazi onslaught. In 1942, Reagan signed a million-dollar contract with Warner Brothers negotiated by legendary MCA agent—and future mogul—Lew Wasserman.[14]

Luce: Changing His Tune Somewhat with America at War

As the U.S. came closer to involvement in the great war taking place in Europe and Asia, Luce's open enmity towards Roosevelt occasionally left him open to attack. In 1941, *TIME* was quite critical of Chilean Popular Front president Pedro Aguirre, writing that the "bushy mustache president Aguirre . . . spent more and more time with the red wine he cultivated." This caused a problem for *TIME* and Luce when Aguirre died right after the issue appeared. In the face of Chilean outrage, Roosevelt pounced. He gave a press conference in which he said that "the government of the United States has been forced to apologize to the government of Chile for an article that appeared in *TIME* magazine," and called the piece a "disgusting lie." Roosevelt added that "the article was a notable illustration of how some American papers and writers are stocking the arsenals of propaganda of the Nazis to be used against us." Luce was taken aback by the directness of the attack, especially at such a fraught period on the international front. His sheepish reply stated that "no one had [previously] said anything in TIME's report was untrue." Perhaps not, but Roosevelt's hit left a mark. Luce wrote in a letter to Roosevelt that "the drubbing you handed out to TIME before December 7 was as tough a wallop as I ever had to take."[15]

By the time Luce had sent his letter, things had changed. The Japanese attack on Pearl Harbor softened Luce's anti-Roosevelt tone somewhat. The letter further stated about the drubbing that, "If it will help you win the war I can take worse ones. Go to it!" Luce even ended the letter with the words, "And God bless you."[16]

Pearl Harbor brought about a brief respite in the animosity between the two men. Even Luce recognized that maintaining a feud with Roosevelt during a war was not wise. *Life* editor and Luce adviser John Shaw Billings wrote in a 1942 memo, "You can't take on the Pres. Of the U.S. in wartime and expect to win."[17]

Even as Luce tried to maintain good relations, sometimes he got in trouble for the actions of his subordinates. In October 1942, Russell Davenport—who had left Luce-world to advise Roosevelt's 1940 challenger Wendell Willkie but returned to *Life* after Willkie lost—wrote a strongly worded "Open Letter" criticizing British slowness in pursuing a cross-Channel invasion. The negative reaction from both Whitehall and Roosevelt was so severe that Luce backed away from Davenport's missive, saying that "I did not write, did not cause to be written," accusing the item of "not having said what we meant as clearly as we should have." Luce's statement alienated Davenport but it did not mollify Roosevelt.[18]

For the remainder of his time in office, Roosevelt would continue to take vindictive actions directed at *TIME* that were really targeted at Luce. In the battle of Guadalcanal, *TIME* correspondent John Hersey—who later wrote the blockbuster *Hiroshima*—saved the lives of several Marines. The commanding general of the First Marine Division put Hersey in for a Silver Star, a recommendation endorsed by Admiral William F. Halsey, the Navy's Board of Awards, and Secretary of the Navy Frank Knox. Roosevelt, however, kiboshed the award, saying that anyone "who had red blood in his veins . . . would do the same thing." Of course, anyone who had indeed done the same thing but had not worked for Luce at *TIME* would have received the well-earned medal.[19]

In 1942, following yet another disagreement on Luce-world's coverage of Latin America, Roosevelt said, "Honestly I think that something has got to be done about Luce and his papers. . . . What to do about this attitude, which is definitely unpatriotic in that it is harmful to the U.S. to a very great degree." FDR aides piled on, with Army Chief of Staff George Marshall summoning Luce for a meeting in which he, per Luce's recollection to an aide, "gave him and the company the devil, just on general principles. . . . Marshall raked up all the past grievances—and warned that the Luce papers must behave themselves." Shortly afterwards, Undersecretary of State Sumner Welles issued a "formal protest with Mr. Luce," warning against pieces "which in any way hurt the Good Neighbor policy with Latin America or tend to promote disunity among any of the United Nations." This coordinated assault by multiple administration actors is reminiscent of the Barack Obama administration's concerted effort against Rupert Murdoch's Fox News, and indicative of the multiple tools an administration has with which it can target a purported opponent when the president wishes.[20]

One last vindictive anti-Luce action that stayed in effect until FDR's death in early 1945 was a travel ban preventing Luce from going to Asia. It was not billed as such, of course. The administration put into effect an order allowing correspondents and photographers to travel to war zones, but not editors, publishers, or news executives. This had the benefit of not only banning Luce, but *Chicago Tribune* publisher Colonel Robert McCormick, whom Roosevelt also hated. Luce tried multiple ways to circumvent the ban, appealing directly to Marshall, and even to Roosevelt himself. No dice. The ban remained until Roosevelt died and Truman took over. Only then was Luce able to visit Asia once again, which he did within a month of Roosevelt's death. Little wonder that even after Roosevelt's death, a still bitter Luce said, "It is my duty to go on hating him."[21]

Once the Japanese attacked Pearl Harbor, World War II became a unifying event in American life. Even committed America Firsters changed their tunes once America was under fire. This unity largely applied to CEOs as well. Those like the Warners, who liked FDR, continued to make films to advance Roosevelt's—and America's—interests. But even CEOs like Ford and Luce sought ways to be accommodating while America was at war. But the accommodations did not change the underlying relationships on either side. Ford still disliked Roosevelt, even as he was running America's most important war production facility. And Roosevelt could still be vindictive towards Luce and enjoy making Ford squirm, even as he benefited from the improved relationships. This period showed CEOs as partners, willing to help the nation with their wares when it suited the nation, and themselves. As for the president, the war elevated both government's role and the president's prominence in American life, bolstering presidential authority over the power of the private sector. Both CEOs and presidents are political animals, and the war showed the degree to which they could all be transactional when they had to be in service to a larger cause.

CHAPTER 6

THE POSTWAR BOOM

Presidents: Harry Truman, Dwight D. Eisenhower, John F. Kennedy

CEOs: Luce, Lew Wasserman, Warren Buffett

With the war over, CEOs had to cope with a new president, and the new realities of postwar American dominance. Government was now bigger and more powerful in the aftermath of the Roosevelt administration, and America was unlikely to retreat again into an isolationist pose. While the 1950s were, like the 1920s, once again a time of peace and prosperity, the now larger federal government meant that hoping to avoid the government was no longer a viable strategy. In addition, the Roosevelt era had shown the limits of disregarding or disrespecting a president as a winning approach. Still, as Henry Luce would learn, there would also be limits to the effectiveness of unbridled friendship as a strategy.

Luce: Blaming Truman for Losing China

From Henry Luce's perspective, Harry Truman had two major advantages over Roosevelt. First, he had ended the travel ban that prevented Luce from going to Asia. Second, and more importantly, he was not the hated Franklin Delano Roosevelt. Luce wrote a letter to Truman in which he said, "I know of no better way to communicate to you my profound good wishes for your Presidency, than to tell you of the confidence which, among themselves, a great number of your fellow citizens already feel in your character and ability." Things appeared to be starting off on the right foot.[1]

Unfortunately for Truman, his two advantages only carried weight for so long. Eventually, Luce became a Truman opponent as well, and on two major fronts, both related to Asia: China and Korea. Luce secured a meeting with Truman shortly after Truman became president. While Luce was more positively disposed to Truman than he was to Roosevelt, Truman brought his own biases to the relationship. He disliked both Luce and *TIME* for their pro-Republican leanings. He also was not predisposed to discuss Asia or China policy with Luce in advance of Truman's upcoming July 1945 summit with Winston Churchill and Josef Stalin in Potsdam. Unsurprisingly, Luce found the meeting disappointing.[2]

Luce would not be happier with Truman after his meetings with the Big Three, either. In May of 1946, Luce and his second wife, Clare Boothe Luce, both signed a letter calling the decisions made by the original big three of Roosevelt, Churchill, and Stalin at Yalta in February of 1945 as being "made behind China's back." He also staunchly backed Chiang Kai-shek's Nationalists in their ill-fated civil war against Mao Tse-tung's Communists. When it was clear that the communists would win and gain control of China, *TIME*'s Max Ways lamented at a *TIME* editorial lunch, "We have lost China." This declaration, made without Luce present, would inspire a potent and far-reaching question that Luce and other China hawks would use to cudgel the Truman administration, "Who lost China?"[3]

With China in the hands of the Communists, Luce soon turned his anti-communist focus to Korea. Following the North Korean invasion of the South in late June of 1950, the Truman administration initially appeared to have "lost" another Asian country to the communists. General Douglas MacArthur's successful landing at Inchon in September of 1950 stopped the communist advance and made MacArthur a hero. It also made MacArthur appear politically untouchable, which was a problem for Truman because of MacArthur's frequent insubordination. He did not listen to Truman's directives, went ahead with policy decisions without getting direction or approval from the president, and generally seemed to operate as if he were not part of any chain of command. Nonetheless,

Truman kept MacArthur in charge in Korea because of MacArthur's popularity and because of the perilousness of the situation on the Korean Peninsula.

In this fight, Luce sided with MacArthur. After MacArthur's eventual recall by Truman, Luce said that "MacArthur as Commander had not only a right but a duty to express his convictions about military strategy." *TIME* criticized Truman harshly in the aftermath, arguing that Truman's foreign policy "denies to the U.S. the efficient use of its power, guarantees to the enemy the initiative he now has, promises that the U.S. will always fight on the enemy's terms. The policy invites the enemy, World communism, to involve the U.S. in scores of futile little wars. . . ." More personally, *TIME* wrote of the firing that "Seldom had a more unpopular man fired a more popular one."[4]

After being relieved, MacArthur returned to the U.S. to great fanfare. He gave a famous speech to Congress on April 19, 1951, in which he said, "Old soldiers never die—they just fade away." MacArthur received an enormous ticker tape parade in New York City, and the criticism of Truman in the press, including *TIME*, was blistering. Luce came to visit MacArthur in this period and described the general in glowing terms: "He looked healthy . . . handsome . . . and more vigorous than any public man I know." Luce pushed MacArthur for *TIME* Man of the Year and for president in 1952. Both efforts failed, and neither endeared him to an already alienated Truman.[5]

Luce: Making the "Case for Ike"

Luce's effort to raise up MacArthur flopped, but he eventually got a president he admired after Truman left office. In getting there, however, the Democrats would need to lose the presidential election in 1952, something they had not done since 1928. After strongly backing Landon and Willkie, Luce had backed Republican Tom Dewey in both 1944 and 1948, although with less effort and less enthusiasm. In 1952, however, Luce was determined to see a Republican back in the White House.

Luce pursued his pro-Republican strategy for a number of reasons. First, he himself was by this point a Republican, and preferred Republican policies, especially in international affairs. Luce was a bold pro-American anti-Communist, whose coinage of the phrase "the American Century" helped define American foreign policy for a good part of the twentieth century. Second, Luce obviously had personal issues with both Roosevelt, whom he hated, and Truman, who did not think much of Luce. But there was also the factor that Luce thought it was bad for the country to have one party rule for too long. Luce "felt that it was of paramount importance to the United States that a Republican should be put in the White House." Following a long interregnum, he felt that Americans "should have the experience of living under a Republican Administration and discovering that they were not thereby reduced to selling apples on street corners."[6]

It is important to remember here that Luce was a patriot, and someone who wanted what he thought was best for America. Yes, he was passionate and forceful, and he could have his hatreds and his feuds, but he did have a larger vision. His advocacy in both the halls of power and in his magazines was not just to serve his considerable ego, or even to advance the interests of his growing company, but to put forth his vision of a powerful America that led the world in the fight against communism, as well as of a democratic nation with shared party rule.

Given his quest to get a Republican in the White House, the question became which one. Ohio senator and *soi disant* "Mr. Republican" Robert Taft did not appeal to Luce, so he began to look elsewhere. In January of 1952, Luce traveled to Paris and met for two hours with Dwight Eisenhower, former commanding general of the Allied forces in World War II. Luce was impressed. He liked both the "sound of the man's voice" and the "the twinkle" in his "brightest blue eyes." Overall, the Paris visit left Luce "under the agreeable spell of a great personality and with a sense of confidence that the Republican Party had a winner."[7]

Of course, wanting Ike to win and getting him over the finish line were two very different things. After all, Luce had tried and failed with both Willkie and Landon, and the Republicans were on a six-election losing streak, a spiral never before or since repeated by the GOP. But Ike was different, and Truman was deeply unpopular. Shortly after the Ike-Luce get together, *Life* wrote a compelling editorial, "The Case for Ike," which argued that Ike was an optimist who could help improve America.[8]

Ike read the editorial and liked what he saw. In a follow-up letter to "Dear Harry"—avoiding FDR's mistake of calling him "Henry"—Ike modestly claimed that the editorial "erred grossly on the side of generosity in your estimate of my capacity." More importantly, Ike later credited the editorial as a factor that "helped influence" him to throw his hat in the ring.[9]

With Ike on board, Luce was prepared to help in a myriad of ways. He provided two speechwriters, Emmett Hughes and C. D. Jackson, as well as campaign adviser John Knox Jessup. Hughes was a Princeton grad who served as a bureau chief abroad for *Time-Life* before coming to New York and becoming editor at *Life*. He would write the most famous line of Eisenhower's campaign, "If elected, I shall go to Korea." The line indicated the seriousness of purpose with which Eisenhower would address the Korean War, a conflict that had frustrated both Truman and the American people. The line helped Eisenhower win the election over Adlai Stevenson, and Ike fulfilled the pledge shortly after his victory.[10]

Jackson also attended Princeton, seventeen years earlier than the younger Hughes. After a stint with the Office of Strategic Services (precursor to the CIA), Jackson became publisher of *Fortune*. He took over Eisenhower's disorganized speechwriting operation and gave it some coherence. Ike thanked Luce for sending over Jackson, calling him a "G-dsend" who saved Ike's sanity, "such part as is salvageable." Like Hughes, he would also join the Eisenhower White House staff.[11]

Jessup was a Yale grad and chief editorial writer for *Life*. He did not go to work in the Eisenhower White House, but loaning him to the campaign was a big deal as Luce valued him so highly. *TIME* editor in chief Hedley Donovan would say of him that, "I think Harry esteemed Jack Jessup, as a mind and as man, as much as anybody he knew, in Time Inc. or anywhere else." Jessup would later write a 1969 book, *The Ideas of Henry Luce*, demonstrating his close understanding of Luce's thinking.[12]

In addition to lending Eisenhower some of his top people, Luce also effectively lent his magazines as pro-Eisenhower organs. *TIME* profiled Eisenhower from his home of Abilene, Kansas, observing that the American people favored Ike "in a way they could scarcely explain. . . . He made them proud of themselves and all the half-forgotten best that was in them and in the nation." *TIME* was so favorable to Eisenhower that Ike's campaign manager Henry Cabot Lodge would distribute copies of the magazine to guests. Lodge wrote a thank you note to Luce, calling him "a tower of strength" and gushing that "one of the lasting satisfactions of this adventure has been the fact that you and I have worked so closely for such a great cause."[13]

In addition to working to get Eisenhower elected, Luce also aimed to shape Eisenhower's policies in a favorable way. In the spring of 1952, Luce had approached John Foster Dulles—the likely secretary of state in an Eisenhower administration—to sketch out a Republican foreign policy vision. The subsequent *Life* article, "A Policy of Boldness," articulated a Luce-friendly, pro-America, anti-communist, foreign policy vision, and would be echoed in the eventual GOP platform that summer. The article called for aggressive policies such as the "liberation of the captive nations," and for hitting opponents "where it hurts, by means of our own choosing." Luce loved it and called it "the embryo of a united Republican foreign policy."[14]

Eisenhower won the presidency, with Luce's help on the press, personnel, and political fronts. Luce was ecstatic, wiring the phrase "Victory, it's wonderful" to selected allies and friends. The benefits of victory came almost immediately: lunch and letters with Ike, invitations to the White House, and staffers like Jackson and Hughes joining the Eisenhower administration. There was some talk of Luce as a possible secretary of state, but Dulles had that in the bag, and Luce did not feel himself qualified for the job, either.[15]

While Luce himself would not join the administration, his wife would. Clare Boothe Luce was a brilliant and vivacious woman, a former actress and former Republican congresswoman who, like her husband, had strong views on foreign policy. She had also extended herself for Eisenhower, campaigning on his behalf in the presidential race. After the election, she met with Eisenhower at the transition offices in the Commodore Hotel in New York to discuss a role in the administration. Eisenhower proposed the secretary of labor position for her, but she demurred. Although she considered herself "certainly smarter and abler" than Frances Perkins, Roosevelt's secretary of labor, she was more interested in foreign policy. They discussed both the Chair of the UN Commission on Human Rights and the Ambassadorship to Great Britain, but both were already taken, before moving on to Ambassador to Italy. There were other competitors for the job, but Clare got it, in part because of Harry, noting that "in honoring the wife, he sought to honor and please the husband!" Regardless, the post was hers, and she would serve there for three and a half years.[16]

With Clare in place in Rome, Luce would have multiple ways to influence the Eisenhower administration and some direct contact with a friendly Ike. Former aides like Jackson and Hughes were in the White House. Secretary of State Dulles was an ally, and his wife was also a good medium for passing on policy ideas and suggestions. And then there was *TIME* Inc., with over 30 million subscribers as a platform for ideas and suggestions to the favorably inclined administration. In many ways, the Eisenhower years were the peak of Luce's influence and the peak of his vision for leadership in the American Century. All of the decades of seeking to be able to influence the presidency seemed to have come to fruition. As Luce later wrote in his never finished memoir, "The eight Eisenhower years were great years for the Republic. . . . Largely by their own efforts, individually or in voluntary association, the American people made giant strides in nearly every field of endeavor under the benign laws of their Republic."[17]

Still, while the 1950s showed the potential benefits of the Luce approach as a model for influencing the president and the presidency, Luce's very success also showed the limitations of the approach. Despite all of his pathways to the president, Luce still was not always happy with the results. While Dulles and Eisenhower were indeed anti-communist, there was no global crusade to liberate captive nations. Ike's Korea policy did not differ much from Truman's, and the Korean War ended in a stalemate. According to Billings, *TIME* editors staged an intervention to "knock down most of Luce's hopeful and unrealistic notions about the Eisenhower Administration." Luce would occasionally complain, "What's wrong with Ike?" but for the most part would disassociate his disappointments with the administration's policies from his admiration for Eisenhower the man and the president.[18]

In addition to the imperfection of the results, there was also the internal strife caused by what staffers like Billings feared was perceived as being "Eisenhower's mouthpiece." The *New York Times'* obituary of "house liberal" Griffith noted the "tumultuous interoffice clashes on major news stories" during this era. He even told Luce that, "It's been traditional at *Time* magazine to sort of twist the news a bit around the time of election. But now it is a four-year job." Griffith was far from the only participant or grumbler. Billings complained during the campaign that "Luce is dazzled by Eisenhower's glamour. . . ." He also observed that *TIME* employees were "moaning and groaning" about the pro-Ike bias. The Adlai Stevenson-backing editor T. S. Matthews asked, "How can Time possibly hope to attain and maintain a real integrity if it's partisanly concerned with getting somebody elected?" Luce listened to some degree, allowing for a get-to-know-you meeting between Luce and key *TIME* staff. But there were limits to how open he was to criticism. He told the staffers at the meeting that while *TIME* was not a Republican organ, he personally favored Eisenhower, and that "I am your boss. I guess that means I can fire any of you." He also forbade Matthews from editing the pre-election cover story on Eisenhower, choosing instead to edit it himself.[19]

Beyond the internal strife was the issue of how the Ike boosterism affected the magazine's reputation. There was a joke that "Time was even-handed during election years: Half the time it praised the Republicans, and half the time it damned the Democrats." Luce's oft-quoted comment on the subject was, "I am a Protestant, a Republican, and a free enterpriser, which means I am biased in favor of God, Eisenhower, and the stockholders of Time Inc.—and if anyone who objects doesn't know this by now, why the hell are they still spending 35 cents for the magazine." Still, Luce biographer Alan Brinkley observed that Luce's overt pro-Ike stance was "crossing a line." The pro-Republicanism opened up a broader vein of *TIME* criticism. The *New York Post*'s Alvin Davis wrote in 1956 that "Time today is the gratuitous sneer and the open mouth of shocked belief, it is the wisecrack of Madison Avenue and the maxim of Main Street, it is the mouthpiece of the Republican party and the spokesman for the American people." And the famed Marshall McLuhan wrote of how *TIME*'s "rapid fire prose" encouraged a "sub-rational response."[20]

McLuhan's high-minded criticism was one thing. But a charge that began to stick was that *TIME*'s bias made it less than fully accurate. This was a charge that

Franklin Roosevelt had leveled directly to Luce as far back as 1923, but it really picked up in the 1950s. The critic Clement Greenberg claimed that *TIME* aimed to "discredit reality." Igor Stravinsky complained that "Every music column I have read in Time has been distorted and inaccurate"; The actress Tallulah Bankhead said publicly, "Don't believe a word you read in Time. . . . It is made up of fakery, calumny, and viciousness"; Democratic senator John McClellan regarded "Time as prejudiced and unfair in its reporting"; and the comic novelist P. G. Wodehouse called *TIME* "about the most inaccurate magazine in existence." And these critiques were not limited to the 1950s, or to those on the left. Libertarian economist Milton Friedman once told his colleague and rival Paul Samuelson that a benefit to writing for *Newsweek* was that "I've been freed from *TIME* phone calls. In my experience they have a very high record for unreliability." Luce got his president, and he got his influence, but they came at a cost.[21]

Lew Wasserman: Building an Empire without Worrying about Washington

Few American industries have been more globally dominant than the entertainment business. The early pioneers in Hollywood helped reshape America's perception of itself—and that same industry has helped convey that sense to the rest of the world. From those early visionaries and legendary bosses to today's new moguls, the one who interacted with U.S. presidents the most—and with the greatest effect—was Lew Wasserman.

One reason Hollywood's founders could tell the American story was because so many of them were immigrants. The town—and the industry—was built by Jewish immigrants in the first part of the twentieth century. From a few studios employing only fifteen thousand people in 1910, Hollywood grew to a $2 billion business by 1940, when 60 million Americans were seeing a movie weekly. Today it is a more than $90 billion a year business. It was this sense of entertainment as a business that first led a reluctant Lew Wasserman to question his early avoidance of Washington.[22]

Wasserman was not part of that first generation of moguls; he was born in America—Cleveland—not Europe. His birth certificate from 1913 has never been found, which has created shades of a mystery. But the fact that he was born in America, albeit to immigrant Russian Orthodox Jewish parents, made him more comfortably American than his famous studio founder predecessors. His friend and protégé Sid Sheinberg later observed of Wasserman that, "He may have over-lapped with some of these historical figures, but it's wrong to say he was one of them. He was something different."[23]

Wasserman was indeed something different. He got his start in the entertain-ment industry early, but in relatively lowly positions, as a theater usher and then a nightclub promoter in Cleveland. By 1936, though, he had attracted the eye of and began to work for Jules Stein, creator of MCA—Music Corporation of America—a talent agency in Chicago. He told his wife Edie that he saw a great future in the job. When she asked, "What's so great about it?" He replied, "Stein is an old man." (Stein was forty at the time.) Two years after that, Wasserman moved to MCA's new office in Hollywood and never looked back.[24]

The tall—6'2"—and slim Wasserman immediately started making his impact on the movie industry. His first two clients were *Gone with the Wind*'s Hattie McDaniel and a former radio announcer named Ronald Reagan. Wasserman was an aggressive agent, not above stealing clients from competitors. According to fellow MCA executive Berle Adams, "Lew decided he was going to go out and take a shot at every star." This entailed violating what was then known as the "Jewish gentleman's agreement" under which agents would not poach clients from other agents. Wasserman not only violated that agreement, but he had a standard method for doing so. He would steal a client, and if there were objections, he would pay the former agent the commission until their deal expired, then negotiate a bigger deal that gave the commission to MCA alone. Wasserman secured his first $1 million contract, for Ronald Reagan, when he was still in his twenties. Because of his aggressive methods, MCA soon controlled 60 percent of the bankable talent in Hollywood, and by 1946 the thirty-three-year-old Cleveland-born child of immigrants was president of MCA.[25]

As president, Wasserman was now in charge of MCA's agents, and he trained them in his methods. One of his iron rules was to stay out of the spotlight at all costs. "Avoid the press," he said: "No interviews. No panels. No speeches. No comment." He conveyed this with a pithy epigram: "Stay out of the spotlight. It fades your suit."[26]

The suit line worked because it related to one of Wasserman's other rules, a strict dress code of a black suit, white shirt, and a black tie. He told his employees that their colorful ties were not appropriate for the office, since "color is for actors." As Wasserman aged, he added a pair of oversized glasses, which completed his trademark look. "Dress British, think Yiddish," he would say. He aimed to change the stereotype of the agent from a sleazy striver often perpetuating anti-Jewish stereotypes to a classy, respected figure. One MCA agent said that it was all part of a larger plan: "Everything was designed to give you the feeling that you were dealing with Ivy League WASPs."[27]

One of Wasserman's great strengths was his farsightedness. He could look ahead and see the changes looming in the industry and adapt to them, not just once or twice, but consistently. He saw that the studio system—in which the studios controlled actors for long periods—could not last and that representing talent was the wave of the future. Then, according to Sheinberg, "He began to embrace television when others weren't," making another correct bet. He even saw the potential in film libraries, acquiring Paramount's library of old films and renting them to hungry-for-content TV stations.

As City University of New York professor and Hollywood historian George Custen observed, Wasserman "saw, before anyone, that studios were eventually going to be just one piece of entertainment conglomerates." Custen said that these insights showed that Wasserman was "the kind of visionary who always saw a few squares ahead on the board." Sheinberg agreed, saying, "There is always the question, to what degree is a person capable of making a successful transition? You may catch one wave, as you hit a certain age, but to be able to catch wave after wave—that's the trick." Wasserman mastered that trick.[28]

It is one thing to see a trend developing. It is another thing to act on the trend before anyone else in a profitable way. Wasserman did this in the way he represented talent. MCA was a pioneer in the concept of "packaging," bundling together clients from one agency into a project in order to get more fees, and more control. He was the first agent to get his client a share of the profits instead of a flat fee. He did this for Jimmy Stewart in 1950's *Winchester '73* and made Stewart wealthy in the process. He also began to see the advantages of running a studio over just having an agency, a decision that would make him even more wealthy and even more powerful. It also put him on a trajectory to clash with Washington.[29]

Katharine Graham: Inheriting an Empire

Katharine Graham was born in 1917 to a wealthy Jewish father, Eugene Meyer, and Agnes, an austere non-Jewish mother. Graham somehow did not realize that she was partly Jewish until she was a student at Vassar. In 1940, she married a talented but troubled Philip Graham, a Harvard Law graduate and Supreme Court clerk. In 1945, Eugene made Phil the publisher of the *Washington Post,* which Eugene had purchased during the Great Depression. Graham was thirty years old at the time. As publisher, Phil befriended multiple presidents. He had the paper endorse Dwight Eisenhower in 1952, even as Katharine was an Adlai Stevenson fan. He became even closer to John F. Kennedy, to whom he gave political advice, and Lyndon Johnson, for whom he—inappropriately—drafted speeches. Phil, who suffered from depression, committed suicide in 1963. This left Katharine in charge of both the *Post* and *Newsweek*, which the family had purchased in 1961.[30]

Graham had minimal experience in journalism or corporate life when she took over. But she had a steely will. After the takeover, she gave a resolute speech to the board of the company emphasizing her determination to remain in charge. She told the board: "I'M NOT SELLING THIS PAPER. And we will get through this together." In her new position, she was the only female in the Fortune 500 at the time.[31]

Some people were more gracious than others after Phil's death and her ascension to the top spot. President Kennedy attended the funeral, and Jacqueline Kennedy wrote a moving condolence note. But Kennedy's top speechwriter, Ted Sorensen, did not see her as right for the job. When she had him over to lunch to discuss the possibility of him becoming a columnist, he responded, somewhat rudely, "The only job I really want is yours. Why don't you move over and let me run the company for you?" She passed on his offer.[32]

Kennedy was assassinated less than four months after Phil's suicide. Graham had inherited an empire but would not get to become comfortable on the throne during the friendly Kennedy administration. Instead, she would have to navigate through the challenges posed by both Lyndon Johnson and Richard Nixon.

Wasserman: Getting Help from a Future President While Clashing with a Sitting One

The early 1950s were a worrisome time for the Hollywood studios. They saw the new medium of television as a threat that would keep audiences out of the theaters and rooted in their living rooms. When box office numbers slumped in the early 1950s, studio executives saw television as the culprit. Wasserman, in contrast, saw TV as an opportunity.

Wasserman wanted to create a subsidiary of MCA that would create prime-time programming for network TV. But he had a problem. The Screen Actors Guild (SAG) had a rule prohibiting agents from being involved in production. The powerful union understandably saw the potential for a conflict of interest. Typically for Wasserman, he saw a way through, via a future president of the United States. Wasserman pushed his client Ronald Reagan, for whom he had secured a million-dollar studio deal with Warner Brothers in 1945, to be president of SAG.[33]

With his grateful client as union president, Wasserman sought a blanket exemption from the rule limiting agencies in production. The union already granted one-time exemptions to the rule on a case-by-case basis, but Wasserman did not want to be encumbered by the rule at all. He made the case that the blanket exemption would create more jobs for SAG employees and help maintain SAG membership. In 1952, Reagan and SAG granted the exemption, allowing MCA to move into television production. MCA established a successful subsidiary called Revue Productions, which created many successful shows for the small screen, including *Alfred Hitchcock Presents* and *Bachelor Father*. In 1953, Revue also created *General Electric Theater*, hosted by Reagan, whose film offers had dried up by this period. *GE Theater* allowed Reagan to re-invent himself as a TV star, which he would remain until entering politics in the mid-1960s. The deal worked out for

Wasserman as well, as by 1958 the subsidiary Revue was making six times what the parent agency MCA was bringing in.[34]

Now that Wasserman had a quasi-studio in the form of Revue, he set his sights on an actual studio. The target was Universal, which had come on hard times since its glory days under founder Carl Laemmle in the 1920s and 1930s. Wasserman had initially targeted the down-on-its-luck studio as early as 1950, and in 1958, he secured a deal that procured cash-strapped Universal's real estate, which he then leased back to the studio. Reagan finished his second stint as SAG president in 1960, and in 1961, SAG withdrew the joint MCA-Revue production waiver. With production revenues now dwarfing what the agency brought in, Wasserman made a strategic move in a new direction. He moved to purchase Decca Records, Universal's parent company, and shed the agency business, allowing the employees to purchase it. All these developments attracted the attention of a new actor in the Hollywood story: the federal government.[35]

For two decades in Hollywood, Wasserman had largely ignored Washington. He had secured a strong stable of talent, become head of the most powerful agency in Hollywood, and even skirted the rules by becoming a force in TV production. His ambitions attracted governmental interest, which would hold profound implications for Wasserman's business. In 1958, Wasserman and MCA were the subjects of two federal investigations and one grand jury. The IRS had made a habit of auditing MCA, although without any findings of wrongdoing.[36]

Kennedy's Federal Communications Commission (FCC) was looking into MCA as well. The FCC was helmed by Newton Minow, who had given a famous speech decrying TV as a "vast wasteland." This blanket condemnation from a senior government official was in itself concerning. But Minow had also received a letter from an advertising executive telling him to target MCA, because its leverage over the television industry "is the basic source of much of the mediocrity on America's TV screens."[37]

If MCA felt it was being hit from all sides, there was a new structural reality behind it. All of these federal probes revealed the array of tools that the government had accrued for regulating business and corporations. It also showed that the Washington players at the top could descend like the deus ex machina of old whenever they wanted to and change the business realities on the ground. When Wasserman made his move for Decca and with it Universal, the Justice Department under one Robert F. Kennedy moved to center stage.

In July of 1962, the Kennedy Justice Department filed suit to prevent the Decca-MCA-Universal deal. Spinning off the agency to its employees was too close to ownership, prompting the DOJ to intervene. The case never made it to trial, but it forced Wasserman and his company into negotiations with the government. The Justice Department exacted a heavy price. They greenlit the deal, but at the cost of MCA's ability to represent talent and to engage in any more acquisitions for seven years. *Variety* breathlessly reported the titanic news on its front page: "MCA Inc.'s talent agency, which only a week ago was the most powerful in the industry, is no more." MCA had acquired Universal and entered the studio business, but in the process was now no longer a talent agency. Wasserman, who had paid little attention to the federal government up to this point, decided he needed to make some friends in Washington.[38]

Wasserman's antitrust defeat hit him hard. Even though he secured a studio, which was his ultimate aim, it was traumatic to part with the agent business he had worked so hard to build for almost three decades. He remembered the painful defeat in later years, calling it "the major surprise of my life . . . a useless, unwarranted act." But Wasserman had not worked so hard to give up his life's ambition because of a failed run-in with the growing federal octopus. He decided to change tack. According to his former executive assistant Jerry Gershwin, he fixed his eyes on politics from that moment, saying, "If you can't beat 'em, you join 'em."[39]

Wasserman's bold entrance into politics did not take long. In June of 1963, less than a year after the unfavorable Department of Justice decision, Wasserman hosted a $1,000-a-plate fundraiser for John F. Kennedy, the president whose Justice Department—under the auspices of his brother—had dissolved Wasserman's agency business.[40]

Wasserman was not a political neophyte. In 1944, he recalled, he hosted a low-key event for Harry Truman, one far less organized—and lucrative—than the 1963 Kennedy dinner two decades later. Wasserman's approach to the Truman dinner had been rather ad hoc: "I invited anybody who would come." He and

MCA also chose not to raise a campaign fund for Roosevelt that year. A self-described "moderate Democrat," Wasserman was not opposed to FDR. He just was not that interested in politics at the time.[41]

Wasserman continued to see politics as something tangential to Hollywood in the 1950s as well. Hollywood is overwhelmingly liberal today; back then, as a moderate Democrat, Wasserman was in the minority among the heavily Republican Hollywood executives of the 1950s. In 1952, Wasserman came under heavy pressure from top Hollywood executives Jack Warner, Sam Goldwyn, and Darryl Zanuck to back the presidential candidacy of Dwight Eisenhower in 1952.

Wasserman and Stein resisted until the general election, saying that they did not get involved in politics. Eventually, they relented slightly. Wasserman let MCA put his name on the Entertainment Industry Joint Committee for Eisenhower-Nixon in 1952, and Wasserman gave $1,500 to Eisenhower's successful election effort. The same trick would not work again in 1960, though, when Warner tried and failed to get Wasserman to back Richard Nixon's 1960 presidential effort. Wasserman was not a Nixon fan, something that became relevant when Nixon did successfully win the presidency in 1968.[42]

With the antitrust defeat still smarting, Wasserman got more involved in politics in the 1960s. At the behest of Arthur Krim, the New York-based chair of United Artists, Wasserman agreed to head the West Coast chapter of Krim's President's Club, a fundraising vehicle for Kennedy's political needs. The club charged $1,000 for membership, which brought with it occasional "seminars" from key administration figures. Krim had concluded that proximity to Washington was important sooner than Wasserman had, and saw membership in the club as a useful investment. In Krim's telling, the club "didn't get you a favor with the government, but it got you an awful lot of fun for yourself and a feeling of being close to the charisma of power." It was exactly what Wasserman was looking for to begin his more serious entrée into the political game.[43]

Wasserman's dinner for Kennedy was a hit. It also showed how far Wasserman had come on the political front in a very short time. The dinner sold ten seats for each eleven-seat table. The empty seat at each table was for Kennedy, who rotated among the tables so that each guest could be told in advance—and later tell others—"You will be sitting with the president." Escorting Kennedy from table to table was Wasserman, who told Kennedy as he approached each table who was who, so that the president would be prepared and could pretend that he knew each guest's name. As a result of this unalloyed political triumph, Kennedy sent Wasserman a note inviting him onto the board of the National Cultural Center in Washington. Wasserman had the note framed. He was hooked.[44]

In addition to helping Kennedy with politics, Wasserman also helped facilitate Kennedy's other main interest. When Kennedy would come to town, Wasserman would go to political events without his wife Edie so that he could escort attractive starlets for Kennedy to pursue. At one event, Wasserman attended with the actress Angie Dickinson as his date, but he did not leave with her. According to Universal executive Frank Price, "Angie was ushered through a side door, where some of the president's men whisked her off."[45]

Although Wasserman was doing all of these favors for Kennedy, he still loathed the president's brother, the attorney general. Wasserman was angered and humiliated by the antitrust action, and he knew who to blame. According to the producer Walter Seltzer, "There was great antipathy between Wasserman and Robert Kennedy after the breakup." Edie Wasserman hated RFK as well. As Seltzer put it, "You cannot mention his name to either Edie or Lew without their going apoplectic." But Wasserman was also learning that pragmatism was essential to politics. You did not have to like someone, or his brother, in order to cultivate political support. And Wasserman seemed genuine in his affection for the older Kennedy, the one who was actually president. Publicist Herb Steinberg of Universal recalled that when Wasserman heard about Kennedy's assassination, "Lew was heartbroken," calling for Universal Studios to be closed in tribute to the fallen president. A story even circulated that Wasserman closed all of Hollywood in the wake of Kennedy's murder, but that was untrue. As powerful as Lew Wasserman was in Hollywood, that was beyond his capabilities.[46]

Luce: Intrigued by JFK

In 1960, Henry Luce was intrigued by the presidential candidacy of John F. Kennedy. While still a Republican, Luce did not have *TIME* weigh in as heavily on Nixon's behalf, which may have helped Kennedy squeak by in a close election. The criticism of the pro-Ike boosterism was a factor, but Luce also had a long-standing relationship with Kennedy, and wrote the foreword to Kennedy's 1940 book, *Why England Slept*. He maintained the relationship over the years, occasionally lunching with the young Senator Kennedy in the 1950s.[47]

Luce watched Kennedy's nomination acceptance speech on TV with Kennedy's formidable father, Joseph Kennedy. As a Republican, Luce did not have nearly the influence in the Kennedy administration that he did under Eisenhower. For his part, Kennedy was also somewhat aloof, telling the *New York Times*, "Like most Americans, I do not always agree with Time, but I nearly always read it." Upon reading, he would take complaints about things he disliked in the magazine directly to Luce. Even so, Luce was rooting for Kennedy, saying, "I don't agree with Kennedy on most things. But I like him." When Luce heard the sad news about Kennedy's tragic assassination, he buried his head in his hands.[48]

CHAPTER 7

UPHEAVAL AND STAGFLATION

**Presidents: Lyndon Johnson, Richard Nixon,
Gerald Ford, Jimmy Carter**
*CEOs: Wasserman, Luce, Lee Iacocca, Jack Welch,
Katharine Graham, Rupert Murdoch*

Just as Roosevelt's death in 1945 ended an era, so too did John F. Kennedy's in 1963. Before that, America seemed on a winning streak economically and geopolitically. But Kennedy's death unleashed something different in American politics, and in terms of the federal government's relationship to American business. Just as the Roosevelt era was marked by both a war and an ambitious domestic effort to increase the size and reach of the federal government, so too were the Lyndon Johnson years. That growth, coupled with the souring of the American attitude, would help shape presidential relations with CEOs for much of the next two decades.

Graham: Navigating Vietnam and Watergate

With John F. Kennedy's administration tragically cut short, Graham quickly went about establishing a relationship with Lyndon and Lady Bird Johnson. She had a friendly tea with Mrs. Johnson shortly after the assassination and continued to see Mrs. Johnson regularly throughout the administration. Her relationship with the president was also friendly at first, and he would even insist in 1964 that she come visit the Johnson Ranch in Texas. It did not last.

Even though the *Post* was seen as generally supportive of the war in Vietnam, Johnson was hypersensitive to criticism about the issue, and Graham recalled that, "The war definitely got in the way of my friendly relationship with Lyndon Johnson."[1]

Despite the coldness, Johnson did not completely shut her out. Initially, he was more apt to berate her than to ignore her. In general, she felt that Johnson's attitude was, "Phil Graham had been loyal. Why was I allowing my paper to report and say such things about his policies?" When Johnson did not like a story in the *Post*, he would tell his aide Jack Valenti to "call Kay Graham and ask her how that stupid SOB could write that." Graham got used to it and was eventually amused by the calls. On another occasion, Johnson summoned her to his White House bedroom at night and berated her about a *Post* article while he undressed for bed. When he reached his underwear, he sensed her discomfort and barked, "Turn around!" then continued the tongue-lashing with her back to him. As things in Vietnam worsened, so did Johnson's mood, and he initiated a "freeze-out" of her that lasted until the end of the administration. As she put it, "By 1966 our relations were definitely distant. I was no longer asked to anything intimate or friendly, and though I was invited to state occasions from time to time, his greeting in the receiving line was frigid or almost nonexistent."[2]

Graham tried different approaches with Johnson. Early on, she tried flattery, explaining that she "admired the legislation he himself had got passed and was for him and wanted to make sure he knew it." She also could be rough: on a 1964 visit to the ranch, Graham was dismayed at the way Johnson berated Lady Bird, and barked at him, "Oh, shut up, er . . . Mr. President." And she tried being rational. In response to the "freeze-out," she wrote him a letter saying, "Because I am responsible for two publications, one or the other of them is probably bound in the nature of things to irritate you or worse at times. And I am always sorry when we add to your problems—whatever reason. I only hope that at other times our support has been of some small pleasure or help." Johnson wrote back to her, but without much substance, saying, "I was, of course, happy to hear from you in your letter. . . . The spirit in which it was written is most welcome. Mrs. Johnson and I are fond of you, as we were of Phil; he is still very sorely missed by those of us who knew him so well." Graham did not think much of the Johnson letter, considering it "a slap in the face." None of her approaches resolved things with the complicated Johnson, but at least the lines of communication remained open. And Johnson softened in his post-presidency. He called her post-retirement and told her that he was coming to Washington for a visit. When she graciously asked, "Can I have lunch for you, or a dinner?" Johnson replied: "Both."[3]

Wasserman: Making Friends with LBJ

When Lyndon Johnson took over as president after Kennedy's death, Lew Wasserman was in far better shape than he had been with Kennedy. Even though Bobby Kennedy stayed on as Johnson's attorney general for a time, he was no longer the brother of the president. In fact, Johnson hated Kennedy, a sentiment that he shared with Wasserman. Wasserman's relationship with Johnson reached back into the 1950s, when Johnson was senate majority leader. In 1960, Wasserman supported Johnson over Kennedy for the Democratic presidential nomination, although, as with most of Wasserman's pre-1962 political commitments, it was decidedly half-hearted.[4]

With Johnson, Wasserman also had a man on the inside. Jack Valenti, a Texas-based PR man who joined President Johnson's team as a special assistant, was a Wasserman fan. He even advocated that Johnson bring Wasserman onto his team. Wasserman passed, but it was not the last time the two men would recommend each other for important jobs. For now, though, having Valenti in the White House became an invaluable resource.[5]

Wasserman continued to help Johnson, remaining a member of the President's Club and regularly raising funds for Johnson. Wasserman did it with eyes wide open, recognizing that he was trading fundraising dollars for access—which he needed after his recent government-caused setbacks. The producer Sam Goldwyn Jr., a longtime friend, recalled that "Wasserman was one of the first to realize that Hollywood could have clout in government." According to Goldwyn, Wasserman said, "We can be an influence—but don't kid yourself, it means patronage." Wasserman got a rude awakening to the transactional nature of things early on in their relationship. A 1964 thank you letter from the White House to Wasserman got returned. It had been sent to an incorrect address, demonstrating the White House's relative unfamiliarity with Wasserman at the time.[6]

Wasserman was undeterred by the letter miscue. He had a larger purpose in mind, and as he became more involved, he increasingly enjoyed the Washington game. Working with politicians brought him into contact with people who had a larger worldview than just the grosses from the weekend releases. The people in Washington were in some ways bigger than those in Hollywood, and Wasserman enjoyed interacting with them. He liked gossiping about the goings-on in Washington instead of just what was happening in Hollywood, and he liked being part of the larger conversation.[7]

It also helped that Wasserman had a personal affinity for Johnson, saying he "was my kind of guy. No sham about him." Their respect for each other started in their first face-to-face meeting in the 1950s. As Wasserman remembered, "He was very gracious, very outgoing, and from my viewpoint we seemed to hit it off immediately. We became friendly after that." Later, when Johnson was president, Wasserman recalled that he "was always very impressed by the fact that, holding the highest office in the world, he was a real person, at least with people who he considered his friends." Despite Johnson's earthy reputation, Wasserman felt that "he was never boorish."[8]

The two men had similar personalities, unyielding inside and tough with close advisers, but with an ability to be charming in public settings. Wasserman recalled that Johnson "was enormously effective in small groups, small groups being any-thing under a hundred, where you could really communicate." Both men also understood power, and how to wield it. As a result, Johnson respected Wasserman, and even included him in political strategy sessions. In one such session, Wasserman demonstrated a level of *chutzpah* that a traditional Washington hanger-on would not have dared. Wasserman did not recall whether the session took place at the White House or Camp David—itself an indication of how fre-quently Wasserman went to both places—but the subject was the impact of California's Proposition 14 on Johnson's political prospects in the Golden State. Proposition 14 was a ballot initiative that overturned a state law forbidding dis-crimination in the sale or purchase of real estate. This may sound like a settled issue to twenty-first century readers, but at the time it was an issue of great controversy, and the initiative was expected to pass.[9]

Wasserman entered the room, and Johnson immediately asked him, "What is this Proposition 14?" Wasserman expressed his disapproval of the measure, but added that it was likely to pass by two million votes, leading another adviser to warn Johnson: "See, you're doomed." Johnson then asked Wasserman how Johnson would do in the state. Here, Wasserman was more bullish, predicting that Johnson would carry California by 750,000 votes. This flummoxed the other advisers, who wondered how the civil rights provision would lose overwhelmingly, but Johnson would still win. Wasserman recalled listening for about five minutes, and then getting up to go, which, he observed, "one does not do in the company of the President." Johnson asked, "Where are you going?" Wasserman, who had just arrived, replied, "I'm going back to California."[10]

The response upset Johnson. "What do you mean, you're going back to California?" he demanded. "I thought we were going to have dinner, and you're staying for the weekend." Wasserman replied, "Well, you know, I live in California. I have the responsibility of some of your activity there. The only place I've heard you identified with Proposition 14 is in this room. Before you get me confused and get me thinking along those lines, I'm going to get out of here." Johnson laughed, and Wasserman stayed. The response was a gutsy one, but Wasserman was right. Proposition 14 passed, and Johnson won the state by a comfortable margin. As the story shows, Wasserman was clever, commanding, and fast on his feet, but he was also quite comfortable with Johnson by this point. He had come a long way from the guy who thought dealing with Washington was not worth his time.[11]

In addition to strategy sessions, Wasserman would also spend time with Johnson in more casual settings. He enjoyed the presidential retreat of Camp David, recalling that "it was very informal, and you had the feeling you were with family, you know." He also spent time at the Johnson Ranch in Stonewall, Texas, by the banks of the Pedernales River. Of those visits, he recalled, "I must say, all the visits we've had at the Ranch have been entirely personal. We visited friends.

We went driving in the countryside; had a barbecue; sat around and looked at some movies; had dinner."[12]

On one ranch trip, Johnson and Wasserman were joined by Henry Ford II. This was Hank the Deuce, grandson of the original Ford and the chairman and CEO of Ford Motor Company. Ford brought a new Mark IV automobile and Johnson, who loved to drive fast, said, "Let's go for a ride." Johnson sped around the ranch's unpaved roads with Wasserman and Ford hanging on in the back seat. After about fifteen minutes of this, Ford said to Wasserman, "You know, Lew, I don't think this car is built for this terrain."[13]

When not speeding around in cars, Johnson and Wasserman would talk, both early in the morning and late into the night. Wasserman recalled that on occasions he was staying in the White House, the very act of asking for his morning coffee would prompt an invitation to see the president. These were informal sessions, in which Wasserman would "come down and have your coffee with him in his bedroom in your robe and slippers, which I did on many occasions. We would chat." In these conversations, they would be "just shooting the breeze, as it were, about movie-making or television programs or about the people in them or what they did."[14]

Johnson was similarly chatty with Wasserman at night. Wasserman recalled one instance in which they were "talking about Hollywood and about movie stars and personalities," and Wasserman "kept asking to go to bed because I thought he looked tired." Johnson did not disengage and go to bed until one or two in the morning, at which point Mrs. Johnson invited Wasserman for a nightcap. Wasserman told Mrs. Johnson that he felt guilty for keeping the president up late, since, "If we hadn't been here the president would have gone to bed at eleven o'clock instead of one. Instead of which, we sat and talked." Mrs. Johnson dismissed his concerns, saying, "Lew, don't you realize this is the only relaxation he gets?"[15]

The stories of Johnson's conversations with Wasserman point to a unique appeal that powerful business leaders can have to presidents. Being president is a lonely job, and everyone seems to want something from you, especially in Washington. No one in the entire government is your peer, which makes business leaders, who can be similarly lonely at the top of their own industries, among the rare people who can relate to presidential loneliness and offer personal thoughts about other personalities and power players.

Given Johnson's connection to Wasserman, it is also not surprising that Johnson wanted to stay in close contact with his mogul friend. Both men loved phones and staying in touch with many subordinates with whom they could check in and milk for information. Wasserman confessed that, "I happen to be a telephone nut, I have telephones everywhere, my car." As *TIME* wrote in a profile of Wasserman, "He is always available by phone to anyone—except possibly to reporters."[16]

Johnson was similar. As senate majority leader, he would brag about being the first legislator to get a car phone. When Minority Leader Everett Dirksen got his own car phone and proudly called Johnson's car on it, Johnson one-upped him, saying, "Can you hold on a minute, Ev? My other phone is ringing." Johnson was so well known among his aides for having phones installed everywhere, including his boat and his bathroom, that after he died, his vice president, Hubert Humphrey, heard a phone ringing in a TV studio and joked, "Don't be surprised if he's calling."[17]

Johnson so valued his connection with Wasserman that he tried to make Wasserman as accessible as his own aides. Even though Wasserman was an early adopter in having a car phone, one day he got a call at the office telling him that someone from the White House Signal Corps was at his house installing a phone in Wasserman's bedroom. Wasserman spoke to the man and said, "I don't know who you are or what you're doing in my home, but I didn't order a phone." The man replied, "Well, the President has ordered the phone put in your room, and I understand I'm standing in your room. Now, would you like it at the head of your bed or at the foot of your bed?" Wasserman continued to protest, saying, "I really wouldn't like it at all," to which the corpsman responded, "Well, we're going to install it, so you may as well put it where you like it." As with most things, Johnson got his way, and the phone was installed.[18]

On another occasion, Johnson called Wasserman from Texas to talk about *TIME*'s 1964 "Man of the Year" issue, an award that Johnson would also win in 1967. While Johnson had scored the accolade and the cover, the issue also had a brief profile of Wasserman, "A New Kind of King," which caught Johnson's attention. According to Wasserman, Johnson teased him about the story and accused him of "stealing his thunder." Wasserman was bemused: "Here he was on the cover and there was a two-page story on the inside." The presidential teasing did not bother Wasserman, who characterized the presidential outreach as "a call from a friend; that was not a call from the President of the United States." [19]

As much as Johnson enjoyed Wasserman's company, Johnson was also getting something tangible from his relationship with Wasserman in the form of Hollywood money. While Hollywood is a key source for Democratic fundraising today, it was not yet so at the time, and Wasserman was instrumental in making it happen. Former Johnson aide Lloyd Hand recalled that Wasserman made great strides in this area in a short period. According to Hand, "Wasserman was not, in the early 1960s, the principal fund-raiser . . . but starting in 1964 Lew became the key guy." The President's Club, which was an important vehicle for fundraising, had five hundred California members, second only to New York. Wasserman's branch of the President's Club sent a $155,000 check to Johnson's reelection campaign in August of 1964. Wasserman himself contributed $28,000 to Democratic candidates that cycle. Jack Warner, who had previously tried to get Wasserman involved in political fundraising—albeit on the Republican side—noticed what Wasserman was doing and approved. He sent Wasserman a note saying, "I am most delighted that you are heading the fund-raising campaign for our esteemed President Johnson's re-election campaign."[20]

Fundraising at Wasserman's level required not only glad-handing and opening checkbooks but on occasion fast thinking. On June 20, 1964, Wasserman planned a President's Club dinner to raise money for Johnson at the Ambassador Hotel in Los Angeles. The event was to take place at the famous Cocoanut Grove nightclub within the hotel, the location that had hosted the Academy Awards in the 1930s and 1940s. Unfortunately, the room had already been booked for that night for a bar mitzvah. Given that the night in question was the only one that worked for the president's schedule, Wasserman called the father of the bar mitzvah boy to ask him if he would be willing to change rooms. The man was initially reluctant to do so, until he heard that it was an event for the president. Even so, the man drove a hard bargain, agreeing to do so only if his son could meet the president. Wasserman agreed, only to have the man call back a few minutes later with an additional request: "Well, if you let the rabbi meet him, it's a deal."[21]

Wasserman's fundraising helped Johnson in his reelection effort, but it also helped Wasserman increase his access in Johnson's second term. After Johnson's victory, Johnson considered Wasserman for the position of secretary of commerce. It did not happen, and the differing accounts for why it did not happen are instructive. One suggestion is that Johnson wanted to be nice to Wasserman but was not serious about the offer. Harry McPherson, an important White House adviser to Johnson, feared that repeated allegations of Wasserman's mob ties—the mob was heavily embedded in the Hollywood unions at the time—would severely complicate Wasserman's path to senate confirmation.[22]

The idea did not work on Wasserman's end, either. Wasserman wanted to remain focused on his business. This makes sense, as he was a kingmaker in Hollywood and would only be a second-tier cabinet secretary in Washington. Wasserman himself suggested personal reasons, saying that he could not pursue the job "because my wife wouldn't move to Washington." Wasserman also said something to Johnson in 1963 that revealed that the conversation about commerce was likely a non-starter from the beginning. In December of 1963, shortly after Johnson's ascension to the presidency, Wasserman and Johnson New York political adviser Ed Weisl met with Johnson at New York's Carlyle hotel. They spoke for a few hours, after which Wasserman said to Johnson, "I'd like to ask you a very important favor." Wasserman recalled that Johnson seemed unhappy and braced himself for the request. Wasserman followed up with, "I want you to promise me that I never have to work for the government." The joke made Johnson laugh, but it also meant that Wasserman for secretary of commerce was unlikely to happen.[23]

Even though Wasserman did not join the president's cabinet, he remained heavily involved in the president's second term, both as fundraiser and political adviser. Most of that involvement happened behind the scenes. Wasserman seemed uninterested in the public perks of being close to the president and did not, for example, want to ride in the president's limousine. This was in line with his "stay out of the spotlight," no-publicity rule. But he did continue to raise money, something that was noticed within the White House. An internal White House memo in 1967 identified the potential for the "the development of a substantial base for political contributions in Southern California." Wasserman had a lot to do with that development.[24]

Wasserman's generosity extended beyond just political giving. He also helped with Mrs. Johnson's Wildflower campaign, part of her highway beautification effort as First Lady, and the LBJ Library, to which he gave MCA stock with an eventual value in the hundreds of millions of dollars. His advice to Johnson from outside the Washington bubble was valuable as well. As Wasserman recalled, Johnson "asked for opinions, for temperature readings about how to cope with the PR problems, as distinguished from whether he had one. I think the President was aware he had a PR problem, certainly in the latter days of the Administration."[25]

Wasserman: Embedding Johnson's Man at the MPAA

Wasserman gave a lot to the Johnson administration, but he got a lot in return as well. He became known as an important player in Washington. He also became an important cog in the Democratic fundraising machine, which brought him more benefits when Democrats were in power, and fewer when they were not. His political problems with the U.S. government seemed to die down as well, although the Justice Department had already prevented him from taking over Universal while keeping MCA. Regardless, being close to the president would help if new problems arose, which was his goal when he initially started paying more attention to Washington to begin with.

Wasserman also got another lasting benefit out of the Johnson administration. In 1966, the Motion Picture Association of America (MPAA) appointed Johnson confidante Valenti as president. The MPAA head had been vacant for five years, ever since Eric Johnston left the position in 1961, as warring studio heads could not agree on a candidate. A few years later, Kennedy and then Johnson speechwriter Ted Sorensen was considered for the position, but he ultimately did not get it. Valenti finally broke the logjam, with Arthur Krim and Wasserman serving as his patrons.[26]

President Johnson did not take well to the initial suggestion of losing his close aide. Johnson had initially suggested someone else, who also did not work out. When Wasserman and Weisl broached the idea of Valenti, saying, "What about Jack?" Johnson "threw us out of his office." Johnson relented shortly afterwards. As Wasserman recalled, Johnson "called me a couple days later and said, 'you can have him.'" Johnson called Valenti a "Benedict Arnold" after the decision was made, but he saw the advantages. According to Johnson's appointments secretary, Jim Jones, "Lew Wasserman had convinced [Johnson] that Jack Valenti could do more for him in fund-raising in the Hollywood community."[27]

For Wasserman, getting Valenti was a huge coup. He and Valenti already had a strong relationship, and Wasserman had been letting Valenti use his Palm Springs home. They were also close enough so that they could be honest with one another, even about areas of disagreement. In 1965, Johnson sent Wasserman a glowing note commemorating the 50th anniversary of Universal Studios, honoring Universal's "many enduring contributions to our national goals." Valenti, however, enclosed his own note to "Dear Lew" with the Johnson letter, warning that "we do frankly have some doubts as to the wisdom of using it in the advertising supplement which you are publishing in the Sunday *New York Times*. It would be a marked departure from past practice to have a Presidential message of this sort used in paid company advertising." Having someone with a close relationship who was also not intimidated by Wasserman made for a strong partnership.[28]

Valenti benefited from having Wasserman as his ally as well. Valenti's first big initiative was to replace the outdated Hays Code governing film standards with the Motion Picture Association's film rating system we have today. It was a controversial move all around, as some studio heads liked the Hays Code, some found it too restrictive, and no one knew how the new system would work. Valenti ushered it in, with Wasserman's assistance being crucial. Valenti later said that Wasserman "was the only one who could have gotten so disparate a group to agree. They respected his judgment." Valenti would go on to serve as the head of the MPAA for thirty-eight years and ally with Wasserman in many important battles over the ensuing decades.[29]

Coda: Luce's Departure and Legacy

By the time Lyndon Johnson became president, Henry Luce had begun to wind down. He stopped running the *TIME* empire in 1964. His 16 percent stake in the magazine was worth $109,862,500, approximately $1 billion in today's dollars. Of his retirement, the *New York Times* observed that "Mr. Luce once played a hard game of tennis and now plays an occasional easy game of golf." He was an admirer of Lyndon Johnson, and his support for Johnson over Barry Goldwater—whom Luce saw as too radical—broke a string of backing Republican presidential candidates that dated back to Hoover in 1932. But he was no longer in the game, enjoying a brief retirement before dying on March 10, 1967.[30]

When Luce died, his company was a powerhouse of influence and reach. It regularly printed fourteen million copies of his magazines— *TIME, Fortune, Life*, and *Sports Illustrated*. Luce's personal and political influence was no less far reaching. His interactions with American presidents began with Herbert Hoover and stretched to Lyndon Johnson. Johnson once remarked, "The magazines that bear his stamp are an authentic part of life in America."[31] Johnson was right. Luce's magazines, and his worldview, shaped mid-twentieth century America. As Luce rose and sought to expand his empire, he realized early on that his journalistic enterprises required an understanding of this occupant of the Oval Office, but only later recognized the importance of those relationships to his business enterprises.

Ultimately, the Luce story is a tale of the limits of power of a media mogul. *TIME* indeed had millions of readers and helped shape both national news outlets and the coverage of the president as an individual. *TIME* also influenced the way America wrote and spoke, bringing words like "tycoon," "pundit," "socialite," and "kudos" into prominence. What it could not do, however, was determine presidential elections. Luce put his best efforts into trying to defeat Roosevelt multiple times, without success. He may have annoyed Roosevelt, but there is little evidence that he significantly damaged Roosevelt's presidency with his enmity. Luce did throw it all in for Eisenhower, but it's not clear that Ike needed the help to get elected, and the blatancy of Luce's efforts harmed Luce and his publications.

Luce ultimately shaped the media landscape far more than he did the political one.

This does not mean, however, that Luce was unimportant or lacking in influence on the presidency. Luce's approach to presidents would live on in how presidents would deal with the media going forward. During the Johnson years, a courier would bring a copy of the new issue of *TIME* to the White House on Sunday nights. Johnson would read it in his pajamas, and if he did not like something he saw, he would wake up *TIME* White House correspondent Hugh Sidey and scream at him over the phone, "Goddamn it, Sidey! You bastards." By personalizing the relationship between presidents and the press, Henry Luce had opened up a whole new venue for presidents who wanted to voice their complaints to members of the media or their bosses, one that would live on long after Luce retired from the scene.[32]

Lee Iacocca: CEO as Lobbyist

Lee Iacocca was one of the most famous CEOs of the twentieth century, working in one of the most storied American industries. He wrote a best-selling autobiography, appeared frequently on TV, and actively flirted with running for president. He was also CEO of two major American car companies at a time of great change for the auto industry, and the industry's many challenges brought him frequently into the orbit of multiple American presidents. Over the course of a long career and a celebrity retirement in which he continued to write books and speak out, he was friendly with at least ten presidents. More importantly, he used his connections with multiple presidents to lobby, with considerable success, for policies that he thought were good for his companies. Later, when he became more famous, he also used his celebrity and presidential connections to lobby for policies that he felt were good for America.

Iacocca may have had an illustrious career, but he came from humble beginnings. Iacocca was born in Allentown, Pennsylvania, in 1924, the son of Italian immigrants. His first name was originally "Lido," which he eventually

Americanized into "Lee." As a child, he admired Franklin D. Roosevelt, who, Iacocca later recalled, "was always willing to try something new. And if that didn't work, he was willing to try something else." As a young man, Iacocca liked Harry Truman, because he "told it like it was." Iacocca "enjoyed having a President in the Oval Office who spoke his mind in plain English." When he grew older, Iacocca too would be known for speaking his mind in plain English.[33]

Iacocca went to Lehigh University, graduating after only three years, and was recruited to work at Ford. He took a leave to get a master's in mechanical engineering at Princeton, but then returned to Ford, where he stayed for thirty-two years. His mentor at Ford was Robert McNamara, who became secretary of defense under John F. Kennedy. Iacocca did not join McNamara in Washington, but he was impressed with Kennedy. In his autobiography, Iacocca wrote that, "The striking contrast between the new decade and the 1950s, between John Kennedy and Dwight Eisenhower, could be summed up in a single word—youth."[34]

Under McNamara's tutelage, Iacocca climbed the corporate ladder and learned how to play politics, both internal and external. He became the number two in the company under Henry Ford II, who liked Iacocca and took him along on a visit to meet Lyndon Johnson. The 1960s were good times for the American auto industry. Iacocca captured the national mood with the cars he helped shepherd through the process, including the Mustang in 1964. The Mustang brought in over $1 billion in profits for Ford and landed Iacocca on the covers of both *TIME* and *Newsweek*. But more challenging times were coming for the auto industry, and politics, both at home and abroad, had a lot to do with them.[35]

When Richard Nixon came into office in 1969, Iacocca was president of Ford Automotive North American Operations and executive vice president of the Ford Motor Company. He represented the company at meetings of Nixon's Cabinet Task Force on Oil Import Control. He also joined Henry Ford II to meet with Nixon to try to fend off one of the chief challenges facing the auto industry in the 1970s: regulatory impositions from Washington.[36]

In 1965, Ralph Nader published *Unsafe at Any Speed*. The book, which specifically focused on the dangers of the Chevrolet Corvair, put the entire automotive industry on the defensive. In addition, increased levels of pollution led to calls for environmental limits on cars as well. At the same time, increasingly expensive union contracts and the development of foreign-made alternatives to American cars were making for tougher times for Detroit after a dominant postwar period. Washington and its policies were becoming increasingly important for the auto-makers, in terms of financing, regulation, and international competition, and those issues brought Iacocca into regular contact with American presidents for the next two decades.

By 1970, Iacocca had ascended to the top of Ford, second only to Henry Ford II. On April 27, 1971, the two men went to the White House to meet with Nixon and his domestic policy adviser, John Ehrlichman. From the outset, Nixon made clear that he was sympathetic to the two men and their industry, and not to Nader. According to Nixon, his own "views are, frankly, whether it's the environment or pollution or Naderism or consumerism, are extremely pro-business." The two visitors were happy to have Nixon rant against "Nader running around and squealing against this and that and the other thing," but they also wanted to address specific concerns. Ford II made a stark pitch that the various regulations in play would impose real costs on American consumers. Ford II told Nixon that, "We think that the prices of cars are going to go up from next year through '75 anywhere from a hundred dollars to, up to maybe seven or eight hundred dollars in the next four years because of the requirements." To address the problem, Ford II said, "We're talking about trying to put some sense into the [Department of Transportation] and how they go about doing their business."[37]

Iacocca was the junior man in the room, but he was not shy. He reported that he had already been meeting, unsuccessfully, with Transportation Secretary Anthony Volpe, and asked him, "Would you guys cool it a little bit? You're gonna break us." Nixon told his visitors that he would look into it, and he did. Ehrlichman reached out to Volpe and told him to suspend the air bag regulation under con-sideration. Volpe pushed back, saying that the Democrat "Mr. Ford isn't your friend." Ehrlichman was unmoved, telling Volpe, "He sure is." The regulation was suspended and air bags would not be mandated on American cars until 1991 legislation that went into effect for model year 1998. The young Iacocca got an early lesson in the potency of cultivating presidential support.[38]

Iacocca appreciated Nixon's backing, but he was also willing to give Nixon some assistance of his own. In September of 1971, Iacocca publicly touted Nixon's economic plan in a speech to the Sales Executive Club of New York. Iacocca, whom the *New York Times* described as looking "more like a football coach than a corporate officer," acknowledged that Nixon's plan "calls for temporary sacrifices," but added that it "imposes them on everybody so that in the end everybody, business, labor, consumers, taxpayers, all of us, can benefit." As Iacocca said, to laughter, "I don't deny that there are inequities. But there are enough inequities to go around."[39]

Iacocca's actions provided an important lesson for CEOs in their role as lobbyists. Sometimes the best way to get what you want is to give them what they want. For Iacocca, backing Nixon's economic plan was a small price to pay for getting the air bag rule suspended.

Graham: In the Thick of It with Watergate

Although Graham's relations with the Johnson White House had rough patches, things got far worse in the Nixon administration. She had personally supported Nixon in the primaries and the general election in 1968, and tried to befriend him once he became president, but Nixon was not interested. He would not attend her dinners, and he ordered his staff not to, either. When she reached out indirectly to get White House Chief of Staff H. R. Haldeman to share a meal with her, he responded to the intermediary, "We don't accept lunches at *The Washington Post*."[40]

Initially, the *Post* was not overtly hostile to the Nixon administration, with the notable exception of the cartoonist Herblock. Herblock had never liked Nixon, and his drawings of a sinister Nixon with a perpetual five o'clock shadow damaged Nixon's image. According to the journalist David Halberstam, Herblock's Nixon drawings "stamped him and defined him as no Democratic politician could." Herblock aside, two major and related incidents would contribute to the larger sense of hostility between the Nixon administration and the *Post*, and Graham had a key role in both.[41]

The first was the Pentagon Papers. On June 13, 1971, the *New York Times* began publishing this revealing series of leaked documents detailing America's increasing involvement in Vietnam during prior administrations. The government asked the courts to stop the publication, and the courts enjoined the *Times* from publishing further documents. But then the *Post* obtained the documents, presenting Graham with the decision of whether to publish them.[42]

It was a difficult decision. The *Post* had just gone public, and there were legitimate concerns about what a fight with the Nixon administration would do to its stock price. In addition, the Justice Department was threatening a criminal prosecution of the *Post* if it went ahead with the publication. If its executives were convicted, the *Post* could conceivably have lost its broadcast licenses. One evening, Graham got a call from the office, where *Post* executives and editors were debating what to do. Graham heard arguments on both sides before weighing in with her eventful decision: "I say we print."[43]

Ultimately, the Supreme Court allowed the publication, sparing the *Post* from criminal penalties and the loss of its licenses. But Graham's decision had other important implications as well. First, it established the *Post* as a serious competitor to the *Times*, at least in terms of its Washington coverage. Second, it made Nixon angry—at the *Post*, at journalists in general, and at leakers of all kinds, leading him to demand the launch of an anti-leak effort that created the Plumbers, a group of internal investigators so designated because they plugged leaks. And, as Graham noted in an overly genteel way, "Needless to say, the minor irritations experienced between the *Post* and the Nixon administration prior to this, which had slowly ratcheted up all atmosphere, had now turned major."[44]

The "irritations" became even worse with the Watergate scandal. Nixon's Plumbers burglarized the Watergate complex in June of 1972, looking for intelligence from the Democratic National Committee headquarters. They got caught, and two *Post* reporters, Bob Woodward and Carl Bernstein, began digging, with support from Graham and *Post* editor Ben Bradlee. Most other news outlets lost interest in the story, but the *Post* kept on it, despite fears that it could harm the *Post*'s reputation as an impartial news source. Graham was subject to an infamous threat from Attorney General John Mitchell, who warned that if the *Post* kept on the story, "Katie Graham's gonna get her tit caught in a big fat wringer." More specifically, there were once again concerns about the company's TV stations, which needed federal licenses to operate. Nixon had even said to aides that, "The main thing is the *Post* is going to have damnable, damnable problems out of this one. . . . They have a television station . . . and they're going to have to get it renewed."[45]

Some Nixon aides were paying attention. In 1974, George Champion Jr., Florida finance chairman of the 1972 Nixon re-election campaign, challenged the renewal of licenses for two *Post*-owned stations in Florida. Ultimately, the renewals went through, and Nixon was forced to resign, but it was not clear all along that that was how things would play out. Graham herself recognized the risks she was facing in allowing the Watergate coverage to continue. At one point during the scandal, she said, "All I know is that 24 months from now, one of us [Graham or Richard Nixon] is going to be in jail." Nixon did not quite go to jail, but he might have if his successor Gerald Ford had not pardoned him. As old Washington hand Clark Clifford put it, "She got into the meanest, toughest fight I've ever seen in this town with the Nixon Administration."[46]

Iacocca: Managing the Chrysler Bailout

In 1978, Iacocca became the head of Chrysler—making him the only man to be at the helm of two of Detroit's Big Three auto companies. His good relationship with Ford II had turned sour, and Ford II fired the increasingly famous Iacocca because he just did not like him, saying, "He's too conceited, too self-centered to be able to see the broad picture."[47]

As Chrysler CEO, Iacocca had a very good sense of the "broad picture," and it was not pretty. The deadly combination of higher union costs, expensive regulations, and increased foreign competition, especially from Japan, had caught up to Detroit. These developments, coupled with terrible economic times under President Jimmy Carter, had Chrysler reeling. Chrysler needed help, and Iacocca went to Washington to lobby for loan guarantees as part of a package to turn Chrysler around. Iacocca visited with Carter during his lobbying effort, although, according to Iacocca, "Carter didn't get very involved in the Chrysler debate, but he did support our cause." Carter also was well aware of Iacocca's presence in a Chrysler TV commercial and his growing public profile. He joked that Iacocca "was becoming as well-known as he was." Carter was not involved in the details of the loan guarantees, but his support was crucial. According to Iacocca, Carter "made it clear that he stood behind us. Without the support of the executive branch, the bill would never have passed."[48]

Iacocca was grateful. He went to the White House for a January 7, 1980, celebration of the passage of the $1.5 billion loan guarantee package. While there, he thanked Carter for his help, claiming that "600,000 jobs have been preserved." Iacocca later wrote that "Jimmy Carter had his drawbacks, but his accomplishments have been underrated."[49]

Iacocca was happy with the package, but he wasn't satisfied. In July of 1980, only six months after the loan guarantee package had passed, he was pressing the Carter administration for a $1,500 tax credit for Americans who purchased American cars. He was angry about Japanese import limits on American cars and felt that American car manufacturers needed a leg up in order to compete. Carter told him to wait for a package next year. But Iacocca was impatient, warning, "Wait for that? We are all going to be dead."[50]

Iacocca was right that waiting was unwise. Carter lost the 1980 election to Ronald Reagan, whose administration was less interested in regulating the automakers, but also less interested in government-sponsored corporate bailouts.

Rupert Murdoch: Learning to Lobby

Media mogul Rupert Murdoch got his start in Australia. He then migrated to England but eventually earned his greatest fame, fortune—and notoriety—in America with Fox News. Even though he had other important media properties, including the *Wall Street Journal* and the *New York Post*, it was Fox News that got the most attention from multiple presidents.

Presidential attention was important to Murdoch, who had longed for it for decades, and had been meeting with presidents since a December 1, 1961, Oval Office visit and interview with John F. Kennedy. Getting in good with government has long been part of Murdoch's business model. Over the decades, he has taken advantage of a variety of regulatory changes and dispensations to build and grow his media empire.[51]

Murdoch was born in 1931, the son of newspaper publisher Keith Murdoch. Sir Keith—he was knighted in 1933—ran multiple papers, but they did not make him rich. His estate even had to sell one of the papers he owned to pay estate taxes, something that rankled his ambitious son. The younger Murdoch went to Oxford and was determined to be more successful on the business side of things. According to Sir Edward Pickering, a newspaper executive who mentored Murdoch, "The great driving force in Rupert's life is the feeling that his father was cheated."[52]

Murdoch apprenticed in London, where he learned how to use sensationalism to build circulation, and then returned to Australia to run the remaining family papers. He also began acquiring papers, including Sydney's *Daily Mirror*. In 1964, he created a nationwide newspaper, *The Australian*, then set his sights on British papers, including the *News of the World* and *The Sun*. He plunged into British politics, backing Margaret Thatcher in 1979, and subsequently getting favorable treatment from British regulators. Following Thatcher, he supported Tory John Major but also Labour's Tony Blair, showing a willingness to back politicians of both parties. He also moved into television news, starting Sky Television in 1990.[53]

Murdoch took the model of buying papers, endorsing politicians, and moving into television to America as well. His first U.S. acquisition was in 1973, but he came to American prominence with his purchase of the *New York Post* in 1976. In 1980, Murdoch had lunch with Jimmy Carter at the White House during Carter's grueling battle with Senator Ted Kennedy for the Democratic nomination. On the same day, he met with Export-Import Bank chairman John L. Moore. Shortly afterwards, the *Post* endorsed Carter in the New York primary, and the bank backed a low interest loan beneficial to Murdoch's business interests. Murdoch claimed these were unrelated, but the episode showed Murdoch's eagerness to engage with American politicians and a brazenness regarding his willingness to be criticized for possible influence peddling. At an early stage in his career, Murdoch had absorbed the lessons of CEO as a lobbyist for his company's interests.[54]

Wasserman: Navigating Washington after Johnson

When Lyndon Johnson left office in the beginning of 1969, Lew Wasserman had a problem. He had ingratiated himself so well with the Johnson administration that it would be hard to get as close to any successor. Wasserman was also so clearly identified as a Democrat that a Republican administration would be a tough environment for him. Furthermore, Johnson's successor was not just any Republican, it was Richard Nixon, someone that Wasserman could not stand.[55]

Back in 1960, Jack Warner had tried to get Wasserman to support Nixon's candidacy. That was a nonstarter, even though Wasserman had perfunctorily backed the Republican Eisenhower in 1952. Now, eight years later, Wasserman was even more closely identified as a Democrat and a crucial partisan who had donated tens of thousands to the Democratic Party and helped develop both Hollywood and California in general for Democratic fundraising efforts.

Furthermore, Wasserman still had business interests that could be affected by Washington. In 1968, his old firm MCA attempted a merger with the Westinghouse corporation. That merger failed as the companies dropped the effort "by mutual agreement"—even after hours of negotiations—because of looming scrutiny from federal regulators. That announcement came in April 25, 1969, three months after the start of the Nixon administration, although the review had begun under Johnson. Another MCA planned merger, this one with Firestone Tire and Rubber Company, was scuttled in September of 1969.[56]

Wasserman's position in 1969 highlights the risk of a CEO going too far in supporting one particular administration or one particular political party. When that party or that administration leaves power, the CEO is left without allies in high places, or worse, can be the target of political resentment. Clearly, Wasserman could not just sit around and wait for a more friendly administration.

As usual, Wasserman had a plan. While he was the company's top Democrat, his colleague Taft Schreiber was a Republican. It was Schreiber who would raise money for Republicans and make friends in the Nixon administration. He was not as big as Wasserman and did not get as close to Nixon as Wasserman did to Johnson, but the arrangement left their bases covered.[57]

Despite the Schreiber arrangement, Wasserman did not completely leave the picture as far as Washington was concerned. In 1971, he helped head a bipartisan Hollywood push for Nixon's proposed tax cut package. His purpose was twofold. Business leaders generally prefer tax cuts, but this tax package would reinstate an investment tax credit for the full cost of making films, including cameras, projectors, and the film itself. The provision was important—and valuable—enough to the industry that it warranted Wasserman allying himself with the Nixon administration for this purpose.[58]

In August 1974, Nixon resigned as a result of the Watergate scandal, and his vice president Gerald Ford took over. With a Republican still in the White House, Wasserman continued to take a back seat to Schreiber on fundraising and relations with the White House, but he still kept his foot in the game. In January of 1975, he and his wife hosted Secretary of State Henry Kissinger for a dinner in his honor at their home. Their house, known as the Foothill Estate, hosted four presidents in addition to Kissinger.[59]

Kissinger had been in regular contact with Wasserman for a while. In June of 1973, when Kissinger was Nixon's National Security Adviser, he had a conversation with Paramount executive Robert Evans about finding a cowboy film to show Soviet Premier Leonid Brezhnev, who was set to visit the U.S. for a week. In addition to finding a film, they wanted to get it subtitled in Russian. Kissinger thought Wasserman might be able to help, telling Evans, "Hugh [sic] Wasserman is dying to get—Remember all that stuff he has about getting into the Russian market?" In the end, Evans had Paramount president Frank Yablans call Kissinger and provide some films, including *Roman Holiday* and *Romeo and Juliet*, but the episode shows that Kissinger was in touch with Wasserman, even if his transcribing secretary did not know Wasserman's first name.[60]

Wasserman continued to stay in touch with Kissinger during the Ford administration, and he and Edie introduced Kissinger to people around Hollywood. Other guests at the Foothill Estate dinner included Alfred Hitchcock, Gregory Peck, Kirk Douglas, and Sid Sheinberg. Kissinger joked that actors and politicians had many similarities, except "politicians play only one role and have a shorter life."[61]

Kissinger loved hobnobbing with Hollywood people. He even dated Jill St. John, an actress who played a "Bond girl" in *Diamonds are Forever.* Evans had introduced the two. Kissinger also liked showing that he was in touch with Hollywood people, even to his boss, President Ford. In January of 1976, Kissinger was discussing the upcoming presidential election and Israel with Ford and cited Wasserman in the conversation: "Lew Wasserman said the only one who could beat you was Kennedy. He said how you should use spots and saturate the media for three days. He is concerned about the Jews. He says the present course in Israel will lead to massive anti-Semitism here and the power of the institutional Jews must be broken."[62]

Wasserman was wrong about the election. Ford would be beaten, not by Senator Ted Kennedy, but by a former Georgia governor named Jimmy Carter.

Graham: Getting a Breather with Ford and Carter

With the onset of the Gerald Ford administration, Katharine Graham and the *Washington Post* could finally enjoy working with a less hostile administration. Ford attended and even spoke at a 1975 dinner Graham hosted for the retirement of White House reporter Carroll Kilpatrick. Ford also graciously—and self-deprecatingly—signed a photo of himself superimposed with a joke about him from *Saturday Night Live*: "I got my job through the *Washington Post*." The signature line read, "To Ben Bradlee and all my friends at the *Washington Post*." Bradlee was impressed with Ford's good humor, writing in his memoir that "I can't think of another president who would have done the same thing." Graham and the *Post* supported Ford's opponent Jimmy Carter in 1976, but Graham later regretted it, telling a reporter that "I think we made a mistake in supporting Jimmy Carter. . . . We were so unhappy about Nixon, I think that's why we went for Carter, but Ford was a better president." When Ford heard this, he remarked, "Well, it's pretty late to do that now." [63]

Regrets aside, Carter was now president, and Graham was unhappy with what she got. Like Nixon, the former Georgia governor had little interest in the Washington social scene, including in Graham's hospitality. She was particularly unimpressed when Carter not only refused to attend a party at her home honoring

Eugene Patterson, a former *Post* staffer with Georgia roots, but he did not even respond to the invitation. At the party, Graham was dismissive of the president's and his team's priorities, saying, "Have you noticed that none of the White House people are here to honor one of their fellow Georgians? They just don't understand. They ought to be in here working this room."[64]

The *Post* also had some silly blowups with the Carter White House. In one instance, Sally Quinn, a sharp-penned *Post* reporter and Bradlee's wife, wrote a snarky profile of Carter national security adviser Zbigniew Brzezinski. Brzezinski was indeed arrogant and abrasive, which the article pointed out, but Quinn also included an unnecessary and insufficiently sourced item: that Brzezinski had unzipped his fly in a dismissive way at a female reporter named Clare Crawford. After the story came out, Crawford denied that it had happened, putting the *Post* in a bind. When told about the incident by Brzezinski and Press Secretary Jody Powell, Carter was irate and told his team: "Go and deal with it." The *Post* issued a retraction, and the White House was gleeful. An anonymous aide (likely Brzezinski or Powell) gloated: "This is the newspaper they made the big movie [*All the President's Men*]. About how they had six sources for everything and how they agonized over what they would print on Watergate. I guess they're more worried about their treatment of criminals than their treatment of the innocent." These tiffs were only part of the reason that Graham was glad to see the Carter team go. [65]

Wasserman: Back in with Carter

Lew Wasserman backed Jimmy Carter early, prompted by his wife Edie. She had met Carter at a fundraiser and called Lew to tell him, "I've just met the next president of the U.S." When Wasserman met Carter, the two clicked. According to the political consultant Bill Carrick, "Wasserman was a New Deal Democrat and so was Carter."[66]

With Carter's 1976 victory, a fellow Democrat was once again in the top spot in the White House. As he had with Johnson, Wasserman raised a lot of money for Carter. According to Democratic strategist and fundraiser Bob Strauss, Wasserman once bailed out the Carter campaign when it was completely broke.

Wasserman quickly invited forty people to an emergency fundraiser and raised the $200,000 the campaign required. As with Johnson, he was no pushover, though. When the Carter people asked to add additional people to the guest list, Wasserman said no: "It's in my home, I want control of the guest list." Strauss saw this as a measure of Wasserman's stature, observing that, "A lot of people didn't speak up to presidential nominees in the way Wasserman did."[67]

As with Johnson, Carter considered Wasserman for secretary of commerce. As with Johnson, the appointment never happened. Wasserman even spent time with Carter away from the White House, once playing the role of bartender at a get together in Carter's home in Plains, Georgia. However, over time, Wasserman soured on Carter and his policy failures. Wasserman and his wife supported the Democrat in 1980, as always, but halfheartedly, and made an effort to revive their relationship with an old friend and client who was about to step into the presidency.[68]

CHAPTER 8

THE REAGAN BOOM

Presidents: Ronald Reagan, George H. W. Bush
*CEOs: Oprah Winfrey, Bill Gates, Warren Buffett, Steve Jobs, Jack
Welch, Murdoch, Wasserman, Iacocca, The Warners (posthumously)*

In 1980, former actor and Lew Wasserman client Ronald Reagan won the presidential election. His era, like those of the 1920s and the 1950s, was also one of peace and prosperity. It would be punctuated for a regulatory retrenchment, a sense that government had gotten too big and interventionist. Reagan himself famously said at a news conference that, "The nine most terrifying words in the English language are: I'm from the Government, and I'm here to help."[1]

While Reagan did not actually shrink the federal government—no president had done that since Coolidge—he did try to make it less interventionist, both in the development of new regulations and in the pursuit of enforcement of antitrust actions. Still, even deregulatory efforts had business implications, as Wasserman and Iacocca would come to learn. In addition, the combination of technological advances and a favorable business environment once again opened up the possibility of new business empires.

Coda: The Warners' Posthumous Appearances
in the Reagan Administration

Jack and Harry Warner were of course long dead by the time Reagan became president, but they remained on his mind. Reagan often told Warner stories as president, including the joke in which Harry Warner famously questioned the prospects for talking pictures by asking, "Who the hell wants to hear actors talk?" Reagan told that joke at least eight times as president. But Jack Warner was the funniest Warner. When Jack heard that Reagan was running for governor, Jack thought for a moment and said, "No, uh-uh—Jimmy Stewart for Governor, Ronald Reagan for best friend." Reagan used that line at least ten times as president.[2] The frequency with which Reagan mentioned them shows that even long-dead CEOs could continue to have an impact on presidents. It also showed, as Wasserman would learn to his advantage, that Reagan's formative years in Hollywood remained important to his worldview decades after his acting career had ended.

Iacocca: Frustrations with Free Marketers after Enmeshing with Government

For Lee Iacocca, one of the great ironies of the 1980s was that they became a period of great fame for him, but they were also a period of great frustration with Washington. Despite his earlier free market arguments during the Nixon administration, Iacocca found himself out of step with the pro-market administrations of Ronald Reagan and George H. W. Bush. In the 1980s, Iacocca had largely moved on from concerns about loan guarantees and safety regulations. He had made his company far more dependent on federal largesse and began to see the federal government as a protector of his business, an entity that could keep out upstart foreign competitors that paid lower wages, had lower health-care costs, and benefited from protectionist trade policies that put American car companies at a disadvantage.

Reagan and Iacocca liked each other and spoke regularly. Iacocca described Reagan as "the sunniest guy I ever met. He didn't have a mean bone in his body." He also appreciated that, "When Reagan heard that my wife Mary was dying, he made a point of calling me to offer comfort and prayers." Reagan appointed Iacocca head of the Statue of Liberty-Ellis Island Foundation in 1982 and reportedly offered him a cabinet slot, which Iacocca declined. In 1983, Reagan had Iacocca over for a small "stag-bull session" dinner at the White House with smart thinkers like Irving Kristol and George Will to discuss the auto industry and Japan's trade practices. Reagan in his diary called the conversation "most informative & useful since we'll be dealing with P.M. [Yasuhiro] Nakasone Tues."[3]

Reagan liking Iacocca did not mean that he went along with Iacocca's wishes. In one instance, Iacocca wanted the Reagan Treasury Department to return to Chrysler warrants from the Carter loan guarantee that allowed the government to purchase Chrysler stock. These warrants were valuable now that Chrysler had regained its footing, and the Treasury Department argued against returning them. The issue made its way to Reagan's desk, and Iacocca argued his case, while Assistant Treasury Secretary Tom Healey made the case for Treasury. Reagan sided with Treasury, saying, "Well, Lee, you know that Tom's right." This angered Iacocca, who called Treasury Secretary Don Regan on his way back to Detroit, "cursing and swearing at the 'young jerk' [Healey] who worked for him and who had the audacity to tell the President of the United States that the warrants belonged to the taxpayers." Iacocca remained angry about this, later writing that, "Their attitude was, 'Screw Chrysler. Let's get every cent we can.'"[4]

The warrants incident was illustrative of a larger disconnect between Reagan and Iacocca. Reagan was a free marketer, while Iacocca wanted a government that acted more in the interests of Chrysler specifically, and corporations in general. He was against regulations that held automakers back, but for taxpayer-funded corporate largesse and trade protections for their products. He understood that the Carter bailout would not have happened under Reagan: "There's no question in my mind that if there had been a Republican administration in 1979, Chrysler wouldn't be around. The Republicans wouldn't even have said hello to us. Chrysler

would have gone bankrupt, and today they'd be writing books about having protected free enterprise." To Iacocca, Reagan and his free-market aides were "living
in the nineteenth century." As a result, while he was once a Republican, he
acknowledged in his memoir that "ever since coming to Chrysler, I've leaned
toward the Democrats."[5]

This policy disconnect exacerbated tensions with the conservative Reagan
team. Iacocca pushed for a gas tax during an Oval Office visit, but Reagan dismissed the idea, saying, "Lee, you're a smart guy, but my pollster tells me I'd commit political suicide if I raised the gas tax." Reagan explained that people would
blame him every week when they filled up their gas tanks, and added, "That's why
you're sitting on that side of the desk, and *I'm* the President."

While Iacocca had once been attracted to Reagan's geniality, over time,
Iacocca lost patience with Reagan's folksy way of dealing with policy disagreements. According to Iacocca, "Anytime you talked to him about something, he
would drift off into an anecdote. And once he gave the punch line, the show was
over and you were out the door." He disliked Reagan's aides—dismissing them
as stooges—and had a particular dislike for Donald Regan, who Iacocca said
"kept me twisting slowly in the wind" regarding his suggestion that the administration celebrate the Chrysler bailouts. After serving as secretary of treasury,
Regan became Reagan's chief of staff. Once that happened, Iacocca's "couple of
times a year" meetings with the president came to a halt. As Iacocca wrote, under
Regan, "they locked the doors at the White House and pulled in the welcome
mat."[6]

Iacocca's cold shoulder at the White House coincided with a remarkable period
of fame and celebration for him most everywhere else. It was a time of
"Iacoccamania." His autobiography *Iacocca* sold 2.7 million copies, becoming
both 1984 and 1985's best-selling non-fiction book. He remained the face of
Chrysler in its commercials, and had a cameo on the hit show *Miami Vice* as Parks
Commissioner Lido, a play on his actual birth name. He was on the cover of *TIME*
twice, and was the third most admired person of 1985, after Reagan and Pope
John Paul II. He also befriended future president Donald Trump. The two men
invested together in a West Palm Beach luxury condominium project, and Trump

may have been inspired by the success of *Iacocca*. The book came out three years before Trump's *Art of the Deal* and even has a concluding chapter called "Making America Great Again."[7]

Inevitably, all this attention led to speculation that Iacocca would run for president, initially in 1984 and more seriously in 1988. Ultimately, it did not happen, although Iacocca, in a revealing use of the passive voice, notes that, "Committees were formed, money was raised, bumper stickers were produced (I LIKE I)." When Iacocca told his friend and Speaker of the House Tip O'Neill about the prospective run—"Tip, they want me to run for president."—O'Neill was dismissive, jokingly asking, "President of what?" More seriously, O'Neill told Iacocca that he was not wired for the job, saying, "You're used to running a big corporation. When you make a decision in the morning, you either earn a profit that day or you don't. You can't run a government that way. It would drive you crazy."[8]

Iacocca did not run, but he remained in the political orbit. He became increasingly concerned about the "insidious Japanese economic and political power within the United States." He even used a Chrysler ad to make the point, saying, "It's time to peel off the Teflon kimono." His Japan-bashing might sound quaint today, but it was in line with populist sentiments in the 1980s and 1990s. Given his rhetoric, it was a little odd that Iacocca accompanied President George H. W. Bush on a trade mission to Tokyo. His hostility was palpable during the trip. When Bush asked what Iacocca thought of a toy bank shaped like a Chrysler minivan, Iacocca said, "I thought we were here to talk about the *big* seven-passenger minivans, not the nickel-and-dime kind."

This was also the infamous January 1992 trip in which Bush, exhausted from the travels as well as a game of tennis earlier in the day, vomited on Japanese prime minister Kiichi Miyazawa at a State Dinner. Iacocca recalled watching *The Tonight Show*'s Johnny Carson joke that, "If you had to eat raw fish, and sit across from Lee Iacocca, you'd throw up, too."[9] That year saw the end of twelve years of Republican presidents and of Iacocca's tenure at Chrysler. The Japan-bashing went too far, harming his image, while Chrysler's many challenges caught up with it. Iacocca retired and spent more time in his house in Tuscany.

Oprah Winfrey: Building an Empire by Staying out of Politics

Oprah Winfrey is not a traditional CEO. In fact, nothing about her is traditional. A Black woman in a world dominated by white men, Oprah rose up from poverty to become one of the richest, most famous, and most popular people in America. Although best known for her work in front of the camera, she is also a multibillionaire who runs a huge business empire that included a media company, a restaurant chain, and WeightWatchers. Along the way, she interacted with multiple American presidents, helped make the presidency of one of them, and was touted as a possible presidential candidate herself. Many CEOs have used their empires to develop platforms, but Oprah used her platform to develop an empire.

"Orpah" Winfrey was born to a single mother in Mississippi in 1954, but was soon called "Oprah" by her family. As a child, she moved to Nashville to live with her father where she became interested in journalism. She had a series of jobs in TV news before launching her famous talk show in 1986 in the second term of the Reagan administration. Her show was initially more scandal-based but she then consciously changed tack to plug into the national psyche of self-help, fitness, and health. Her "Live your best life" mantra was born of this and even became a part of the national lexicon.

In her show's early days, therefore, it was not serious enough to be political. Politics, however, did occasionally come up. In 1988, for example, a young real estate developer named Donald Trump appeared on the show to discuss his interest in replacing Ronald Reagan after the 1988 election. Trump had spent $100,000 on newspaper ads criticizing American foreign policy, raising questions that he might be interested in running for president. In his Oprah interview, Trump teased the possibility of a run, telling her that he gets "tired of seeing what's happening with this country. And if it got so bad, I would never want to rule it out totally, because I really am tired of seeing what's happening with this country—how we're really making other people live like kings, and we're not." He acknowledged that he was unlikely to run, but he did not completely rule it out, saying that if he did, "I would say that I would have a hell of a chance of winning, because

I think people—I don't know how your audience feels—but I think people are tired of seeing the United States ripped off."[10]

The Trump interview, however, was an exception. Oprah largely stayed away from politics as she built her show into a daytime powerhouse. In many ways, being apolitical was a wise strategy, as it did not alienate people with differing political beliefs. But there was another reason as well. She thought politicians were poor interviews who did not provide what she was looking for as an interviewer. As she later said, "I didn't want to delve into the world of politics because I felt I lost control." She felt as if she could not "get them to actually respond because a skilled politician knows how to give the answer they want."[11]

Oprah occasionally got involved, but only with non-controversial issues. In 1993, she went to the White House for a ceremony in which Bill Clinton signed the National Child Protection Act, a bill that helped facilitate background checks for childcare providers. Mostly, however, when it came to politics, she just stayed away.[12]

Jack Welch and the Rise of the Celebrity CEO

Like Lee Iacocca, Jack Welch was the CEO's CEO—a new type of celebrity executive in the age of twenty-four-hour cable news. Welch had the fortune of running America's largest company during a period of remarkable peace and prosperity, which brought him to the attention of multiple presidents. At the same time, he also had the misfortune of running a company that was at its heart an electric products enterprise at the very same time that the hot new development in electronics was the personal computer.

Welch's General Electric was a colossus that employed four hundred thousand people. GE focused on electric power and things that could be done with that power at the time. Its primary products were appliances like televisions, refrigerators, and toasters, but it also made jet engines and nuclear reactors. Before Welch, GE was known as "Generous Electric" for its comfortable compensation packages and near lifetime employment positions. Welch would change that reputation with his outsourcing of jobs and his tough management techniques that required managers to regularly assess and fire their lowest-ranked performers.

Welch was born an only child in Peabody, Massachusetts, in 1935. His father was a railroad conductor and his mother a homemaker. Welch earned a PhD in chemical engineering from the University of Illinois at Champaign and then went on to work at GE in 1960, steadily attaining jobs of increasing responsibility. After a challenging and competitive selection process, he ascended to the position of CEO in 1980. His new approach of layoffs, acquisitions, and outsourcing earned him the name "Neutron Jack" from *Newsweek*, a nickname he disliked, to a degree. "I hated it, and it hurt," he recalled of the nickname, adding, "But I hated bureaucracy and waste even more."[13]

The first president Welch worked with, Ronald Reagan, also hated bureaucracy and waste. Welch liked Reagan and saw him as an improvement over his predecessor Jimmy Carter. In 2016, Welch recalled the economic dynamism and job growth unleashed by Reagan as an "incredible surge." Reagan liked Welch as well, and there were rumors of him joining the administration in a cabinet position. In Reagan's diaries, he refers to a dinner he had with Welch at the home of John and Ann McLaughlin in 1986; he, the host of the popular inside-the-Beltway show *The McLaughlin Group*, and she a senior Reagan official who became secretary of labor in 1987. Reagan described Welch as "the new & sensationally successful head of G.E." and the dinner—also attended by the actor Charlton Heston—as "a lot of fun."[14]

The mutual admiration between the two men was helpful to Welch's business success. Welch's strategy to increase the value of GE's stock in part through buybacks and acquisitions of new businesses also benefited from Reagan's easing of regulatory barriers. In 1982, Reagan's Securities and Exchange Commission allowed stock buybacks, which had previously been illegal. In addition, GE's 1985 purchase of RCA only happened because the Reagan administration discarded an outdated consent decree from the 1930s that had specifically forbidden the two companies from merging. With the consent decree gone, part of a Reagan-era effort to scrub unnecessary or outdated rules, GE made the $6.28 billion purchase of RCA on December 11, 1985. *Washington Post* reporter David Vise characterized the move as part of "merger-mania's 1985 sweep through the broadcasting industry."[15]

Welch continued with his stock-growing approach through the administration of George H. W. Bush, with whom he was of course also friendly. Welch played golf with Bush and joined Bush for a showing of the Melanie Griffith *Wall Street* comedy *Working Girl* at the White House theater.

While Welch was a longtime Republican, he befriended the business-friendly Democrat Bill Clinton. Clinton chief of staff Mack McLarty invited Welch to a series of White House lunches to discuss policy with corporate leaders. Welch also played golf with Clinton. In August of 1997, Welch, Clinton, GE general counsel Ben Heineman and regular Clinton golf partner Vernon Jordan played together in Martha's Vineyard. The foursome, which included the head of the world's biggest economy and the head of the world's biggest company, finished eighteen holes and then agreed to play another round. They only stopped after twenty-seven holes because Heineman had to catch a ferry off the island.[16]

Steve Jobs: Staying out of Politics

He wasn't an engineer. He wasn't a programmer. But Steve Jobs shaped the personal computing revolution because of a relentless focus on usability, design, and excellence. Jobs created an iconic company in Apple, lost it, and then returned to take the company to unequaled heights of dominance and impact. Over his all-too-short life, Jobs created the Macintosh, the iPod, the iPhone, and the iPad—products that helped shape both the late twentieth century and then the twenty-first century. Jobs accomplished this while disdaining politics and for the most part stayed away from it altogether, seeing it as a waste of time and resources.

Many CEOs, including John Rockefeller, Lew Wasserman, and Bill Gates, mistakenly thought that they could ignore Washington if they grew their companies and industries big enough. Jobs succeeded where they failed. He largely ignored Washington with little cost to him or his company. But presidents and policymakers paid careful attention to him, his ideas, and his products.

Steve Jobs was born in San Francisco in 1955 and raised by adoptive parents. He attended Homestead High School, where he met Stephen Wozniak. The two of them became close friends and collaborators. Wozniak was the more talented engineer, but Jobs was the visionary. Jobs attended Reed College but dropped out in 1973 to pursue his general but as yet undefined interest in computers and their potential. He and Wozniak formed a company in 1976, created the Apple II in 1977, and Apple entered the Fortune 500 in 1982. No company has ever had a faster rise.[17]

In February of 1985, Wozniak, who was more interested in engineering than managing, declared that he was leaving the company. Around that time, both he and Jobs went to the White House, where they received the National Medal of Technology from President Ronald Reagan. At the ceremony, Reagan referenced the advent of the first phone in the White House, which Alexander Graham Bell gave to Rutherford B. Hayes in 1877. Reagan quoted Hayes, who said at the time, "An amazing invention, but who would ever want to use one?" Then, making a self-deprecating joke about his own advanced age, Reagan said, "I thought at the time that he might be mistaken." Interestingly, Apple did not even have a dinner to highlight the award, perhaps because of the awkwardness around Wozniak's departure. If the company had been more focused on Washington and its importance, they likely would have held such a celebration, regardless of the timing.[18]

A few months later, Jobs would meet Vice President George H. W. Bush in Paris at a trade show. Bush was focused on the Cold War, and pressed Jobs to get his computers into the Soviet Union so that they could "foment revolution from below." Bush's words had an impact on Jobs, who later told a U.S. embassy official about the importance of getting Macs into Moscow since, he said, "By putting Macs in the hands of Russians, they could print all their newspapers." When Bush became president, he thought highly enough of Jobs to put him on the President's Export Council, an unpaid position where he served from 1991 to 1993. By this time, Jobs had left Apple, and there is little evidence that he contributed much to the Export Council, but his FBI file, compiled for the purpose of the appointment, did provide historians with some interesting tidbits. According to the 191-page file, Jobs had a history of drug use, was secretive and unhelpful with investigators, and "will twist the truth and distort reality in order to achieve his goals."[19]

Graham: Personal Friendships Trump Ideological Differences, Most of the Time

Ronald Reagan and his administration were far more conservative than Katharine Graham or the *Washington Post,* which endorsed Jimmy Carter in the 1980 presidential election. Reagan and Graham, however, had a preexisting relationship. Graham was also quite friendly with Nancy Reagan, and those relationships went a long way in Reagan's Washington. In addition, the Reagans, especially Nancy, were far more interested in the Washington social scene over which Graham presided than their immediate predecessors had been.

Graham had met the Reagans through the writer Truman Capote. When Reagan was governor of California in the 1960s, Capote told Graham, "Honey, I know you won't believe me, but you'd really like them." The Capote introduction initiated what Graham called "a long friendship that puzzled many in Washington."[20]

On December 12, 1980, the Reagans joined Graham for dinner at her R Street home. A photographer snapped a picture of her and Reagan embracing, which the *Wall Street Journal* described as "a photograph that may upset arch-conservatives almost as much as the famous one of Jimmy Carter bussing Leonid Brezhnev at the Vienna summit." Conservative Caucus head Howard Phillips criticized Reagan at a meeting of conservative activists, warning that, "You cannot always have Kay Graham going to your cocktail parties and smiling at you. If by June the Washington establishment is happy with Ronald Reagan, then you should be unhappy with Ronald Reagan."[21]

The Reagans ignored the warnings. Nancy would have lunch with Graham five or six times a year, and Reagan himself went to multiple dinners at her house. The *Post* was a liberal paper, and was often critical of the Reagan administration, but the disconnect did not break the relationship because both sides recognized that there were both benefits and limits to the friendship. In one instance, CIA director William Casey tried to get Reagan to intervene to prevent the *Post* from running a story about a U.S. communications espionage effort against the Soviets called Ivy Bells. Reagan called Graham to discuss the matter, and she said that she deferred to the *Post*'s editor on these decisions. They left the matter there, and the *Post* ran the story, but changed it somewhat to address the national security concerns. In another instance, Graham considered calling Nancy to let her know what a *Post* reporter had picked up about the extent of Soviet preparations for an upcoming summit, but she wisely followed the cues of her staff and thought better of it.[22]

Reagan was generally used to press criticism, but Nancy was more sensitive, which at times tested the relationship between Graham and the Reagans. *Post* style writer Sally Quinn was quite critical of Nancy as well, and the *Post* criticized Nancy over her hair, her clothes, and her White House china. Graham assuaged her, explaining that attacks against Nancy came from young feminist writers who "couldn't identify with you. . . . You represented everything they were rebelling against." According to First Lady press secretary Nancy Reynolds, who knew both women, Nancy "knows, I think, or feels, that Kay is separate from all the negative things that the *Post* might write." They did have a brief falling out during the 1984 reelection campaign—the *Post* endorsed Reagan opponent Walter Mondale—but they patched things up during Reagan's second term. As Nancy wrote of Graham with only slight exaggeration in her memoir, "Ronnie and I never allowed politics to stand in the way of our friendship with her."[23]

In 1988, as the Reagans were preparing to return to California, they had one last dinner at Graham's house. Someone spilled a drink, and Reagan got down on his hands and knees to clean it up. Graham was nonplussed, but Nancy had seen it before. When he was hospitalized after being shot in 1981, he made a mess in the bathroom and moved to clean it up, fearing that his spill might get the nurse in trouble. A different president might have grumbled more about the *Post*'s coverage, but a different president also would not have bent down to clean up a spilled drink at a Katharine Graham party. Graham never again had as close a relationship with a president or a first couple as she did with the Reagans.[24]

Wasserman: Rekindling the Relationship with Reagan

Although Wasserman and Reagan had been friends and collaborators during Reagan's time at the Screen Actors Guild, they drifted apart after Reagan's tenure there. There were a number of reasons for this. The first was professional. Reagan felt that Wasserman had not represented him well towards the latter part of his career, in which Reagan's acting roles had largely dried up. Reagan was displeased with the role Wasserman found for him in 1964's *The Killers*—a rare role in which Reagan played a villain. It was Reagan's last film role, and he was unhappy that Wasserman had delegated representing Reagan to MCA's Arthur Park at such a difficult moment in Reagan's career. For his part, Wasserman was irked that Reagan was not more grateful to MCA for managing to find any part for the hard-to-employ actor.[25]

As Reagan drifted away from acting and into politics, the political differences between the two men drove them further apart. Wasserman backed Reagan's opponent, incumbent governor Pat Brown, in the 1966 California gubernatorial race. Reagan won, with support from MCA Republicans like Taft Schreiber and Jules Stein. The Democratic Wasserman also disliked Reagan's policies, including his budgetary savings and his law-and-order approach to student protests. The two men were largely out of contact when Reagan served in Sacramento.[26]

When Reagan emerged as a serious challenger to Carter in the 1980 presidential election, Wasserman realized that he needed to repair the relationship with his former client. He and his wife Edie would work on this project together. Even as Wasserman had previously moved apart from Reagan, Edie had worked to maintain the relationships with both Reagan's ex-wife Jane Wyman as well as Reagan's second wife Nancy Reagan. As for Wasserman, he still backed Carter, but according to a senior MCA executive, "In 1980, Lew hedged his bets; he put a little tentacle out [to Reagan]." One manifestation of this hedge was helping the Reagan campaign find Republican donors. He could not donate directly because of his support for Carter, but he could and did use his skills as a master political fundraiser to help in a typically behind-the-scenes way.[27]

The maneuvering worked. Wasserman and Edie attended Reagan's inauguration, with Edie being at least as responsible as Lew for the invite, and Reagan let Wasserman back into the fold. Reagan would have him visit the Oval Office and offer his strategic advice, just as he had with Johnson. Reagan also watched some of Wasserman's MCA/Universal hit movies, such as *E.T.*, *Back to the Future*, *The Secret of My Success*, and *Dragnet*, all of which were screened at Camp David. *Back to the Future* even made an appearance in Reagan's optimistic 1986 State of the Union address, when Reagan said, "As they said in the film *Back to the Future*, 'Where we're going, we don't need roads.'"[28]

Wasserman availed himself of his opportunities with Reagan to help the movie business. He would talk to the president about his vision that the movie studios would merge or at least partner with the cable networks, and make sure Reagan administration policies did not get in the way of Wasserman's vision. Wasserman's hard-fought and reclaimed ability to speak to Reagan would have a profound impact on the movie studios' bottom line. In 1982, Reagan's Federal Communications Commission proposed a major change to the way Hollywood had operated up to that point. The three TV networks of the time, ABC, CBS, and NBC, had been prohibited since 1970 from participating in the syndication of TV shows. These rules were called the Financial Interest and Syndication Rules, but were typically referred to by the abbreviation "fin-syn."

Under fin-syn, the studios would produce the shows, and the networks would pay a fee for airing the shows. The fee would be less than the cost of the show, but the studios would have the possibility of making up for it in syndication fees, derived from selling the show to local stations. Syndication fees could be incredibly lucrative, and the networks resented being forbidden from having a chance to earn those fees by producing shows of their own. The studios feared, with some justification, that networks would be more likely to air network-produced shows than ones that came from the studios. Reagan's FCC, under the leadership of Chairman Mark Fowler, wanted to put an end to fin-syn as part of the Reagan administration's deregulatory efforts. In June of 1982, the FCC voted unanimously to explore the possibility of repeal.[29]

If the studios wanted to stop fin-syn repeal, they had their work cut out for them. Valenti, Wasserman's man at the MPAA, led the uphill battle. In his typically hyperbolic way, Valenti fulminated that, "If the networks take over this, it will absolutely be the end of competition." He also noted that this issue had united the famously fractious studio heads that it was his job to corral. According to Valenti, "In the seventeen years I've been on this job, I've never seen the mutually antagonistic industry that I preside over so unified."[30]

Valenti had his arguments and his studio heads aligned, but he also had a secret weapon in the form of Wasserman. Valenti called Wasserman and asked him to speak directly to Reagan. Valenti knew about Reagan's long-standing, albeit interrupted, friendship with Reagan, and thought that a direct appeal was needed to stop a deregulatory effort in the deregulatory-minded Reagan administration. According to Valenti, he did not, however, check back with Wasserman to see if he connected with Reagan for a very Washington reason: "It's what the CIA calls 'deniability.'"[31]

While Valenti never acknowledged that Wasserman came to see Reagan about the issue, White House deputy chief of staff Michael Deaver did. According to Deaver, Wasserman requested and got a White House visit on the subject. As Deaver explained, "They were friendly, and Lew was very powerful, and he spoke for the industry. And Reagan *loved* that industry," Deaver emphasized. "He would talk about it, much more than about the presidency."[32]

Once Wasserman spoke to Reagan, things began to change on the fin-syn front. What once seemed like an almost certain repeal became more doubtful. The Departments of Justice and Commerce, which once favored repeal, now reversed their positions. While these were important players, the rule change was under the auspices of the FCC, which is an independent agency. In October of 1983, Reagan took the highly unusual step of meeting directly with FCC Chairman Fowler at the White House.[33]

The meeting was Fowler's first visit to the Oval Office. Others attendees included Counselor Edwin Meese, Chief of Staff Jim Baker, Deputy Chief of Staff Dick Darman, communications aide David Gergen, and Fowler aide Willard Nichols. An anonymous aide told the *Washington Post* at the time that the forty-five-minute meeting was innocuous: "There were no policy indications. It is more accurate to say Reagan was briefed." Congressional sources, however, framed the meeting more starkly, telling the *Washington Post* that Reagan took "Fowler to the woodshed."[34]

The lobbying effort worked. Fowler backed down. The repeal discussion was initially delayed for two years, and the rules would stay in place until 1994. By that time, Wasserman was on his way to retirement, and the business had changed sufficiently that the studios could handle the repeal. Wasserman's way had won out. Others recognized Wasserman's role. According to Warner Brothers head Robert Daly, "The relationship between Lew and Reagan was really the thing." Reagan played a part, too. Reflecting on the lobbying effort that took place, Reagan made a humorous reference to how he and Wasserman had drifted apart over Reagan's faltering acting career: "If I had this much attention from so many studio heads, I never would have run for office!"[35]

Wasserman benefited a great deal from the relationship with Reagan, but he gave back as well. He was impressed with Reagan's foreign policy and was subsequently more helpful on Reagan's 1984 campaign than he had been in 1980. He also helped raise money for the Reagan Library. In 1985, he threw a star-studded tribute to Nancy Reagan, attended by stars such as Charlton Heston, Burt Reynolds, Frank Sinatra, and Elizabeth Taylor. When Reagan moved back to California after his two terms as president, his first lunch back in Los Angeles was with Wasserman.[36]

Wasserman even offered the retired Reagan a chance to get back into the movies. In 1989, Wasserman reached out to Reagan with an offer to play the mayor of Hill Valley in *Back to the Future III*. Reagan seriously considered the offer but eventually declined, and the part went to journeyman actor Hugh Gillin. Perhaps Wasserman knew that Reagan would never take the part, but at least he showed that unlike in the 1960s, he could get Reagan movie roles once again.[37]

Back in Los Angeles, Wasserman showed Reagan a deference he granted to no one else. The famously time-obsessed Wasserman, who limited calls to thirty seconds and did not like wasting time on hello and goodbye, also could not abide tardiness. In the early 1990s, Wasserman and Edie were spotted at Chasen's, the Hollywood power lunch spot. The two of them were sitting at a table for four, and Wasserman was glaring at his watch and rumbling, "Our guests are fifteen minutes late." The guests, who arrived shortly afterwards, were Ronald and Nancy Reagan. Waiting was not something that Wasserman liked to do, but for Reagan it was worth it: he had saved Wasserman's industry from fin-syn repeal.[38]

Bill Gates: Hoping to Avoid Washington's Gaze

William Henry "Bill" Gates III could be viewed as a modern John D. Rockefeller. Both entered the workplace when particularly young. They founded companies at the early, chaotic stages of a new industry. And both were initially ignored by the presidential administrations during which they established their empires. In bringing their companies to dominant, even monopolistic, positions within their industries, they undeniably brought life-changing products to consumers that were cheaper, higher in quality, and unleashed productivity that fueled economic opportunity and growth for millions.

At the same time, they also faced angry competitors and U.S. government investigations that led to lawsuits, and both men retired early to pursue philanthropic interests even as they were both forever associated with the firms they had created. Finally, both had their monopolies ended by the federal government, even as external forces were already in the process of moving their respective industries away from being dominated by the companies they had created.

Unlike Rockefeller, however, Gates was born into privilege, the son of a successful attorney and a schoolteacher. Gates knew almost from his first encounter with a computer that he was destined to work with them, while Rockefeller encountered the emerging oil industry when he was already in the working world. The world of information was also much different in Gates's day, making it harder for a new company or industry to emerge without attracting attention. In addition, the role of the federal government was so much vaster in Gates's time that there was no chance of avoiding the federal gaze. And finally, the writings of antitrust theorist Robert Bork held that large entities that produced benefits for the consumer in terms of lower prices and higher quality goods were not necessarily something that needed to be curtailed. As a result, the definition of monopoly had changed: big was not necessarily bad. Gates benefited from entering the marketplace during a favorable policy environment for innovation.

Gates, born in a Seattle suburb on October 28, 1955, was a smart and competitive boy with a passion for reading. He read the entire encyclopedia in his youth and would as an adult preside over the creation of a digital version of the encyclopedia called Encarta, an innovation that would be successful for a time until supplanted by Wikipedia.

As a child, Gates had an active mind and a quick tongue. Once, when his mother asked him what he was doing, he said, "I'm thinking." When she queried, "You're thinking?" He responded, "Yes, Mom, I'm thinking. Have you ever tried thinking?" Such snappishness would occasionally get him into trouble in his battles with the government, but it was the active mind, and its early attraction to computers, that set him on his path in life. By eighth grade, he was programming in BASIC. He developed early computer versions of games like tic-tac-toe and Risk, and began collaborating with his lifelong friend, Paul Allen.[39]

Their first commercial interaction with computers was when they worked with a company to debug its software in exchange for what was then valuable computer time. In tenth grade, Gates built a program for allotting class assignments, one that secretly let him share classes with attractive girls in the school. Another program, with more commercial application, measured municipal traffic.[40]

When Gates went to Harvard, Allen tried to turn their software interest into a business endeavor. Like Mark Zuckerberg would in a later generation, Gates dropped out of Harvard to pursue the business, founded in 1975 as Micro-Soft. One joke about Gates and his short Harvard career was that he had gone there to learn from people smarter than him, but left feeling disappointed. The joke reveals an arrogance that was pronounced in the entrepreneur's early years.[41]

In 1981, Gates and Allen developed the software that would make IBM's new personal computer run—MS-DOS, or Microsoft Disk Operating System. This program, bundled inside every IBM PC, positioned Microsoft to build a solid but quiet monopoly. Furthermore, in a move reminiscent of Rockefeller and the South Improvement Company over a century earlier, some of Microsoft's contracts called for Microsoft to receive royalties on every computer processor sent out, even if the processor included a different operating system.

Unlike Rockefeller and Standard, Microsoft and Gates did not employ spies and agents with strong-arm tactics, just a bundled package of software to accompany hardware in the growing market of personal computers. The bundle allowed Microsoft to create content in such a way that would leave the competition behind.

An internal Microsoft programming joke was, "DOS ain't done till Lotus don't run." IBM's Lotus was a competing product, and Microsoft's ability to write the operating system for all PCs allowed it to maximize the compatibility of its own products and minimize the compatibility of others. Externally, the jokes were more bitter. One went, "Q: How many Microsoft employees does it take to change a lightbulb? A: None. Bill Gates just redefines Darkness as the new industry standard."[42]

Microsoft was able to establish its dominant position in the Reagan administration for two primary reasons. At the time, the new field of computer software was a largely unknown one. Most people did not understand the business or how important it would become, not to mention the degree that mere keystrokes would be the mechanism by which a company could establish dominance.

Another reason for Microsoft's ability to attain dominance without initial federal scrutiny was the Reagan administration's approach to antitrust policy. Early in the Reagan administration, the Department of Justice's Antitrust Division would drop its thirteen-year lawsuit against IBM. The suit, which had continued through parts of four administrations, both Democrat and Republican, was the longest ongoing lawsuit on record, costing both the government and the company millions. In 1982, though, Reagan-era associate attorney general for antitrust William Baxter dropped the suit as "without merit," recognizing that in the thirteen long years of the lawsuit, the original economic conditions no longer applied. Of course, part of the reason for IBM's loss of dominance may have been the pressures of the suit itself, which caused the company to lose focus at the very time that Microsoft was on the rise. Regardless of the reason behind it, the fact was that IBM's dominance had faded, and so had the rationale behind the lawsuit along with it.[43]

That initial case against IBM reflected the old way of thinking about monopolies: big was inherently bad. But Bork's theories held sway in the Reagan administration, during which he was nominated for the Supreme Court. His nomination failed after an ugly battle in the Senate that foreshadowed the bitter fights that have come to define Supreme Court nomination battles. Bork did not make it onto the Supreme Court, but his antitrust theories have influenced the legal and economic debate for decades.

The IBM case did not mean that the Reagan administration was hostile to the idea of antitrust. It just had a different theory of the case. Baxter's antitrust division pursued an action against AT&T, ultimately reaching a settlement that broke up AT&T's longstanding monopoly. But here the administration was acting in a deregulatory vein. The AT&T monopoly that had dominated the phone industry for too long was the opposite of an enterprise that benefitted consumers. It kept prices high and innovation low. After the government broke up AT&T and deregulated the phone industry, options for consumers multiplied, allowing not only today's basically free long-distance calls, but also the entire cell phone industry that has made the once dominant AT&T monopoly a relic of the past.

Throughout the Reagan administration and even through much of Reagan's successor, George H. W. Bush, Microsoft remained under the radar. In 1989 though, newly elected President Bush appointed Janet Steiger as chair of the Federal Trade Commission. Steiger had previously been chair of the Commission on Veterans Educational Policy. Her late husband, Bill Steiger, was a Republican congressman from Wisconsin, and the Steigers and Bushes were close family friends. Bush had signaled that he planned to be tougher on antitrust policy than the Reagan administration had been, and Steiger's appointment was an element of that new policy, along with stiffer fines and enhanced scrutiny and enforcement of mergers. Steiger herself had lamented that under Reagan, antitrust policy had become "a pale shadow of what it once was."[44]

In 1991, under Steiger's leadership, Bush's FTC launched a probe of Microsoft's domination of the $7 billion software industry. At the time, Microsoft controlled about 85 percent of operating software for personal computers, with $2.8 billion in revenue, and that dominance also helped its applications such as spreadsheets and word processing programs. Microsoft's competitors had begun to complain about the company's hardball tactics and elbowing of competition out of the software market, particularly by writing the operating software in such a way as to limit the compatibility of competitors' programs. The approach came from the top down, led by the volatile and hard-charging Gates.[45]

The Gates that built a software empire was different than our current perceptions of Gates as the friendly but geeky philanthropist. As early as 1981, Gates had developed a reputation as being difficult to work with, "notorious for not being reachable by phone and for not returning phone calls," as an industry newsletter put it. As the company grew more powerful, Gates became even more dismissive of others. According to former Microsoft employee Scott McGregor, "Bill would go to a very senior person at these other OEMs [original equipment manufacturer] whether it was DEC or Tandy or Compaq or whoever and yell at them or tell them it had to be this way, or if you don't do this we'll make sure our software doesn't run on your box." Faced with this ultimatum, the hardware manufacturers had little choice. As McGregor recalled, "What do you do if you're one of these OEM guys? You're screwed. You can't have Microsoft not support your hardware so you better do what they say." [46]

As with Rockefeller and Standard Oil, Gates and Microsoft had built a dominant monopoly while attracting little attention from the presidents in office when it happened. Lotus Development founder Mitchell Kapor once even jibed that Gates wanted to be the Rockefeller of the Information Age. But if Microsoft competitors and collaborators had no choice in the business world, the federal government provided an option that did not exist in Rockefeller's time. Gates's competitors could raise their complaints to the federal government. In doing so, they effectively engaged in a cost shift, making the government pay for the litigation rather than themselves. At the same time, they also supplemented the government's work, providing material and evidence to bolster the FTC's case. As one lawyer employed by a Microsoft opponent said, "Any lawyer inside any federal agency, if they can get outside people to work for them, why not?"[47]

The Steiger FTC inquiry did not resolve the issue of whether Microsoft had built an illegal monopoly. With one of the commissioners recused, the five-member commission remained deadlocked for over three years on whether to bring administrative charges against Microsoft and seek changes to their business practices. Gates himself became frustrated and angry over the lengthy investigation. At one point, he yelled at an FTC official, "You don't know what you are talking about." Worse, he lost his temper and told Commissioner Dennis Yao that his ideas were "socialistic," and "communistic" as well. The FTC had two votes

over whether to continue the investigation against Microsoft, but could not ultimately resolve the issue, both times ending tied at 2-2, with both Yao and Steiger
voting against Microsoft. In starting the discussions, however, the FTC teed up
the question of Microsoft's business practices for the incoming Clinton
administration.[48]

Warren Buffett: Billionaire Path to Oracle Status

Warren Buffett was born into a political family, but he was drawn to investing
rather than politics. As he grew wealthier and more prominent, the multi-
billionaire realized that his stature gave him a platform, and he used his newfound
prominence to promote his ideas more than specific political candidates. More
important than his policy ideas was his abiding belief in America and the
American economy, as well as his desire to keep his business and his politics separate. As Buffett himself said in 2020, "I do not believe in imposing my political
opinions on the activities of our businesses."[49]

As a smart boy growing up in Nebraska, Buffett loved following the news. At
an early age, he showed his industrious streak delivering three different newspapers. Buffett also loved numbers, memorizing baseball statistics and excelling at
bridge. Those three tendencies, a focus on the news, a facility with numbers, and
an entrepreneurial spirit, would prove essential strengths for his outsized success
in the investing world.[50]

Buffett's father was a conservative Republican congressman who loathed
Franklin D. Roosevelt. Buffett earned his undergraduate degree from the
University of Nebraska. He also studied at University of Pennsylvania's Wharton
School, and received his MBA from Columbia.

Like his father, Buffett started as a Republican but would later lean left. As a
young man, he became an ardent supporter of civil rights and an opponent of
antisemitism, but he did not become a Democrat immediately, or completely. He
supported Gene McCarthy in his upstart primary challenge to incumbent president Lyndon Johnson in 1968, and backed Hubert Humphrey over the Republican
Richard Nixon in that year's general election. In 1972, however, Buffett initially
supported Nixon's Democratic challenger, George McGovern, but soured on him

when McGovern called for a universal $1,000 stipend for every American. The frugal Buffett pulled the lever for Nixon instead.[51]

By the 1980s, Buffett's steady value-based investment strategy had made him a billionaire well-respected for his farsightedness. That's when he began interacting with presidents regularly. In 1987, he went to Walter Annenberg's Palm Springs estate for a weekend with Ronald and Nancy Reagan, where he paired with Reagan for a round of golf. He also developed a close relationship with Reagan's successor, George H. W. Bush. Buffett would needle Bush, a former first baseman at Yale, about being left on deck in the 1948 college baseball World Series when the batter before him hit into a triple play to end the game. As Buffett said about it, "He's the nicest guy in the world, and he still gets mad about that play."[52]

Murdoch: Insufficient Attention from Republicans before Fox News

Although Rupert Murdoch backed Jimmy Carter in the 1980 Democratic presidential primaries, Murdoch and the *Post* actively supported Ronald Reagan in the general election. Reagan's team credited Murdoch with helping Reagan win New York state, which was still contested in presidential politics then. Reagan thanked Murdoch personally for his support and even gave him a plaque commemorating Murdoch's assistance. Still, Murdoch felt like he received insufficient attention from the Reagan administration. In 1983, he asked that Reagan visit Murdoch's *Boston Herald* on a trip to the city, but the Reagan team passed. Murdoch was angry, and asked New York attorney and fixer Roy Cohn to let them know. The White House apologized, but the incident suggests that the relationship was not the close presidential friendship Murdoch was seeking.[53]

Still, the Reagan relationship was sufficiently close that Murdoch received regulatory dispensation from the administration to acquire his first American television stations. These came under the umbrella of Metromedia but soon were consolidated into the fledgling Fox network. Murdoch got an even bigger regulatory gift from the Reagan administration in 1987. The Reagan FCC, under Chairman Mark Fowler, put an end to the Fairness Doctrine, a provision that limited ideological content on television. Congress tried to reimpose the Fairness

Doctrine legislatively, but Reagan vetoed it. The end of the Fairness Doctrine allowed the appearance of openly conservative content over the airwaves. Conservatives had long complained that the mainstream media outlets leaned left, but that content was considered news and therefore not subject to Fairness Doctrine limitations. The elimination of the Fairness Doctrine opened the pathway for both conservative talk radio and for Fox News Channel, which Murdoch launched in October of 1996. FNC was helmed by long-time Republican media guru Roger Ailes, who had provided crucial TV appearance advice over the years to Richard Nixon, Ronald Reagan, and George H. W. Bush.[54]

Murdoch got another regulatory break under Reagan's successor, George H. W. Bush. The Bush administration suspended the so-called fin-syn rules which forbade networks from syndicating their own content. By suspending those rules, Murdoch was able to build the Metromedia stations and the 21st Century Fox Studios, which he had also acquired in 1985, into Fox, the fourth network. The new regulatory reality let him generate profits from producing shows that would appear on the network and then syndicating them to local stations. This move did not attract a lot of political attention at the time, but it would end up having enormous implications once Murdoch expanded further into the area of twenty-four-hour cable news. That development would roil American politics and demonstrate a new way in which CEOs could exercise influence, but also open up CEOs in that space to dangerous pushback from aggrieved presidents.[55]

CHAPTER 9

AFTER THE COLD WAR

Presidents: Bill Clinton, George W. Bush
CEOs: *Jamie Dimon, Mark Zuckerberg, Gates, Jobs, Winfrey, Buffett,*
Murdoch, Wasserman, Iacocca

B ill Clinton was the first president elected after the fall of the Berlin Wall. America's victory in the Cold War against communism signaled to some that "the end of history" was upon us. But history, as it turned out, still had a lot to say. Clinton and his immediate successor, George W. Bush, can be seen in retrospect as "CEO-friendly" presidents. Clinton's moderate liberal centrism appealed to many CEOs, and his first White House chief of staff, Thomas "Mack" McLarty, had himself been a CEO of a natural gas company before joining the Clinton team. Bush was our first MBA president and his pro-free trade, pro-immigration stances appealed to CEOs but differed from the direction in which the GOP would go less than a decade after he left office. Even in this era, though, it was still dangerous for CEOs to lose sight of what was happening in Washington as globalization, regulations, and increasing partisanship affected the business landscape. As Bill Gates and Microsoft would learn, even in a supposedly business-friendly environment, the government, particularly the Justice Department's antitrust division, had the capacity to impose great costs on companies it targeted.

Jobs: Talking to Presidents When He Had To

Steve Jobs was at NeXT computers during Bill Clinton's first term. The two men had a *de minimis* relationship at the time, although they did meet up occasionally, both in California and at the White House. In the spring of 1996, Jobs sent a check supporting the Democratic National Committee, for which Clinton sent him a nice note, thanking him for the contribution and saying, "I've enjoyed having the chance to talk with you." Their relationship intensified towards the end of 1996 and into 1997 as a result of three factors: Clinton's reelection effort, Jobs's return to Apple, and Chelsea Clinton's attendance at Stanford University in California.[1]

In late 1996, Clinton won reelection by defeating former senate majority leader Bob Dole. Jobs sent Clinton a note of congratulations, along with some unusual personnel recommendations. He recommended Dean Ornish for surgeon general and Andy Grove for secretary of defense. Ornish was a doctor and creator of the Ornish Diet, while Grove was the CEO of Intel. Jobs must have known Ornish was a long shot, as he wrote that he hoped that Ornish "will not be lost among more 'traditional' candidates for this super-important job." As for Grove, Jobs felt that he "could be a secret weapon to change our perspectives and thinking about defense as our nation faces new world roles and fiscal limitations." Clinton wrote back a note thanking Jobs for the recommendations, but neither one of Jobs's picks joined the administration.[2]

Shortly afterwards, Jobs returned to Apple. This time it was Clinton who sent the congratulatory note, a handwritten letter in which Clinton looked "forward to four good years of working together." Despite the note, they did not work together that closely in Clinton's second term. Once Chelsea started going to Stanford, Jobs offered his nearby home as a place for the Clintons to stay when they went to visit their daughter. After Jobs died, Clinton recalled how much he appreciated that, saying that Jobs "gave me a priceless gift: the opportunity to see my child while I was still a very public figure, so I'm highly biased in his favor."[3]

Less appreciated was Jobs's advice during the Monica Lewinsky scandal. On a phone call, Jobs told Clinton that if he had indeed had sex with the young White House intern, he should get it out there: "I don't know if you did it, but if so, you've got to tell the country." Clinton did not respond.[4]

THE INFANT HERCULES AND THE STANDARD OIL SERPENTS.

President Theodore Roosevelt depicted as a baby Hercules strangling the two-headed snake of Standard Oil's John D. Rockefeller and U.S. representative Nelson W. Aldrich. The cartoon shows the degree to which Rockefeller was demonized by politicians and the press alike. (*Frank Arthur Nankivell, Puck Magazine Cartoon*)

Henry Ford (right) leaves the White House after a meeting with President Franklin Roosevelt. The meeting took place after many failed attempts to bring the two men together. Neither man much liked the other, but they did find common cause in World War II, as Ford built Willow Run, the nation's most famous munitions facility. (*Harris & Ewing photographer*)

Rupert Murdoch meets with President John F. Kennedy in the Oval Office in 1961. Murdoch has long wanted close relations with presidents, but has often found that to be an elusive goal. Going into the 2024 election, both sitting President Joe Biden and challenger and ex-President Donald Trump actively disliked Murdoch. (*Cecil Stoughton, White House Photographs, John F. Kennedy Presidential Library and Museum, Boston*)

Katharine Graham and President Ronald Reagan talk at a White House dinner party. Graham ran a mostly liberal paper and angered presidents on both sides of the aisle with her paper's reporting. At the same time, she was the social queen of Washington and generally maintained good personal relationships with every president during her tenure except one: Richard Nixon. (*White House / Ronald Reagan Presidential Library*)

Hollywood mogul Lew Wasserman talks with Ronald and Nancy Reagan at the reception for Lady Bird Johnson receiving the Congressional Medal. Wasserman initially stayed away from Washington until government antitrust actions forced him to get involved. He then became a fundraiser and adviser to multiple Democratic presidents while mostly staying away from Republicans. The only exception to that was Reagan, his former client. (*White House / Ronald Reagan Presidential Library*)

Steve Jobs is awarded the National Technology Award from President Ronald Reagan in 1985. He hated those sorts of things and generally managed to keep Washington's gaze off of his products during his two tenures at Apple. (*White House Photographic*)

Bill Clinton and auto magnate Lee Iacocca sit in a meeting in the Oval Office. Although he started meeting presidents as a regulation-criticizing Republican, he later became a pro-subsidy, pro-tariff Democrat in the face of international competition. (*Ralph Answang for the White House; photo archived in Clinton Presidential Library*)

Elon Musk gives President Barack Obama a tour of SpaceX at Cape Canaveral. The Obama administration helped make Musk's companies SpaceX and Tesla, but Musk later became persona non grata among Democrats over his dealings with Donald Trump and his purchase of Twitter, which he rebranded as X. (*Chuck Kennedy, President Barack Obama tours SpaceX launch pad*)

President Barack Obama and Bill Gates talk at the U.N. Framework Convention on Climate Change. Before becoming an avuncular philanthropist and friend to presidents on both sides of the aisle, he engaged in a fierce battle with the Clinton administration over its antitrust case against Microsoft. (*Official White House Photo by Pete Souza*)

President Barack Obama awards Oprah Winfrey with the Presidential Medal of Freedom in 2013. Winfrey carefully stayed away from politics for decades, but she left the political sidelines to endorse Obama's 2008 run for president. (*Official White House Photo by Lawrence Jackson*)

Warren Buffett and President Barack Obama talk in the Oval Office. Buffett became a friend and adviser to presidents on both sides of the aisle, taking the approach that "if any president asks me for help in any way, I mean, that's part of being a citizen." (*Official White House Photo by Pete Souza*)

Donald Trump and Tim Cook shake hands at an Apple manufacturing plant in Austin, Texas. Many tech CEOs shunned Trump, but not Cook, of whom Trump said, "The only one that calls me is Tim Cook." (*Official White House Photo by Shealah Craighead*)

Mark Zuckerberg and Donald Trump shake hands in the Oval Office. Zuckerberg and Trump seemed to have an understanding while Trump was president, but their relationship worsened after the 2020 election. Unfortunately for Zuckerberg, Joe Biden did not like him that much either, characterizing the Facebook founder as "a real problem." (*Official White House Photo by Joiyce N. Boghosian*)

Given how most CEOs used time with presidents at least in part for business-related reasons, it is striking to see how little Jobs's interactions with Clinton had to do with Apple-related matters. Jobs did invite Joel Klein, Clinton's antitrust head who was pursuing the case against Microsoft, to Palo Alto to discuss strategy. Jobs advised Klein to keep Microsoft entangled in litigation in order to enable Apple and competitors to "make an end run" around Microsoft by offering new products. As for Clinton himself, he and Jobs were more in the friend zone, as characterized by a note Clinton sent Jobs in July of 2000, with six months left in his second term. Clinton, who was an avid solver of the *New York Times* crossword puzzle, noticed that Jobs was an answer and sent him a note reading, "Dear Steve—Congratulations! You made the NY Times Crossword puzzle—94 Across—Hope you're all well—Sincerely, Bill."[5]

Jobs did not have much to do with Clinton's successor, the Republican George W. Bush. He did reengage somewhat once the Democrat Barack Obama entered the White House, but he did it on his terms. By now, Jobs's second stint with Apple was a massive success, and Jobs had created the historic trifecta of the iPod, the iPhone, and the iPad, the last of which hit the shelves during Obama's first term. Apple was still less focused on lobbying than other tech companies. In 2009, for example, Apple spent far less than other media and tech companies on federal lobbying, only about $1.5 million, compared to $4 million for Google, $7 million for Microsoft, and $15 million for AT&T. But Jobs was focused on what mattered to him, making products that people wanted, and he therefore tried to avoid distractions such as politics. As Clinton recalled of him, "He was a very determined man. He probably had the most intense powers of concentration I ever saw."[6]

Gates: Grappling with Clinton's Antitrust Team

Bill Clinton's administration followed twelve years of Republican rule. Clinton promised a new technocratic administration, seemingly in line with the new technological revolution Gates and others were leading on the West Coast. Both men were Ivy League-educated baby boomers, although Clinton was almost a decade older than Gates. They seemed to share a similar sensibility about smarts dominating a new meritocratic and globalizing America. Clinton specifically campaigned on a platform of increasing American competitiveness by aiding America's new high-tech companies, such as Microsoft. He also specifically cultivated CEOs and business leaders to show he was a new type of Democrat.[7]

At the same time, Clinton also promised a new approach to antitrust. One of his transition advisers, Robert Pitofsky, had authored a textbook that Clinton assigned while teaching law school at the University of Arkansas. Pitofsky believed that Reagan and Bush had offered "about as minimal an antitrust program as can be imagined." Pitofsky wanted to change that. He offered a different vision, one in which "antitrust enforcement would be more vigorous. Close questions in all areas would more often lead to government challenges." And yet, at the same time, Pitofsky signaled that there would also not be longstanding vendettas against individual companies. As he put it, in this new environment, "Unjustified non-enforcement at the federal level would end."[8]

Pitofsky would become Clinton's FTC chairman, replacing Janet Steiger. Even though Pitofsky's vision helped shape Clinton's new technocratic approach to antitrust, Clinton himself was less involved in the issue than Roosevelt had been with Standard Oil nearly a century earlier. For one thing, the government was so much larger and more powerful by this point and had so many more things to deal with. For another, the specter of a president personally getting involved in policy towards a specific company seemed increasingly inappropriate. What this meant for Clinton was that the Justice Department could be the bad cop; the president himself did not have to get personally involved.

The head of the Department of Justice's Antitrust Division had enormous powers that did not necessarily rely on presidential or even White House involvement. In contrast to an independent agency like the FTC, the Department of Justice is an executive agency, and therefore directly answerable to the president. Yet the norms around legal scrutiny of governmental actions had grown to the degree that presidential and White House involvement in decisions on specific governmental actions could trigger criticism and even legal action. As a result, it was now far better to keep this issue out of the White House and leave decisions up to the Justice Department, which soon became more interested in pursuing the allegations against Microsoft.

The Clinton administration's policies towards Microsoft would initially be in the hands of Anne Bingaman, a lawyer and, like Steiger, the wife of a federal legislator. Bingaman was married to New Mexico Democratic senator Jeff Bingaman. She wanted to revitalize the Antitrust Division and reassert Justice's role over the FTC in antitrust enforcement. The first female law professor at the University of New Mexico, she moved to Washington with her husband and was practicing law at Powell, Goldstein, Frazer, & Murphy when Clinton selected her for the Antitrust position. Once in the job, Bingaman successfully made the case for additional resources to Congress, arguing that the Antitrust Division was the same size that it had been at the end of World War II, when the U.S. economy was a quarter of the size. She also hung up a drawing of Teddy Roosevelt, signaling to all that the Antitrust Division was on the hunt once again. Part of her revitalizing effort was taking on the Microsoft case from the FTC, something that was not ordinarily done, especially given that the FTC had deadlocked on the question of referring the Microsoft case to the DOJ.[9]

Bingaman was not alone in wanting the DOJ to take up the case. Prominent senators, including Utah Republican Orrin Hatch and Ohio Democrat Howard Metzenbaum, both members of the Senate Judiciary Committee, also pushed for the DOJ to get involved. And Microsoft's competitors continued to press the case. Novell Inc., a company with a competing operating system, argued to the department that, "Microsoft's practices are those of a classical monopolist bent on preserving and extending its market power by unlawful means."[10]

Both Bingaman and the case against Microsoft had their detractors as well. MIT economist Frank Fisher warned that, "You don't want to confuse Microsoft's success with monopoly." Rob Shapiro, an economist at the Clinton-allied think tank the Progressive Policy Institute, argued that the case would hurt the U.S. software industry and that Microsoft's market dominance was proof that that the "market is working well." Inside the department, Attorney General Janet Reno often clashed with Bingaman, convinced she was only there because she was the wife of a senator. On the other hand, Deputy Assistant Attorney General Robert Litan was well respected within the administration and had known Bingaman for a decade, making him an important internal advocate.[11]

Then there was the White House. Clinton and Vice President Al Gore presented themselves as tech-savvy, future-oriented centrist Democrats, as opposed to the old school tax-and-regulate liberals. Clinton and Gore had both been part of the Democratic Leadership Council, a group that was trying to get Democrats to win elections by moving back towards the center. Siccing the government on the most prominent high-tech firm in the world appeared contrary to the direction in which the Clinton-Gore administration wanted to go. Bingaman seemed aware of the criticism and dismissed it, saying, "I'll tell you the truth. I've never had a problem with the White House at all in any of this. This is a figment of the press' [imagination] to me."[12]

Bingaman opened an investigation against Microsoft in 1993, relying in part on the earlier FTC investigation materials in her decision. She filed suit in 1994. Microsoft's competitors cheered. Washington lawyer and antitrust expert Jeffrey Schmidt told the *Washington Post* that, "Microsoft is viewed as such a behemoth. . . . Any chinks that the commission could put in their armor—a lot of firms would like to see that done." While other firms were counting on Washington to help them, Microsoft, as well as Apple, had largely hung back from Washington engagement.

Apple's Steve Jobs, a friend and rival of Gates, hated politics and thought lobbying to be a waste of time and resources. Together, the two men seemed to believe that Washington and the regulatory state were not their concern, that they were too big to have to worry about Washington. Gates would later regret this. Years later, he told a young Mark Zuckerberg not to ignore or alienate Washington. "Get an office there, now," he said, giving advice that he wished a younger version of himself could have followed.[13]

Bingaman's suit was settled in 1994, after hours of personal on-the-phone negotiations between Bingaman and Gates. The consent decree ended Microsoft's "per processor" license agreements with PC makers that required a payment from the OEM to Microsoft for each microprocessor shipped, even if the processor did not contain Microsoft's operating software. While these agreements were indeed outrageous, they were not the sum total of Microsoft's sharp-elbowed practices.

Bingaman and her team celebrated the settlement, but critics thought Bingaman had gone too soft on Microsoft. Gates, it should be said, agreed, internally belittling Bingaman and her team by saying to his staff that Microsoft would not change its behavior at all as a result of the settlement. He also said, dismissively, that he supposed he would have someone at Microsoft read the agreement. In the four months following the initial settlement, Microsoft stock rose almost 30 percent, from $48 to $62 per share.[14]

Murdoch: The Rise of the Fox News Empire and Democratic Enmity

Rupert Murdoch launched Fox News in October of 1996, one month before Bill Clinton's reelection. The new news network has had enormous implications for American politics and America's CEOs. It would empower the conservative movement, but it would also contribute to the raising of the temperature in American politics. The 1990s would be, like the 1920s, 1950s, and 1980s, a period of peace and prosperity, but it would also be a period that saw Congress change hands, a president impeached, and the further encroachment of politics into American life, increasingly involving American businesses in the process.

Clinton and Murdoch were not personally hostile to one another, but the myriad of Clinton scandals, coupled with the end of the Fairness Doctrine, created a huge opportunity for the new conservative news network to establish itself. The mainstream media outlets initially downplayed the swirl of accusations around Clinton, mostly about financial improprieties related to Clinton's Whitewater real estate investments. Seeing this, Ailes and Murdoch filled the vacuum. According to former NBC president Bob Wright, "We were not paying much attention to it at NBC News. And MSNBC wasn't. CNN wasn't. And what Fox did was say, 'Gee, this is a way for us to distinguish ourselves.'" When the Monica Lewinsky scandal emerged in 1998, which the mainstream outlets did cover in greater depth, FNC already had a leg up in covering the Clinton scandal beat, and an audience that knew it could look to FNC for the latest tidbits on Clinton misdeeds.[15]

Gates: More Antitrust Troubles in Clinton's Second Term

Unfortunately for Bill Gates, Microsoft's antitrust troubles were not over with the 1994 Justice Department settlement. In February of 1995, Federal Judge Stanley Sporkin rejected the Bingaman-Gates deal, saying that, "It is clear to this court, that if it signs the decree presented to it, the message will be that Microsoft is so powerful that neither the market nor the government is capable of dealing with all of its monopolistic practices." He had read James Wallace's book *Hard Drive: Bill Gates and the Making of the Microsoft Empire* and was concerned that the consent decree had not addressed certain practices that were alleged in the book. But a mere four months later, the D.C. Circuit Court of Appeals reversed Sporkin and remanded the case to the District Court, with instructions to enter the decree. In fact, the D.C. Circuit was so troubled by what Sporkin did that it kicked him off the case and ordered that the case be reassigned to a different district judge.[16]

Still, the grumbles against Microsoft continued. Bingaman said that her division had become a "Microsoft complaint center," and continued to press the issue, investigating Microsoft's planned launch of the Microsoft Network along with its new Windows '95 OS. With the commercial potential of the internet becoming apparent, early entries into that market such as AOL and CompuServe feared that Microsoft would use its operating system advantages to take over the online world just like it took over the desktop. Gates's reaction to the continued investigations into his company echoed Bork's theory on antitrust, "It's kind of funny that it's the computer industry, where the prices come down and products get better and nobody has a guaranteed position, that's the one that somebody would look into."[17]

By the end of Clinton's first term, the internet had emerged as a force in America. In the 1996 election, Clinton's opponent Bob Dole had tried to seem cutting edge by telling viewers of the presidential debate to visit his website, "www. dolekemp96.org." (Gates, per long-standing practice, had stayed neutral in the race, which probably did not endear him to Clinton.) Even though the seventy-three-year-old Dole was the first presidential candidate to give a URL on national television, it was the younger Clinton and Gore who were seen as more capable of building what Clinton called a "bridge to the twenty-first century."

The focus on the emerging internet extended to the world of antitrust as well. Joel Klein, Clinton's second term antitrust head, would take up the Microsoft case again, this time focusing on the emerging new area of internet browsers. The World Wide Web was becoming the new tech frontier, and Gates and Microsoft had been late to adapt to it. But Gates was determined to reclaim lost ground. On December 7, 1995, Gates had targeted Netscape, the company that was dominating the browser market. Gates reportedly even used the word "jihad" internally to capture how fervently he wanted his team to be in going after their rival. Gates and Microsoft used its size and leverage to gain on Netscape and within a year had fully caught up in the browser market. By 1997, it had pulled ahead, owning three quarters of the browser market.[18]

To the Antitrust Division, Microsoft's aggressiveness in this space signaled that it had abrogated its agreement with Bingaman. Klein filed a contempt case in late 1997, alleging that Microsoft had violated the terms of the 1994 consent decree that it had agreed to. Klein argued that Microsoft's actions to catch up in the browser market constituted "precisely the sort of improper use of [its] market power to protect and extend its monopoly that [the consent decree] sought to prevent." Klein wanted Microsoft to stop bundling Microsoft's Explorer browser in its operating system and threatened to fine the company a million dollars a day unless it complied. Gates, not irrationally, saw this as anti-progress mandates from the supposedly pro-technology Clinton administration. He posed a probing question in a public forum, asking, "Are we allowed to continue to innovate in products, and in Windows itself?" In June of 1998, the Court of Appeals for the D.C. Circuit determined that Microsoft had not violated the 1994 consent decree.[19]

The Court of Appeals decision did not end Microsoft's legal woes, as Klein filed a monopolization case in May 1998 that made many of the same allegations. It was this case that went to trial in late 1998, with attorney David Boies taking the lead for the government. Klein and Boies made villainizing Gates personally a central part of their strategy. At the 1998 trial, Microsoft attorney John Warden claimed that Boies, arguing for the government, was trying to "demonize Bill Gates," playing eight hours of Gates's testimony at the trial, aiming to make Gates the face of the Microsoft monopoly. Gates, of course, contributed, mocking his interlocutors along the way. In one deposition in a related case, Gates told a young Justice Department attorney, "That's a silly question." The attorney responded, somewhat cheekily, "Those are my specialty," to which Gates acidly observed that, "You are not unique." Gates also struck many people as odd with his unusual behavior, rocking back and forth as he engaged in wordplay and the occasional insults. Gates may have enjoyed getting his digs in, but his snarky and unhelpful responses did not help his case when Boies played back the tapes.[20]

Klein was not alone in seeing Gates as a nefarious figure. Silicon Valley had long viewed Gates in this way. Netscape co-founder Marc Andreessen described a June 21, 1995, meeting with Gates as "like a visit by Don Corleone," adding that he "expected to find a bloody computer monitor in my bed the next day." But it was one thing for Microsoft's competitors to depict Gates in this way. It was another thing entirely for the U.S. government to do it.[21]

In the end, Gates's tactics did not work, and Klein's leveraging of the government did. In 2000, Judge Jackson ruled in favor of the DOJ and against Microsoft, and issued a remedy order breaking the company into two units. Microsoft appealed, and in June 2001, the Court of Appeals issued a decision mostly upholding the district court's liability determination but overturning the remedy. In an echo of its 1995 decision, the Court of Appeals criticized Jackson's conduct and kicked him off the case, ordering that the matter be reassigned to a different district judge.[22]

In this period, Microsoft faced challenges from both the private and public sectors. In the marketplace, Microsoft's products were no longer cutting edge, hurting their competitiveness and their business. At the same time, the government's resolve against the company had hardened. The administration became more unified on behalf of Klein than it had been with respect to Bingaman. One big reason for this change was that Reno was openly supportive of Klein. She jokingly introduced him at an event in 2000 by saying, "Now I'd like you to meet again one of the busiest men in Washington, Joel Klein."[23]

More importantly, the White House, and particularly President Clinton, were on board as well. Reno recalled in an oral history that she had concerns and "wanted to make sure that what we did would not have an adverse effect on the economy unless we understood what it would be and the impact it would have." Given those concerns, she "thought it was appropriate to talk to the White House about that and make sure we had input from Treasury and that we handled it correctly." Even with that White House input, though, Reno emphasized that, "I'm not saying that you can veto this. If this is an important action that must be taken under the law then we should do it, but we should understand the consequences before we do it and have a plan of action to deal with it if necessary." Showing her faith in Klein, she also noted that he "did an awful lot in terms of talking those issues through the White House and working with the White House on that."[24]

All this work with the White House was helpful in getting the president on board. In 1998, as the case was proceeding, Clinton was asked at a press conference about Microsoft's claim that Justice's preventing Microsoft from distributing Windows '98 would have a deleterious impact on both the software industry itself and U.S. economic growth as a whole. Clinton's response was a master class in acknowledging the economic challenge, demonstrating the necessary distance from the case, and still signaling his support for pursuing the case.

Clinton began by stating that as "a general principle, I have taken the view that I should not comment on matters within the jurisdiction of the Justice Department that could be the subject of legal action." He then added, "At this time, I do not think I should depart from that policy on this case," but still recognized that "it obviously will have a big impact on an important sector of our economy." Having mentioned the economic concerns, he then supported the team at Justice, saying, "I have confidence in the way the antitrust division in the Justice Department has handled the matter." In one short answer, Clinton skillfully managed to check all the boxes.[25]

Clinton went on, making similar points once again. He claimed he was not commenting on the case (even though he effectively was) but he did "want to reserve the right at some time in the future, if I think it's appropriate, to make a comment." The reason he wanted to reserve the right, he said, was that. "This is not just an open-and-shut case of one party sues somebody else. This is something that would have a significant impact on our economy." Despite that, he said,

"Based on what I know, I have confidence in the way the antitrust division has handled this." Finally, after delivering this, he closed by saying, "While it's pending at this time, I think I should stick to my policy and not comment."[26]

Clinton's comments showed remarkable message discipline. He had three points he wanted to make, he made them, and then he made them again, in order, with the cameras rolling and the microphones in his face. Such message discipline revealed a great deal about where the top of the administration stood regarding the Antitrust Division's pursuit of a company that was an enormously important part of the American economy, and that had become, on Clinton's watch, the first corporation to exceed a market capitalization of over $500 billion. The comments also revealed that while the Clinton White House was briefed on what the Antitrust Division was doing, the era of a president specifically directing these policies seemed to have gone away.[27]

All told, the Department of Justice investigation took thousands of man hours—14,000 attorney hours, 5,500 paralegal hours, and 3,650 economist hours and over a million pages of documents. In June of 2000, Judge Thomas Penfield Jackson ruled against Microsoft and moved to break up the company. Both candidates in the 2000 election weighed in on the issue. Texas Governor George W. Bush sounded pro-Microsoft, saying that he planned to "stand on the side of innovation—not litigation," concerned what would happen "if this company were to be broken apart—this engine of change, engine of growth." Ultimately, Bush said, "We'll see what the courts say on the issue," but his comments made clear where he stood. Bush's opponent Al Gore, vice president in the Clinton administration, was in a tougher spot. In a speech to Microsoft employees in Redmond, he acknowledged feeling their pain in a classic Clintonian way: "You're naturally going to feel put upon if a judge, looking at the antitrust laws and how they apply to a fact situation that involves your workplace, decides in the findings of fact that the law's been crossed." Gore's overall message was that he was ok with the pursuit of the case, saying, "The values that are inherent in the antitrust laws are ones that are sound, in my opinion."[28]

Ultimately, the company remained intact, but it did take a severe hit. In 2002, in the Bush administration, Microsoft and the Department of Justice reached a settlement in which the company had to share some of its programming with competitors. The subsequent years were less kind to Microsoft, even though its market capitalization is now over $3 trillion. Its stock price dropped significantly after the judge's ruling against it and did not reach the same level again until 2015. And it never came close to achieving the same dominance in web browsers and internet services as it had with operating systems. In some ways, this stemmed from the decade long fight with the government, but it also was a result of competition from new Silicon Valley entities such as Google. Google's search engine was just flat out more popular with users than Microsoft's. Microsoft went from having 94 percent of the browser market in 2002 to 5 percent of it in 2021.[29]

One other thing came out of the battles with the government: the end of Gates's tenure as CEO. He stepped down in the summer of 2000, while Clinton was still president. The fight with the Justice Department was not stated as the cause, but even Gates's friends thought it had to have played a role. Berkshire Hathaway chairman Warren Buffett put it gently, telling the *Wall Street Journal*, "I know the government thing obviously has been no fun. When something isn't much fun, he might look for things that are more fun." Shortly afterwards, Microsoft took a different tack, as new general counsel Brad Smith advised the company to "make peace."[30]

As for Clinton, he marked Gates's departure by complimenting Gates as "a genius with technology," and praised Gates's charitable work. The Gates Foundation had launched in 1994, and Gates, while staying on as chair of the Microsoft board, planned to devote more time to the foundation. As for the antitrust case, Clinton remained his studiously neutral self, saying, "The judge's opinion is there and they have to argue about the remedy, which as anybody knows in an antitrust case is completely different from finding whether somebody violated the laws or not." Always on message, he added, "I hope they'll do what's best for the American economy and American consumers."[31]

When asked about Gates's resignation a few days later on CNBC, Clinton praised the Bill and Melinda Gates Foundation's efforts "to help minority young people go on to college and the massive commitment they've made to make vaccines more available to poor people throughout the world." Clinton ended by saying, "I wish him well, and I want to encourage him to do more of that." No mention was made of the suit against Microsoft, or of his Justice Department's efforts to demonize Gates in its antitrust investigations.[32]

Gates: Compartmentalizing through the Microsoft Investigations

Despite Microsoft's battles with the Justice Department, Clinton and Gates somehow became friends. Throughout much of the time that the Antitrust Division was investigating Microsoft, the new tech billionaire Bill Gates was building a personal relationship with Bill Clinton, separate and apart from his company's struggles with Clinton's administration. Gates was beginning to develop a reputation as an ambassador from the strange new world of high tech to Washington. In this, he did not seem to be representing his embattled company so much as this unfamiliar new industry.

In August of 1994, Gates and Clinton even played golf. A Martha's Vineyard foursome was set up by Clinton pal Vernon Jordan, who was a Clinton adviser and ambassador to the business world. Warren Buffett joined to round out the foursome. Interestingly, at the time, Gates was in second place in a nationwide poll of most admired executives. Chrysler's Lee Iacocca was first, and Clinton was only fifth. Real-estate mogul and future president Donald Trump was third, two slots ahead of Clinton, but one behind Gates.[33]

In the golf game, Clinton, typically, hit a poor first shot and took a mulligan. Clinton was so notorious for taking these "extra shots" that he even joked about granting "Presidential pardons" to mis-hit golf balls. His partners did not always appreciate the habit. Once, when golfing with former president Gerald Ford and golfing legend Jack Nicklaus, Clinton claimed that he had shot an 80. Nicklaus whispered to Ford in response, "Eighty with fifty floating mulligans."[34]

Clinton opponent Bob Dole tried to make the mulligan issue into one of presidential character. On the campaign trail in 1996, Dole complained in response to Clinton's claim of shooting an 83 that, "I don't know whether he shot an 83 or a 283 or a 483. You'll never really know."[35]

Gates was competitive at golf as he was at most things, but there is no indication that he was unhappy with the mulligan. Still, the two men did not appear exactly to have a meeting destined for the creation of a beautiful friendship. Clinton was the master of the personal schmooze, while Gates was more interested in discussing technology. They also had dinner together that night at the home of the *Washington Post*'s Katharine Graham, but they did not appear to bond.[36]

Clinton would cite Gates in speeches occasionally, even as his Justice Department was pursuing the investigation and lawsuit against Microsoft. In April of 1996, Clinton referred to Gates as "the American computer wizard" and favorably cited Gates's book *The Road from Here.* Clinton credited Gates with observing that, "The changes we are now experiencing in communication are the most profound the world has experienced in 500 years since Gutenberg printed the first Bible in Europe with a printing press," and this observation became a recurring theme in multiple Clinton speeches. On another occasion, he referred to Gates's wisdom in discussing Clinton's efforts to reinvent government. According to Clinton, Gates had said, "You know, our world works three times faster than normal business, and Washington works three times slower. That puts them behind by a factor of nine."[37]

In addition to citing Gates as guru, another safe space for Clinton was to praise Gates's philanthropy. In February of 1996, Clinton specifically referred to Gates's gift of $10 million for technical schools in Washington state as "a shining example of the kind of partnership between businesses and public institutions that we need more of in America."[38]

The interesting thing about all these compliments and references is that they were taking place as Clinton's Justice Department was not only investigating Gates but also making him the face of Microsoft's allegedly predatory practices. As with all presidential addresses, Clinton's speeches had to go through the White House staffing process, which means they had to be approved throughout the White House, including by the White House Counsel's office, which was aware of the actions taken against Microsoft. This presidential praise for the CEO of a company under DOJ investigation was somewhat unusual. It is hard to imagine Roosevelt complimenting Rockefeller during the investigations into Standard Oil. It is even harder to imagine Roosevelt playing golf with Rockefeller as Clinton and Gates did. Even William Howard Taft, who was far less hostile to Rockefeller than Roosevelt had been, was warned off golfing with the oil mogul by Nellie Taft, his politically wary spouse.

The compartmentalizing was not always perfect. On April 4, 2000, Clinton held a summit at the White House with nonprofit and high-tech executives aimed at bridging the "digital divide" between haves and have-nots in the twenty-first century. At the event, Clinton hosted a panel of CEOs that not only included but led off with Gates. In his introduction, Clinton praised Gates for his philanthropic work, noting that the "Gates Foundation has made some phenomenal commitments to the education of minorities in America."[39]

Clinton may not have been comfortable praising Gates's building of his successful company, but Gates was not shy about what he had done in the business world. In his rather lengthy remarks, Gates talked about the dream he and Paul Allen had in making the personal computer "an essential tool of the American productivity revolution." In what was perhaps a nod to Bork's consumer benefit lens on antitrust policy, Gates added that, "We've seen its power double every eighteen months. Its price fall. And its importance grow as an empowering tool in our lives." He was also somewhat prescient in predicting "breakthroughs that will allow computers . . . to be in a tablet form connected up to a wireless network that you just carry around with you." Clinton's response was once again careful, focusing not on Microsoft's technological advances but on the future of pharmaceutical innovation, one of the goals of the Gates Foundation.[40]

The incongruity of Clinton and Gates appearing together at the same time in which the government was targeting Gates's company was not lost on the White House press corps. At a press briefing that day, a reporter asked White House economic adviser Gene Sperling, "Isn't it a little unusual to have Bill Gates at a White House conference two days after the Justice Department applauded a decision which accuses his company—or found that his company engaged in illegal business practices?" Sperling responded with a bracing example of compartmentalization in the modern era. He said that, "The truth is that an administration, any administration, is engaged with a variety of companies and CEOs, on a variety of topics at any time. The majority, the overwhelming majority of most top companies and top CEOs have some form of business or some form of regulatory or enforcement issue in front of the government at some point. And the only way that the administration can function properly in that setting is to do what we do, which is to not comment on independent or enforcement proceedings as they are going on."[41]

The reporter seized on Sperling's assertion that the only approach is to "not comment on independent or enforcement proceedings," noting that the administration had indeed commented on the Microsoft case. Sperling responded, somewhat less comfortably, "I'm saying that in the White House we do not—in the White House—I said for independent—obviously, that is an issue which is a mixture, an antitrust division enforcement is a mixture, in some sense—is not entirely an independent agency, but it is an enforcement proceeding. We do not make regular comments—I'm not saying we never, ever will, but that has not been our general practice."[42]

Sperling then added that, "Obviously we support the position of our Justice Department and there's no question about that." More broadly, though, he said, "The issue is whether or not we can continue to hear from somebody, talk with them or consult with them on issues such as relating to best ways to address the global divide in terms of health, infectious diseases, or the divide that might be created in changes in technology. Clearly, Mr. Gates has much to offer in terms of his point of view. We aren't endorsing or necessarily disagreeing with all sorts of things people are going to say."[43]

Sperling was right to acknowledge that there might be disagreements with Gates. That same month, despite the friendly panel, Gates was publicly criticizing the Clinton administration's plan to break up Microsoft as "anti-consumer." He also visited Capitol Hill, where Republicans and even some Democrats took Microsoft's side in its fight against the Justice Department. Republican house majority leader Dick Armey said he'd "rather break up the Justice Department," while Democratic New Jersey senator Robert Torricelli said that, "Only the United States would consider breaking up a company that has done this much economically to advance our national interest." Gates also told congressional Republicans that he was hoping for a friendlier approach if there were a new Republican administration after the November elections.[44]

Both Gates's and Sperling's comments after the friendly White House CEO panel reveal the limits of the compartmentalization approach. Clinton could laud Gates's philanthropic efforts and tech guru status, but that did not change the fact that his administration's Justice Department was trying to break up Gates's company. And Gates could appear on all the White House panels he wanted, but that would not change the administration's stance on the antitrust issue, nor stop the DOJ's efforts to make Gates the face of Microsoft's modern-day monopoly. Clinton and Gates could play golf and even establish an amicable relationship of sorts, but the bottom line was that the Clinton administration had taken a big chunk out of Microsoft, and Gates was no longer CEO of America's biggest tech company.

Coda: Graham's Legacy

Katharine Graham had good relations with both George H. W. Bush and with Bill Clinton, who attended a dinner at her home shortly after his 1992 election. Other than that, and seeing the Clintons on Martha's Vineyard, Graham recalled having "little contact" with the Clintons, noting that, "They have been polite but are of a younger generation, so it's perfectly normal." George W. Bush was the last president of her lifetime, and he did attend one of her Welcome to Washington dinners at her home, where they were joined by Washington luminaries as well as CEOs Bill Gates and Warren Buffett.[45]

Graham died in 2001, Bush's first year in office. In 2002, he gave her a posthumous Presidential Medal of Freedom, calling her "a forceful, courageous, and deeply principled newspaper publisher." As publisher, she had interacted with nine presidents, and eight of them—all but Nixon—had come to her house for one of her famous get togethers. While her paper was liberal, her relationships with presidents did not follow ideological lines. Perhaps it is a quaint sentiment in these extremely partisan times, but she genuinely believed, as she wrote in her memoir, that "people who may disagree on politics must still be able to communicate, and it's crucial for all of us in the press to listen to all sides."[46]

Her paper wrote about—and was read by—presidents and their top aides every single day of her tenure. Her decisions about what to publish—and what not to publish—pleased, infuriated, and even brought down presidents. But her power was not unilateral: presidents had their own ways to flatter, criticize, and punish her and her paper. Throughout all her battles and alliances, she could be sure of one thing: that at some point the president would leave the White House, but the *Washington Post* would still be there.

Wasserman's Last Hurrah with Clinton

Hollywood and Washington may have been looking ahead to the days after Lew Wasserman, but he was not done yet. For starters, he remained an essential source of political cash for Democrats. From 1991 until his death in 2002, Wasserman made $1.4 million in political donations, over 95 percent of which went to Democrats. His prodigious giving and fundraising made him attractive to Democratic politicians, including Arkansas's young and talented governor, Bill Clinton.[47]

Clinton had originally reached out to Wasserman in his capacity as governor. According to Clinton, "I asked him if he would give me some advice about how I could get more movies made in Arkansas." At the time, Clinton was the little-known governor of a small state that had never produced an American president. According to Clinton, "At that time, only my mother thought I would ever become president, so there was nothing in it for Lew to spend forty-five minutes talking to a politician from a state which for all I know he had never visited—but he did." As Clinton recalled, "He didn't know me from Adam. He certainly couldn't have known I would be president. And he sat and talked to me for thirty or forty-five minutes, like I was the most important person in the world."[48]

In spending that time with Clinton, Wasserman revealed a lot about why he was good at what he did. Clinton was unknown at the time, but Wasserman—and Edie—had a good sense of people's potentials. As the Hollywood writer Dominick

Dunne observed, "Edie and Lew could smell power, whether it was in Hollywood, Washington, or Arkansas." In addition, Wasserman always took the prospect of giving advice seriously. He told politicians what he thought and did not sugarcoat matters. He also had a skillful way of presenting tough advice. When Clinton asked what he could do to get more films made in Arkansas, Wasserman was brutally honest. According to Clinton, "He said in a very elegant and brief language, 'Not much.' And to compound the irony, he actually made me like it—I mean, I enjoyed the meeting."[49]

As had happened with so many others beforehand, Wasserman became both a key adviser and fundraiser for Clinton. As many politicians had discovered previously, Wasserman was tremendously talented at both. Bob Strauss had observed that when Wasserman did a fundraiser, it was done right: "If it was supposed to be $200,000 for a fund-raiser you'd show up and it wouldn't be $203,000 or $197,000, it was $200,000." Clinton needed someone with those talents. He called Wasserman while riding on his presidential campaign bus and asked him to help with fundraising. Wasserman responded as Wasserman did, raising $1.7 million for Clinton at a $10,000-a-couple dinner at the Wasserman home. Wasserman bragged that it was "the most successful dinner in a private home in American political history."[50]

The bragging was unlike Wasserman, but when it came to Clinton, he was smitten. Wasserman even admitted it, saying, "I am crazy about him." According to Wasserman, "If you get me going on the subject of Bill Clinton, I'll sound like a love-struck teenager." Once Clinton became president, they would speak for hours at a time on all manner of subjects. Clinton valued the older man's counsel, later reflecting that Wasserman helped him look at the presidency via the predecessors Wasserman had known: "He talked to me about other presidents. He wasn't a gossip. He told stories to illustrate how he thought things ought to be done, how he thought problems ought to be solved. I always hated to leave when I was at his home." At Wasserman's memorial, Clinton said, "Lew helped me become president, he helped me stay president, he helped me become a better president."[51]

In his second term, when Clinton got into political trouble because of his affair with White House intern Monica Lewinsky, Wasserman stayed on Clinton's side.

He raised money for Clinton's legal defense fund, and he stood up for Clinton publicly. In September of 1998, Wasserman told the *New York Times's* Bernard Weinraub that Clinton remained beloved in Hollywood, scandal notwithstanding. "He outdoes JFK," Wasserman said, adding, "He works the crowd here, and he sees them as friends. They genuinely like him. There's no decline in support. So he made a mistake. He said he was sorry. What else can you do?"[52]

Wasserman got a lot out of the relationship as well. In 1993, Clinton attended a special Washington screening of *Schindler's List*, a Universal-distributed film. Wasserman was of course in attendance. In 1995, Clinton awarded Wasserman the Presidential Medal of Freedom. When told about this, Wasserman's response was that the award "just came out of the blue," adding, "I'm astounded and honored." Perhaps he need not have been so surprised.[53]

Clinton was also personally solicitous of the Wassermans. One day, when Wasserman was leaving for work, he saw a man in his backyard. Wasserman's butler told his curious boss, "That's a Secret Service man, sir. . . . The President is coming to visit, sir." At that moment, Wasserman realized that Clinton was coming to visit Edie, who was under the weather. A regular person would have stopped and waited for the president's visit. Wasserman, accustomed to presidential attention for three decades by this point, continued on his way to work.[54]

Despite his closeness to the president, Wasserman did not get everything he wanted from the Clinton administration. In December of 1993, the Clinton administration was engaged in a series of international trade negotiations on the General Agreement on Tariffs and Trade (GATT), known as the Uruguay Round. The movie industry, led by Valenti, wanted the administration to get rid of what was known as "the cultural exception," a provision that European countries used to limit the access of American films to European markets. Siding with the studios, the U.S. had targeted the cultural exception, within limits. At a certain point, U.S. negotiators saw that they could get an overall deal if they kept the cultural exception the studios wanted to eliminate. Mickey Kantor, Clinton's trade representative, called the president from Geneva to brief him on the difficult question.

Clinton had two responses, one mischievous and one serious. On the humorous side, when Kantor said that Valenti wanted to call the whole negotiation off unless the exception was eliminated, Clinton said, "If we do that, everyone will think I've been sleeping with Sharon Stone." More seriously, on the issue of whether to proceed with the deal without killing the exception, Clinton said, "Look, call Lew, see what Lew thinks and then call me back."[55]

It was 4:00 a.m. in Geneva, 8:00 p.m. in Los Angeles, when Kantor reached Wasserman. Wasserman, Kantor recalled, was, of course, "an old friend of mine." While Valenti was unyielding on the issue, Wasserman was more philosophical and farsighted, saying, "Mickey, isn't this the largest trade agreement in history?" When told that it was, Wasserman continued, "The movie industry is just fine. We have 80% of the market in Europe. Technology is going to override anything you would do or not do there. We'll be just fine and we shouldn't stand in the way of this agreement." In conclusion, Wasserman gave him the go-ahead, saying, "I appreciate your call, tell the President thank you, but go do what you have to do, go get the agreement." Kantor later told an unhappy Valenti what Wasserman had said. According to Kantor, "Valenti blanched."[56]

Ultimately, Valenti was the lobbyist for the movie industry, but Wasserman had his eye on the whole picture. He saw the greater value in getting the agreement and gave his ok. As Kantor said of Wasserman, "It wasn't just that he had power and was the head of a major studio and was shrewd and smart. He was a very thoughtful, impressive human being. You know, sometimes you ask big contributors for advice to feed their egos. But people actually wanted to hear from Lew."[57]

The Uruguay Round was a loss for Hollywood. It was far from the only loss for Hollywood, though, even after Wasserman got involved in politics. There were the antitrust actions preventing the MCA mergers in 1969, but also actions by the Carter and Reagan Justice Departments that prevented other MCA mergers that would have taken the company into the cable business. Overall, though, Wasserman piled up many more wins than losses once he got the political bug. Even when an issue did not go his way, as with the Uruguay Round, Wasserman knew that the first instinct of presidents when faced with tough issues having to do with Hollywood would be the same as Clinton's: "Call Lew." The frequency with which those two words were used were Wasserman's ultimate win from having made the decision to enter the political game.

Buffett: Increasingly Vocal on Political Matters

Like Bill Gates, Warren Buffett got to know Bill Clinton by playing golf with him on Martha's Vineyard and dining with him periodically. He advised Clinton at a lunch with CEOs to raise taxes and cut spending to bring down the deficit.[58]

The first president Buffett criticized with his expanded reputation as a wise man was George W. Bush. Buffett disliked Bush's plan to reduce estate taxes and noted that he was against the idea of passing on wealth from generation to generation. "I don't believe in dynasties," he said, which could have been seen as a dig on the estate tax repeal, on Bush as a son of a former president, or both. Buffett became active on the issue, writing op-eds in the *Washington Post* and meeting with the Senate Democratic Policy Committee about it. He even appeared to break his rule about mixing politics with business, writing in Berkshire Hathaway's 2004 annual report that, "If class warfare is being waged in America, my class is clearly winning." It was here that Buffett started using the now famous talking point about how his secretary Debbie Bosanek paid higher effective tax rates than he did.[59]

Following the financial meltdown of 2008, Buffet provided statesman-like advice to inject optimism into the economy. He wrote in a *New York Times* op-ed, "In short, bad news is an investor's best friend. It lets you buy a slice of America's future at a marked-down price." The event also helped revise his opinion of President Bush. After Bush left office, Buffett noted on multiple occasions that Bush handled the 2008 financial crisis well, and he praised Bush's call to action— "If money doesn't loosen up, this sucker will go down"—calling it "the greatest economic statement of all time."[60]

Oprah: Dipping Her Toes in Political Waters

In 2000, as part of a larger evolution, Oprah Winfrey made an important adjustment in her policy on politics and her show. With the election to replace Bill Clinton shaping up to be a close contest between Texas governor George W. Bush and Al Gore, Oprah invited both men to appear on her show. Trump's 1988 tease notwithstanding, this was her first invitation to official presidential candidates. Gore appeared first, on September 11, 2000. The highlight of the interview was when she asked Gore his "favorite thing to sleep in," to which Gore responded, "A bed." This was a sly dig at his boss Bill Clinton, who had shocked people when he answered a "boxers or briefs?" question with "usually briefs" in a 1992 MTV interview. More important than the substance of the interview was the result. A *Newsweek* poll that appeared after Gore's Oprah appearance—as well as an appearance on *Late Night with David Letterman*—had Gore with a twelve-point lead. This was a surprising development in an exceedingly close race.[61]

Bush went next, eight days later. At the start, Oprah acknowledged her shift, saying, "I stayed away from interviewing politicians for 15 years because I thought it would be really difficult to break through the wall of sound bites and what appeared to be practiced answers." She explained her change of heart by saying that she hoped "to ask questions that will help reveal the real man so you can decide who feels like the right candidate for you."[62]

Oprah got what she was looking for. Bush charmed her, kissed her on the cheek, talked about his struggles with alcoholism, and revealed that his favorite song was "Wake Up, Little Susie." When Oprah pressed him on his seeking forgiveness for his past, saying she was looking for specifics, he said, "I know you are, but I'm running for president." On the *Newsweek* poll that came out after Bush's *Oprah* appearance, he had closed back to within two points. As *Salon*'s Joyce Millman observed, "The road to the White House goes through Oprah."[63]

Despite these campaign interviews, Oprah still remained reluctant to get involved in politics. In 2002, she turned down an invitation from Bush to tour schools in Afghanistan. But after nearly two decades on the air, Oprah had finally begun to recognize her political power.

Welch: Bigger than a Cabinet Post

Despite his friendship with Bill Clinton, Jack Welch remained a staunch Republican. When Welch read that Clinton aide George Stephanopoulos was looking to join NBC News, he faxed a copy of the article with a drawing of his middle finger on it to the network's president, putting an end to that possibility. He also showed his partisan preferences on election night 2000, actively rooting for George W. Bush over Clinton vice president Al Gore. It was an exceedingly close election, and Welch pushed NBC executives to declare Bush the winner, saying, "Okay, how much do I have to pay you a$$holes to call this thing for Bush!"[64]

Welch liked Bush—at one point calling him "good sh**"—and was a fan of the entire Bush family. He was in touch with Bush during the transition, and was widely rumored to be in the mix for the position of Secretary of the Treasury, a job that ultimately went to another CEO, Paul O'Neill, who had recently retired from Alcoa. Welch, however, was uninterested, explaining that the reason "CEOs don't often make great cabinet officers is they've been the chief executive for the last, in my case, 21 years. Going to be a staff man for somebody else's policies is not something that appeals to me in any way, shape or form."[65]

Another reason that Welch was uninterested in a Cabinet slot is that he was in the process of retiring from GE and moving into a new phase of his career, that of all-purpose management expert. He retired in September of 2001, just as his book *Jack: Straight from the Gut* came out, on the same day as the 9/11 terrorist attacks. Over the course of Welch's time in office, GE stock rose by 4,000 percent, and GE became the world's first $500 billion company. Welch's final pre-retirement pay package brought him $122.5 million.[66]

Coda: Iacocca's Post-Retirement Relationships with Presidents

In September of 1993, Democratic president Bill Clinton woke a retired Lee Iacocca at 2:00 a.m. in Italy to ask him to come to the White House. When Iacocca got back to Washington, D.C., on September 23, Clinton asked for Iacocca's help to sell NAFTA—the North American Free Trade Agreement. Clinton saw Iacocca as a helpful foil to Ross Perot, another CEO-turned-political-actor who

(Continued)

was regularly railing against the pending free trade deal. Iacocca joined Clinton at an October 1993 White House event promoting NAFTA, where Clinton praised the former auto executive for being "such an eloquent spokesperson for NAFTA." NAFTA passed on December 8, 1993, and Iacocca later praised Clinton's "passion for governing, his openness, and his respect for people from all countries and all walks of life."[67]

Iacocca thought less of Clinton's replacement, George W. Bush, though. While he supported Bush in 2000, in large part because of his relationship with Bush's father, he disapproved of Bush's administration. He backed Bush's opponent John Kerry in 2004, and he published a book in 2007 that was harshly critical of Bush. Iacocca wrote that Bush "doesn't have common sense" and characterized Bush's team as "a gang of clueless bozos steering our ship of state right over a cliff." In response, White House spokesman Alex Conant retorted the administration "does not do book reviews."[68]

In 2008, Iacocca, by now in his eighties, liked both the Republican John McCain and the Democrat—and eventual winner—Barack Obama. He described Obama as "one of those stars who seem to come from nowhere to capture the imagination of the nation." He was disappointed in Obama's presidency and backed Mitt Romney—son of former auto executive George Romney—in 2012. Iacocca knew Joe Biden from Biden's long career in the Senate and thought that there was "some great experience in that man—much of it in foreign affairs—if we're willing to take advantage of it." Iacocca did not live to see Biden's presidency, dying on July 2, 2019, after typifying the increasing entanglement of CEOs and American presidents. While he initially pushed to get government off his company's back, he spent his later years trying to get more government intervention on behalf of his business interests. Iacocca's evolution from anti-regulation lobbyist in the Nixon days was reflective of the shift made by CEOs in the twenty-first century. While they once wanted government off their backs, many now increasingly wanted government on their sides.[69]

Jamie Dimon: Pitching in to Help Save the Economy

Jamie Dimon and his twin brother Teddy were born in Queens in 1956. Dimon's grandfather was a Greek immigrant who came to the United States to pursue the American dream. The Dimon family would see that play out with generations of increasing success. Dimon's father ascended to the position of executive vice president at American Express—working for another legend of Wall Street, Sanford Weill. When Dimon graduated from Harvard Business School in 1982, he followed in his father's footsteps by working for Weill.

Weill eventually moved on from American Express, and Dimon went with him. He learned from the older man how to manage financial operations, which he did for Weill at places like Primerica, Smith Barney, and Salomon Brothers. Dimon did not lack confidence. He routinely challenged his elders—including Weill himself. When Weill would ask, "Does anyone have a problem with that?" Dimon did not mind saying, "I do." Unfortunately for Dimon, Weill did mind, and fired him in 1998. But Dimon learned a lasting lesson. Upon leaving Weill's employ, he told a friend, Guy Moszkowski, "I'm never going to work for anyone else again."[70]

Dimon kept that pledge. He went to work at the helm of troubled Bank One in 2000 and helped turn it around. He then merged Bank One with another drifting bank, JPMorgan Chase, in 2004, becoming CEO of the larger entity in 2005. As CEO, he had a reputation as a hands-on manager who read everything and retained it as well. As his colleague Steve Black said, "He reads it and remembers." He has a reputation as a domineering boss who sometimes gets into trouble by not listening to others, but he is also known to learn from his mistakes and seldom make them again.[71]

As CEO of JPMorgan Chase, Dimon brought a storied company to even greater heights. In 2004, the top U.S. banks at the time, including JPMorgan Chase but also Citigroup, Bank of America, and Wells Fargo, had earnings of $27.6 billion, $4 trillion in assets, and employed over 300,000 people. To be at the head of one of those banks was to be at the very pinnacle of the American financial system, listened to by presidents and business leaders. It seemed to be an enviable position.[72]

Dimon: Dealing with Paulson on the Financial Collapse

The good times would not last. In the fall of 2007, the Dow Jones Industrial Average hit a peak of 14,165. From there, it began a steady fall, plummeting to 6,926 in March of 2009. The recession, exacerbated by a credit collapse due to over-leveraged mortgage-based securities, hit Wall Street hard. In March of 2008, Bear Stearns collapsed. JPMorgan Chase, with strong encouragement from the Bush administration, purchased Bear for a mere two dollars a share—a 93 percent discount over its valuation the week before. Even at that rate, JPMorgan Chase needed both the federal encouragement and a $30 billion loan from the Federal Reserve to make it happen. This kind of federal intervention had not happened since the 1930s. Dimon was gracious if not fully optimistic afterwards, saying that "Bear Stearns' clients and counterparties should feel secure that JP Morgan is guaranteeing Bear Stearns' counterparty risk. We welcome their clients, counterparties and employees to our firm, and we are glad to be their partner."[73]

In September of 2008, Merrill Lynch lost more than $50 billion in toxic mortgages, prompting a quick sale to Bank of America. Then Lehman Brothers collapsed. This put the entire economy on the precipice. It was no longer a matter of bank ups and downs. The federal government began to get involved in major and unprecedented ways.[74]

George W. Bush, a largely free-market, pro-business Republican was president at the time. The first term of his administration had already been roiled by the terrorist attacks of September 11, 2001. Early in his second term, Hurricane Katrina had hit New Orleans—and the response from local, state, and federal officials was disastrous. Bush could not believe he was facing another massive crisis on his watch with barely three months left in his presidency. When he assembled his top advisers in the White House's Roosevelt Room on September 18, 2008, he asked a stark question that indicated both his shock and his disappointment: "How did we get here?"[75]

Bush had to deal with more than most presidents, but he was fortunate in the selection of his advisers for this latest national crisis. His treasury secretary was Henry "Hank" Paulson, former head of Goldman Sachs, who not only knew Wall Street but had personal relationships with the heads of the nation's top financial institutions. His Federal Reserve chairman, Ben Bernanke, was a well-respected academic who had done his dissertation on the causes of the Great Depression of the 1920s and 1930s. Bernanke had specifically looked at what the federal government had done wrong in that era. He was determined to learn from the past to make sure that history did not repeat itself.

Bush recognized that his top advisers had greater expertise in taking on this challenge than he did. Consequently, Bush had Paulson take the lead on the federal response. As Paulson recalled, Bush was a "boss" who "understands that when you're dealing with something as unprecedented and fast-moving as this we need to have a different operating style."[76]

With Paulson in charge, it was he who had the talks with the top Wall Street executives, including Dimon. Dimon was a Democrat and not a huge fan of Bush. When JPMorgan Chase made its government-aided purchase of Bear Stearns, which failed to stop the economic turmoil, Dimon had called it "Mission not accomplished." This was both a dig at the government's inability to contain the problem as well as a callback to Bush's landing on the aircraft carrier USS Abraham Lincoln welcomed by a banner prematurely declaring "Mission Accomplished" in the second Iraq War. Over the next three years, the nation would learn the Iraq mission was far from over. So Dimon's quip was a reminder—and a warning—that the Bear Stearns acquisition was just the beginning and more pain was to come.[77]

Dimon may not have been close to Bush, but he was in close contact with Paulson. On September 17, Dimon told Paulson that "the markets are frozen." The next day, Paulson and Bernanke presented a rescue plan—the Troubled Assets Relief Plan (TARP)—which entailed Congress creating a $700 billion bank rescue fund. The plan initially failed in Congress, sending markets on a downward spiral before lawmakers recognized the danger and passed the plan on the next try.[78]

Even though Dimon had encouraged Paulson to come up with a rescue plan, he was not eager to have his company participate in it. He felt that JPMorgan Chase did not need the funds. Paulson knew this, believing Dimon was in "the best shape of the group." In addition, Dimon feared both government strictures attached to taking the money and public anger about so many taxpayer dollars going to Wall Street banks. He also feared that some of his colleagues would not take the money, which Dimon was only agreeing to take to prevent the needy banks from being stigmatized upon receipt of the funds.[79]

When it came time to sign a document accepting the government funds and the amount they had accepted, Dimon was wary. He told Treasury General Counsel Bob Hoyt to hold his signature in escrow until the other CEOs signed. He asked Hoyt to notify him via his personal cell phone once all the signatures were in, but the brusque Dimon was not looking to make a new friend. Dimon said to Hoyt, "Call me and tell me when everything is done. Then throw this number away after you use it."[80]

Overall, the plan worked, and the threat of a collapse ended, although the recession continued into 2009. On October 17, 2008, Bush spoke to the U.S. Chamber of Commerce and said, "The government moved to protect the American people. We prevented a disorderly failure of these large, interconnected firms—and we did so in a way that protects taxpayers and does not shield executives from the consequences of their irresponsible decisions."[81]

Even so, Dimon was right to have been concerned about his own company's participation in the plan. By accepting the funds, Dimon created the perception that JPMorgan Chase was bailed out, even though it did not need the funds at the time. In addition, the government strictures Dimon feared did impose unwanted limits on his business operations, something that he complained about in the administration of Bush's successor Barack Obama. Moreover, Dimon proved right in his deepest fear: the plan ignited public outrage against Wall Street, which contributed to the general unhappiness both political parties had with Wall Street and corporations in general in the 2010s and 2020s.[82]

On the plus side of the ledger, Dimon's business came out of interactions with the government in an arguably better position. It acquired Bear Stearns, even with all its problems, at a very low price. Dimon claims that the company lost $5 to $10 billion on the deal and said, in 2012, "Would I have done Bear Stearns again knowing what I know today? It's real close." Others are not so sure. Boston University Finance professor Mark Williams said in 2012 that, "It was the best risk-sharing negotiation Jamie Dimon has ever done. So for him to come back now and say it was a bad deal is just posturing." The ensuing decade bears that out as well. JPMorgan

Chase stock, which went to as low as about fourteen dollars a share, reached a high of over $163 in 2021. Dimon's personal net worth is over $2 billion.[83]

Zuckerberg: Monetizing the Internet

Mark Zuckerberg invented a platform used by three billion people around the world. Henry Ford likely never dreamed of selling three billion Ford cars. The Model T sold about fifteen million cars in its lifespan. Nor did Henry Luce think he would get three billion subscribers to *TIME,* although his magazines did reach thirty million people at the company's apex. There are obviously more than three billion users of oil-based products, but that's like saying there are more than three billion people who eat food or breathe oxygen. In any event, Standard Oil, long broken up, does not provide the oil for three billion people, and did not do so even in its heyday. But Mark Zuckerberg, still barely forty, has come closer than any of his predecessors to making a product that has taken over most of the world. But in the process, he has made a great many enemies, culturally and politically, including some American presidents, on both sides of the political aisle.

Zuckerberg was born in 1984 to a comfortable family in White Plains, New York. His early biography is well-known. He started coding at a young age. He attended the ultra-elite Phillips Exeter Academy, followed by Harvard. A close review of his biography reveals themes in his life that would recur often in adulthood in his capacity as the CEO of a trillion-dollar company.

The first is that he liked to understand how things tick. Zuckerberg taught himself how to code at age eleven from the book *C++ for Dummies.* The reason he dove into programming flowed from his love of seeing his projects come to life. "I just liked making things," he would later say. "Then I figured out I could make more things if I learned to program." Like his hero Bill Gates decades earlier, one of the first things Zuckerberg designed was a program for the game Risk, which also revealed a lifelong love of military strategy. Later, Zuckerberg would view his battles with both competitors and with Washington through that lens of military strategy.[84]

Zuckerberg's dentist father noticed his affinity for programming and hired him a tutor. While at Exeter, Zuckerberg and a friend developed a program called

Synapse that would suggest musical selections based on what the user had previously listened to. The program did well, and a number of companies, including Microsoft, looked into buying it for a reported price of around $2 million. Nothing came of it, as Zuckerberg was not interested in ceding control. As he later said, "What they really wanted was for us to come and work for them. We didn't want to do that." So not only did he want to build things, he wanted to shape popular tastes—and that came with a strong desire to remain in charge of whatever he was doing.[85]

Zuckerberg's time at Harvard taught him additional lessons about the cutthroat world of business. Three famous episodes, all well-known from the 2010 Zuckerberg biopic *The Social Network*, stand out. First was his initial foray into programming notoriety with the Facemash program. This program allowed users to rate the attractiveness of their fellow Harvard students. It caught on like wildfire, but also caused a backlash among people offended by what he did and the not quite legal way in which he hacked into existing databases to secure the pictures. Zuckerberg had to face a hearing of the Harvard Administrative Board, which let him off with a warning after he agreed to take down the site. This episode showed Zuckerberg's ability to create a viral product, the backlash his work could create, and how to appease regulators in such a way as to escape serious harm from the backlash. After he survived the hearing, he and some friends drank champagne to toast his narrow escape.[86]

The next famous incident was the dust up with the Winklevoss twins, Tyler and Cameron. The two popular student athletes had asked Zuckerberg to set up a social networking website for them after seeing his Facemash site written up in the *Harvard Crimson*. Zuckerberg agreed to do it but instead produced his own site, "TheFacebook," which quickly took off. The Winklevosses objected and tried to get Zuckerberg disciplined by the Harvard administration. When that failed, they sued Zuckerberg and eventually secured a $65 million settlement. They made millions, but Zuckerberg made billions. The entire incident highlighted Zuckerberg's willingness to outmaneuver outside competitors in his quest to create a high-tech behemoth.[87]

The third incident had to do with an internal challenge. Zuckerberg started "The Facebook" with a Harvard classmate named Eduardo Saverin. Zuckerberg did the programming and Saverin put up seed capital and initially handled the business side of things. Zuckerberg would leave Harvard to pursue the business full-time, following in the footsteps of his idol, Bill Gates, thinking, "Like Bill Gates had said: 'If Microsoft didn't work out, he could always go back to Harvard.'"[88]

While Zuckerberg moved to Silicon Valley, Saverin would stay and graduate at Harvard. To Zuckerberg, this showed a lack of commitment to their joint endeavor. The two men quickly developed different visions for the company, and Zuckerberg would show little remorse in maneuvering Saverin out of a leadership role, and out of much of his equity. In one conversation, Facebook adviser Sean Parker marveled at Zuckerberg's work with Facebook investor Peter Thiel on a stock re-evaluation that cut out Saverin. Parker said, "I bet Thiel learned that from [venture capitalist] Mike [Moritz]." Zuckerberg's bloodless response: "Well, now I learned from him, and I'll do it to Eduardo."[89]

With the inside and outside competitors pushed aside, Facebook became a phenomenon. User numbers exploded across Harvard, other elite schools, and then across the university system in general. After launching at Harvard in February of 2004, Facebook started at Columbia, Stanford, and Yale that same month. By June of 2004, Facebook was at forty schools, with over 150,000 users. Within four years, it would have seventy million users.[90]

In short order, Zuckerberg would turn down multiple early offers for Facebook, including $75 million from MTV in 2005 and a billion dollars from Yahoo in 2006. According to Yahoo's incredulous Terry Semel, Zuckerberg's attitude was, "This is my baby, and I want to keep running it, I want to keep growing it."[91]

If keeping it as his baby meant parting with old friends, Zuckerberg was ok with it. Facebook was, and would remain, as Zuckerberg put it on the original Facebook site, "A Mark Zuckerberg production." A close friend told a reporter that, "Ultimately, it's 'the Mark show.'" This desire for control manifested in the structure of the company. He controlled everything: the board, the equity, the strategy. Another friend said that, "It really is like dealing with the court of a king. You had different factions and different interests, but they don't really challenge the king." Zuckerberg's early business card summed it up: "I'm CEO—Bitch." [92]

The concentration of power in one person brought with it advantages and disadvantages. Zuckerberg could not be threatened internally, but he could also not count on his people to give him bad news. Not just kings, but CEOs and presidents have all faced this challenge of how to get honest feedback from someone who controls the livelihoods of everyone around them.

Zuckerberg's centrality within the company also made him, as the *New Yorker* called him, "the Face of Facebook." He was becoming a celebrity, but also a target. In 2008, *Rolling Stone* profiled Zuckerberg, somewhat unfavorably, and even compared him to future president Donald Trump. His sharp elbows drew attention as well. Journalist Kara Swisher asked, "How many people has he burned and he's only 24?" By 2010, Zuckerberg had made it to number one on *Vanity Fair*'s New Establishment power ranking, beating out far more established titans like Steve Jobs and Rupert Murdoch, and getting dubbed "our new Caesar" in the process.[93]

Zuckerberg: Looking to Washington Early

While Zuckerberg idolized Gates and modeled himself after the Microsoft founder, he also sought to avoid some of Gates's mistakes. One of those was paying insufficient attention to the regulators in Washington. When Gates met Zuckerberg, he gave him clear and stark advice: "Get an office there, now." Many people receive advice, but they don't always take it.

When his idol spoke, Zuckerberg listened. Gates noticed, later saying, "And Mark did, and he owes me."[94]

Even without Gates's advice, Zuckerberg would likely have opened a Washington office early in his tenure. The tech companies were growing too big, too fast, and attracting Washington's attention in the process. Silicon Valley had seen what happened to Microsoft in its fight with the Clinton Justice Department, with its stock halved and its founder stepping down. In addition, the mood in Washington was getting increasingly less friendly towards corporations in general, and Silicon Valley in particular. This, coupled with the enormous increase in the number of arrows in the government's quiver that could be deployed against corporations, meant that Washington could not be ignored. The record of other titans who had tried the approach of ignoring Washington was dismal. Recall

Rockefeller refusing to engage in public relations, despite aides telling him he needed to, and Gates's dismissal of Washington's antitrust officials as "socialistic." In return, both had seen their companies diminished by directed government action.

Like those predecessors, Zuckerberg had almost complete autonomy within his organization. This meant that things were on his shoulders, but it also meant that he could pursue whatever strategy he wanted to protect the company from government encroachment. Luce, when asked what he would do if everyone in the company wanted to vote another way, responded that *TIME* would go with what Luce said. In the years ahead, Facebook would go ahead with what Zuckerberg said, even if it alienated his extremely progressive workforce.

Zuckerberg knew he lacked expertise in the ways of Washington, so he was willing to find it elsewhere. He was also willing to learn. In 2005, the *Washington Post* almost acquired 10 percent of Facebook, a deal that would have made the company billions of dollars. It did not work out, but Zuckerberg befriended the *Post*'s chairman Don Graham, who would go on to serve on Facebook's board. In 2006, Zuckerberg was visiting Graham at the *Post*, and a *Post* reporter gave Zuckerberg a copy of his new book on politics. Zuckerberg was dismissive of the gift, telling Graham, "I'm never going to have time to read this." At the time, Zuckerberg did not even follow the news.[95]

Graham saw this as a teachable moment. According to Graham, "I teased him because there were very few things where you'll find unanimity about, and one of those things is that reading books is a good way to learn. There is no dissent on that point." To Zuckerberg's credit, Graham acknowledged, he was willing to listen. Graham added that "Mark eventually came to agree with me on that, and like everything he did, he picked it up very quickly and became a tremendous reader." In later years, Zuckerberg even had a copy of Chinese leader Xi Jinping's book of essays on government strategically placed on his desk for visiting Chinese reporters to see. It's likely that Zuckerberg was never as anti-reading as Graham's story suggests, but it does illustrate that Zuckerberg's interest in personally engaging with political or cultural topics was limited. He wanted to be the influencer— not the influenced.[96]

The next year, Zuckerberg would show that he was willing to learn from people as well as books. He hired Sheryl Sandberg, who had served previously as the chief of staff to Obama treasury secretary Larry Summers. She initially oversaw Facebook's political operations. A few years later, she would bring in Joel Kaplan to replace Marne Levine as head of policy. Kaplan, who had served as deputy chief of staff in the George W. Bush White House, would build up the Facebook Washington office into a formidable political operation, employing both Democrats and Republicans. He also saw the benefit of deploying his well-known CEO as a political asset, and would successfully work to get Zuckerberg more personally involved in advocating on behalf of the company in Washington.[97]

CHAPTER 10

BIG TECH DOMINATION

Presidents: Barack Obama, Donald Trump, Joe Biden

CEOs: Elon Musk, Tim Cook, Zuckerberg, Gates, Jobs, Buffett, Murdoch, Oprah

Jobs: Telling Obama What He Thought till the End

After Barack Obama became president, legendary Silicon Valley investor John Doerr told Obama he should meet with Jobs to get his views on American competitiveness. Obama agreed, but Jobs was reluctant, telling his wife Laurene: "I'm not going to get slotted in for a token meeting so that he can check off that he met with a CEO." When Jobs did go ahead with the meeting, it was after a five-day delay in responding to the presidential invite. He and Obama met in the fall of 2010 near the San Francisco airport, and Jobs spoke to Obama in stark terms for forty-five minutes, telling him, "You're headed for a one-term presidency." Jobs complained about regulations, America's subpar education system, and the teachers' unions.[1]

Jobs offered to put together a group of six CEOs who could make recommendations for improving America's business environment. White House advisers Valerie Jarrett added her own names to the list, irking the prickly and by now sick-with-cancer Jobs, who did not make the trip to Washington. He did, however, join Obama at another dinner organized by Doerr, this one in Silicon Valley in February of 2011. At this dinner, also attended by Facebook's Mark Zuckerberg,

(Continued)

Google's Eric Schmidt, and Oracle's Larry Ellison, among others, Jobs once again complained about America's lack of competitiveness, and particularly about America's lack of trained engineers. After the dinner, Jobs was annoyed with Obama, who, he said, is "very smart, but he kept explaining to us reasons why things can't get done. It infuriates me." Jobs was right that Obama failed to solve the problem, but his point struck a nerve, as Obama told his team multiple times afterwards that "we've got to find ways to train those 30,000 manufacturing engineers that Jobs told us about." [2]

Jobs would not get to see the engineer problem solved. In October 2011, he died of cancer. He was one of the nation's most influential CEOs in terms of his impact on American society, but he intentionally steered away from the roiling waters of politics, and even tacked away from American presidents. In 2022, President Joe Biden awarded Jobs the Presidential Medal of Freedom posthumously, likely sparing Jobs the annoyance of having to go to the White House to receive it.

Jobs differed from other CEOs in how he was able to steer clear of government and presidents for much of his career. His luxury-style products were somewhat less subject to regulation than other products: if one did not want to buy an Apple product, there were plenty of cheaper alternative products to choose from. His period away from Apple helped as well. By leaving and then having his triumphant return to the company he created, he did not seem to be a monopolistic empire builder as Rockefeller or Gates did. In addition, he died in 2011, just after the Clinton-Bush era and before the full emergence of the populist period of bipartisan anticorporatism that we are in currently. These factors helped Jobs largely avoid Washington and even criticize presidents as he saw fit. His successor would almost immediately have to take a different approach.

Elon Musk: Initially Benefitting from Government Largesse

Elon Musk has been a CEO at multiple companies—in areas as disparate as electric cars, tunnel digging, electronic payments, space exploration, and social media. He is an entrepreneurial capitalist who had multiple businesses dependent on government contracts, loans, and regulations. Despite these close governmental links, he is a Democrat loathed by Democrats. He is also a father of ten children—by three different women.

Musk is full of contradictions, something that he himself acknowledges. On *Saturday Night Live* on May 9, 2021, he joked, "To anyone I've offended, I just want to say: I reinvented electric cars and I'm sending people to Mars in a rocket ship. Did you think I was also going to be a chill, normal dude?" His quirky mix of interests, opinions, and talents, as well as his companies' varying degrees of dependence on government, has also understandably shaped his relationship with American presidents.[3]

Elon Musk was born in Pretoria, South Africa, in 1971. After his parents divorced, he moved to Durban with his mother, but then returned to Pretoria to be with his father. At ten years old, he first saw a computer and prevailed upon his father to buy him one. His father got him a VIC-20 with a five-kilobyte memory. The computer came with a book that included lessons on programming in BASIC. According to Musk, "It was supposed to take like six months to get through all the lessons. I just got super OCD on it and stayed up for three days with no sleep and did the entire thing." Musk was hooked.[4]

At age seventeen, Musk left South Africa for Canada. After a year of traveling the country and working low wage jobs, he began attending Queen's College. From there he transferred to the University of Pennsylvania. Musk briefly went to Stanford for graduate school before succumbing to the allure of Silicon Valley. He started his first company, Zip2, in 1995. It used the still-in-its-infancy internet to help customers find services near them. He netted $22 million when Compaq bought his company in 1999 for $307 million. Musk then worked on an electronic payments startup where he was CEO until Peter Thiel organized a successful putsch against Musk while Musk was on his honeymoon. Musk was angry, complaining that "this activity is heinous," but he came out ok, making about $175 million when eBay bought PayPal for $1.5 billion.[5]

Now that Musk was wealthy, he could do whatever he wanted. He had long told people that the three areas where he wanted to have an impact were space travel, the internet, and renewable energy, but acknowledged that, "It probably sounded like super-crazy talk." Musk went about making his talk not so crazy, moving to Los Angeles and focusing his efforts in those areas. All of his areas of interest would lead to encounters with American presidents.[6]

Musk now used his money rather than just his sweat equity to make an impact. He invested $10 million in Solar City, $70 million in Tesla, and $100 million in SpaceX. All seemed like risky bets, but Musk had both a high tolerance for risk and a sense that things would always work out for him. Thiel recalled Musk crashing and destroying his $1 million McLaren while they were driving to a meeting. Musk told Thiel that, "I had read all these stories about people who made money and bought sports cars and crashed them. But I knew it would never happen to me, so I didn't get any insurance."[7]

At Space X, Musk got a massive early boost from President Barack Obama. The George W. Bush administration had promised a return to the moon, but the incoming Obama administration kiboshed the project. In 2010, Obama still wanted to signal support for space exploration, but had little to highlight besides the forthcoming launch of a classified spaceplane called the X-37B. So Obama's team suggested a visit to the Kennedy Space Center and specifically the launch site for SpaceX, Musk's private-sector space exploration company. SpaceX was focused on providing a competitive solution in launch vehicles. In this effort, the company was heavily reliant on government contracts, so the company and its CEO were thrilled at the prospect of a visit by the company's biggest target customer. The selection of SpaceX as the site for a presidential visit, which Musk later characterized as "a sheer accident," was a triumph for SpaceX, generating priceless photos of young tech guru Elon Musk with the young tech-savvy president. Obama made no public statement, but it did not matter. The pictures were invaluable to the then little-known space company and to its leader. Obama still was not sure about the company, though. Throughout the meeting, Musk felt that Obama was studying him carefully, noting that, "I think he wanted to get a sense if I was dependable or a little nuts."

Whatever sense Obama got from that 2010 meeting must have been a good one, as the meeting launched an ongoing relationship between Musk and Obama. In May of 2012, Obama called Musk to congratulate him on the first successful private launch of a mission to the International Space Station. Musk recalled being inundated with congratulatory calls that day, and Obama's call came from a blocked number. Musk almost ignored it before taking the call and was glad he did. Musk tweeted about the incident in an epic humblebrag: "The President just called to say congrats. Caller ID was blocked, so at first I thought it was a telemarketer."[8]

In April 2014, Obama and Musk had their only private one-on-one meeting. The meeting was on Hyperloop, a company aiming to develop high-speed city-to-city transport. Musk later said that they also discussed the nascent area of artificial intelligence and the need for AI to have ethical guidelines and controls. In 2016, Obama exuberantly praised Musk on SpaceX's successful rocket landing on a drone ship. In response to the news, Obama tweeted, "Congrats SpaceX on landing a rocket at sea." He also added words that had to have delighted Musk, saying, "It's because of innovators like you & NASA that America continues to lead in space exploration."[9]

By this time, Obama had other reasons to see Musk as a helpful partner. Musk's electric car company, Tesla, made the Obama administration look good in another challenging high-priority area: green energy. In July of 2006, Musk introduced impressed onlookers to the beautifully designed Tesla roadster with the honest admission that, "Until today, all electric cars have sucked." A few years later, Obama was looking to tout taxpayer-funded investments in green energy, and the electric car that didn't suck seemed to be a promising bet. While the 2006 Roadster was too costly to be popular, the $50,000 Model S had potential. The George W. Bush administration had initiated a loan program for alternative fuel projects at the Department of Energy, and the Obama administration wanted to show that such a program could work. It announced two promising projects, for the solar company Solyndra, and then shortly after for Tesla, which would get $465 million from the Department of Energy to build two plants. Tesla would also be the tremendous beneficiary of federal and state taxpayer incentives that rewarded consumers for purchasing electric vehicles. These subsides—often more than $7,500—enabled liberals who had done well to do good by buying the now-trendy Tesla.[10]

Now, a decade and a half later, with almost three million Teslas on the road, it's clear that Tesla was a good bet. But it was far from a sure thing back then. Tesla had lost money every year since its founding. Solyndra got even more money from the federal government—$528 million, but it went bankrupt in 2011. Republican presidential challenger Mitt Romney saw these Obama administration investments as a vulnerability and made criticizing them a standard part of his case against Obama.

In October of 2011, Romney wrote an op-ed in the *Orange County Register* criticizing Obama's spending on green projects, writing that, "Like Solyndra, these loans are turning out to be historic opportunities to line the pockets of major campaign fundraisers." Romney also brought up the topic the next year in his successful first presidential debate against Obama, saying, "You put $90 billion— like 50 years' worth of breaks—into solar and wind, to Solyndra and Fisker and Tesla and Ener1. I mean, I had a friend who said, you don't just pick the winners and losers; you pick the losers." Romney was right about Solyndra, but ended up being wrong about Tesla. The company paid back its loans in 2013 and is now worth more than $600 billion.[11]

In 2012, Obama won re-election—and Musk supported him. (Musk would also vote for Hillary Clinton in 2016 and Joe Biden in 2020.) Obama's praise for Musk continued in his second term and reflected gratitude for a reliable Democrat, one who helped the administration out in two high priority areas of concern. The Elon Musk of the Obama years endeared himself to Democrats by showing how corporations could serve the interests of a tech and green-friendly federal government. As for Musk, his bold investments in those areas made him one of the richest men in the world.[12]

Gates: Attaining "Ambassador" Status Post-CEO

For Bill Gates, subsequent presidential administrations would be somewhat friendlier to Microsoft than the Clinton administration had been. In 2002, a new settlement that imposed some restrictions but did not break up the company resolved the antitrust question. This new settlement was too late for Microsoft, and for Gates. The company would no longer maintain its earlier dominance, and Gates was now more focused on his foundation than on his previous job of running the company. As head of the Gates Foundation, though, he would have far more frequent and friendlier interactions than he had had with presidents up to that point. In those interactions, there was a different Bill Gates than the heavy-handed monopoly maker who threatened competitors and did not return phone calls. Now, the world would see a changed Bill Gates. There had been hints of this Gates emerging in the Clinton years, as his philanthropy and his policy guru status grew. But in the post-Clinton years, the charitable guru became the entire persona. The sharp-elbowed entrepreneur would become a creature of an increasingly forgotten past.

In 2011, Barack Obama joked about this new incarnation of Bill Gates when he awarded the Presidential Medal of Freedom to Warren Buffett. In recalling how he upgraded the "thrifty" Buffett's tie, Obama then joked that "when Bill Gates came, he wanted one too." The next year, when Obama was in El Paso talking about immigration, he cited Gates as someone who agreed with Obama on immigration policy. According to Obama, "Bill Gates gets this. He knows a little something about the high-tech industry," adding, "The United States will find it far more difficult to maintain its competitive edge if it excludes those who are able and willing to help us compete."[13]

Obama continued to cite Gates during his reelection campaign in 2012, proving that unlike with Rockefeller, the Gates name did not "cut like a knife" with voters. At a fundraiser in Medina, Washington, Obama said that on the issue of energy production, "Ultimately, Bill Gates is right. What we need to actually solve the problem is a massive technological breakthrough." A few months later, at another fundraiser in Studio City, California, Obama cited not just Gates, but two of his other high-tech colleagues, saying, "I told a roomful of folks, some of whom work for Microsoft, Bill Gates is a genius, Steve Jobs is a genius, Mark Zuckerberg, amazing what they've accomplished." Obama tempered this compliment with a plug for the government, adding that "the Internet doesn't exist unless all of us together make an investment in something called DARPA that helped develop the Internet." These interactions show that Obama liked to use Gates to make his own policy and political points, but the friendly way in which he cited Gates proved that there was no political cost, and there may have even been political benefit, in citing the formerly demonized Gates.[14]

In Obama's second term, the mentions and the direct interactions with Gates became even more frequent. In 2014, Obama cited Gates twice in off-the-cuff question-and-answer sessions, suggesting that Gates was on Obama's mind and not just a prop in staff-written prepared remarks. In July of 2014, Obama cited Gates in making the case that wealth was ok, but that the government needed to remain vigilant on antitrust so as to maintain opportunities for the next generation of entrepreneurs. According to Obama, "If you're successful—if you are a company like Apple that innovated and—or a company like Microsoft that came up with a new concept—you should be able to get big and you should be able to be successful, and those who founded it, like Bill Gates, should be wealthy." Shifting gears, Obama added, "But what you also want to make sure of is, the next generation—the Googles or the Facebooks—that they can be successful too in that space."[15]

A few months later, at a town hall in Princeton, Indiana, Obama noted that he had recently had lunch with Gates and used him as an example of someone who will not increase consumption should he get additional dollars: "I had lunch with Bill Gates the other day. Now, Bill Gates has got a lot of money. And he's doing great things with it, by the way, doing great charitable work. But the truth of the matter is, is that if Bill Gates gets an extra million dollars, it's not like he's going to spend more money on food or go and buy an extra car or buy a new refrigerator, because he's already got everything he needs." In contrast to Gates, though, Obama said, "If somebody who is a low-wage worker gets a raise, first thing they're going to do is they're going to spend it, maybe on a new backpack for the kids or finally trade in that old beater for a new car."[16]

Obama referred to Gates's interest in technological innovation to solve the climate problem in 2015 and in 2016. He also referred to Gates as an inspiration for entrepreneurs in a 2016 town hall meeting in Vietnam, saying, "Bill Gates, who started Microsoft, he didn't start off thinking, 'I want to be a multibillionaire.' He started off thinking, 'I really like computers, and I want to find out how I can create really neat software.'"[17]

Obama granted the Presidential Medal of Freedom to Gates and his then-wife Melinda in 2016. The award was given for their philanthropic work, not the development of Microsoft, but this was still a far cry from Gates's experience with the previous Democratic administration. Obama did refer to Gates's background in lightly mocking him on his initial approach to Melinda. Obama told the crowd that when Gates met Melinda, "Bill's opening line was, 'Do you want to go out two weeks from this coming Saturday?' I mean, he's good with computers, but . . . " Regardless of the jibe, or the focus on the philanthropic side, the award provided further proof that Obama's Democratic administration harbored no ill will over Gates's antitrust fights with an earlier Democratic team.[18]

Oprah: Capitalizing on Her Political Power

In 2004, Oprah Winfrey encountered a candidate who got her to wield her newly recognized political power on his behalf. Oprah, along with much of the country, was mesmerized by Barack Obama's spellbinding speech at the 2004 Democratic convention. She interviewed the candidate for *O Magazine* that year, writing that Obama had "captured the attention of John Kerry, which landed him on the world stage for one of the most extraordinary speeches I've ever heard." In 2006, she had Senator Obama on her show. And in 2008, she broke a longstanding policy against endorsements and supported Obama for president. The endorsement, she recalled, "came from such a pure instinctive place."[19]

Unlike her previous caution, when it came to the Obama endorsement, she "didn't even think about it in terms of business or viewership." She had spent years building a show, a brand, and then a media empire by carefully avoiding political disputes. But Obama captivated her to such a degree, and she presumably now felt secure enough with her show and businesses, that she followed her conviction to go public for Obama.[20]

Her endorsement was big political news. The *New York Times's* Jeff Zeleny covered it, writing that, "It is the first time that Ms. Winfrey has endorsed—not to mention thrown her brand behind—a political candidate." She explained her decision on Larry King, saying that, "I think that what he stands for, what he has proven that he can stand for, what he has shown was worth me going out on a limb for—and I haven't done it in the past because I haven't felt that anybody, I didn't know anybody well enough to be able to say, I believe in this person." She even campaigned for Obama, attending events for him in Iowa, New Hampshire, and South Carolina. And she was well aware of the power of her endorsement. When asked if she planned to contribute to Obama's campaign, she said, "I think that my value to him, my support of him, is probably worth more than any check."[21]

Oprah was right. Obama won the 2008 election, and Oprah became a regular presence at the White House. She interviewed Barack and Michelle Obama in the Green Room in 2012. In 2013, Obama gave her the Presidential Medal of Freedom, calling her "the pinnacle of the entertainment universe." In 2016, she went to the White House for a United State of Women Summit with Michelle Obama. Oprah had made one endorsement in her entire career to that point, but she sure made it count.[22]

Welch: Seeing an Old Friend Become President

Barack Obama was an outspoken critic of CEO pay, as both Jack Welch and Jamie Dimon would learn. Therefore, it was not a surprise that Welch was not a big fan of Obama and what he called Obama's "nasty, nasty, nasty" comments about business. From his newfound perch as pundit and CNBC commentator, Welch regularly criticized Obama. In September of 2010, Welch derided Obama's handling of the economy, saying that, "I think the economy has been terrible, and they have not done things to move the economy forward," adding of the administration that, "They don't have the foggiest idea about business." Welch did take the opportunity to praise Bill Clinton and the way Clinton tacked back to the center after a poor start and a loss in the 1994 midterm elections that brought Republicans to power and made Newt Gingrich the first Republican Speaker of the House in four decades. Welch hoped that Obama would have a "Bill Clinton type conversion from 92 to 94." As Welch put it, "Bill Clinton certainly came around and became a hell [of a] president with Newt Gingrich for six years." Clinton's golf games with Welch probably did not hurt Welch's recollection of the Clinton presidency.[23]

Welch was on shakier ground in 2012, when he accused the Obama administration of fiddling with the unemployment statistics. In reaction to the October jobs numbers, Welch tweeted "Unbelievable jobs numbers. These Chicago guys will do anything . . . can't debate so change numbers." This notion of "Chicago guys" sounded conspiratorial, and mainstream economists criticized Welch for the accusation. At least one person, however, liked it, and that was Donald Trump. Trump called Welch's allegations "100 percent correct" and added, "I don't believe the number and neither do any of the other people that have intelligence."[24]

Trump and Welch had a long-standing personal and professional relationship. In the 1990s, GE Finance, one of the GE divisions that Welch cultivated as CEO, worked with Trump on New York Central Park's Trump International Hotel and Tower. In 1999, when Trump was doing one of his considerations of a presidential run, he touted Welch—"probably the greatest corporate leader in history of a major company"—as a possible running mate. Welch guest-starred on Trump's *The Apprentice*—an NBC and therefore GE-owned show—and touted his appearance with a joint Trump-Welch visit to NBC's *Today Show*. The men had an on-air mutual admiration society, with Welch saying, "Donald has been extremely helpful," and Trump adding, "There's nobody better than Jack."[25]

With Trump finally serious about running for president in 2016, Welch was a cheerleader for his long-standing friend and collaborator. He told CNBC that he wanted "a strong economy that creates jobs," and he felt that Trump would provide that. "I have no ax to grind with the Clintons," he said, adding, "I'm supporting an agenda. It's Donald Trump's agenda, and I'm for it." Welch had some qualms when Trump's offensive *Access Hollywood* comments came out in October of 2016, but he remained supportive, meeting with Trump multiple times in the White House, once again eschewing interest in a possible cabinet opportunity floated by Trump, and

(Continued)

joining, along with Jamie Dimon, Trump's Strategic and Policy Council. Of one visit to see his longtime friend in the White House, Welch said, "We had a hell of a meeting . . . I've been coming down here since 1980, and this was the first presidential meeting I've ever had where it was like talking to a peer."[26]

The post-Welch years have not been kind to GE. The company now has half the number of employees that it did under Welch, and a market cap a third of the size of its $500 billion landmark valuation under Welch. Some of the decline is due to Welch's decisions, but more of it stems from the shift in the consumer electronics business. The micro-electronics industry became far more about smart products, computers, tablets, and phones. GE, once the great innovator of the American economy, was left behind. As for Welch, his mostly friendly relations with presidents were directed towards keeping the government's hand off the tiller. For most of his tenure, Welch enjoyed policies that didn't directly undermine business— which contributed to his steady success as CEO. In his dealings with presidents, Welch addressed the challenges he knew about, but he— and they—did not see the global tectonic shifts that would eventually end GE's dominance.

Musk: Alienating Silicon Valley with His Trump Ties

As Obama left the White House and Donald Trump entered it, there was every reason to believe that Musk would be another anti-Trump Silicon Valley CEO. He had befriended Obama and publicly opposed Trump's election, saying in November of 2016 that Trump "is not the right guy. He doesn't seem to have the sort of character that reflects well on the United States." Yet a number of factors came together to make Musk's relationship with Trump defy expectations.

First was Musk's increasing success and fame, something that always appealed to Trump. From 2010 to 2020, Musk steadily moved from wealthy tech entrepreneur to multi-billionaire to household name. Another factor was Musk's willingness to cooperate with Trump once he became president, something that was likely influenced by the degree to which Musk's businesses were intertwined both with government contracts and, importantly, government regulations. Finally, Musk was also influenced by changes on the left during the Trump period, during which free speech declined as a value, and overall conformity, especially in attacking Trump, became the expectation. These new developments concerned Musk.[27]

Musk met with Trump twice after his election, once during the transition, and once after Trump became president. Trump also appointed Musk to two of his advisory councils, and called him for advice on NASA, telling him, "I want to make NASA great again." Despite criticism from employees and a left that was increasingly intolerant of dissent, Musk justified his cooperation with Trump by saying he was lobbying for better environmental and immigration policies. In February of 2017, he tweeted, "Activists should be pushing for more moderates to advise President, not fewer. How could having only extremists advise him possibly be good?" Musk's rebuttal revealed an early shift in both his position and the way he was perceived on the left. Yet Musk was also willing to criticize Trump. In June of 2017, he left the policy councils over Trump's decision to exit the Paris Climate Accords, tweeting, "Am departing presidential councils. Climate change is real. Leaving Paris is not good for America or the world." He also criticized Trump on tariffs, tweeting in March of 2018 that, "I am against import duties in general, but the current rules make things very difficult. It's like competing in an Olympic race wearing lead shoes."[28]

Trump and Musk also complimented one another. On *60 Minutes* in December of 2018, Musk acknowledged his disagreements with Trump but praised the idea of Trump's Space Force and noted that Trump was "amazingly good at Twitter." Trump, for his part, told CNBC in January 2020 that, "You have to give him credit" for Tesla and that, "He's also doing the rockets. He likes rockets. And he's doing good at rockets too, by the way." Trump even called Musk "one of our great geniuses," along with inventor Thomas Edison. The Covid-19 pandemic revealed additional commonalities between the two men. When Americans were blocked from leaving their houses and threatened with arrest, Musk exclaimed: "This is fascist. This is not democratic. This is not freedom. Give people back their goddamn freedom." When Musk fought California's state government in May of 2020 over its Covid-related restrictions, Trump sent a supportive tweet, saying, "California should let Tesla & @elonmusk open the plant, NOW. It can be done Fast & Safely!" An appreciative Musk replied, "Thank you!"[29]

The Trump-Musk relationship would remain complicated after Trump's presidency, with implications for both men. In response to the January 6, 2021, takeover of Congress, both Twitter and Facebook banned Trump from their platforms. Musk, who was increasingly concerned about free speech limitations on social media, used the Twitter ban on Trump as part of his rationale for acquiring Twitter—now renamed X—and eliminating many of the platform's speech guidelines. Musk said that he would allow Trump back on the platform, but Trump had an exclusivity deal with Truth Social and did not return, even after Musk's $44 billion purchase of the company. Yet Trump also called Musk a "bullshit artist," claiming that Musk's statement that "I've never voted for a Republican" contradicted his telling Trump that he had voted for Trump. (Musk denied saying that he'd done so.)[30]

In 2022, Musk said that Trump should not run again, prompting Trump to lash out at length on Truth Social, writing, "When Elon Musk came to the White House asking me for help on all of his many subsidized projects, whether it's electric cars that don't drive long enough, driverless cars that crash, or rocketships to nowhere, without which subsidies he'd be worthless, and telling me how he was a big Trump fan and Republican, I could have said, 'drop to your knees and beg,' and he would have done it." The sentiments would sound familiar to Mark Zuckerberg, who received similar post-administration treatment from Trump, but they also revealed the degree to which tech CEOs have to be careful about alienating government leaders.[31]

Gates: Testing the Limits of Bipartisanship in the Trump Years

For most of his career, Bill Gates had worked hard to maintain his bipartisan credentials, and on his ability to befriend politicians on both sides of the political divide. An early profile of him in *TIME* noted that Gates "vaguely considers himself a Democrat," but it seemed that the vagueness was the more important part of the sentence than the "Democrat" part. Gates even remained neutral in the 1996 presidential election, when it arguably might have helped him to back the heavily favored Clinton in an effort to get better treatment from the Department of Justice's Antitrust Division in a second Clinton term. In 2015, Melinda Gates told *Bloomberg* that the Gateses would not be endorsing Hillary Clinton, or anyone, in the 2016 campaign, despite the fact that they had worked closely together with Clinton and admired her work for women. As Melinda said, "We're going to work with whoever is in office. We never endorse a candidate." The coming of Donald Trump would test Gates's studied efforts at bipartisanship.[32]

For the first few years of the Trump administration, the interactions between Trump and the tech-giant-turned-philanthropist were largely as they had been with previous administrations. Shortly after receiving the Medal of Freedom from Obama, Gates came to visit President-elect Trump at Trump Tower during the transition. Although Gates had noted during the campaign that Trump "hasn't been known" for charitable giving, that did not preclude a friendly, hour-long post-election meeting on a wide range of topics. According to Gates, "We had a good conversation about innovation, how it can help in health, education, the impact of foreign aid and energy, and a wide-ranging conversation about power of innovation." Gates also compared Trump to Kennedy and his work to build a space program. Gates said that "in the same way President Kennedy talked about the space mission and got the country behind that, I think whether it's education or stopping epidemics . . . [or] in this energy space, there can be a very upbeat message that [Trump's] administration [is] going to organize things, get rid of regulatory barriers, and have American leadership through innovation." Given the hysteria over the Trump election in the high-tech world at the time, Gates's warm words about the incoming president were quite bold.[33]

Gates's supportive comments helped him maintain access to the new administration. In February of 2017, White House press secretary Sean Spicer reported that Trump and Gates met in the White House to discuss "their shared commitment to finding and stopping disease outbreaks around the world." Spicer added that, "The President particularly commended Mr. Gates for the Gates Foundation's work in global health and health security." Little did anyone know at the time that they were discussing the very issue that would at least temporarily put an end to Gates's political neutrality.[34]

Gates would continue to meet with Trump in order to press him on Gates's priorities. In March of 2018, Gates came to the White House again to argue for foreign aid from a health security perspective. According to Gates, "The preparedness we have for a pandemic, either a naturally caused pandemic or a bioterrorism, intention-caused pandemic, we don't have the tools, the preparedness, the capacity to deal with that." Gates was trying to convince Trump of the benefits of foreign aid for U.S. interests, even discounting the humanitarian side of things. Gates did appear to take a slight dig at Trump afterwards, but it was a gentle one. He told *Politico* after the meeting that, "It's hard for me to understand the notion that helping people that are poorer than we are is a bad thing. It's kind of in the Bible." Later that spring, Gates again made an understated joke at Trump's expense, saying on MSNBC that Trump had trouble telling HPV and HIV—two very different diseases—apart. According to Gates, "Both times he wanted to know if there was a difference between HIV and HPV, so I was able to explain that those are rarely confused with each other."[35]

Gates's Bible and HPV comments aside, his careful effort to stay on Trump's good side appeared to be working, at least from the perspective of providing access to the White House. On a 2018 visit, Trump even offered Gates the job of White House science adviser. Gates turned him down, saying that it was "not a good use of my time." As late as 2019, *USA Today*'s Marco della Cava noted that Gates "has never directly criticized President Donald Trump." Della Cava noted that while Trump and Gates had some policy differences, particularly on foreign aid, Gates was careful not to be seen as critical of Trump. On the question of American isolationism, della Cava noted that Gates had been diplomatic in saying, "If you interpret America First in certain ways, it would suggest not prioritizing the stability of Africa and American leadership." That diplomatic approach would soon change.[36]

Gates: Covid Prescience and the
Straining of the Trump Relationship

In 2015, Gates warned of the significant threat of a pandemic on the horizon. In a 2015 TED talk on the subject, Gates said that, "If anything kills over 10 million people in the next few decades, it's most likely to be a highly infectious virus rather than a war—not missiles but microbes." Gates also wrote a 2017 op-ed for *Business Insider* in which he warned that "epidemiologists say a fast-moving airborne pathogen could kill more than 30 million people in less than a year. And they say there is a reasonable probability the world will experience such an outbreak in the next 10 to 15 years."[37]

When the Covid-19 outbreak occurred in March of 2020, Gates's prescient warnings gave him a significant degree of credibility on the subject of pandemics. His foundation was also heavily involved in international health security and was the second largest funder of the World Health Organization, after the U.S. government. In April of 2020, Trump alienated Gates by announcing that the U.S. would be reducing funding for the WHO, saying at a press briefing, "We have not been treated properly. . . . The WHO pushed China's misinformation about the virus." Trump's WHO cut pushed Gates too far, and from then on, Gates broke with his carefully maintained neutrality. He and Melinda issued simultaneous and identical tweets to their tens of millions of followers, saying, "Halting funding for the World Health Organization during a world health crisis is as dangerous as it sounds. Their work is slowing the spread of COVID-19, and if that work is stopped, no other organization can replace them. The world needs @WHO now more than ever."[38]

With that rebuke issued, Gates emerged as a more frequent critic of Trump, breaking a multi-decade policy of not criticizing American presidents. In May, he told the *Wall Street Journal* that he had specifically warned Trump of the dangers of a pandemic in their 2016 post-election meeting at Trump Tower. In June, he told CNN that Trump's claim that the U.S. had more Covid cases than other countries because the U.S. was doing more testing was "completely false." He added that U.S. efforts to fight the pandemic were "not even close" to being sufficient. In August, Gates said that most U.S. Covid tests were "completely garbage," and for good measure complained about Trump's position on Microsoft's potential acquisition of TikTok, saying, "Having Trump kill off the only competitor, it's pretty bizarre." [39]

In October, as the presidential election neared, Gates increased the frequency of his critiques. He told *Meet the Press* that the U.S. was "running the worst testing system" of any country and warned of "lots of additional deaths coming if we don't get our act together." On October 14, he told CNBC that, "Most governments take advantage of their scientists and listen to them. They don't undermine them and attack them." He did not mention Trump by name but did not have to in order to make his point. Gates was even more direct on October 15, when he criticized White House coronavirus adviser Dr. Scott Atlas, telling *Yahoo Finance* that, "We now have a pseudo-expert advising the president." He added that he considered Atlas to be "off the rails." [40]

All of Gates's critiques had an impact, as he became a target for pro-Trump forces. Anti-Gates conspiracy theories proliferated, and the *New York Times* reported in April, shortly after the critiques started, that Gates "has effectively assumed the role occupied by George Soros, the billionaire financier and Democratic donor who has been a villain for the right." It was therefore with a palpable sense of relief that Gates tweeted on November 7, 2020, "Congratulations to President-Elect Biden and Vice President-Elect Harris. Thank you to the election officials and campaign workers who worked tirelessly to ensure a record number of Americans could cast a ballot and have it counted during such a challenging time for our country." The tweet itself was a rebuke, as Trump had not yet acknowledged the results of the election—he of course still has not—and Gates's tweet was a signal that he recognized that Trump had lost. [41]

With Trump out of office, Gates could return to his normal—and preferred—mode of presidential interaction, that of friendly outside adviser and philanthropist. It did not take long before that longstanding mode reasserted itself. On Inauguration Day, January 20, 2021, Gates wasted little time in making clear his interest in working with the new president on the pandemic and on climate issues. Gates issued a series of four tweets, signaling his interest in cooperation with the Biden administration and praising it for rejoining the Paris Climate Accord. When the senate confirmed Jennifer Granholm as Biden's energy secretary, Gates was her first meeting with a private citizen, within twenty-four hours of confirmation. The two would meet again a month later, on March 30, 2021.[42]

Gates's interactions with and on behalf of the Biden administration in its first few years were on a par with the frequency of his criticisms of the Trump administration in its last year. In April of 2021, Gates attended and spoke at Biden's global climate summit, which was designed as an apparent rebuke of the Trump-era environmental policies. In May of 2022, Gates spoke at the Biden-hosted Global COVID-19 Summit, where he committed $125 million in Gates Foundation money to the fight against the pandemic and thanked "the Biden administration for your efforts to secure more funding for global pandemic response." In July of that year, he lobbied West Virginia Democratic senator Joe Manchin on behalf of Biden's misnamed Inflation Reduction Act. The bill was instead mostly a climate-related bill, and Gates's intervention helped get Manchin to stop holding out and join the rest of his fellow Democrats in supporting it.[43]

Coda: Gates as Compartmentalizing Chameleon

In more than three decades of dealing with Washington and specifically with presidents, Bill Gates has shown a remarkable level of agility. His initial attitude of arrogance towards Washington led him to first ignore Washington and then lash out in anger when he felt his company was being targeted. As the Clinton administration progressed, he developed the strategy of compartmentalization, continuing to work against the Clinton administration—and even with its Republican opponents—on the antitrust action against Microsoft, even as he developed a friendly relationship with Clinton himself. When Gates stepped down as Microsoft CEO, he cultivated the image of an avuncular, non-partisan philanthropist, building relationships with presidents of both parties. This approach extended even initially to Trump, despite Trump's unpopularity in the philanthropic, high-tech, and Pacific Northwest realms that Gates occupied. Then, as Gates became increasingly disenchanted with Trump's approach to

(Continued)

Covid-19, he turned, issuing the most blistering criticisms he had ever publicly made of a U.S. president.

When Biden won, Gates reverted back to his friendly-to-all-presidents persona, although perhaps so much so as to preclude him from working closely with Republican presidents in the future.

Gates also continued to be an inspiration to other tech gurus trying to find their way in the second web-based wave of the American high-tech revolution. Mark Zuckerberg considered Gates his idol, and in the early days of Facebook would ignore the attention of interested women for a chance to gape at Gates. Zuckerberg would also take Gates's hard-won advice to develop a substantial Washington presence early on. Zuckerberg was not the only one who looked to Gates. Netflix CEO Reid Hoffman followed Gates's and Jeff Bezos's example in developing a succession plan in which they left the CEO slot to become company chairs after finding appropriate replacements.[44]

Bill Gates's chameleon-like approach to working with presidents brought with it significant benefits, but also had its limitations. He was unable to stop the antitrust effort against Microsoft, at great cost to his company but also to his personal reputation and perhaps even to the point of stepping down from his position as CEO. He did manage to befriend the Trump administration initially, but without much luck in getting his own policy priorities enacted. He then both turned on Trump and embraced Biden to a degree that raises questions over whether the non-partisan Gates of the first two decades of the twentieth century is still his preferred operating system.

Buffett: An Increasingly Political Player in an Increasingly Partisan Era

Buffett liked what he saw in Barack Obama. As early as 2005, Buffett said of Obama, "I've got a conviction about him that I don't get very often. He has as much potential as anyone I've seen to have an important impact over his lifetime on the course that America takes." Obama praised Buffett as well, saying that, "Warren

Buffett is one of those people that I listen to." Buffett raised funds for Obama's 2008 campaign, although he had also contributed to Hillary Clinton in the Democratic primaries. Obama spoke to Buffett frequently once he won the White House, and called him "one of my favorite people." On one of Buffett's White House visits, Obama, making fun of Buffett's well-known frugality, gave him a new tie as the one Buffett had on looked tattered.[45]

Obama and Buffett shared common cause on federal tax policy. Obama called his proposal to impose a minimum 30 percent tax on anyone earning over $1 million annually "the Buffett rule," based on Buffett's comparison with Bosanek's tax rates. Buffett wrote a *New York Times* op-ed praising the rule named in his honor. Obama did not get the rule passed, but he did get a potent talking point. As for Buffett, he would get the Presidential Medal of Freedom from Obama in 2010.[46]

Buffett was less enamored of the next two presidents, particularly Donald Trump. He criticized Trump in the 2016 campaign, calling on him to release his tax returns and disapproving of Trump's attack on a gold star family. Once Trump won the election, though, Buffett was more careful, telling CNN, "I support any president of the United States." In 2017, when asked why he was not more critical of Trump, Buffett said, "I'm not in the business of attacking any president, nor do I think I should be." Trump was similarly careful around Buffett, doing his classic mix of criticism and praise when he said in 2020 that, "Warren Buffett sold airlines a little while ago. He's been right his whole life, but sometimes even someone like Warren Buffett—I have a lot of respect for him—they make mistakes. They should have kept the airline stocks because the airline stocks went through the roof today."[47]

In 2020, Buffett surprised people by neither endorsing Joe Biden nor donating to his campaign. Buffett was less active as he approached his nineties, and his approach to politics was generally cautious. His business did not need help from Washington, nor was it threatened by federal policies. Buffett had certain policy preferences, and he promoted those on occasion, but he generally preferred his role as "the Oracle of Omaha" over the role of being yet another lobbyist for business or industry. As for direct interactions with presidents, Buffett has become more reflective in his later years, recalling that he had thus far lived under fifteen, or one third, of our nation's forty-five presidents, and he had "bought stocks under 14 of the 15." Buffett was willing to help if asked, but it was not his main goal. As he put it in 2016, "I've never called a president in my life. So I don't initiate 'em. But . . . but if any president asks me for help in any way, I mean, that's part of being a citizen."[48]

Oprah: No Longer Able to Stay out of Politics

After helping Barack Obama get elected in 2008, Oprah Winfrey could no longer cite her longstanding policy as a reason for staying on the sidelines. In 2016, she backed Hillary Clinton, using the slogan "I'm with her" while promoting the Oprah Winfrey Network show *Greenleaf* on *Entertainment Tonight*. Oprah couched her endorsement in terms of female empowerment, saying of Clinton's campaign, "Regardless of your politics, it's a seminal moment for women." She also got even more animated than she had for Obama, telling talk show host T. D. Jakes, "You get in conversations—and there's not a person in this room who hasn't been in the same conversation—where people say, 'I just don't know if I like her.' She not coming over to your house! You don't have to like her. You don't have to like her. Do you like this country? Do you like this country? You better get out there and vote."[49]

It was a political and business decision more than a personal one. Oprah had known Clinton's opponent, Donald Trump, for almost thirty years. Trump often praised her, even suggesting in 1999 that she serve as his vice president should he run for president. Trump had told Larry King, "I love Oprah," adding, "Oprah would always be my first choice." Trump went on, saying, "She is a terrific woman. She's somebody that's very special," and that, "She's popular. She's brilliant. She's a wonderful woman." He followed up with a 2000 book, *The America We Deserve*, in which he wrote that his "first choice for vice president would be Oprah Winfrey." He sent Oprah a copy of the book, and got a nice note from her in return, in which she wrote, "Too bad we're not running for office. What a team!"

She was also sentimental, writing to Trump, that "I have to tell you your comments made me a little weepy." But sixteen years later, Oprah knew that Trump, who was highly unpopular with female voters, was bad for her brand. As Trump lamented, "Sadly, once I announced for President, she never spoke to me again."[50]

Once Trump was president, her unhappiness with him was such that she even allowed Oprah for President speculation to emerge. At the 2018 Golden Globes, Seth Meyers joked that Trump ran in 2016 because of Meyers's 2011 White House Correspondents' Dinner routine saying that Trump was not qualified to be president. Leaning into the joke seven years later, Meyers said, "Some have said that night convinced him to run. So, if that's true, I just want to say: Oprah, you will never be president! You do not have what it takes." The joke led to lots of chatter among Democrats desperate to defeat Trump about what a formidable candidate Oprah would be. Unlike in previous boomlets, Oprah did not shoot down the speculation, tweeting out an article encouraging her to run and adding, "Thanks for your VOTE of confidence!" Trump noticed, and told reporters, "Yeah, I'd beat Oprah," but adding that, "Oprah would be a lot of fun. I know her very well . . . I like Oprah. I don't think she's gonna run."[51]

Trump was right. She did not run, although she had pitched Mitt Romney on running as an independent, with her as his running mate. Trump's replacement, Joe Biden, had also known Oprah for decades. After the 9/11 terrorist attacks, Biden, who was then chairman of the Senate Foreign Relations Committee, pitched Oprah on having him do the show so that he could deliver a positive message about how the U.S. could do anything if its people came together. She agreed, having him on the show and calling him "a key player in helping determine how our country will respond to these attacks."[52]

Unlike with Trump, Oprah was happy when this old acquaintance became president. On November 7, 2020, the day when Biden was declared the winner of the election, she tweeted: "Character rises. Decency rises. The Soul of America gets a reset. And it starts now: #BidenHarris." She also did separate town halls with Biden, and with his vice-president elect, Kamala Harris. *O Magazine*, her flagship publication, wrote an article "celebrating the rise of decency" and giving "Congratulations to President-elect Joe Biden and Vice President-elect Kamala Harris!" Oprah had long been reluctant to let herself and her businesses get involved in politics, but by 2020 things had changed so much that for someone with Oprah's female fan base, staying out of politics no longer seemed like a viable option.[53]

Murdoch: Coping with the War on Fox News

Fox News took a much friendlier approach to the George W. Bush administration than it had to the Clinton administration. Murdoch and his outlets—he acquired the *Wall Street Journal* in 2007—backed Bush politically and in his efforts to fight the War on Terror following the September 11, 2001, terrorist attacks on New York and Washington. Murdoch saw an opportunity in the mainstream media's regular bashing of Bush, who he felt was "persuasive, strong and articulate" in person. In 2007, Murdoch said in a public speech that apart from the *Post* and the *Journal*, "There's a sort of monolithic attack on him every day of the year." Fox News was the favorite outlet of the Bush administration, and was regularly displayed on televisions in the White House and other executive agencies during the Bush years.[54]

In 2008, though, Murdoch found Barack Obama to be "a phenomenon" and even considered endorsing him for president. Roger Ailes, however, understood that the Fox News audience would not go for it, even threatening to resign if Murdoch had gone ahead with the endorsement.[55]

Obama, for his part, had no such mixed feeling about Murdoch, nor did his administration. Obama's communications director Anita Dunn specifically targeted FNC as a hostile entity. Dunn told the *New York Times's* Brian Stelter that, "We're going to treat them the way we would treat an opponent. As they are undertaking a war against Barack Obama and the White House, we don't need to pretend that this is the way that legitimate news organizations behave." White House chief of staff Rahm Emanuel echoed a similar line, saying that, "It is not a news organization so much as it has a perspective." Obama himself weighed in, saying, "If media is operating basically as a talk radio format, then that's one thing, and if it's operating as a news outlet, then that's another." The White House accentuated its rhetorical attack by sending Obama for a round of interviews with all of the Sunday shows, except for the one on Fox.[56]

Obama's war on Fox News got some pushback. Stelter, who was sympathetic to the Obama administration, noted that this targeting of one news organization was "unusual." Fox News anchor Chris Wallace, who maintained a reputation as a non-partisan newsperson during his time at Fox, called the Obama team "the biggest bunch of crybabies I have dealt with in my 30 years in Washington." Murdoch, however, seemed unbothered, telling a group of shareholders that the White House war on Fox had led to higher ratings. His apparent apathy failed to capture the totality of the situation. Yes, Murdoch had built a powerful and political media platform, but he had also alienated a political party and made him a target in the process.[57]

Dimon: Buying into the Program under Obama

In 2008, Jamie Dimon supported Barack Obama for president. Dimon was on board with Obama's top priorities: infrastructure spending, green energy, and universal health care. Dimon and his wife had given over half a million dollars to Democrats over the preceding two decades. He donated $50,000 to Obama's inauguration and attended three days of festivities surrounding Obama's swearing in. The very fact that Dimon was a Wall Street Democrat appealed to Democrats who felt—not always correctly—that Republicans dominated the financial industry. Powerful House Democrat Barney Frank noted that Dimon was "one of the few Democratic C.E.O.'s in that line of work."[58]

Dimon also knew Obama from Chicago, where Dimon worked when he was at Bank One. Dimon knew other key Chicagoans as well. He was friendly with Chief of Staff Rahm Emanuel from Emanuel's time in the Clinton administration. In addition, when Dimon wanted to bolster government relations at JPMorgan Chase, he hired Bill Daley, a Chicago Democratic fixer who served as co-chair of the 2008 Obama campaign (and later became Obama's second chief of staff). Dimon was even on the short list to be Obama's secretary of the treasury.[59]

Given all of these close ties, it was little wonder that things started out smoothly for Dimon in the Obama administration. Dimon started coming to Washington twice a month, instead of his previous practice of twice a year. He met with top Obama officials, including Treasury Secretary Tim Geithner and White House economic adviser Larry Summers. He was in regular email contact with Emanuel and, when Geithner could not speak to Dimon's board at a meeting in Washington, Emanuel agreed to do it, although he later withdrew when the press criticized the planned appearance. The *New York Times* referred to Dimon as "President Obama's favorite banker."[60]

Yet despite the promising beginning, things soured in the relationship between Dimon and the Obama administration. In his typically far-sighted way, Dimon had predicted they would. The Obama administration saw the acceptance of TARP funds as a mechanism with which it could regulate corporate behavior. Dimon complained about TARP-imposed limits on hiring of foreign workers as well as executive compensation packages. He argued that he had reluctantly accepted the funding and had only done so to help the government get the program to work. These arguments did not sway the Obama administration, but Frank worked with Dimon to allow JPMorgan Chase to repay its $25 billion in June of 2009, thereby exiting the TARP program and giving it additional breathing room.[61]

But the damage was done. Protest movements from both sides of the political divide—the Tea Party on the right and Occupy Wall Street on the left—would point to the TARP program and use it as fuel for their own critiques—creating pressure that further pushed the Democratic and Republican parties apart on policy, but together in calling out Wall Street.

The protests complicated matters for Dimon. He liked Obama, but he did not like Obama's anti-bank rhetoric, part of which flowed from his left flank's increasing anti-Wall Street sentiments. In December of 2009, Obama went on *60 Minutes* and said, "I did not run for office to be helping out a bunch of fat-cat bankers," adding that, "What's really frustrating me right now is that you've got these same banks who benefited from taxpayer assistance who are fighting tooth and nail . . . against financial regulatory control." Over the course of the interview, Obama said that the financial meltdown was "caused in part by completely irresponsible actions on Wall Street." Obama was particularly miffed by the strategy of paying back TARP to escape its strictures, especially on executive compensation. JPMorgan Chase had done this, putting Dimon in Obama's cross hairs.[62]

Overall, Obama thought the banks were clueless. He noted that the continual paying of bonuses "I think tells me that the people on Wall Street still don't get it. They don't get it. They're still puzzled, why is it that people are mad at the banks?"

Obama went on to channel and even foster some of the bitterness that has emerged towards Wall Street over the last decade, saying that, "You guys are drawing down $10, $20 million bonuses after America went through the worst economic year that it's gone through in decades, and you guys caused the problem. And we've got ten percent unemployment. Why do you think people might be a little frustrated?"[63]

Obama's *60 Minutes* interview appeared one day before Obama met Dimon and other CEOs at the White House. Three of the executives, Goldman Sachs's Lloyd Blankfein, Morgan Stanley's John Mack, and Citigroup chairman Richard Parsons, did not make the meeting in person as their planes were delayed by bad weather. All three had flown commercial so as not to highlight their extravagant lifestyles. The self-assured Dimon, in contrast, flew private, but he made the meeting, as his more wary peers participated via conference call. [64]

Dimon disapproved of Obama's comments on CEOs. He chastised Obama, saying, "President Lincoln could have denigrated all Southerners. He didn't." If Dimon's comment was supposed to get Obama to tone down his rhetoric, it failed. After the meeting, Obama told the press that, "I made very clear that I have no intention of letting their lobbyists thwart reforms necessary to protect the American people. If they wish to fight common-sense consumer protections, that's a fight I'm more than willing to have."[65]

Despite their differences, Dimon was back at the White House a month later for lunch with Obama in January of 2010. This visit was in advance of Obama's State of the Union address. Dimon visited the White House twenty-two times between Obama's inauguration and the beginning of the second term. Nevertheless, the two never quite clicked. Dimon saw it as his role to challenge Obama when he disagreed with him—the same impulse that had led to the fallout with his mentor Sanford Weill. For his part, Obama seemed unfazed. He continued to criticize Wall Street bankers and pursue policies with which Wall Street disagreed.[66]

One of the problems that the two men faced in trying to maintain a relationship despite their differences was the progressive left. After the "fat cats" kerfuffle, Obama gave an interview with *Business Week* in which he appeared to soft pedal his criticisms of Dimon and his fellow Wall Street executives. When asked about

Dimon's $17 million bonus and Blankfein's $9 million one, Obama praised both men as "savvy businessmen" and surprised many by saying, "I, like most of the American people, don't begrudge people success or wealth. That is part of the free-market system."[67]

This apparent softening in his approach angered many of Obama's allies on the progressive left. MIT economist Simon Johnson said the comments make it sound like Obama "doesn't care, doesn't understand, doesn't get it." Leftist *New York Times* columnist Paul Krugman asked, "[H]ow is it possible, at this late date, for Obama to be this clueless?" George Goehl, executive director of the protest group National People's Action, saw the comments as a reason to doubt Obama's commitment to progressive causes, observing that, "It's as if his heart isn't in it, like he's chomping down some broccoli or his least favorite vegetable at the end of the dinner."[68]

The White House recognized that Obama's comments had created a political headache. It claimed that the remarks were taken out of context and put out a blog post clarifying that Obama disapproved of the sizable bonuses. In addition, press spokeswoman Jen Psaki tried to explain that not "begrudging" the bonuses did not indicate approval: "The President has said countless times as he did in the interview that he doesn't 'begrudge' the success of Americans, but he also expressed 'shock' at the size of bonuses and made clear that there are a number of steps that need to be taken to change the culture of Wall Street."[69]

Beyond the policy disagreements themselves, the very fact of the relationship between the two men led to questions. After Obama's January lunch with Dimon and five other CEOs, Obama press secretary Robert Gibbs got pushback from the press corps on the mixed message between Obama's words and his actions. Bloomberg News's Julianna Goldman specifically called out Dimon, asking, "What sort of message does it send that on Friday the president—last week the president says he's fighting against Wall Street, but then today he has Jamie Dimon here for lunch as part of the group of six CEOs?" Gibbs had to do some artful maneuvering to explain to the left the cognitive dissonance, saying, "There are a lot of people in that lunch that have said things that are in disagreement with what the president has talked about, but that doesn't—simply because they may disagree on some issues doesn't mean they're not going to talk on a whole range of issues relating to the soundness of our economy."[70]

Throughout the rest of the administration, Obama and his team continued to face political peril in consulting with Dimon. Dimon, for his part, saw engagement with the White House as an important part of his leadership. The long-standing relationship with Obama dating back to Chicago was only one of many that Dimon had developed with lawmakers via consistent and strategic outreach. Rick Lazio, a former New York Republican Congressman who headed JPMorgan Chase's government relations office during the Bush years, recalled Dimon hosting elected officials monthly in New York. He also encouraged his senior team to do similar types of relationship building. According to Lazio, "Jamie intellectually understood the importance of engaging with Washington," adding that, "I never got the sense that anybody was doing anything exceptional to help JPMorgan, it was more about creating a dynamic where there was a good exchange of ideas and some level of trust."[71]

To Dimon, if Obama got criticized for speaking with him, that was Obama's problem, not his. Yet the noise around Obama's interactions with Dimon was part of a larger narrative and ideological trajectory that led Democrats to express, often vehemently, their hostility to Dimon and his industry. A Senate Permanent Subcommittee on Investigations report regarding JPMorgan Chase's relationship with regulators portrayed Dimon and his team as contemptuous of government officials. One executive even called bank examiners "stupid." Dimon's reputation for bluntness contributed to the perception. As Daley, who had served as Obama's chief of staff from 2011 to 2012, said of Dimon, "He's a direct guy. That's what's charming about him, though some people interpret it as arrogance."[72]

Dimon's frustration with the Obama administration—and the ascent of the class-warfare left in particular—was such that by 2012, he was describing himself as "barely a Democrat." Dimon was particularly irked when the New York State attorney general sued JPMorgan Chase over what Bear Stearns had done with mortgage-backed securities in 2006 and 2007. From Dimon's perspective, JP Morgan Chase had done the government a favor by rescuing Bear Stearns, lost money in the process, and was now getting sued and demonized over what Bear

Stearns had done before JPMorgan Chase acquired it. Dimon had even warned regulators at the time of the acquisition about this eventuality, saying, "Please take into consideration when you want to come after us down the road for something that Bear Stearns did, that JP Morgan was asked to do this by the federal government." Dimon sounded huffy when he told a reporter, "We didn't participate with the Federal Reserve, OK? Let's get this one exactly right. We were asked to do it. We did it at great risk to ourselves." Dimon then added, "I think the government should think twice before they punish business every single time things go wrong." This last comment suggested that his anger with "government" went beyond just the actions of New York's opportunistic attorney general.[73]

The disagreements fed on themselves. An administration official told a reporter about Dimon and his industry, "They don't really understand how toxic they are." Dimon described an administration plan to get back bailout funds as a "punitive bank tax." The White House snubbed Dimon by not inviting him to a State Dinner attended by some of Dimon's peers. Dimon later referred to Obama's Treasury Secretary as "Timmy" Geithner rather than "Tim." At one point, the administration retaliated by keeping bank representatives out of discussions about a financial reform plan. Dimon complained to his friend Emanuel about anti-business rhetoric and told him, "Washington doesn't get it!" Emanuel responded, "You guys don't get the anger out there. Jamie, you're asking the American people to bail out the industry. And if they're going to bail out the industry, it's got to change its habits."[74]

Emanuel had a point. Dimon and company were seen as toxic, especially by Occupy Wall Street, the angry protest movement that started in 2011. In fact, Occupy specifically targeted Dimon, aiming to "visit" him at "one of his many skyscrapers." Dimon happened to be traveling in Asia at the time, so he was spared the unwelcome "visit," but the fact that Occupy was looking at him by name suggests bankers' unpopularity in twenty-first-century America.[75]

Dimon's notoriety did not completely shut off his access. He still got to go to the White House on occasion, and he maintained his carefully managed relationships with a host of government officials inside and outside of Washington. After Obama's reelection, Dimon's name was once again bandied about as a possible

Treasury Secretary, including by Warren Buffett, but it did not happen. The fraying of the policy relationship with the Obama administration took its toll. Even with Dimon's early support and personal efforts, the breakdown speaks volumes and demonstrates the degree of the interrelationship between business and government in the twenty-first century; despite their differences, the two sides could not easily separate.

Still, the Obama administration's embrace of the progressive critique weakened Dimon's influence. The administration's responses to the progressive left also revealed the degree to which anger about Wall Street, the financial world, and industry in general shaped—and warped—the conversation between the public and private sectors.[76]

Zuckerberg: Digitizing Presidential Campaigns

The digitalization of the presidential campaign began before Facebook. In 2004, the Bush-Cheney reelection campaign, helmed by Ken Mehlman, successfully used microtargeting of potential Bush voters to enhance turnout among its supporters. This new but not yet online tactic cross-referenced data from multiple databases on personal habits and preferences in order to identify outlets like smaller cable channels or niche magazines in which to advertise to reach potential voters. Going into the 2008 presidential campaign, experts predicted that microtargeting would be the go-to political tool for both the Democratic and Republican campaigns.[77]

What the experts predicted, however, was a mere drop in the bucket from an industry that was to transform politics—and the economy. In 2008, the presidential campaign of first term Illinois senator Barack Obama would deploy newer tools, previously unfamiliar to political operatives, to win an upset nomination victory over New York senator and former First Lady Hillary Clinton, and then win the presidency. The Obama campaign was staffed with tech-savvy aides from Silicon Valley, including Facebook cofounder and Zuckerberg pal Chris Hughes. The Silicon Valley presence was so prevalent that *The Atlantic* called the Obama 2008 campaign "the year's hottest start up." Hughes and his colleagues used the new technologies of MySpace, YouTube, and especially Facebook to attract and energize young voters and create a tremendous appetite for Obama. Hughes worked in the campaign's New Media Department, which handled the campaign's online presence and its fundraising. Their efforts helped Obama gain five million followers across fifteen different social media platforms. Half of them came from Facebook, leading the 2008 campaign to be dubbed "the Facebook election."[78]

Facebook and its liberal staff liked Obama, but they did not just help the campaign for altruistic or even for political motives. The 2008 campaign was a business opportunity for Facebook. Zuckerberg's sister Randi, who worked for Facebook, observed that Facebook use during the election signaled that the platform was evolving into "an indispensable tool for everyone, including those who wanted to do something really important, such as influence the outcome of a presidential election. This was also an opportunity for Facebook to expand its audience and influence."[79]

In 2008, Facebook was being deployed in the presidential race by the media as well. Randi Zuckerberg noted that Facebook's U.S. Politics app had garnered a million users by the start of 2008. The January 5, 2008, Democratic primary debate was co-sponsored by ABC and Facebook. Randi Zuckerberg talked about how thrilled they were at Facebook headquarters to hear ABC's Diane Sawyer take statistics from Facebook users live on air and to see the Facebook logo on the moderator's platform.[80]

After Obama's victory, Facebook worked with CNN to cover the 2009 presidential inauguration. Chris Hughes, the Facebook co-founder who had been embedded in the 2008 Obama campaign, told the Facebook staff afterwards that, "This project was Facebook at its best. It was a win for Facebook, a win for CNN, and a win for President Obama." Randi Zuckerberg saw it as a win as well, quadrupling CNN's viewership and getting an astounding twenty-six million concurrent video streams for Facebook. She later wrote that, "We had shown how innovation and politics could go hand in hand. We had proved that technology, when combined with broadcast television, could become a potent and entirely new force for engaging and mobilizing voters."[81]

In addition to the business advantages, there were political benefits to Facebook's 2008 role in multiple facets of the presidential race as well. Facebook had helped Obama get over the top, and Obama knew it. In 2016, in his eighth year as president, he shared a stage with Zuckerberg for a Global Entrepreneurship Summit held at Stanford University. During his remarks, Obama spoke directly to Zuckerberg about how he had benefited from the 2008 campaign's digital efforts. Obama said that, "People remark on my 2008 campaign and how we were really early adapters of so much technology. It wasn't because I knew what I was doing. It's because a bunch of 20-year-olds came to me and said, hey, there's this new thing called MySpace." The audience laughed as Zuckerberg winced, and Obama got another laugh by acknowledging, "That was just a little dig."[82]

Obama continued in that vein, saying, "[T]he point is that they had all this stuff that I had never heard of. And if I had tried to maintain control and said, 'No, no, no, we're going with pamphlets because I'm used to pamphlets, and I can control what's in the pamphlet,' then I might not be sitting here." Obama's self-awareness regarding how much his initial effort had been helped by the new digital campaign experts was reminiscent of John F. Kennedy's reaction to seeing a tape of his televised performance in the 1960 presidential campaign: "We wouldn't have had a prayer without that gadget." The two men, both from Harvard and both young junior senators from liberal states, had taken advantage of new technologies to help secure them the presidency. In contrast to Kennedy, though, in Obama's case it was one dominant company that had led the way.[83]

Zuckerberg: "Palling Around" with Obama

The Stanford event was far from the only event Obama would do with Zuckerberg in his two terms as president. In 2011, the Obama White House reached out to Facebook to ask if the company would be willing to host a Facebook Live event with the president. This request was part of the Obama communications team's hyper-focused selection of friendly platforms for presidential communications. CNN producer Jonathan Wald had observed that under Obama, "The White House is very careful who it picks for which message." The selection of Facebook Live for this particular event targeted both youth and high-tech workers. The audience inside the auditorium was small, but it was available on video to what was then Facebook's user base of five hundred million people.[84]

Interestingly, this was not the first time that a president had visited Facebook headquarters. In December of 2010, former president George W. Bush, who had been president when Facebook started in 2004, met with Zuckerberg to promote his memoir *Decision Points*. The event reached 6,500 people, who got to hear Bush give Zuckerberg advice that would come in handy: "It just comes with the territory. When you're president, or when you're a successful CEO, you get criticized."[85]

The timing of the Bush meeting was instructive. It took place one month after Republicans had won the House of Representatives in Obama's first midterm election. This led the political analyst Maury Litwack to speculate that Facebook, which was well aware of its liberal reputation and its well-publicized role helping Obama in 2008, was trying to develop credibility with the newly ascendant Republican congressional majority. To Litwack, Facebook had a purpose in the meeting that went beyond a desire to promote the former president's memoir: "I don't know if President Bush sold any books, but Facebook likely gained some powerful friends with a clever association that should give their lobbyists something to talk to legislators about in the coming year."[86]

The timing for the Obama event was advantageous for the administration and Facebook. It boosted the White House's reach to target audiences and provided a presidential imprimatur for Facebook. Randi Zuckerberg, who helped set up the event, later wrote that, "For Facebook, this was a defining moment. The president had every distribution channel available to him to communicate to the country. But out of every website, every TV channel, every radio station at his disposal, he had chosen Facebook as the best way to speak directly to the nation."[87]

At the event, Obama began by ribbing Zuckerberg. He introduced himself by saying, "My name is Barack Obama, and I'm the guy who got Mark Zuckerberg to wear a jacket and tie," scoring big laughs in the hall. This was both a public and a private joke. Everyone knew of Zuckerberg's predilection for casual clothes in the form of t-shirts, sneakers, jeans, and hoodies. But only Obama knew that the twenty-six-year-old Zuckerberg had been nervously sweating backstage in anticipation of being on stage—and on screen—with the president of the United States. Seeing how uncomfortable Zuckerberg was in his unfamiliar suit and tie, Obama recommended that both men relax by removing their jackets.[88]

Later, when hawking his budget proposals, Obama took a dig at Zuckerberg's newfound wealth, saying, "And then what we've said is let's take another trillion of that that we raise through a reform in the tax system that allows people like me—and, frankly, you, Mark—for paying a little more in taxes." When Zuckerberg responded, "I'm cool with that," Obama got another laugh from the crowd with the rejoinder, "I know you're okay with that." At the end, Zuckerberg thanked Obama by giving him a Facebook hoodie. Obama responded jokingly, "This is a high-fashion statement right here. This is beautiful." CNN's Mark Milian would describe their interactions as "palling around."[89]

Randi Zuckerberg recalled that the event "had been Facebook's biggest ever live-streaming event. The numbers were off the charts." But the White House benefited as well. It not only got the targeted audience it was looking for, but it also got to control the questions. According to CNN's Milian, using a Google platform for these kinds of events had enabled audiences to ask uncomfortable questions that the White House did not want asked. Using Facebook allowed the White House to let Facebook screen the questions. Given Facebook's interest in keeping Obama and the White House happy, this let the White House avoid questions that might have emerged on a more open platform.[90]

Zuckerberg: Facebook's Integration into the 2012 Obama Campaign

Facebook would become even more intertwined with—and even more essential to—Obama's 2012 campaign. According to Obama campaign operative Lis Smith, by 2012, digital was no longer just that strange activity engaged in by Silicon Valley types but an essential part of the entire presidential campaign operation. While digital was a separate unit in 2008, in 2012, "it was fully integrated into every aspect of the campaign." It was also an area of significant Obama advantage over his opponent, former Massachusetts governor Mitt Romney. Even though Facebook hosted a Republican debate in 2012—and would do so again in 2015 for the 2016 cycle—the Obama campaign took far better advantage of the new platforms than its Republican challenger. According to Smith, "We completely dominated Romney across every platform in terms of followers and engagement.

Obama had 20M followers on Twitter to Romney's 1.5M; 29M followers on Facebook to Romney's 8M; 233K subscribers on YouTube to Romney's 21K; and 1.4M followers on Instagram to Romney's 38K." It made a difference. Obama's Project Narwhal digital election monitoring effort propelled him to victory. Romney imitation Project Orca—thus named because orcas are predators of narwhals—was a buggy and costly flop.[91]

Obama's 2012 campaign had fully embraced digital, and Facebook in return embraced Obama back. And it was not just Facebook. On Election Day 2012, Obama official David Plouffe bragged of Google's executive chairman, Eric Schmidt, "On election night he was in our boiler room in Chicago." Schmidt had backed Obama in 2008, in a personal capacity of course, and the Obama and Google teams were closely linked. Google employees were regular visitors to the Obama White House, with Google lobbyist Johanna Shelton having 128 visits, far more than her colleagues at other companies. Over the course of the Obama administration, fifty-five Google employees moved into federal government, and 197 government employees went from government to Google. And in 2012, shortly after the Google and Schmidt-aided Obama victory, an FTC examination into Google fizzled out.[92]

Of course, Facebook was helpful to the Obama campaign as well. According to Media Director of Obama for America Carol Davidsen, the Obama campaign used Facebook information to get key insights into potential voters. Davidsen recalled that Facebook knew what the Obama campaign was doing, but allowed it, even as the practice violated Facebook privacy policies. According to Davidsen, the Obama campaign received a special exemption from Facebook to mine this data, and Facebook staffers "were very candid that they allowed us to do things they wouldn't have allowed someone else to do because they were on our side." Davidsen would not reveal this until 2018, when public opinion, and many Democrats, had turned against Facebook. Facebook was fine in 2012, but by 2018 she considered the data mining effort to be "creepy."[93]

Cooperation between Facebook and the Obama White House would continue in Obama's second term. In 2014, a public complaint from Zuckerberg about government surveillance programs spurred the White House into action, and

Zuckerberg scored a valuable call from President Obama to discuss the issue. A few days after Zuckerberg's surveillance-themed post, which carefully criticized the U.S. government but not specifically the Obama administration, Obama hosted a White House meeting with key tech executives, including Zuckerberg, to discuss the issue. The meeting was the second one on the topic in only four months, raising questions of whether Facebook and the White House were working together behind the scenes on it. The meeting gave Zuckerberg an opportunity to look strong on privacy, an issue on which he and his fellow tech executives were vulnerable. Silicon Valley was already being suspected of using private data for political and other purposes. A joke about Zuckerberg and privacy is indicative of the popular sentiment on the young mogul: "A boy walks up to Mark Zuckerberg. The boy says: 'My daddy said you were stealing our information.' Mark Zuckerberg replies: 'He isn't your dad.'"[94]

Following the call, a Facebook spokeswoman told reporters that Zuckerberg had "brought his concerns . . . directly to the president." She also praised the administration but said more needed to be done to protect privacy, implying that Facebook was on the side of doing more: "While the US Government has taken helpful steps to reform its surveillance practices, these are simply not enough . . . Facebook will keep urging the US Government to be more transparent about its practices and more protective of civil liberties."[95]

In 2016, Facebook also cooperated with the Obama administration on developing tools to identify Islamic radicals sympathetic to the Islamic State terror group. Obama had previously sent key members of his national security team, including his chief of staff, counterterrorism adviser, and secretary of Homeland Security to Silicon Valley to meet with tech executives to discuss the challenge of Islamic radicalism online. This meeting led to a January 8, 2016, summit, attended by Sandberg, where Facebook announced the new tools. In the campaign, as in the administration, the Facebook and Obama teams were working hand in glove.[96]

Facebook's cooperation with the 2012 campaign and the second Obama administration pushed the bounds of political partisanship, but the Facebook staff did not care. They liked the candidate and they liked the result. In 2016, a different candidate would find a new way to use Facebook in ways beneficial to his campaign, with very different results. The Facebook team, and the rest of Silicon Valley and the mainstream media, would look much less favorably on Facebook's behavior in that instance.

Dimon: Coping with Trump and Populism from the Right

In the Trump administration, Jamie Dimon faced a different populist critique, this time from the right. Unfortunately for Dimon, the electoral turn did not diminish the ire on the left; it even seemed to stoke it. The result was new anti-corporate rhetoric and policies on the right that had the possibility of bipartisan support. This new anti-corporate coalition created a novel threat for corporations, as they could no longer rely on Republicans to push back against Democratic assaults on business.

Like most analysts, Jamie Dimon did not expect Donald Trump to defeat Hillary Clinton in the 2016 election. In addressing attendees at a JPMorgan Chase conference in October of 2016, he stated, "I hope the next president, she reaches across the aisle." The crowd cheered. Aside from this uncharacteristic miss on a political prediction, his expression of hope that a Democratic president would reach "across the aisle" indicated he saw a worrisome ideological change in the party that went beyond the Obama years. Dimon likely expected his "barely a Democrat" status to continue. Ironically, his alienation from the Democrats helped in the initial transition to a new Republican administration.[97]

After Trump's unexpected victory a month later, Dimon pivoted. During the transition, Dimon expressed support for Trump's selection of prominent people from the business world for top administration posts as "a good reset." He also used the opportunity to praise business and defend it from some attacks proliferating on the left and in the Obama administration. According to Dimon, "I think it's a mistake for the American public to constantly be told that if you work for an oil company or you work for a bank, that automatically makes you bad." As for the Trump appointees, he was positive without being specific, saying, "I think a lot of these people are very qualified people who are patriots. They're going to want to help the country. They're not going to try to help their former company. These are people with deep knowledge that will hopefully do a great job."[98]

Dimon continued in the same vein in Davos, at the annual gathering of elites at the World Economic Forum. At a private lunch shortly after Trump's inauguration, Dimon provided an optimistic perspective on things in general, and on Trump in particular. According to Dimon, "Trump has put some professional people around himself. Experienced. Successful . . . they are knowledgeable and smart and they've been around the world. And hopefully when we go from one-liners—forget the one-liners and tweets—to serious policy, maybe we'll do the things that help America grow better and help the average American." Although the lunch was technically "private," Dimon agreed to allowing his remarks to be placed on the record.[99]

Dimon knew that his words would attract attention, and he further knew that the new president loved praise, especially from top business leaders he respected. It's a safe bet that he had prepared the remarks in advance and always planned to let the private remarks be placed on the record. If so, the plan worked. Dimon's name was once again bandied about as a possible secretary of the treasury, although once again it did not happen. More importantly, on February 3, Dimon was among a number of CEOs invited to the White House to discuss Trump's economic plans. Other CEOs in the group, labeled the "Strategic and Policy Forum," included Blackstone's Stephen Schwarzman, General Motors' Mary Barra, Tesla's Elon Musk, GE's former CEO Jack Welch, and Disney's Bob Iger.[100]

On the day of the meeting, Trump issued an executive order pledging an overhaul of the onerous reporting requirements from the 2010 Dodd-Frank financial overhaul. At the meeting, Trump saluted Dimon's expertise on the subject, saying, "There's nobody better to tell me about Dodd-Frank than Jamie, so you're going to tell me about it." Trump added that, "We expect to be cutting a lot out of Dodd-Frank, because, frankly, I have so many people, friends of mine that have nice businesses that can't borrow money—they just can't get any money—because the banks just won't let them borrow because of the rules and regulations in

Dodd-Frank." Here, Dimon made a smart bet, as Trump signed a partial Dodd-Frank repeal in May of 2018.[101]

With his early, strategic praise and his appearance at the White House, Dimon emerged at first with the informal designation of "the president's banker," an honorific previously bestowed on legendary financial figures such as Citicorp's Walter Wriston under Ronald Reagan and Bank of America's Hugh McColl under Bill Clinton. Dimon also continued to praise Trump in public, crediting him in March with releasing the economy's "animal spirits" and in April dismissing expectations of "there to be smooth sailing" early in an administration as "silly."[102]

Dimon appeared to have recovered from his difficulties with Obama and was back at the center of Washington developments. With Donald Trump, however, things were never simple. By May, Dimon was already being pressed by shareholders to respond to the demands of an anti-Trump letter-writing campaign that he leave Trump's "Strategic and Policy Forum." Dimon responded with a simple "no." He then added that he saw Trump as "the pilot flying our airplane. We're trying to help. I would try to help any president of the United States because I'm a patriot."[103]

In June, Trump took the U.S. out of the Paris Climate Accords. This increased the pressure on the CEOs in the "Strategic and Policy Forum"—most of whom were often hypersensitive to criticism in the mainstream media. Disney's Bob Iger resigned over the decision, while Tesla's Elon Musk also left. Dimon remained, but he made clear that he disagreed with Trump's decision on the climate deal. Despite this difference in policy, Dimon held firm on his patriotic rationale for staying on the advisory group, saying, "We have a responsibility to engage our elected officials to work constructively and advocate for policies that improve people's lives and protect our environment."[104]

The Strategic and Policy Forum was finally disbanded in August of 2017 after a white supremacist demonstration in Charlottesville, Virginia. A racist murdered one counter-protester, and Trump caused an uproar with his comment that "you also had people that were very fine people, on both sides." Trump claimed the comment was taken out of context, but the noise was too great for the members to stomach. Dimon never actually resigned from the council, as its members agreed to disband it, sparing the CEOs from angering Trump by issuing resignations. This also allowed Trump to claim that he had been the one to disband it. Dimon wrote a letter to employees explaining his actions, saying that "I strongly disagree with President Trump's reaction to the events that took place in Charlottesville over the past several days. Racism, intolerance and violence are always wrong. . . . It is a leader's role, in business or government, to bring people together, not tear them apart."[105]

This was the second letter Dimon wrote to employees on the matter. The first one, issued two days earlier, did not mention Trump. It said in part, "The violence was a stark reminder that we must recommit ourselves every day as a society to stand up and uphold the values that bind us as Americans." The existence of the two letters shows the intensity of the cross pressures on Dimon. He was trying to find a path where he would not alienate the sitting president but also assuage his angry employees. The incident shows the difficulty of maintaining CEO-president relations in the era of social media. Someone will always be outraged, and there will always be pressure to justify one's relationships in Washington.[106]

Dimon's careful management of the optics worked, to a degree. In February of 2018, Trump invited Dimon to a small private dinner with two other CEOs at the White House to discuss the economy. The other two CEOs in attendance were Eastman Chemical's Mark Costa and Cummins' Tom Linebarger. All three of them were there as representatives of the prestigious Business Roundtable, but Dimon was clearly the most prominent of the three. His attendance indicated that he was still willing to engage with the president after the Strategic and Policy Forum disbanded, and that Trump was still willing to engage with him.[107]

The Business Roundtable dinner notwithstanding, the Trump-Dimon relationship was not as warm as it had been in those early days of the administration. In September, Dimon made a rare misstep, bragging that he could beat Trump if he ran against him, adding that, "I'm as tough as he is, I'm smarter than he is. . . . He could punch me all he wants, it wouldn't work with me. I'd fight right back."

Dimon also signaled his continuing frustrations with the progressive left, saying, "I can't beat the liberal side of the Democratic Party."[108]

Dimon quickly realized that he had gone too far. He walked back his comments, saying both that he was not running and that his intemperate comments proved why. The *mea culpa* did not deter Trump, who always relished the opportunity to counterpunch. He fired off a Twitter assault on Dimon, writing that, "The problem with banker Jamie Dimon running for President is that he doesn't have the aptitude or 'smarts' & is a poor public speaker & nervous mess." Typically, Trump topped the comment off with a joke, adding, "Otherwise he is wonderful." Trump concluded the tweet with self-praise saying, "I've made a lot of bankers, and others, look much smarter than they are with my great economic policy!"[109]

Trump's designation of Dimon as "banker" Jamie Dimon demonstrated how both parties saw an opportunity to score quick political points by railing Wall Street and the financial industry. The Trump administration may have given Dimon better policies for his industry than the Obama administration, but the animus towards his industry was now firmly entrenched and endorsed by Republicans and Democrats.

Dimon: Resented on the Left for Working with Trump

Donald Trump's apparent souring on Dimon did not help Dimon with his own party. Many Democrats viewed Dimon with distaste, as the self-described "barely a Democrat" that he was. In the 2018 midterm elections, the Democrats were big winners. They took charge of the House of Representatives and they invited Dimon to testify at a hearing looking back a decade after the financial crisis. The hearing was titled "Holding Megabanks Accountable," indicating the new majority's perspective on things.

Maxine Waters, the California Democrat chairing the hearing of the House Financial Services Committee, started the proceedings with a warning for Dimon, "I understand that there is some attempt to get Mr. Dimon, per the press reports, to speak for everybody. We know that he is very smart. We know that he has been around for a long time. But this is not just his show today." The message was clear:

the friendly greetings and the monthly meetings with lawmakers were now a thing of the past. For both political parties, taking shots at Wall Street was far more popular than partnering with it.[110]

The election of Joe Biden had the potential to tone things down somewhat, but it did not change the overall ideological dynamic. Biden knew Dimon for a long time. Both of them had been on the national stage for decades, and Dimon had long taken outreach to lawmakers seriously. Biden, as had his predecessors, invited Dimon to meetings at the White House on the economy. In an October 2021 White House event on the public debt limit, Biden introduced Dimon as "my old buddy Jamie Dimon up there at JP Morgan." When told by Biden that he could call him "Joe," Dimon wisely stuck with the respectful "Mr. President." Biden set Dimon up with a question on the importance of raising the debt limit, and Dimon dutifully gave a five-point answer explaining Wall Street's perspective on the importance of the U.S. honoring its debts. Dimon also praised the administration on its China policy, telling reporters in 2023 that, "I think if you listen to Secretary Blinken, Secretary Yellen, national security adviser Jake Sullivan, the president—they're talking about the right things." Overall, thanks to his cooperative approach, Dimon was one of the four most frequent CEO visitors to the White House in the first year of the Biden administration.[111]

Despite these positive interactions, there was no bromance with Biden, nor membership in a "Strategic and Policy Forum," as with Trump. Both sides were being cautious in this new environment. Politicians were wary of associations with Wall Street, and Wall Street was wary of getting burned by anti-Wall Street rhetoric and policies. Dimon, as always, had a good sense of the challenge that lay before him. In 2023, CNN's Poppy Harlow asked Dimon if he thought a second term of Trump would be good for the economy. Dimon, facing a no-win situation, said, "I'm not going to answer that question." Harlow followed up and asked why. Dimon, by now used to the worsening tide of political vitriol from Washington, said simply, "I don't want to."[112]

Coda: Dimon and the Limits of Bipartisanship in a Hyperpartisan Era

Jamie Dimon's bipartisan approach to politics was perfect for the Clinton-Bush era in which he first came to politics. Even though he was a Democrat, the quintessential Wall Street executive befriended politicians on both sides of the aisle, while his massively profitable bank became increasingly enmeshed with an increasingly powerful and demanding federal government. He was the CEO nearly everyone looked to for signals regarding the direction of Wall Street and how business could relate to Washington.

Yet Dimon's skillful navigation of Washington and Wall Street in the Clinton and Bush years was more challenging in the subsequent period of scapegoating Wall Street and CEOs on both the left and the right. While his careful approach allowed him to maintain ties in a period of increasing political partisanship, even he was not immune to the class warfare and bipartisan critiques of the financial sector that typified America in the 2020s. For CEOs in this period, perhaps the best one could hope for was a low profile.

Tim Cook: The Operator Sees the Need for Political Involvement

In contrast to Apple founder Steve Jobs, Tim Cook was not a product creator. He was a manager whose executive leadership skills helped lift Apple to new heights. Cook focused on adding value through strong management and logistics, which led him to be more involved in Washington than Jobs was. In the highly regulated twenty-first century economy, Cook recognized the potential of getting favorable treatment from Washington. This strategic shift made Cook far more likely to interact with presidents, regardless of party affiliation, than Jobs had patience for.

Cook took over Apple in August of 2011, two months before Jobs lost his battle with cancer. Cook, who had been Apple's chief operating officer for 6 years, was a behind-the-scenes guy, someone who avoided the spotlight, but kept things crisp.

When Jobs tapped Cook to be his replacement, it was like "Think different," one of Apple's early ad campaigns. Jobs knew Cook had different skills and temperament. Cook saw it, too, telling Charlie Rose, "He knew, when he chose me, that I wasn't like him, that I'm not a carbon copy of him."[113]

Cook was born in Alabama in 1960. As a sixteen-year-old, he won a utility-company essay contest on "Rural Electric Cooperatives—Challengers of Yesterday, Today, Tomorrow." As part of his prize, he got to go to the White House and hear President Jimmy Carter speak. Three decades later, as Apple's CEO, he would return to the White House more regularly, where he would be speaking, and not just listening, to presidents.[114]

Unlike Jobs, Cook saw value in interacting with the nation's chief executive. In 2012, when Cook was still new to the CEO role, President Obama called him to discuss the looming "fiscal cliff," a combination of tax hikes and spending cuts threatening to come together on January 1, 2013. Speaker of the House John Boehner, who was on the Republican side of the negotiations from Obama, had already met with Cook to brief him on the situation. Obama and Boehner eventually came to an agreement without any particular input from Cook, but the incident revealed how Cook was already on the speed dial of the country's top political leaders. Jobs likely would have had little patience with either side.[115]

Cook wasn't just a neutralist. He had strong opinions on privacy and security, which were core to Apple's long-term business interests. In 2013, Cook, along with AT&T's Randall Stephenson, Google's Vint Cerf, and other executives, participated in a White House meeting on what White House officials described as part of a "national dialogue about how to best protect privacy in a digital era." Despite his inclusion in the 2013 meeting, Cook had concerns with the government's approach to privacy issues and was willing to call out those disagreements on behalf of Apple. In a 2015 speech at a cybersecurity summit organized by the White House, he warned that "history has shown us that sacrificing our right to privacy can have dire consequences."

Cook, speaking before Obama at the summit, was worried about Apple being asked to cooperate with law enforcement efforts to break the encryption of personal devices. According to Cook, "If those of us in positions of responsibility fail to do everything in our power to protect the right of privacy, we risk something far more valuable than money. We risk our way of life." Cook's speech, coming just before Obama spoke, was seen as a challenge to Obama and his administration's more law enforcement-centric approach.[116]

Cook continued to speak out on this issue. In December of 2015, the previously press-averse Cook went on *60 Minutes*, where he made the case that Americans should not have to choose between privacy and digital security, saying, "We're America, we should have both." Two weeks later, in a private meeting with senior administration officials in Silicon Valley, he criticized the Obama team for being unwilling to advocate for unbreakable encryption with "no backdoors." Attorney General Loretta Lynch pushed back on behalf of the administration, calling for the need for "balance" between privacy and security. Cook's inclusion in meetings like these did not mean that he liked the result. In 2016, towards the end of the Obama administration, Cook went on ABC's *World News Tonight* to express his disappointment in how the Obama administration ultimately handled the privacy vs. security challenge. After an Islamist terrorist killed fourteen people in San Bernardino in December of 2015, the Obama administration pursued a court order to force Apple to decrypt the terrorist's phone. Apple learned about the administration's filing from the press, which caught Cook off guard. He expressed his disappointment. Ultimately, Cook realized that appearing to be on the side of a terrorist over law enforcement was a tough place to be, acknowledging that, "Some things are hard, some things are right, and some things are both. This is one of those things."[117]

Zuckerberg: "The Facebook Election"

Even before the 2016 election took place, there were widespread concerns that Facebook could sway the election in favor of the chaos candidate Donald Trump. The concerns manifested both inside and outside of Facebook. Back in 2014, *Buzzfeed*'s Ben Smith, a savvy media analyst, speculated that Facebook would soon be the primary election battleground in American politics. In a *Buzzfeed* article called "The Facebook Election," Smith wrote that "Facebook is on the cusp—and I suspect 2016 will be the year this becomes clear—of replacing television advertising as the place where American elections are fought and won."[118]

Smith's essay used Facebook sentiment data to look at the prospects of eight potential GOP candidates for 2016. None of the eight was the eventual winner. As it turned out, that winner would not only roil American politics in general, but he would also particularly frighten liberal voters in Silicon Valley, precisely the sort of people who worked for Facebook.[119]

On March 4, 2016, an internal Facebook question generated for a Q-and-A session with Zuckerberg asked, "What responsibility does Facebook have to help prevent President Trump in 2017?" The question was revealing on many levels. It certainly had not emerged earlier, when Facebook was providing assistance and even violating its own policies to aid the campaign of Barack Obama. The question revealed what many people already recognized: a heavy liberal tilt among the Facebook workforce as well as Silicon Valley. [120]

Beyond the liberalism of the workforce, the question also revealed what Facebook employees believed were the platform's true capabilities. Facebook, and implicitly its all-powerful CEO, they were saying, had the ability to determine the outcome of a presidential election. Within any other company this might be seen as arrogance. When it came to Facebook, it was probably closer to a form of realism.

Cook: Complications under Trump

Things got more complicated for Cook in the Donald Trump administration. Of course, Cook was not alone in having complicated relations with the Trump White House. But with Apple and Trump, the complications began during the presidential campaign, and regarding the same problem that Apple was having with the Obama White House. At a South Carolina campaign stop in February of 2016, Trump called for a boycott of Apple products based on the company's position on the terrorist's iPhone. Trump attributed Apple's position to Silicon Valley liberalism, saying that, "Tim Cook is looking to do a big number, probably to show how liberal he is." Neither the Obama nor the Trump opposition changed Apple's view on the matter. Ultimately, the FBI decrypted the terrorist's iPhone without Apple's assistance, but the incident seemed poised to put Apple and Trump in a potentially bad place.[121]

Further complicating matters was the fact that Cook opposed Trump in the 2016 campaign. He donated a quarter of a million dollars to Hillary Clinton-affiliated groups in that cycle. Given Trump's unpopularity in Silicon Valley and the near universal predictions of a Hillary victory, supporting Hillary seemed to be a smart bet. Trump, however, surprised nearly all prognosticators and won the election, putting Apple in a potential bind. Jobs might have remained disengaged but Cook took the opposite tack, working hard to develop a relationship with the new president.[122]

Cook began coming to Washington regularly, every four to six weeks, to meet with Trump and other senior officials. He impressed Trump economics adviser—and former Goldman Sachs head—Gary Cohn by not focusing exclusively on Apple's needs in those meetings. According to Cohn, "Our dinners weren't talking all about Apple tariffs and technology. I'd say 75% was talking about life. To be a good CEO, to get things accomplished, you have to be personable, you have to be a good communicator and a good listener, and Tim was all of those things." As part of his Trump charm offensive, Cook also went to White House CEO summits and visited Trump at his golf club in Bedminster. Trump happily told the *Wall Street Journal* in 2017 that Cook promised to build "three big plants, beautiful plants" in the U.S. Cook's efforts bore fruit. When Trump threatened to impose tariffs on China, Cook reached out to Trump's son-in-law Jared Kushner and asked for a chance to argue against the tariffs to Trump. The two spoke on the phone, and shortly afterwards Trump exempted iPhones from his tariff plan.[123]

Cook continued to cooperate with the Trump administration through 2018 and 2019. They met regularly, and Cook went to Trump's first State Dinner for the French president Emmanuel Macron in April of 2018. A few months before the invitation, Cook publicly credited the Trump tax cuts with leading Apple to repatriate $38 billion in taxes on money held overseas, and to invest $350 billion in the U.S. economy. Trump loved this acknowledgment, tweeting in response that, "I promised that my policies would allow companies like Apple to bring massive amounts of money back to the United States. Great to see Apple follow through as a result of TAX CUTS. Huge win for American workers and the USA!"[124]

Cook did not agree with everything Trump did, criticizing his decision to leave the Paris Climate Accords and disagreeing with him on aspects of immigration policy. But he kept the lines of communication open. He did not get upset when Trump called him "Tim Apple" at a meeting of the American Workforce Policy Advisory Board in March of 2019. Later that year, Cook welcomed Trump to an Apple factory in Austin, Texas, where Trump bragged about creating American jobs. When asked in August of 2019 why he had such a good relationship with Cook, Trump was quite clear about what Cook brought to the table: "That's why he's a great executive because he calls me, and others don't. Others go out and hire very expensive consultants, and Tim Cook calls Donald Trump directly. Pretty good. And I would take their call, too, but the only one that calls me is Tim Cook."[125]

Cook's efforts differed from other tech CEOs, and from his predecessor Jobs as well. Cook not only went to Washington more, but he also had Apple spending more on lobbying. From 2017 to 2019, Apple spent $18 million on lobbying, still half of what Amazon and Alphabet were spending, but considerably more than it had been spending under Jobs. And while Jobs would have snubbed or ignored Trump, Cook kept on reaching out. Some of Apple's liberal employees noticed and grumbled, but Cook did not face an all-out revolt, as Zuckerberg would when Trump posted, "When the looting starts, the shooting starts," during the George Floyd protests in 2020. Here Cook had two advantages over Zuckerberg. Apple was not a content provider, so it did not have to make decisions about giving Trump access to its platforms. Second, Cook was incredibly beneficial to Apple's bottom line, as the company became the world's first trillion-dollar company in the Trump years. Whatever Cook was doing, it was working, and the employees were reaping the benefits. Of course, so was Cook, who became a billionaire as a non-founding CEO, a relatively rare accomplishment.[126]

When Joe Biden became president, Cook said that he did not plan to change his approach. In early 2021, he told podcast host and tech journalist Kara Swisher that, "Our focus is not on the politics of it. It's on the policy. That's what we did during President Trump's administration. That's what we'll be doing during President Biden's administration." It helped that Cook already knew Biden from the Obama administration. In 2012, at a meeting with tech leaders in Palo Alto, Vice President Biden asked Cook why Apple could not make iPhones in the U.S. The question put Cook on the spot, but it also helped him learn what Biden liked, and he acted accordingly when Biden became president. In 2021, Cook announced that Apple would be making some Macintoshes in America. In 2022, he went to an event with Biden in Arizona where he announced that Apple would be buying U.S.-made microchips. And in 2023, Cook joined Indian prime minister Narendra Modi, who also had a close relationship with Cook, for two events at the Biden White House: a CEO technology meeting on artificial intelligence and another State Dinner.[127]

Tim Cook was a steward, not an inventor, but a very successful steward. He recognized that managing the world's most valuable company in twenty-first-century America required good relations with a powerful federal government that had many tools with which it could punish companies or shape corporate behavior. When Cook changed tactics from Jobs and began engaging more seriously with Washington, he did not do it because he wanted to, he did it because he had to.

Murdoch: Skeptical of Trump but Wary of His Audience

Murdoch initially did not want to see Donald Trump as Obama's replacement. Early in 2015, Trump had invited Murdoch to lunch to inform him of his planned presidential run. Murdoch, who remembered Trump talking of running but not following through in previous election cycles, was skeptical, and told him that, "You have to be prepared to be rapped up badly." Ailes was also skeptical, but he recognized that Trump was good for ratings. Trump watched Fox regularly and would get angered by criticism from Fox personalities, including Brett Baier, Stephen Hayes, and Megyn Kelly.[128]

Once Trump emerged as the likely winner of the GOP primary, Murdoch and Fox began treating him better. The two had dinner at Trump's Aberdeen golf course, along with Murdoch's then- wife Jerry Hall, Jared Kushner, and Ivanka Trump. Once Trump won the presidency, Fox became even more pro-Trump, and Trump reciprocated, often praising Murdoch in his speeches. Multiple Fox employees, including Bill Shine and Heather Nauert, joined the administration.

Trump took Murdoch's calls immediately, once yelling at his assistant Madeleine Westerhout, "Never put Rupert Murdoch on hold! Never!" Beyond the personal side, there were regulatory benefits as well. Trump's Justice Department slowed down AT&T's acquisition of FNC rival CNN via its Time Warner merger, although the deal eventually went through.[129]

With Trump, Murdoch had found the close relationship with a president that he had long wanted, but it came at a cost. While always conservative, Fox had also tried to remain a serious news organization. In the Trump administration, Murdoch and the network became too cozy with the administration, leading serious news people to question whether its "fair and balanced" slogan remained operative."[130]

The close relationship came apart on election night 2020, when Fox was the first network to call Arizona, a crucial and closely contested state, for Trump's challenger, Joe Biden. Fox later called the election for Biden as well, although it was not first on that front. Trump continued to claim that he won the election, a stance that "dismayed" Murdoch. Murdoch thought that Trump would go away following his defeat, telling a friend after the election that, "In another month Trump will be becoming irrelevant and we'll have lots to say about Biden, Dems, and appointments." He was wrong. Trump stayed on the scene, and Fox's net favorability ratings dropped precipitously among conservatives. Fox downplayed Trump and tried to push Florida governor Ron DeSantis, but Trump stayed very much in the picture, dominating the 2024 Republican primaries.[131]

Murdoch ended up with the worst of both worlds. Fox had hurt its reputation and had to pay over $750 million for slandering Dominion Voting Systems as its on-air talent continued to press the case that Trump had been cheated in the election, something that Murdoch did not believe. He had alienated Trump, even as Trump remained the driving force in Republican politics. And the new president, Joe Biden, saw Murdoch as an enemy, calling him "the most dangerous man in the world." Even anti-Fox strategist Anita Dunn was back, working as a top adviser in the Biden White House. With Trump and Biden emerging as the two most likely candidates to run in a rematch, Murdoch found himself in a situation where both leading candidates for president despised him. Murdoch, not coincidentally, stepped down from his CEO slot in the summer of 2023. Yes, he was old and that was a factor in his decision. But the degree to which the apparent heads of both major American political parties hated him had to have played a part in his decision as well.[132]

Facebook and Trump: Swaying the Race for a Less-Favored Candidate

Facebook had previously claimed that it was not seeking to sway American politics. In 2014, Sandberg declared that, "Facebook would never try to control elections." But even this statement revealed that perhaps Facebook could control elections, if only it got over its internal aversion to trying.[133]

As for the aversion to trying, perhaps that aversion would go away if only the company's CEO felt strongly enough. Zuckerberg had not minded when the company helped Obama in 2008 and 2012. It was not quite controlling the election, but it was putting the thumb on a scale in a nation where presidential elections were being decided by a few thousand votes in key areas. And in this case, Zuckerberg made it rather clear how he felt about the 2016 race. In April of 2016, perhaps with the internal employee question in mind, Zuckerberg said at a developer conference, "I hear fearful voices calling for building walls and distancing people they label as 'others.' I hear them calling for blocking free expression, for slowing immigration, for reducing trade, and in some cases, even for cutting access to the internet." The statement did not mention Donald Trump by name, but no one had any doubt regarding who Zuckerberg was referring to.[134]

Even with the possibility of Facebook affecting the election, most credible observers did not see what was coming. In August of 2016, the *Washington Post*'s Jim Tankersley wrote that, "Hillary Clinton is running arguably the most digital presidential campaign in U.S. history. Donald Trump is running one of the most analog campaigns in recent memory." Tankersley added that, "The Clinton team is bent on finding more effective ways to identify supporters and ensure they cast ballots; Trump is, famously and unapologetically, sticking to a 1980s-era focus on courting attention and voters via television." What Tankersley and the *Post* did not know was that the Trump campaign had just hired Cambridge Analytica to identify both potential Trump voters and shaky Clinton voters. The analytics company used this data to shape a $70 million monthly advertising campaign on Facebook that was designed to attract those potential Trump voters and discourage those shaky Clinton voters with targeted messaging. The messaging was designed to get potential Trump voters to the polls, and to keep shaky Clinton voters away.[135]

Cambridge Analytica's work played a role in Trump's 2016 victory. The campaign's Project Alamo effort developed a database of twelve to fourteen million emails, credit card and contact information for 2.5 million donors, and helped raise $275 million for the campaign. Overall, the Trump campaign would purchase more than 5.9 million Facebook ads in 2016, spending $44 million in the process. Both Facebook and Trump benefited from the relationship.[136]

Trump campaign strategist Steve Bannon said just before the election that, "I wouldn't have come aboard, even for Trump, if I hadn't known they were building this massive Facebook and data engine." Bannon explained that he was aware of what Facebook could do from his experience at Breitbart News, where he had been executive chairman. Between 2015 and the 2016 election, Breitbart's reach exploded, going from 100,000 to 1.5 million likes, and passing the *New York Times* in user interactions. Facebook, which featured Breitbart, powered this explosion. According to Bannon, "Facebook is what propelled Breitbart to a massive audience. We know its power."[137]

Something was happening with Facebook, and the company notified Obama's national security team about it. In June of 2016, Facebook told the FBI about its suspicions that Russian intelligence was trying to spread fake news via Facebook. Russian accounts purchased over three thousand ads on Facebook—a tiny fraction of the ads purchased by the Trump campaign—during the campaign, a clear effort by Russia to interfere with American elections. The Russian interference story remains a hotly debated one, and while Russia did not appear to sway the 2016 election, it remains the case that Russia did try, and saw Facebook as one mechanism for doing so.[138]

Even if stories of the impact of Russian interference were overblown, the fact of Facebook's impact was not. The Trump campaign successfully used Facebook and Cambridge Analytica during the campaign, and this in itself was as shocking to Democrats and Silicon Valley as the Russian interference allegations. Some Facebook employees took a week off from work to grieve over Hillary Clinton's defeat. Managers sent emails about how terrible the defeat was for women and minorities. One of those grieving was Sandberg, who unhappily attended a meeting of tech execs at Trump Tower shortly after Trump's victory. Trump told the group that, "Everybody in this room has to like me," but Sandberg definitely did not see herself in that category.[139]

Facebook's assistance to presidential campaigns in 2008 and 2012 had been celebrated. In 2016, it was mourned. In their shock and anger over the election defeat, some Facebook employees turned their ire on Zuckerberg. He said shortly after the election that the idea that Facebook had swayed the election to Trump was "crazy." Others in the company were not so sure, and even formed an internal group to look into the question. For his part, Obama also thought Zuckerberg was not taking the issue seriously enough. He pulled Zuckerberg aside at a Lima, Peru, conclave of world leaders to issue a warning that he needed to take a harder look at the issue of disinformation on Facebook and that the problem could worsen in future election cycles. At the end of Trump's first year in office, *New York Magazine*'s Max Read wrote that, "Not even President-Pope-Viceroy Zuckerberg himself seemed prepared for the role Facebook has played in global politics this past year." [140]

Part of the shock was due to revulsion towards Trump himself. But there was more. In Silicon Valley, and among Democratic partisans more generally, there was a belief that the digital world was their world and that it could be used in perpetuity to help Democratic campaigns, leaving the Luddite Republicans behind. 2016 changed that. The belief that this was the new normal ran aground because the new normal does not stay the same in presidential politics. Things change, parties adapt. In 1988, Democrats were despondent at having lost a third consecutive presidential election, as analysts fretted that the electoral map permanently favored Republicans. In 1992, Bill Clinton changed that, with an assist from Independent Party candidate Ross Perot, who received 19 percent of the popular vote. But now the political assumptions were being rejiggered once again, and Zuckerberg would have to figure out how to navigate things in the new New Normal.

The Zuck and Trump Show

With Trump now in the White House, Facebook had to recalibrate for the post-Obama era. The picture of grieving staff mourning Trump's win was not a good look for the company or for Silicon Valley in general to the new group in power. Joel Kaplan, the former Bush aide, accompanied Sandberg on her meeting to Trump Tower. With Republicans in the White House, Kaplan warned both Sandberg and Zuckerberg that they needed to improve their relationships with Republicans. Kaplan was well-suited to do this. A former Marine and Supreme Court clerk for conservative justice Antonin Scalia, Kaplan demonstrated his GOP bona fides by interviewing with the transition team at Trump Tower for the position of Director of the Office of Management and Budget. Kaplan did not pursue the job beyond that, but the very fact of the interview showed that he was a well-regarded figure in Republican circles.[141]

Under Kaplan's tutelage, Zuckerberg increasingly took on the role of emissary to Washington from the company. Sure, Facebook was known as a liberal company in liberal Silicon Valley, but it did have some points separating it from its high-tech competitors. Facebook had, of course, helped the Trump campaign in 2016. Intentionally or inadvertently, it mattered little: Facebook was part of the win. As for Kaplan himself, he was close friends with Brett Kavanaugh, Trump's second of three picks for a Supreme Court seat. When Kaplan appeared in the hearing room sitting behind Kavanaugh at his contentious 2018 Senate confirmation hearings, he said he was there supporting his friend, but many Facebook employees saw it as a signal that Facebook was endorsing Kavanaugh.[142]

In addition, Facebook was an important engine for the dissemination of conservative ideas. As the journalist Max Chafkin wrote, "Facebook wasn't biased against conservative media; it was conservative media." While Google adjusted its algorithm to promote mainstream, mostly liberal, news services, Facebook let vox populi rule. Whatever was trending was promoted, and this gave conservative stories and conservative outlets more oxygen than they got from other tech platforms.[143]

One of the reasons that Facebook kept this popularity contest feature was board member Peter Thiel. In contrast to most senior Silicon Valley executives, Thiel was a libertarian conservative, and he had even backed Trump in the election. He served as a kind of ambassador to the conservative world from Facebook, which help add to the company's credibility with conservatives. In May of 2016, when news leaked of an internal Facebook effort to suppress conservative stories, Thiel put together a meeting of Zuckerberg and sixteen key conservative thought leaders to tamp down the controversy. Tucker Carlson, Glenn Beck, and Dana Perino were among the attendees. From their perspective, the dinner was a success. Afterwards, Zuckerberg posted a declaration of continued political neutrality, saying, "We built Facebook to be a platform for all ideas. Our community's success depends on everyone feeling comfortable sharing anything they want." To progressives and many Facebook employees who wanted to see some of Trump's comments restricted, the message read quite differently, indicating that Trump and other conservatives would continue to have the ability to post what they wanted on the platform.[144]

Thiel was helpful to Facebook and Zuckerberg with the right in other ways as well. He served as a liaison to senior people in the Trump administration, including most especially Trump's son-in-law and top aide, Jared Kushner. The connection was sorely needed. In June of 2019, Trump had ranted about the tech companies, calling them "all Democrats" and "totally biased towards Democrats." He then issued a classically vague Trumpian threat, saying, "Look, we should be suing Google and Facebook and all that, which perhaps we will, OK?" A generation earlier, a government lawsuit had grievously wounded Microsoft. Facebook took notice. In September, Zuckerberg came by the Oval Office for a surprise meeting with Trump. It was the first time the two had met, and Trump tweeted a photo saying it was a "nice" meeting.[145]

A month later, in October of 2019, Thiel joined Zuckerberg and Kushner for a secret dinner at the White House. In the background were the Democratic presidential primaries, which had taken a decidedly anti-Facebook turn.

Democratic presidential hopeful Elizabeth Warren was threatening to break up Facebook, which Zuckerberg would come to view as "an existential threat." Some inside the Trump administration, including Attorney General Bill Barr, were warning Trump about "the effects that concentrated power has on our society and culture." Barr even told Trump before taking the job that, "One of my top priorities would be looking at the large online platforms from an antitrust perspective." Still, Zuckerberg feared Warren more, and with good reason.[146]

The friendly dinner led to an apparent deal. Facebook would continue to allow political speech without fact-checking, a filter that hurt Trump both because of the liberal bias of the fact checkers and Trump's tendency to make unfounded claims. In exchange, the Trump administration would not pursue onerous regulations against Facebook and the tech platforms.[147]

Following the dinner, Facebook continued to provide equal access to conservative sites on its platform. Zuckerberg and Kushner spoke regularly, and Thiel pressed the idea to conservatives that Facebook was a better actor than many of the other tech platforms. When the dinner became public a year later, Zuckerberg expressed somewhat friendly words towards the third president he had met: "One of the things that I found interesting is that he's kind of exactly the same in person as you'd expect him to be from the stuff that he says publicly."[148]

Zuckerberg: Unfriending Trump in 2020

Zuckerberg and Facebook would adhere to its part of the deal until the insanity of 2020. The year started out relatively normal, with Trump praising Zuckerberg on CNBC's "Squawkbox." In the interview, Trump said of Zuckerberg, "I heard he's going to run for president. That wouldn't be too frightening I don't think. But he does have that monster behind him." The "monster" was not defined, but presumably Trump was referring to Facebook and its largely anti-Trump employee base. In addition, Trump seemed pleased with Facebook's continued willingness to show political ads regardless of ideology, saying, "He's done a hell of a job when you think of it. And he's gonna do what he has to do." This statement would seem to support the idea of the October dinner "deal" wherein Facebook would not limit Trump ads and Trump would not target Zuckerberg's company.[149]

Trump's praise of Zuckerberg continued into February. Of course, Trump being Trump, the praise came in the context of how well Trump was doing on Facebook. On February 14, Trump tweeted, "Great honor, I think? Mark Zuckerberg recently stated that 'Donald J. Trump is Number 1 on Facebook.'" The playful "I think" reflected the disdain he and his base had for Silicon Valley, in general, but that was pretty light criticism for Zuckerberg.[150]

Trump would elaborate on this theme of his popularity on Facebook six days later at a "Make America Great Again" rally in Colorado Springs. At the event, Trump described the October dinner between him and Zuckerberg, saying, "We had dinner recently just because I want them to pay taxes. I wanna find out what's going on. But he walked in, he's smart, and he said, 'I just wanna congratulate you.' Small dinner, a few people. He said, 'You're number one in the world in Facebook.'"[151]

Trump being Trump, he then asked Zuckerberg, "Who's number two?" When Zuckerberg told him that it was "Prime Minister Modi of India," Trump responded, "'Wait a minute, wait a minute. He's got 1.5 billion people and we have 350 so he should be number one.' But we're never gonna give up that position of number one in the world for our country, for Facebook, for Twitter, for anything, and they still haven't figured it out. They have not figured it out." Trump was clearly proud to report his number one status, and he praised Zuckerberg by calling him "smart," but he also got his digs in, saying he wanted them to pay taxes and implying that Silicon Valley did not want America to be number one. They did not know it yet, but Trump's rally riff on Zuckerberg would be the high point of their relationship.[152]

Zuckerberg: Navigating Trump's Final Months

Over the course of the remaining eleven months of Trump's presidency, Facebook and Trump would be on the opposite sides of a series of flashpoint issues. The relationship between Trump and Zuckerberg that had seemed friendly in late 2019 and early 2020 frayed, raising the question of whether Facebook internally made a strategic decision to change directions and become an outright Trump opponent.

Things began to deteriorate at the end of May of 2020. The nation was roiling from prolonged Covid lockdowns and the killing of George Floyd by Minneapolis police. Protests broke out across the country, many but not all of them violent. Trump added to the controversy when he tweeted and posted his "looting starts, shooting starts" comment, as it was a fraught phrase echoing back to its uses in the 1960s by Miami Police chief Walter Headley and segregationist presidential candidate George Wallace. Twitter, which had become increasingly more likely than Facebook to censor Trump on its platform, put a warning on the tweet, raising the question of what Facebook would do about the similar post in its platform. To raise the stakes, Trump had hit back at Twitter, tweeting that, "Twitter is doing nothing about all of the lies & propaganda being put out by China or the Radical Left Democrat Party. They have targeted Republicans, Conservatives & the President of the United States. Section 230 should be revoked by Congress. Until then, it will be regulated!" [153]

Trump had just issued an executive order targeting social media companies, specifically mentioning Facebook for practicing "selective censorship." Facebook and Kaplan had worked hard to maintain amicable relations with the Trump administration—too hard in the eyes of many of its staff—and the explosive situation threatened that careful balance.

Facebook called the White House to express its concern about the post. The White House heard the call differently, as if Zuckerberg was trying to cover himself in the face of a rebellious staff. Zuckerberg even said, "I have a staff problem," a phrase that stuck with the White House staffers listening to the call. White House staffers jokingly characterized Zuckerberg's attitude as, "Mark doesn't think there's anything wrong with" what Trump had posted, "but his staff is going to kill him."[154]

That afternoon, Trump called Zuckerberg's cell phone. Zuckerberg later said that he was more direct this time to Trump about his discomfort with the "divisive and inflammatory" post. Still, Zuckerberg allowed the post to stay up. Trump then amended the post to add that the comment was "spoken as a fact, not as a statement," adding, "I don't want this to happen." These softening words put the original post more safely inside Facebook's user policies, ending the question of whether it needed to be taken down.[155]

Zuckerberg put out his own post, saying that he had "been struggling with how to respond to the President's tweets and posts all day," and that he personally had "a visceral negative reaction to this kind of divisive and inflammatory rhetoric." But he also defended free speech, saying, "I'm responsible for reacting not just in my personal capacity but as the leader of an institution committed to free expression." He then contrasted Facebook with its competitor, saying, "Unlike Twitter, we do not have a policy of putting a warning in front of posts that may incite violence because we believe that if a post incites violence, it should be removed regardless of whether it is newsworthy, even if it comes from a politician." Finally, he acknowledged that he had been talking to the Trump administration about the issue, noting, "We have been in touch with the White House today to explain these policies as well." [156]

Zuckerberg's actions tamped down a potential employee revolt. In addition to the post, Zuckerberg also hosted an internal town hall to explain his decision. There was still internal disagreement: Over a thousand Facebook employees reported in an internal poll that Facebook was wrong to have kept Trump's post up. Hundreds of employees staged a virtual walkout, and some posted fist avatars, but the worst of it was over. [157]

In July, Zuckerberg would be more directly critical of Trump, this time regarding the Covid-19 crisis. Four months earlier, in the early stages of the pandemic, Facebook had created an "information center" to highlight authoritative information about the virus. Zuckerberg had justified this move from a free speech perspective by saying, "You don't allow people to yell fire in a crowded room, and I think that's similar to people spreading misinformation in the time of an outbreak like this." This was an implicit dig at Trump, who had highlighted unproven therapies for Sars-Cov-2 and once even suggested ingesting bleach as a possible therapy. In response, Zuckerberg revealed his own positions by hosting an interview with coronavirus task force member Dr. Anthony Fauci of the National Institutes of Health. During the interview, Zuckerberg said, "At this point, it is clear that the trajectory in the U.S. is significantly worse than in many countries and that our government and this administration have been considerably less effective in handling this." He also got a little cheeky when he responded to a comment by Fauci with, "I think you might be quite generous in your description of the government's response here." CBS's Irina Ivanova characterized Zuckerberg's "blunt criticism" during the interview as "a departure from his typically more reserved remarks about the Trump administration." The interview was an indication of the degree to which Trump-Zuckerberg relations had declined since their May phone call.[158]

Things got worse as the political campaign between Trump and Democratic nominee Joe Biden heated up. In the fall of 2020, a bizarre story came out in the *New York Post* that Biden's troubled son Hunter had left a computer for repair at a Delaware computer shop. Hunter never picked up the laptop, and the store owner revealed that the laptop contained embarrassing information that was potentially incriminating regarding Hunter. The strangeness of the laptop's emergence led many in the media and Silicon Valley to claim that the *Post* story must be Russian disinformation or a Republican dirty trick and consequently to call for the suppression of the story. Almost every media outlet and tech company complied, and soon the story was only available on conservative news platforms.

At Facebook, Director of Communications Andy Stone announced the decision of what to do about the laptop story. Stone was a former Democratic staffer on Capitol Hill who had previously worked for Senators Barbara Boxer and John Kerry. Stone said that Facebook would not distribute the story until Facebook's third-party fact-checkers verified it. This served as a virtual guarantee that Facebook would go along with the mainstream media consensus not to allow for distribution of the story. Facebook also adjusted its internal algorithms in such a way as to limit the laptop story's spread. Facebook had not gone as far as Twitter, which blocked the *New York Post* from Twitter, but it did effectively participate in the broader effort to shut down the story.

The Trump administration noticed, and was not happy. One unnamed Trump official noted that Joel Kaplan's wizardry could no longer help manage the relationship, saying, "Joel's conservative credentials couldn't make up for what the company was doing."[159]

Only in the spring of 2022 did the *New York Times* and *Washington Post* finally admit that the laptop story was real. As strange as the way the story became public was, Hunter had indeed left his laptop at a computer repair store. By the time the mainstream media made this admission, Biden was safely ensconced in office. In closing ranks on the issue of suppressing discussion of the story, the media companies and tech companies, Facebook among them, had done Joe Biden and his campaign a real service. In a close election, suppression of the negative information about Biden's son and the Democratic candidate's role in a web of corruption could have made a difference.[160]

Beyond helping squelch the laptop story, Zuckerberg would do one other thing that put his heavy thumb on the scale for Biden in a significant way. Like many of the creator CEOs who had come before him, Zuckerberg created a philanthropy to both help distribute his wealth and potentially create some good will for himself. The Chan Zuckerberg Initiative—Zuckerberg was married to Priscilla Chan—was founded in 2015 as an LLC, rather than the traditional 501(c)(3) foundation structure. This alternative tax designation put it more on the category of philanthrocapitalism—which looks for returns on its charitable "investments" than traditional philanthropy. It also lets the organization get involved in politics in ways that foundations cannot.

CZI's political involvement took a number of forms. One was direct political support or opposition to specific California ballot initiatives, including one pushing stricter sentences for criminal offenses (opposed) and another in support of public school funding (supported). After 2020, CZI announced that it would no longer engage in this kind of direct political involvement. But CZI had another political mission, one arguably more influential and that would have an impact on the 2020 election.

In September and October of 2020, CZI donated $419 million to the Center for Tech and Civic Life and the Center for Election Innovation and Research. Both of these entities were ostensibly dedicated to facilitating voting in the challenging pandemic year of 2020, and went to pay for masks, gloves, and equipment for processing mail-in ballots. The grants became controversial because the groups in question were run by progressive activists, which led to accusations that the grants were designed to promote voting by people in places inclined to vote for Democrats. In October of 2021, Trump said that in making these grants,

Zuckerberg was a "criminal" and that he had "change[d] the course of a Presidential Election."[161]

There is no basis for saying the grants were criminal in any way, but Trump was not the only one on the right to raise concerns about them. The Capital Research Center, a conservative research group, issued a report in December 2021 that found that, "New discoveries reveal that Zuckerberg funneled $328 million through the Silicon Valley Community Foundation, the largest community foundation in America and a notable donor to left-wing causes." The CRC added that, "Zuckerberg is perhaps the single largest donor to the foundation, dumping close to $2 billion into the pass-through since 2010."[162]

In her book *Rigged*, conservative writer Mollie Hemingway analyzed this effort and concluded that "Zuckerberg didn't just help Democrats by censoring their political opponents. He directly funded liberal groups running partisan get-out-the-vote operations. In fact, he helped those groups infiltrate election offices in key swing states by doling out large grants to crucial districts." In 2023, Elon Musk would say that, "My understanding is that Zuckerberg spent $400 million in the last election nominally in a get out the vote campaign but really fundamentally in support of Democrats."[163]

Zuckerberg denied that there was any partisan component to the donations and went on to claim the funds went to more Republican districts than Democratic ones. But the denials did not matter. The notion that these "Zuckerbucks" affected the election result became received wisdom on the right. The idea of the donations, coupled with Zuckerberg's clear souring on Trump in the second half of 2020, washed away the impact of Kaplan and Zuckerberg's efforts throughout most of the Trump administration to have Facebook be seen on the right as a different kind of tech company. Zuckerberg recognized the political impact of the donations as well. In 2022, Zuckerberg spokesman Ben LaBolt—a former Obama and future Biden communications official—acknowledged that the CZI no longer planned to donate to the Center for Tech and Civic Life and the Center for Election Innovation and Research. "They have no plans to repeat that donation," LaBolt said. But based on Zuckerberg's consistent effort to shape the public taste and be an influencer, it is likely some other evolution in his efforts could be expected in the future.[164]

After Trump lost the 2020 election, Zuckerberg acknowledged to his staff that Biden would be the next president. Although he did not issue a public congratulations at that time, the acknowledgment was enough to annoy Trump. He also alienated Trump after the January 6, 2021, riots at the Capitol, joining Twitter in removing Trump's account in response to Trump's irresponsible actions in the lead-up to and on that day. Although Trump behaved poorly, indefinitely suspending him from the platform did raise questions of why Trump was banned but assorted dictators and American enemies around the world faced no such sanctions. In January of 2023, Facebook, now named Meta, ended the suspension, allowing Trump to return to both Facebook and Instagram, which the company owned as well.[165]

Musk: The Consequences of Alienating the Left

The final stages of the Trump administration broke the Trump-Musk relationship. Unfortunately for Musk, that rupture did not help him with Joe Biden's administration. Musk's early cooperation with Trump, his loud pushback against the Covid lockdowns, and most especially his removal of speech guidelines following his acquisition of Twitter/X, infuriated the left, which did not like billionaires to begin with. Musk's occasional jibes at Biden, including calling him "a damp sock puppet," did not help, either, nor did Musk's attempts to keep his workforce union-free. The fact that Musk had voted for Biden and tweeted early on that, "I'm super fired up that the new administration is focused on climate" did little to increase his popularity in Biden-world.[166]

Musk's pariah status on the left had a real-world impact on his businesses. When Biden had a climate summit in August of 2021, the head of the largest electric car manufacturer in the U.S. went conspicuously not invited. Biden further snubbed Tesla when he said, implausibly, that General Motors "electrified the entire automobile industry," although the comment had the added impact of making the octogenarian Biden seem out of touch. Musk even complained, to little avail, that, "This administration has done everything it can to sideline & ignore Tesla."[167]

Musk was further annoyed when a Biden Super Bowl tweet got twenty-nine million views, dwarfing the nine million views Musk received for his own

Super Bowl tweet. He had his engineers adjust Twitter's algorithm so that it would amplify Musk's own tweets by a factor of one thousand. Musk could to some extent control how his own tweets were amplified, but he could not stop a regulatory regime that now had him in its sights. After an Obama administration that wanted to boost Tesla and a Trump administration that was largely uninterested in heavily regulating business, Tesla started to feel the regulatory boot in the Biden years. The National Highway Traffic Safety Administration launched an investigation into Tesla's AI software and issued eight safety recalls of Tesla's popular Model 3 vehicle. Other probes or assaults on Musk businesses came from Biden's Justice Department, his National Labor Relations Board, his Fish and Wildlife Service, and his Federal Trade Commission. There was no indication that Biden himself had ordered all these probes, but he did not have to. As the *Wall Street Journal* wrote, "We doubt any order from on high has been sent, but it doesn't need to be when a figure becomes Progressive Enemy No. 1." The lesson for all CEOs, not just Elon Musk, was clear: alienating an administration and its regulatory apparatuses could be extremely harmful to a company.[168]

With both the former and current president hostile to him and his companies, Musk backed Florida Republican governor Ron DeSantis for president in 2024. Unfortunately for Musk, Trump and Biden were at the time the most likely candidates to win the 2024, leaving Musk with a far lower percentage option. Trump and Biden's domination of their respective party primaries revealed the degree to which Musk's risk-taking, let-it-all-hang-out, say-what-you-think approach to presidential-CEO relations has its downsides. For someone whose companies rely on both government contracts and a favorable regulatory environment, his alienation of presidents—and the ideological foot soldiers that staff their administrations—put him in an increasingly challenging situation with the multi-tentacled regulatory state.[169]

Zuckerberg: The Biden Administration's Cold Shoulder

With Biden coming into office, Facebook took quick steps to ingratiate itself with the new administration. The increasing actions against Trump in late 2020 and early 2021 were not enough. Most Democrats, including the new president-elect, were skeptical of the company, regardless of its 2020 action. Within a few weeks of the election, Facebook was in the midst of planning a "charm offensive" to win over the incoming team. This PR effort included actively encouraging users to take the newly approved coronavirus vaccine—a high priority for the Biden administration, and to promote content touting the Paris Climate Agreement, which Trump had left and Biden planned to rejoin forthwith. It also planned to rely heavily on Vice President of Global Affairs Nick Clegg, a former deputy prime minister in Britain, who had worked closely with Vice President Biden during the Obama administration.[170]

Clegg was more favorably viewed by the Biden administration than Kaplan, but that did not solve Facebook's problems. According to one senior Facebook employee, "A lot of the Democrats simply hate Facebook right now. We know Nick Clegg is not going to save us from that, but at least he will help us get a hearing."[171]

One of those Facebook haters was Biden himself. The Biden campaign was unhappy with Facebook's more pro-free speech approach compared to the other tech companies, viewing that as a pro-Trump stance. Throughout the 2020 campaign, the Biden team complained to Facebook about its approach, even as the company was being more critical of Trump. When Biden met with the *New York Times* editorial board, his views on Facebook were stark, and of no small concern to the company. Biden said, "I've never been a fan of Facebook, as you probably know." He also personalized things, adding, "I've never been a big Zuckerberg fan. I think he's a real problem."[172]

Biden was even starker on Section 230, the provision that gave tech firms protection for what was written on their platforms. According to Section 230, the tech firms were not considered publishers and therefore did not have the same responsibilities as publishers. This provision was existentially vital to the social media companies, and threats to it were threats to the heart of their business models. Biden told the *Times* that, "Section 230 should be revoked immediately." He added, in his inimitable logorrheic way, "That's right. Exactly right. And it should be revoked. It should be revoked because [Facebook] is not merely an Internet company. It is propagating falsehoods they know to be false, and we should be setting standards not unlike the Europeans are doing relative to privacy. You guys still have editors. I'm sitting with them. Not a joke. There is no editorial impact at all on Facebook. None. None whatsoever. It's irresponsible. It's totally irresponsible."[173]

With the skepticism of Facebook coming from the very top, Facebook faced serious challenges from the Biden administration. Biden's Justice Department was looking into an antitrust action against the company, and Lina Kahn, Biden's chair of the FTC, was a severe critic of the company as well. Furthermore, the standard plays in the playbook—cozying up via friendly staff, philanthropic efforts, partnering on administration priorities—did not seem to be working. In addition, Biden was now committed to the path of Elizabeth Warren, who according to polls was popular with his voters. He made his criticisms of Zuckerberg public, so there was no hint of the "palling it up" relationship Zuckerberg had built with Obama developing with Biden.[174]

At the same time, Trump, still the leading figure in the Republican Party, had decidedly cooled on Zuckerberg as well. He still liked to describe the dinner with Zuckerberg, but he now did so in very different terms. At a Pennsylvania campaign rally in 2022, Trump told the crowd that "the weirdo—he's a weirdo—Mark Zuckerberg came to the White House, kissed my ass all night." Trump then mimicked the conversation he had with Zuckerberg for the crowd, saying, "'Sir, I'd love to have dinner, sir. I'd love to have dinner. I'd love to bring my lovely wife.' All right, Mark, come on in. 'Sir, you're number one on Facebook. I'd like to congratulate you.' Thank you very much, Mark. I appreciate it." In his photo book of his administration, Trump included a picture of the dinner with Zuckerberg, Jared Kushner, Ivanka Trump, and Trump with a caption reading: "Mark Zuckerberg would come to the White House and kiss my ass." Where he had once bragged about the Zuckerberg dinner as a sign of his own popularity, now he was using it as a way to belittle Zuckerberg for being obsequious.[175] In 2024, after Trump secured the Republican nomination, he opposed the bipartisan push to ban TikTok because he felt it would help the man he now called "Zuckerschmuck". Clearly four years had not reduced his ire over the 2020 election.

Coda: Friendless in Washington

The party standard bearers' disdain for Facebook was indicative of how both parties felt about the company in the 2020s. Republican FCC commissioner Brendan Carr observed that Facebook "has lost all their friends in Washington." When Facebook tried to reach out, even offering direct engagement with Zuckerberg, lawmakers did not want to hear it. One Democratic lawmaker rejected repeated entreaties from the company, recounting that Facebook staff said, "Come have dinner at his place, with his wife! Sheryl can come!" The lawmaker's devastating retort: "I don't want to meet with him. We're not friends." Oregon senator Ron Wyden went so far as say that, "I think [Zuckerberg] ought to be held personally accountable, which is everything from financial fines to—and let me underline this—the possibility of a prison term."[176]

The dislike for Facebook went beyond just government officials and politicians. According to *Reason*'s Robby Soave, "Pundits on both sides of the ideological spectrum can routinely be found railing against Facebook" and its fellow tech companies. And then there was the public at large. A 2022 poll listed Zuckerberg as the least popular public figure in America, with 53 percent of Americans having a negative view of him and only 8 percent having a positive view. A parodic headline in *The Onion* summed up Facebook's predicament: "Facebook Announces Plan to Break Up US Government Before It Becomes Too Powerful."[177]

In 2024, two decades after Mark Zuckerberg founded it, Facebook—or Meta as its rebranding has it—faced a hostile president and the very real prospect of additional hostile presidents in the foreseeable future. Through sheer force of will, Zuckerberg brought three billion people onto a single platform that he controlled completely. Unfortunately for him, he also managed to make many if not most of those people hate him in the process.

CONCLUSION

C EOs engage with Washington, and particularly presidents, in an effort to help their companies. Many of the stories in this book describe successful efforts by CEOs to advance the interests of the companies, be it Elon Musk getting helpful funding for Tesla during the Obama administration, Lew Wasserman prevailing on Ronald Reagan not to change the financial interest and syndication rules, or Lee Iacocca getting a major bailout for Chrysler during the Carter administration.

On other occasions, CEO efforts to affect events have hurt companies. Henry Luce failed to dislodge Franklin Roosevelt from the White House, despite his constant carping against the Roosevelt administration. When Luce changed tack and backed the Eisenhower administration editorially and personally, that hurt him as well, since the magazine's overly pro-Ike stance damaged its reputation among elites and trendsetters. Elon Musk may have helped himself in the Obama administration, but his purchase of Twitter (now X) and efforts to make it a free-speech platform made him a pariah to the Biden administration and to Democrats as a whole, who did not like the new direction in which he took the social media company.

Sometimes a CEO's engagements with presidents have been for a national purpose. Jamie Dimon collaborated with the Bush administration at a time when the economy was teetering, taking a bailout he did not need in order to make sure that the financial system maintained its stability. J. P. Morgan helped bail out Teddy Roosevelt in the panic of 1907, despite Roosevelt's manifest hostility towards him. Henry Ford reluctantly put away his dislike of Franklin Roosevelt and built the largest plant building vehicles for military use in World War II.

Interestingly, some CEOs have attained so much fame that they continued to have an impact long after their departure from the corner office. Jack Welch and Leo Iacocca became management gurus and general advisors to presidents. Lew Wasserman continued to be a top fundraiser for Democrats, as well as a strategic advisor to a young Bill Clinton, even after Wasserman retired. Bill Gates built an enormous foundation that collaborated with multiple presidents on a host of health-related initiatives. These stories, and others from the long history of CEOs playing in Washington, allow us to discern some key lessons for how CEOs should consider the challenge of engaging in Washington, recognizing that if you do not move Washington, Washington will be moving you. Yet for all of the stories of CEOs trying to cozy up to presidents, CEOs of major corporations are not patsies. Some want to push back against presidents—and Washington in general—more than others. This history helps us discern certain rules of thumb that can help CEOs—and their advisers—figure out how to proceed in their dealings with presidents.

When CEOs do fight, they need to be careful. It should not be done lightly, and if done, it must be done with a purpose in mind. Former Attorney General and GTE General Counsel William Barr wrote in his memoir of being interested in working at GTE because CEO Chuck Lee wanted to push back against the regulatory state. As Barr wrote, "One of the problems with regulated companies is that they kowtow too often to the regulators and shy away from standing up for themselves because they are afraid the regulators will retaliate. Some act like hostages suffering from Stockholm syndrome." Lee, Barr made clear, did not have that view. According to Barr, Lee "wanted me to fight hard and would back me up." Engaging in tiffs with a president because of personal dislike, as Ford or Luce did, is never productive. Furthermore, in these days when corporations are unpopular and government has so many more tools than it once did, it is downright dangerous. [1]

However CEOs choose to engage, they need to realize that doing it successfully takes tremendous skill and agility. CEOs must be clear on their company narrative, focused in pursuing the company's goals, and be well-rehearsed in articulating their vision, priorities, and contributions. This takes work. CEOs cannot show up in Washington on a whim and read talking points prepared by someone else for the first time in the limo on the way to the White House. They need to internalize their arguments and be prepared to present them cogently and in their own words, in a way that will be compelling to government officials with different interests and different constituencies. Practice is essential for making this happen.

Beyond practicing the messaging itself, the engagements will also require repetition. CEOs cannot wait for a crisis or an emergency to begin engaging with Washington. As John D. Rockefeller and Bill Gates learned, starting to focus on Washington after Washington has already focused on you is too late. This is why Tim Cook and Mark Zuckerberg made real efforts to engage with Washington, even as doing so went against their natural inclinations. Cook specifically got good marks for not only increasing his engagement, but also focusing on the policymakers' concerns, rather than just his own company's needs. Engagement doesn't usually mean going toe-to-toe with a sitting commander in chief, but it does mean committing to being present in Washington dialogue and issues. As Woody Allen famously said, "80% of success is showing up." According to Mack McLarty, himself a former business executive and White House chief of staff under Bill Clinton, the CEOs who are most successful at engaging with presidents "combine a deep understanding of their businesses from top to bottom and a willingness to commit to their fundamental beliefs without bending to the current political winds." In short, the smart ones have a plan for Washington before they encounter a problem.[2]

CEOs must also be sure to take the reins personally. As Tim Carney, AEI fellow and author of *The Big Ripoff: How Big Business and Big Government Steal Your Money*, warns, CEOs "often make the mistake of ceding all government relations to lobbyists." Yet lobbyists, he warns, "have a different interest than the shareholders do." According to Carney, "Under Jeff Immelt, GE spent more than any other company on lobbying, and they lost more value than any other company in the Dow Jones." McLarty also favors a direct approach, citing the wisdom of former senator and former White House chief of staff Howard Baker, who used to say, "You just have to be there." [3]

CEOs should also recognize that their fame lets them expand the universe of tactics. Some are so well-known that they can compete with the president in trying to shape the narrative on an issue, as Tim Cook tried to do with questions over iPhone privacy protections. People like Ford, Dimon, and Rockefeller were looked to for their expertise on the economy. When they spoke, it could move markets and sway public opinion. CEOs should recognize that power and deploy it strategically to their advantage.

Although these lessons can help, CEOs must constantly be aware of the degree to which corporate unpopularity creates significant vulnerabilities for companies and even entire industries. This awareness is more important than ever because corporations and their well-compensated CEOs are extremely unpopular in Washington these days. McLarty told me that, "There is little doubt that large corporations are as unpopular as they have ever been in recent times in the United States. This truly feels unprecedented in my lifetime."[4] According to a report in *The Dispatch*, the Biden administration expressed its dissatisfaction with the tech industry by hiring tech critic Lina Khan to head the Federal Trade Commission and appointing *The Curse of Bigness* author Tim Wu to the White House National Economic Council. With these two opponents of economic integration in place, the Biden administration engaged in unusual actions directed against big tech from both Khan's FTC but also from the Justice Department. Furthermore, the Democratic-controlled Senate aimed to bolster the staff of the FTC, no doubt to allow it to pursue more actions against companies. These actions point to the vast array of tools that government has developed over the last century and a half to govern corporate behavior. While the companies have cooperated with the government to a great extent in developing this apparatus, an administration intent on using regulatory actions to target a company or an industry now has many arrows in its quiver.[5]

In the past, corporations and their CEOs might have looked to Republicans to defend them and the importance of free markets and level playing fields. But while Khan certainly has her critics on the right, companies are not that popular with Republicans these days, either. As McLarty observed, GOP support for companies "has dropped significantly—driven in part by concerns over CEOs and corporations taking public stands on social issues such as voting rights and support for LGBTQ individuals."[6]

The roots of such skepticism go back farther than recent social controversies. Carney thinks GOP skepticism of big business fits in with a larger anti-institution sentiment in American society. According to Carney, "Americans have generally soured on all large institutions, from churches to governments to corporations," but "[w]hat's changed since the Bush Era is that Republican and conservative commentators and politicians have started training their fire on corporate America." Carney agrees with McLarty on recent developments, noting that "corporate America more openly took the side of the Left in the culture wars," but adds that the seeds of Republican disdain for corporations goes back to 2008, when "the Wall Street bailouts happened and Big Business lined up behind Barack Obama in the 2008 elections and in his push for a stimulus and Obamacare."[7]

Carney and McLarty are from different sides of the political aisle, but they both recognize that actions by business are responsible for the challenging situation in which companies find themselves today. In some ways, it is the very closeness of presidents and CEOs that has helped foster the resentment of many Americans toward corporations. A CEO palling around with the president gets access and opportunities that an ordinary American does not get. But the mere closeness of the relationships alone does not explain the recent hostility. Another aspect is the degree to which CEOs and the corporations they head often seem to be in cahoots with the government. Regulations that keep the little guy out can have the impact of keeping CEOs and corporations on top and even prevent new players from entering the marketplace. Yet CEOs will tell you that it's a hyper competitive environment, and as GE discovered, a corporation on top one day can lose its position surprisingly quickly.

CEOs face a Hobson's choice. They must interact with presidents because there is now so much that Washington can do to harm them or to bolster their competitors. Government now regulates so much more than it once did in the days of Rockefeller, that CEOs have to monitor and shape what Washington does as much as possible. At the same time, the coziness between CEOs and Washington, and the degree to which corporations and government have a symbiotic relationship, breeds resentment from voters, and then therefore politicians on both sides of the aisle.

CEOs have helped create an environment in which government tells corporations what to do, but in doing so, it helps the corporations maintain their dominant positions in the marketplace. It is this symbiosis, widely recognized or not, that helps explain the bipartisan resentment we see these days. Government regulations tie small businesses in knots, but allow corporations with large lobbying offices, legal teams, and compliance departments to gain a leg up. CEOs themselves can engage presidents to keep a system in place, advantage their company, and attain generational wealth—even as a majority of Americans struggle. Meanwhile, the government incurs trillions in debt without solving the problems of average Americans.

At the same time, there is no doubt that CEOs are more powerful than ever, running massive conglomerates that provide nearly every product that Americans rely on to eat, sleep, travel, communicate, or entertain themselves. These corporations band together within their industry associations to influence policy and even culture. And with the advent of technology, big tech dominance has made it possible for government and corporations to reach more deeply into private lives than at any point in human history.

The creation of smart products now means that companies can—and do—monitor our every action in ways that even George Orwell never considered. It is imperative that citizens understand both government and business goals—as well as how to keep them accountable. As powerful as they are, CEOs are themselves subject to a variety of forces—including the whims of presidents. The president is important to that accountability because our nation's chief executives preside over agencies and executive powers that govern nearly everything corporations do:

who they hire, which products they are allowed to sell, with which companies they can trade, what kind of energy they use. In many instances, the government is the driver of how and when businesses share their data as part of government investigations and surveillance operations.

This entanglement does not limit their companies' profits or their own salaries, both of which are considerable. But it does mean that the government can leverage corporate power to attain its own political ends. The corporations go along in part because the government rules make doing business so complicated and so costly that only big players can afford the compliance costs, thereby limiting the development of competitors by making it hard for new market entrants to emerge. The other reason they cooperate is because of the power the government has to turn up the heat on their own businesses, using the vast array of regulations and enforcement officials it has at hand.

Whatever they do, given the current environment and the tools government can use against them, companies cannot give up on Washington. CEOs who are willing and good at engaging are often a corporation's best weapon, and will continue to be so. They will also find that presidents and CEOs are often kindred spirits, both subject to the loneliness of leadership. CEOs reading this book can see the importance of their role and learn from those who have grappled with presidents on the biggest issues. Moreover, every reader, not just CEOs, will have seen in these pages the importance of strong and confident leadership in corporations that values competition and innovation. We need corporate leaders like that, just as we need presidents who are clear that these are the foundations for the success of our nation and opportunity for all Americans.

Our current moment in the intertwined relationship between government and business is the culmination of the century-and-a-half long story—much of it shaped by expanding government[8] and the interactions between CEOs and U.S. presidents. A CEO who alienates the president, as Elon Musk has learned in recent years, can suddenly find himself subject to costly governmental interventions that may never be explicitly ordered, yet can still wreak havoc on the bottom line. In other words, CEOs cooperate with presidents because they both want to and because they have to. As the CEOs of this era have learned, making friends with presidents is good business. Whether it's good for the American people is another matter entirely.

APPENDIX 1

CEO MODELS OF ENGAGEMENT

Big-name CEOs have used a variety of engagement strategies with American presidents to help themselves, their companies, and on occasion the country. Some have been more successful than others, but all of their approaches derived from the specific skills, talents, and corporate assets that the CEOs brought to the table.

John D. Rockefeller: Mistaken Distance-Keeper—John D. Rockefeller built his monopoly with little interference from a federal government that lacked the tools that today's policymakers have for reining in corporate behavior. While he did not garner much attention from Presidents Ulysses Grant and Rutherford Hayes in those years in which he was developing his empire, what attention he did receive made him an object of public scorn. Benjamin Harrison signed the first legislation to curb corporate power, but it did not end Rockefeller's dominance. William McKinley was a rare political friend in private, but when he was assassinated, his replacement, Teddy Roosevelt, engaged in frequent attacks on Rockefeller from the bully pulpit. Once retired, Rockefeller finally began efforts—some successful—to improve his public reputation, but he waited for too long to begin those efforts.

J. P. Morgan: Patriotic Dealmaker—J. P. Morgan served as a lifeline for both Grover Cleveland and Theodore Roosevelt during crises that threatened to upheave the American economy. A frequent political donor—mostly to Republicans—Morgan's collaboration with presidents did not prevent him from facing antitrust actions at the hands of those whom he had personally assisted.

Henry Ford: Reluctant Partner—Henry Ford provided some measure of support to every president from Woodrow Wilson to Franklin Roosevelt, friend or foe, consciously or not. His endorsement of Wilson and his photo ops with Warren Harding, Calvin Coolidge, and Herbert Hoover boosted their political images; his production of military vehicles stocked Roosevelt's war machine during World War II, a contribution made despite his vehement opposition to Roosevelt's economic policies. He also had an anti-Semitic newspaper, *The Dearborn Independent*, which both William Howard Taft and Woodrow Wilson denounced. Although Ford was a thorn in the side of several presidents, inducing political headaches with his sharp tongue, his industrial prowess and popularity also made him useful to multiple presidents.

Henry Luce: Competing with the President—Henry Luce created the industry of national news publications in founding *TIME* and serving as its editor in chief. Along the way, his presidential interactions spanned almost half a century, from Herbert Hoover to Lyndon Johnson. Luce harbored a particular hatred for Franklin Roosevelt and the New Deal, and had an enormous platform for making his views known. But Roosevelt had his own platform, and he was not shy about pushing back hard against Luce and his magazines. Luce's use of his magazines to push his political agendas and relationships would hurt both his company's reputation but also the news media writ large.

Harry and Jack Warner: Enthusiastic Boosters—Harry and Jack Warner, the immigrant heads of a top Hollywood film studio, wanted the respect of the Washington establishment, and they were willing to use their products to secure it. They produced films calculated to appeal to Franklin D. Roosevelt, including pro-New Deal films during the Depression and pro-war films during the run-up to and the prosecution of the Second World War. They also actively campaigned for Roosevelt, helping to set up Hollywood's continuing symbiotic relationship with the Democratic Party. Roosevelt, for his part, used the studio heads more than he befriended them. Their efforts on his behalf did not stop the Roosevelt administration from challenging the studios under the Sherman Antitrust Act, nor from going after the Warners for tax evasion.

Lew Wasserman: Purposeful Adviser—For decades, Lew Wasserman was focused solely on the film business and was uninterested in Washington. When he learned that Washington could disrupt his business plans, he began engaging with presidents in his typically thoughtful and strategic way. He first made himself indispensable by serving as a prodigious political contributor and fundraiser, but then made himself even more indispensable as a provider of sage advice to multiple presidents. Along the way, he found that the relationships he forged with presidents helped him shape policies beneficial to his industry.

Katharine Graham: Society Maintainer—Katharine Graham ran a powerful media platform that was read daily by presidents and nearly all of official Washington. She learned that what her paper published could generate presidential enmity, but what she seemed to want most of all was presidential friendship. She saw herself as part of the glue holding Washington's social scene together, and was interested in maintaining relationships with presidents of both sides of the aisle. Sometimes, as with Richard Nixon and the *Post*'s Watergate coverage, this proved impossible. Yet she also was able to stay close to Ronald and Nancy Reagan even as her paper relentlessly criticized the Reagan administration. Her vision of maintaining social ties despite political disagreement seems increasingly quaint in today's hyper-partisan times.

Rupert Murdoch: Conservative Promoter—Rupert Murdoch had long wanted to cozy up to presidents. He's been meeting with presidents since a December 1, 1961, Oval Office visit with John F. Kennedy. In the 1980s, he desperately wanted a relationship with Ronald Reagan, only to find himself snubbed. He then built an alliance with TV guru Roger Ailes, who helped elect Richard Nixon, prepped

Reagan for his debates with Walter Mondale, and advised George H. W. Bush on his televised takedown of Dan Rather. Together, Murdoch and Ailes built Fox News, which became the bête noire of multiple Democratic presidents, including Barack Obama, by offering right-wing voices a platform in an environment where they were seldom represented. Murdoch also tried and failed to stop the rise of Donald Trump, only to change course and make his Fox News Channel one of Trump's top allies before the hectic fallout from the end of the Trump presidency threatened Murdoch's place as one of the Republican Party's most prominent powerbrokers.

Lee Iacocca: Spirited Lobbyist—Lee Iacocca was adept at navigating Washington's halls of power. He directly lobbied Richard Nixon against seatbelt regulations, Jimmy Carter for a bailout, and Ronald Reagan (albeit unsuccessfully) to return valuable stock warrants to Chrysler—and was so well-liked that many Americans wanted him to run for president. He could also be a sharp critic, penning a book that harshly criticized George W. Bush, and complaining about Barack Obama as well. While not quite a kingmaker, Iacocca was still coveted for his political endorsements in his later career post-retirement.

Warren Buffett: Outside Oracle—Warren Buffet has openly endorsed multiple Democratic presidential candidates, including Barack Obama and Hillary Clinton. He also served as an unofficial economic guru for Democrats, including for the Obama administration. But despite his liberalism, he views the presidency as an important unifying institution, even saying so during the Trump presidency, which he opposed. Once he became famous, Buffett used his platform to advance his political agenda while trying to maintain his ability to influence presidents with whom he clearly disagreed. His Nebraska-based efforts have not helped the financial industry as a whole, though, as both Democrats and Republicans these days are equally apt to denounce "Wall Street bankers."

Jack Welch: Celebrity Manager—Jack Welch's tremendous success in increasing the value of GE helped him become a celebrity CEO and management guru. His fame made him sought after by presidents, who wanted his advice on a host of issues. He also knew his limitations, eschewing multiple queries about serving in government, something he knew would be a bad fit both for him and for the government.

Bill Gates: Aggressive Compartmentalizer—Bill Gates has had avuncular relationships with multiple presidents, including Jimmy Carter (as ex-president) and Joe Biden. He also supports philanthropic causes like vaccine development and disease eradication. But in the 1990s, Gates engaged in a titanic battle with Bill Clinton's administration over Microsoft's then-domination of the software industry, even as he and Clinton played golf and participated in panel discussions together. Gates's failure to anticipate the way government could affect his business model would influence a later generation of tech giants to engage earlier and more powerfully with Washington than Gates had.

Oprah Winfrey: Cultural Kingmaker—Oprah Winfrey chose to stay on the political sidelines throughout much of her meteoric late-twentieth-century rise. At the turn of the millennium, though, Oprah's platform became a forum for both nominees during the 2000 election, and she figured as a deeply impactful pro-Obama voice in 2008. Oprah's support of Hillary Clinton in 2016 did not tip the scales in Hillary's favor, though, and Oprah's continued advocacy for Democrats thereafter led to her estrangement from Donald Trump, a former friend, and made her political voice less powerful than it had once been.

Steve Jobs: Unaffiliated Innovator—Steve Jobs fits neatly into no box, neither as a CEO nor in his relationships with presidents. Never much interested in dealing with Washington, Jobs nevertheless had the ear and attention of the White House. After taking a minor role under the George H. W. Bush Administration of which little came, his kind gestures to Bill Clinton were reciprocated and well received, even if his political advice was not. Though quiet during the George W. Bush years, he would emerge as a simultaneous supporter and critic of Barack Obama. An untimely death prevented Jobs's increasing sway in the White House from growing further.

Jamie Dimon: Wall Street Whisperer—Jamie Dimon worked to embody himself as the voice of Wall Street for multiple presidents. He was the most important CEO to accept the 2008 federal bailout. Even though his bank did not need the rescue, his participation signaled that it was ok to receive the federal assistance. As a Democrat, Dimon was generally aligned with President Obama, but he was also willing to criticize Obama over his excessive anti-Wall Street rhetoric. And while Donald Trump may not have been to his liking, he was willing to work with the Trump administration to make sure that Wall Street's voice was heard at a time of populist disdain for big banks from both sides of the aisle. While Dimon of course made the case for his own bank, he was also quite conscious of his role representing Wall Street as a whole in the corridors of power.

Elon Musk: Policy Opportunist—Elon Musk's SpaceX fueled the rebirth of American space exploration to the effusive praise of several presidents, and his championing of electric vehicles further ingratiated him to Democratic presidents—as did his political support of them. However, Musk's willingness to speak his mind, especially on issues regarding free speech and the Covid pandemic, alienated Democrats and left him with few true friends in Washington. His friendless status created regulatory complications for his many businesses.

Tim Cook: Pragmatic Participant—Tim Cook gave Washington far more attention than his celebrity predecessor Steve Jobs had, emphasizing Apple's bottom line over his own political convictions. Despite having supported Barack Obama's presidential campaigns, Cook stood his ground against Obama when his policies on privacy and security ran counter to those of Apple. When most CEOs ran away from Donald Trump, the Democrat Cook developed a close relationship with him; Trump returned Cook's praise, throwing in some beneficial policies as a sweetener. Cook's policy of supporting the president has continued into the Biden era, in which Apple continues to experience extraordinary financial success.

Mark Zuckerberg: Early Influencer—Mark Zuckerberg recognized the need to engage not only Washington, but the White House in particular, much earlier than his mentor Bill Gates had. The liberal head of a liberal company, Zuckerberg aided the Obama campaign and administration, yet he also had a love-hate relationship with Donald Trump, having multiple meetings with him but eventually banning him from Facebook's platform. He used his company's wealth and influence to try to prevent Washington from targeting the tech giants, but made Facebook and its fellow tech companies extremely unpopular in the process. As Trump and Bush 41 Attorney General Bill Barr observed, "For all our disagreements, Americans on the Right and the Left agree on one thing: Big Tech has too much power."[1]

APPENDIX 2

DEVELOPMENT OF FEDERAL TOOLS FOR INFLUENCING PRIVATE SECTOR ACTIVITY

When John D. Rockefeller built his monopoly in the 1870s, the federal government had no tools for shaping or constraining his activities, even if it had wanted to do so. Over the past century and a half, the federal government has developed a wide array of tools for shaping private sector activity and behavior. While Rockefeller and his monopoly may have served as an impetus for the initial development of these new federal powers, the vision of the federal government as a key player in the private sector has grown exponentially since then, as have the methods that the federal government developed to shape that activity. This graph is an attempt to visualize the way that the nature of the relationship between the private sector and the federal government has changed since that time.[1]

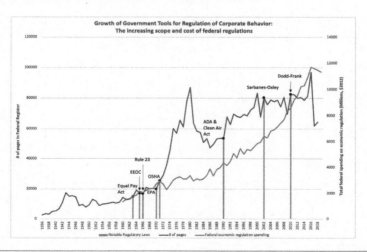

APPENDIX 3

CEO JOKE FILE

One way to measure the degree to which CEOs have become part of the popular consciousness is through humor. Humor, particularly political humor, is predicated on a shared understanding of a person or a concept. The degree to which these jokes by and about CEOs are still understandable today reveals the degree to which big-name CEOs, like presidents, have become part of the American political landscape.

Warren Buffet

"As one investor said in 2009: 'This is worse than divorce. I've lost half my net worth—and I still have my wife.'"—Warren Buffett in a 2010 letter to shareholders

Tim Cook

A journalist asked Tim Cook why iPhones are so expensive.

"Well," said Tim Cook, "that's because the iPhone replaces a whole bunch of devices. A phone, a camera, a watch, a music player, a video player, a PDA, a voice recorder, a GPS navigator, a flashlight, a calculator, a portable gaming console, and many other things. Surely, a high price is worth paying to replace so many devices!"

"Then why are Androids so much cheaper?" asked the journalist.

"Because," said Tim Cook, "an Android replaces just one device. The iPhone."

Apple CEO Tim Cook wants you to know he's in on the joke after President Donald Trump mistakenly called him "Tim Apple" during a recent event at the White House. He changed his name on Twitter to do just that—or, rather, Tim and the Apple logo.

Why do iPhone cameras look like a stove top?
Because Tim Cooks.

Why did Tim Cook go to the ophthalmologist?
Because he had an iProblem.

Jamie Dimon

"The Communist Party is about to celebrate its 100th anniversary. So is JPMorgan. I bet we last longer."—Jamie Dimon

"The problem with banker Jamie Dimon running for President is that he doesn't have the aptitude or 'smarts' & is a poor public speaker & nervous mess. Otherwise he is wonderful."—Donald Trump

Headlines written following a $2 billion trading loss at J. P. Morgan Chase under Jamie Dimon:
"Dimon in the Rough."
"Shine On, You Crazy Dimon."
"Simple Dimon"
"Dimon Rings"
"Dimon Necklace"

Henry Ford

"I'm currently reading a book about the life of Henry Ford. It's an autobiography."—Henry Ford

"Two boys save Franklin Roosevelt from drowning. When Roosevelt offered to reward the boys, one asked for and received a job for his unemployed father. The other one, however, was inconsolable, telling the president that 'If I tell my father who I pulled out of the water, he'll kill me!'" —Henry Ford

Henry Ford drives by a cemetery and notices a gravedigger preparing an enormous grave. Ford asked whether the grave was for a whole family, but the gravedigger responded that it was for one man, who asked in his will to be buried in a Ford. The reason? A Ford had gotten him out of every hole to date, and he was confident it would pull him out of this one.

Henry Ford dies and goes to heaven, where he meets Adam, the first man. Ford asks, "Hey, aren't you the inventor of the woman?" Adam says yes. "Well," says Ford, "You have some major design flaws in your invention: 1. There's too much front end protrusion. 2. It chatters at high speeds. 3. The rear end wobbles too much. 4. And the intake is placed too close to the exhaust." In response, Adam tells him: "It may be that my invention is flawed, but according to the stellar computer, more men are riding my invention than yours."

A little spark, a little coil, a little gas, a little oil, a piece of tin, two inch of board, put 'em together, and you have a Ford.

Ford takes a pitch for a new invention called the air conditioner from three Jewish brothers named Greenberg. Hyman Greenberg, the eldest of the three, says, "We have a remarkable invention that will revolutionize the automobile industry." The second brother, Norman Greenberg, tells Ford to enter a sweltering car. When Ford says, "Are you crazy? It must be two hundred degrees in that car," the youngest brother, Max, says, "Sit down, Mr. Ford, and push the white button." Ford does so and is instantly cooled. Impressed, Ford offers to buy the patent, but the brothers want the name "Greenberg Brothers Air Conditioning" to be stamped right next to the

Ford logo. Ford, says, "Money is no problem, but no way will I have a Jewish name next to my logo on my cars!" They haggle back and forth for a while and finally they settle. Eventually, they come up with a solution: whenever you enter a Ford vehicle, you will see those three names: Hi, Norm, Max.

Bill Gates

Bill Gates met Arnold Schwarzenegger at a party.
He asked him if he had upgraded to Windows 10 yet.
Big Arnie replied: Ah still love Vista baby . . .

Did you hear that Bill Gates lost a dance contest to Al Gore?
    He didn't have the Al Gore Rhythm.

Bill Gates walks into a bar and everyone inside becomes a billionaire . . . on average.

Did you hear about the Bill Gates divorce?
    Melinda kept the house and Bill kept all the windows.

My mom used to tell me not to laugh at another's condition because we may be in their position one day. So I laugh at Bill Gates's condition every day.

What shirt size does Bill Gates wear?
    Excel.

How many Microsoft employees does it take to change a lightbulb?
    None. Bill Gates just redefines Darkness as the new industry standard.

Why did Bill Gates drop out of Harvard?
    He went there to learn from people smarter than him, but left feeling disappointed.

"DOS ain't done till Lotus don't run." —Internal Microsoft programming joke

Katharine Graham

"I got my job from the Washington Post." —Gerald Ford

Lee Iacocca:

In January, 1992 George H. W. Bush traveled to Japan with Lee Iacocca. On the trip, Bush, exhausted from the travels as well as a game of tennis earlier in the day, vomited on Japanese prime minister Kiichi Miyazawa at a State Dinner. On *The Tonight Show* Johnny Carson joked: "If you had to eat raw fish, and sit across from Lee Iacocca, you'd throw up, too."

It was the first day of school and a new student named Suzuki, the son of a Japanese businessman, entered the fourth grade. The teacher said, "Let's begin by reviewing some American history. Who said 'Give me Liberty, or Give me Death?' She saw a sea of blank faces, except for Suzuki, who had his hand up. "Patrick Henry, 1775," he said. "Very good! Who said 'Government of the people, by the people, for the people, shall not perish from the earth'?" Again, no response except from Suzuki: "Abraham Lincoln, 1863." The teacher snapped at the class, "Class, you should be ashamed. Suzuki, who is new to our country, knows more about its history than you do." She heard a loud whisper: "Screw the Japanese." "Who said that?" she demanded. Suzuki put his hand up. "Lee Iacocca, 1982."

What does "Iacocca" stand for?

I am Chairman of the Chrysler Corporation of America.

Steve Jobs

Steve Jobs would've been a better president than Trump. But I guess comparing apples to oranges is unfair.

Why did Steve Jobs eat all the cookies?

Mac users have no CTRL.

Why doesn't Steve Jobs build his own house?

Because he refuses to install windows.

Henry Luce

"Time was even-handed during election years: Half the time it praised the Republicans, and half the time it damned the Democrats."

"Backward ran sentences until reeled the mind." —Wolcott Gibbs, on *TIME*

J. P. Morgan

J. P. Morgan, upon learning that Theodore Roosevelt would be going on safari in Africa, hoped the lions would perform their duty.

Elon Musk

I hope Elon Musk never gets involved in a scandal. Elongate would be really drawn out.

New Teslas don't come with a new car smell. They come with an Elon Musk.

If Elon Musk's space company establishes a Mars colony, and you have a girlfriend on Mars but later break up because of the long distance, she'd be your SpaceX.

Why did Elon Musk go broke?

Because his car insurance rates were astronomical.

"To anyone I've offended, I just want to say: I reinvented electric cars and I'm sending people to Mars in a rocket ship. Did you think I was also going to be a chill, normal dude?"—Elon Musk, on *Saturday Night Live*

Rupert Murdoch

Rupert Murdoch walks into a bar.

The barman says, "Don't worry about it mate, we haven't got Sky either."

The last front page of the final *News of the World* reads: "Thank you and goodbye." Rubbish. I'd have gone with: "You have no new messages."

"You might think I don't like Rupert Murdoch. That's simply not true. How can I dislike a guy who makes me look like Harry Styles?" —Joe Biden

John D. Rockefeller

Will Rogers, after losing to John D. Rockefeller at golf: "I'm glad you beat me, John. The last time you were beaten I noticed the price of gasoline went up 2 cents a gallon."

Writing in the voice of Satan, Mark Twain jibed in a Harper's essay that, "Since the Board daily accepts contributions from me, why should it decline them from Mr. Rockefeller, who is as good as I am?"[1]

Harry Warner

"Who the hell wants to hear actors talk?" –Harry Warner on talking pictures

Jack Warner

When Jack Warner heard that Ronald Reagan was running for governor, he thought for a moment and said, "No, uh-uh—Jimmy Stewart for Governor, Ronald Reagan for best friend."

Jack Warner, upon his consideration by Franklin Roosevelt for an overseas post: "I might have been the first Jewish ambassador to Ireland!"

Lew Wasserman

Jesse Armstrong, about the joke that inspired him to write *Succession*: "I read that Sumner Redstone made the same speech that Lew Wasserman also made. They all made this joke about what they would do when they retired. They all said that they weren't going to retire and they weren't going to die."

"When it comes to Lew Wasserman, I think everyone in this room shares the same emotion—Fear." —Johnny Carson

Lew Wasserman to Lyndon Johnson: "I'd like to ask you a very important favor. I want you to promise me that I never have to work for the government."

Oprah Winfrey

What's the best thing about an Oprah Winfrey joke?
  You get the joke! You get the joke! You all get the joke!

Mark Zuckerberg

Why would Mark Zuckerberg be a very good taxi driver?
  You get in the car and he already knows your name and where you live.

A boy walks up to Mark Zuckerberg. The boy says: "My daddy said you were stealing our information." Mark Zuckerberg replies: "He isn't your dad."

Mark Zuckerberg is really upset that Facebook is about to be fined $5 billion by the FTC for misusing users' personal data.
Please respect his privacy at this challenging time.

"My name is Barack Obama, and I'm the guy who got Mark Zuckerberg to wear a jacket and tie."—Barack Obama

ACKNOWLEDGMENTS

I have been working on and thinking about this project for four years and I have had a lot of excellent help along the way. First on the list is my friend and editor, the talented Matt Robinson, who has discussed this book with me at every step. In addition to Matt, I am fortunate to have many close friends with whom I can discuss my ideas, including Jonah Goldberg. Ben Sasse, Alan Rechtschaffen, Jeremy Katz, Noam Neusner, Seth Leibson, Roger Zakheim, Rob Andrews, Larry Frankel, Noam Wasserman, Juleanna Glover, Mark Lagon, Matt Gerson—also a cousin—and title maven Dan Huff. Eli Lake, James Glassman, Veronique de Rugy, Doug Feith, Harold Furchtgott-Roth, Scooter Libby, Matt Rees, and Adam White attended an early Mercatus workshop on the book concept and provided helpful thoughts. Thanks to the great team at Mercatus for helping with the workshop and so much else, including Martha Anderson, Ben Klutsey, Dan Rothschild, Garrett Brown, David Masci, and Kyle Precourt.

This of course could not have happened without Daniela Rapp, Tony Lyons, Rachel Marble, Janina Krayer, and the team at Skyhorse. Tom Spence also gets credit for seeing the merits of the project, as did Keith Urban, who encouraged me even if he would not represent me. There's always my next book.

My brother Gil Troy read the manuscript and provided helpful advice, and thanks to his wife Linda for putting up with all of the projects he undertakes. Other readers included my good friends Vincent Cannato and Larry Haas. Together the three of them formed a formidable triumvirate of moderate, conservative, and liberal historian reviewers.

I have had some terrific and resourceful researchers work on this project, including Ryan Nickols, Jake Walsh, Arielle Butman, Jacob Rosenzweig,

Chloe Kauffman, Kaelyn Milby, Mallory Bedingfield, Yakov Sundel, and Gavriel Buchwald. I am expecting great things from all of them.

Thanks to the team at the Bipartisan Policy Center, including Margaret Spellings, Steve Scully, Lisel Loy, Matt Weil, Erin Meade, Amelia Sandhovel, Katie Harvath, Kyle Huang, and Phenan Kidane. I am grateful to my BPC supporters, including Michael Gleba and Mongomery Brown at the Sarah Scaife Foundation, John Krieger and Les Lenkowsky at the Achelis & Bodman Foundation, Todd Walker at Altria, and Dan Bryant and Jonathan Burks at Walmart. Thanks as well to my new colleagues at Yeshiva University's Straus Center, including leader Rabbi Meir Soloveichik, Rabbi Dr. Stuart (Stam Stu) Halpern, Sarah Wapner, and Yisroel Ben-Porat.

My pal Jonathan Baron and the smart folks at Baron Public Affairs helped me think through some key aspects of the book. Thanks as well to Jeremy Furchtgott, Jonny Fluger, Dyana Engelman, and Benjamin Burke.

Writing a book is a solitary endeavor, and I could not have done it without the various social outlets that helped maintain my sanity: My bother Dan Troy provided legal and publishing guidance, as well as regular companionship at our Thursday night action movies. His wife Cheryl fed me at many of these sessions, which I appreciate as well. My daily minyan buddies include Jason Unger, David Taragin, Dean Grayson, David Lowenstein, and Rabbi Weinberg. The Saturday night MSMN crew includes hosts Judge Matthew and Lisa Solomson, Jay and Jessica Eizenstat, and Chad and Melissa Miller. Thanks for letting me make the selections. Regular tennis pals include Todd Hanik, Dan Moshinsky, the ageless Ira Thompson, Steve Sandberg, Rafi Cohen, David Lesnoy, Arnie "Call Gloria" Sherman, Aaron Branda, Eddie Snyder, Tim Goeglein, Daniel Lippman, Ari Fridman, Kenny Handwerger, Neil Roland, Andrew Stein, Yossi Kovacs, Jonathan Horn, and Ari "Coach" Goldberg. Ozzie Burnham is a fantastic drash partner.

A final thank you goes to my family. My ninety-four-year-old father, Bernard Dov Troy, sat with me as I edited parts of the book. My supportive in-laws, Drs. Vita and Ray Pliskow, contribute with her copyediting and his jacket photo. My cousin Adele Raemer survived, and I am so very grateful for that. I have a great collection of nieces and nephews, some of whom are doing the dangerous work of defending western civilization from deadly enemies.

Last but absolutely not least comes my immediate family. I had four kids when I started this project—Ezra, Ruthie, Rina, and Noey—but am pleased to now have Ezra's wife Ellie enter the fold. They are all happy to point out when I am being a nerd—not a very challenging task—and they are of course egged on and joined in this task by my funny and talented wife of twenty-five years, Kami. I read two versions of a sentence in this book to her to see which one read better, and she responded: "I fell asleep." (Hopefully the rest of you find it more interesting.) I keep promising her that each book I finish will be my last. Maybe someday I will keep that promise.

NOTES

Introduction

1 Tyler Cowen, *Big Business* (New York: St. Martin's Press, 2019), 167–72. While it is admittedly a huge sum, Cowen points out that it pales next to the $200 billion in annual corporate spending on advertising. GM alone spends about as much in advertising annually as all corporations spend on lobbying.

2 "Guide for the Perplexed: Key Trends in Government Relations," April 10, 2023, in *Political Risk Brief* podcast, episode 16, published by Baron Public Affairs, https://www.baronpa.com/podcast/guide-for-the-perplexed-key-trends-in-government-relations.

3 Xiaomeng Lan et al., "President Trump vs. CEOs: Who Is More Likely to Influence the Media Agenda?," UF College of Journalism and Communications, October 5, 2020, accessed August 9, 2023, https://www.jou.ufl.edu/insights/president-trump-vs-ceos-who-is-more-likely-to-influence-the-media-agenda; Paul Weaver, *The Suicidal Corporation* (New York: Touchstone Books, 1989), 165–167.

4 Felix Gillette and John Koblin, *It's Not TV: The Spectacular Rise, Revolution, and Future of HBO* (New York: Penguin Random House, 2022), eBook. For more on Cook, see Section VII spotlight on him.

5 Note: FAANG stands for Facebook (now Meta), Amazon, Apple, Netflix, and Google (owned by Alphabet).

Chapter 1: The Blank Slate

1 Susan Berfield, *Hour of Fate: The Story of Theodore Roosevelt, J. P. Morgan, and the Battle to Transform American Capitalism* (London: Bloomsbury Publishing, 2020), 33–34.

2 Ibid., 36.

3 Gilbert King, "War and Peace of Mind for Ulysses S. Grant," *Smithsonian Magazine*, January 16, 2013, www.smithsonianmag.com/history/war-and-peace-of-mind-for-ulysses-s-grant-1882227/.

4 Berfield, *Hour of Fate*, 39.

5 William Magnuson, *For Profit: A History of Corporations* (New York: Basic Books, 2022), 192.

6 Ibid., 192.

7 Silas Hubbard, *John D. Rockefeller and His Career* (New York: self pub., 1904), 42.

8 Ibid., 92.

9 Ron Chernow, *Titan* (New York: Vintage Books, 1998), 202.

10   Ari Hoogenboom, *Rutherford B. Hayes: Warrior & President* (Lawrence: University Press of Kansas), 519.

11   John Thomas Flynn, *God's Gold: The Story of Rockefeller and His Times* (United Kingdom: Harcourt, Brace, 1932), 54–55.

12   Ibid.; Chernow, *Titan*, 210–11.

13   "President Benjamin Harrison Acknowledges J. Pierpont Morgan's Primacy in the New York Financial World," August 5, 1892, The Raab Collection, www.raab collection.com/presidential-autographs/harrison-morgan.

14   Lewis Corey, *The House of Morgan: A Social Biography of the Masters of Money* (New York: G. H. Watt, 1930), 187.

15   H. W. Brands, "Upside-down Bailout: J.P. Morgan Rescued the U.S. Treasury from Near Bankruptcy and Got Nothing but Grief for His Efforts," *American History*, 45, no. 3 (August 2010): pp. 26+, *Gale General OneFile*, link.gale.com/apps/doc /A228661041/ITOF?u=duke_perkins&sid=summon&xid=a14a46c0.

16   Ibid.

17   Richard B. Baker et al., "From Plutocracy to Progressivism? The Assassination of President McKinley as a Turning Point in American History," Yale Department of Economics, September 2014, economics.yale.edu/sites/default/files/hilt.pdf; Ron Chernow, *The House of Morgan: An American Banking Dynasty and the Rise of Modern Finance* (New York: Atlantic Monthly Press, 1990), 77–78; Susan Berfield, *Hour of Fate*, 12–15.

18   Hubbard, *John D. Rockefeller and His Career*, 178. Rockefeller's comment was a parody of the saying, "I care not who makes the law, provided I write the songs of the nation," by the seventeenth century Scottish writer Andrew Fletcher.

19   Allan Nevins, *Grover Cleveland: A Study in Courage*, vol. 1, (Norwalk: The Easton Press, 1932) 77; Hubbard, *John D. Rockefeller and His Career*, 147; Flynn, *God's Gold: The Story of Rockefeller and His Times*, 54–55, 255–57.

20   Chernow, *Titan*, 297.

21   Harry Sievers, *Benjamin Harrison: Hoosier President* (Newton: American Political Biography Press, 1996), 268; Peter B. Doran, *Breaking Rockefeller: The Incredible Story of the Ambitious Rivals Who Toppled an Oil Empire* (New York: Penguin Publishing Group, 2017) 188; Daniel Yergin, *The Prize: The Epic Quest for Oil, Money & Power* (New York: Free Press, 2008), 94.

22   Chernow, *Titan*, 334–36.

23   David Zeiler, "How Big Money in Politics Bought a Presidential Election - in 1896," Money Morning, June 29, 2016, https://moneymorning.com/2016/05/20/how-big -money-in-politics-bought-a-presidential-election-in-1896; Steve Weinberg, *Taking on the Trust: How Ida Tarbell Brought Down John D. Rockefeller and Standard Oil* (New York: Norton, 2008), 194. Even though Rockefeller effectively retired and stopped coming to the office, he retained his title as president for another decade, which helped maintain his status as a political target.

24   Flynn, *God's Gold*, 369.

Chapter 2: The Rise of the Progressives

1   Gabriel Kolko, *The Triumph of Conservatism: A Reinterpretation of American History, 1900–1916* (London: The Free Press, 1977), 2–10.
2   Hubbard, *John D. Rockefeller and His Career*, 178.
3   Chernow, *Titan*, 432.
4   Flynn, *God's Gold,* 369. Rockefeller was not wrong to fear assassination. The 1919 anarchist mail bombs that hit Attorney General A. Mitchell Palmer's house had targeted Rockefeller, among others, as well.
5   Arthur M. Johnson, "Theodore Roosevelt and the Bureau of Corporations," *The Mississippi Valley Historical Review* 45, no. 4 (March 1959): 571–90; Edmund Morris, *Theodore Rex* (New York: Random House, 2001), 206. The Bureau of Corporations was the precursor to the modern Federal Trade Commission.
6   Flynn, *God's Gold*, 386–90; Magnuson, *For Profit*, 192–93.
7   Flynn, *God's Gold*, 386–90.
8   Magnuson, *For Profit*, 192–93.
9   Flynn, *God's Gold*, 386–90.
10 Tevi Troy, *What Jefferson Read, Ike Watched, and Obama Tweeted* (Washington, DC: Regnery History, 2013), 61.
11 Theodore Roosevelt, "Address of President Roosevelt at the Laying of the Corner Stone of the Office Building of the House of Representatives (The Man With The Muck-Rake)," April 14, 1906, https://voicesofdemocracy.umd.edu/theodore-roosevelt-the-man-with-the-muck-rake-speech-text/.
12 Kathleen Dalton, *Theodore Roosevelt: A Strenuous Life* (New York: Knopf, 2002), 298.
13 Magnuson, *For Profit*, 192–93.
14 Bill Markley, "Theodore Roosevelt, That Damned Cowboy," True West, May 10, 2018, https://truewestmagazine.com/article/theodore-roosevelt-that-damned-cowboy; Grant Segall, *John D. Rockefeller: Anointed with Oil* (New York: Oxford University Press, 2000), 88.
15 Morris, *Theodore Rex*, 355, 360.
16 Ibid., 355, 361.
17 Ibid., 361, 363; Johnson, "Theodore Roosevelt and the Bureau of Corporations," 571–90.
18 Chernow, *Titan*, 519.
19 Susan Berfield, *Hour of Fate*, 25; Chernow, *The House of Morgan*, 82.
20 Baker et al., "From Plutocracy to Progressivism?"; Susan Berfield, *Hour of Fate*, 141–47.
21 Chernow, *The House of Morgan*, 105–08; Berfield, *Hour of Fate*, 207–08.
22 Steven H. Gittelman, *J. P. Morgan and the Transportation Kings: The Titanic and Other Disasters* (Lanham: University Press of America, Inc., 2012), eBook, 195–96, 203–207.
23 Johnson, "Theodore Roosevelt and the Bureau of Corporations," 571–90.
24 Theodore Roosevelt, "Special Message to the Senate and House of Representatives," May 4, 1906, The American Presidency Project, https://www.presidency.ucsb.edu/documents/special-message-393.

25   David E. Sanger, "The Nation: Big Time; From Trustbusters To Trust Trusters," *New York Times*, December 6, 1998, https://www.nytimes.com/1998/12/06/weekinr eview/the-nation-big-time-from-trustbusters-to-trust-trusters.html; Johnson, "Theodore Roosevelt and the Bureau of Corporations," 571–90; Chernow, *Titan*, 537.

26   Morris, *Theodore Rex*, 495.

27   Chernow, *Titan*, 519.

28   Robert H. Wiebe, "The House of Morgan and the Executive, 1905–1913," *The American Historical Review* 65, no. 1 (1959): pp. 49–60, https://doi.org/10.2307 /1846601; Robert Bruner and Sean Carr, *The Panic of 1907: Heralding a New Era of Finance, Capitalism, and Democracy* (Hoboken: Wiley, 2023), 203–205.

29   Chernow, *The House of Morgan*, 111–12.

30   Segall, *John D. Rockefeller*, 90–91; Chernow, *Titan*, 544. Twain's joke appeared in *Harper's*. Writing in the voice of Satan, Twain jibed that, "Since the Board daily accepts contributions from me, why should it decline them from Mr. Rockefeller, who is as good as I am?"

31   Chernow, *Titan*, 544.

32   Morris, *Theodore Rex*, 495; Chernow, *Titan*, 545.

33   Morris, *Theodore Rex*, 495. Foraker's disgusting remark, which I am loathe to repeat, was, "All coons look alike to me." Roosevelt's on-stage retort, showing his revulsion towards racism, was, "Well, all coons do not look alike to me."

34   Morris, *Theodore Rex*, 536–37.

35   Ibid.

36   Flynn, *God's Gold*, 436–37.

37   "Oil King Rockefeller has President Roosevelt Nervous," United Press International, October 31, 1908, https://www.upi.com/Archives/1908/10/31/Oil-king-Rockefeller -has-President-Roosevelt-nervous/1942711015038/.

38   Morris, *Theodore Rex*, 535.

39   Chernow, *Titan*, 554.

40   Doran, *Breaking Rockefeller*, 234; Robby Soave, *Tech Panic: Why We Shouldn't Fear Facebook and the Future*. (New York: Threshold, 2021), 84.

41   For more detail on Bork and antitrust, see section on Bill Gates, pages 141-143, 156, 164.

42   Segall, *John D. Rockefeller*, 99–100.

43   Ibid.

44   Berfield, *Hour of Fate*, 300; Susie J. Pak, *Gentlemen Bankers: The World of J. P. Morgan* (Cambridge, Massachusetts: Harvard University Press, 2013), 35. eBook, https://ebookcentral.proquest.com/lib/duke/detail.action?docID=3301314.

45   Henry Ford, *Henry Ford: My Life and Work* (Garden City: Doubleday, Page & Co., 1922), 22–28.

46   Magnuson. *For Profit*, 154.

47   Burton W. Folsom, "Ford Did Indeed Have a Better Idea," Mackinac Center for Public Policy, July 7, 2003, https://www.mackinac.org/V2003–20.

48   Magnuson. *For Profit*, 165–175.

49   Ibid., 175.

50   Ford, *Henry Ford: My Life and Work*, 266. Note: originally published in 1922.

51   Ibid., 16–17.

52   Ibid., 17.

53   Hillary Mannion, "Motor Cars Come to the White House," White House Historical Association, 2010, https://www.whitehousehistory.org/motor-cars-come-to-the -white-house.

54   Reynold Wik, *Henry Ford and Grassroots America* (Ann Arbor: University of Michigan Press, 1973), 39.

55   Steven Watts, *The People's Tycoon: Henry Ford and the American Century* (New York: Vintage Books, 2006), 210.

56   Wik, *Henry Ford and Grassroots America*, 39.

57   Erica Gunderson, "Author Makes Case for Edith Wilson as 'Madam President.'" WTTW, November 14, 2016, https://news.wttw.com/2016/11/14/author-makes -case-edith-wilson-madam-president.

58   Vincent Curcio, *Henry Ford* (New York: Oxford University Press, 2013), 86–90.

59   Watts, *The People's Tycoon*, 281; A. J. Baime, *The Arsenal of Democracy: FDR, Detroit, and an Epic Quest to Arm an America at War* (Boston: Mariner Books, Houghton Mifflin Harcourt, 2015), 30.

60   Baime, *The Arsenal of Democracy,* 30; Ford, *Henry Ford: My Life and Work,* 331.

61   Frank Ernest Hill and Allan Nevins, *Henry Ford's Peace Ship* (Boston: New Word City, 2017).

62   Ford Model T joke postcard circa 1915, Benson Ford Research Collection, The Henry Ford, https://www.thehenryford.org/collections-and-research/digital-collections /artifact/313207#slide=gs-219667.

63   Ford jokes continued to be a thing for decades. See Appendix 3, pages 272–4.

64   Baime, *The Arsenal of Democracy,* 30; Ford, *Henry Ford: My Life and Work,* 331; Hill and Nevins, *Henry Ford's Peace Ship.*

65   Hill and Nevins, *Henry Ford's Peace Ship*; Jeff Guinn, *The Vagabonds: The Story of Henry Ford and Thomas Edison's Ten-Year Road Trip* (New York: Simon & Schuster, 2021), 59–60.

66   Baime, *The Arsenal of Democracy,* 31; Guinn, *The Vagabonds,* 61.

67   Baime, *The Arsenal of Democracy,* 286; Hill and Nevins, *Henry Ford's Peace Ship.*

68   Hill and Nevins, *Henry Ford's Peace Ship.*

69   Guinn, *The Vagabonds,* 61.

70   Ford, *Henry Ford: My Life and Work,* 331; Curcio, *Henry Ford*, 92.

71   Watts, *The People's Tycoon,* 10; Guinn, *The Vagabonds*, 65.

72   Flynn, *God's Gold,* 456–57.

73   Watts, 297–98.

74   Wik, *Henry Ford and Grassroots America,* 169; Watts, *The People's Tycoon,* 298.

75   Curcio, *Henry Ford*, 97; Watts, *The People's Tycoon,* 298.

76   Wik, *Henry Ford and Grassroots America,* 169.

77   Curcio, *Henry Ford*, 174–76.

78   Roosevelt was anti–Henry Ford, not Ford automobiles. In 1911, he had cheered on Ford driver Frank Kulick in an upset in a race against a six-cylinder Knox automobile. As Roosevelt watched Kulick's comeback victory, he shouted from the stands, "Marvelous, marvelous, marvelous." Wik, *Henry Ford and Grassroots America*, 39.

79   Richard Snow, *I Invented the Modern Age: The Rise of Henry Ford* (New York: Scribner, 2014), 286; Curcio, *Henry Ford*, 176; Eric Felten, "History Lesson: Henry Ford Was the World's Biggest Sore Loser," *Washington Examiner*, November 27, 2018, https://www.washingtonexaminer.com/weekly-standard/history-lesson -henry-ford-was-the-worlds-biggest-sore-loser.

Chapter 3: The Roaring Twenties

1   Ellen Terrell, "When a quote is not (exactly) a quote: The Business of America is Business Edition," *Inside Adams* (blog), Library of Congress, January 17, 2019, https://blogs.loc.gov/inside_adams/2019/01/when-a-quote-is-not-exactly -a-quote-the-business-of-america-is-business-edition.

2   Wik, *Henry Ford and Grassroots America,* 4; Curcio, *Henry Ford*, 188–89; Watts, *The People's Tycoon*, 217–18, 333; David Lanier Lewis, *The Public Image of Henry Ford: An American Folk Hero and His Company* (Detroit: Wayne State University Press, 1976), 129.

3   "Taft Flays Story of Zion Protocols," *New York Times*, December 24, 1920, https: //timesmachine.nytimes.com/timesmachine/1920/12/24/103519170.html ?pageNumber=4; David W. Dunlap. "Exposing the 'Protocols' as a Fraud," *New York Times*, October 27, 2016, https://www.nytimes.com/2016/10/28/insider/1920 –21-exposing-the-protocols-as-a-fraud.html; Theodore Roosevelt died on January 6, 1919. Had he been alive in 1921, he would likely have joined the three other presidents in signing the statement denouncing Ford's anti-Semitism.

4   At a speech to convicts at Sing Sing prison in Ossining, New York, Ford clumsily said, "I'm so glad to see you all here." Vincent Curcio observed on his poor speaking that, "It gives one pause to think how history might have been altered if Henry Ford had possessed the ability to speak even reasonably well in public." Curcio, *Henry Ford*, 187.

5   Watts, *The People's Tycoon*, 333. Burroughs was also friends with Theodore Roosevelt, who was no friend of Ford.

6   Guinn, *The Vagabonds*, 169.

7   Ibid., 181.

8   Curcio, *Henry Ford*, 187–88; Guinn, *The Vagabonds*, chapter 8.

9   "The Presidency: Mr. Coolidge's Week: Sep. 17, 1923," *TIME*, September 17, 1923, http://content.time.com/time/subscriber/article/0,33009,727363–1,00.html.

10   Joseph Kip Kosek, "Henry Ford for President!," History News Network, https: //historynewsnetwork.org/article/138750; Guinn, *The Vagabonds*, chapter 8; Watts, *The People's Tycoon*, 440–41.

11   Guinn, *The Vagabonds*, 232–36; Note: Coolidge's other son, Calvin Jr., died after getting a blister while playing tennis without socks on the White House tennis courts. The blister became infected and Cal died, devastating Coolidge.

12   Guinn, *The Vagabonds*, 236–38.

13   Isaiah Wilner, *The Man Time Forgot: A Tale of Genius, Betrayal, and the Creation of Time Magazine* (New York: Harper Perennial, 2007), 32.

14   W. A. Swanberg, *Luce and His Empire* (New York: Charles Scribner's Sons, 1973), 52.

15   Ibid., 73; Wolcott Gibbs, "Time . . . Fortune . . . Life . . . Luce," *The New Yorker*, November 20, 1936, https://www.newyorker.com/magazine/1936/11/28 /time-fortune-life-luce.

16   Arthur F. Fleser, *A Rhetorical Study of the Speaking of Calvin Coolidge*, (Lewiston: Edwin Mellen Press, 1990), 87.

17   Alan Brinkley, "Henry Luce and the Launch of Time Magazine," *Vanity Fair*, May 23, 2014, https://www.vanityfair.com/news/2010/05/time-magazine-henry-luce.

18   Ibid.

19   Alan Brinkley, *The Publisher: Henry Luce and His American Century.* (New York: Alfred A. Knopf, 2010), 168–69.

20   Brinkley, *The Publisher,* 168–69; Gibbs, "Time . . . Fortune . . . Life . . . Luce."

21   Graham Daseler, "The Fall of the House of Warner: The Warner Brothers," *Bright Lights Film Journal*, April 17, 2019, https://brightlightsfilm.com/the-fall-of -the-house-of-warner-the-warner-brothers/#.YQg-h45KjIU; Michael Schulman, *Oscar Wars: A History of Hollywood in Gold, Sweat, and Tears* (New York: HarperCollins, 2023), 35.

22   Daseler, "The Fall of the House of Warner."

23   Tevi Troy, *Shall We Wake the President: Two Centuries of Disaster Management from the Oval Office* (New York: Lyons Press, 2016), 66.

24   Kat Eschner, "Before 1929, Nobody Thought the President Needed a Telephone in his Office," *Smithsonian Magazine*, March 29, 2017, https://www.smithsonianmag .com/smart-news/1929-nobody-thought-president-needed-telephone-his-office -180962646/.

25   Brian Corey, "Henry Ford Dedicates the Thomas Edison Institute," This Day in Automotive History, October 21, 2016, https://automotivehistory.org/october -21-1929-henry-ford-dedicates-the-thomas-edison-institute/.

26   Watts, *The People's Tycoon*, 503–04.

Chapter 4: The Great Depression

1   Watts, *The People's Tycoon*, 536–37.

2   Ibid.; Wik, *Henry Ford and Grassroots America,* 4; Curcio, *Henry Ford*, 186–87.

3   Watts, *The People's Tycoon*, 536–37.

4   Conrad Black, *Franklin Delano Roosevelt: Champion of Freedom* (New York: Public Affairs, 2003), 202; Michael Roberts, *The Long Depression: How It Happened, Why It Happened, and What Happens Next* (Chicago: Haymarket Book, 2016), 46.

5   Jack Warner, *My Hundred Years in Hollywood* (New York: Random House, 1965), 208; Lara Jacobson, "The Warner Brothers Prove Their Patriotism," *Voces Novae* 10, article 2 (2018), https://digitalcommons.chapman.edu/vocesnovae/vol10/iss1/2; Stephen Talbot, "On with the Show." *Washington Post*, January 21, 2001, https: //www.washingtonpost.com/archive/lifestyle/magazine/2001/01/21/on-with-the -show/942fbf33–6800-42f2-b07b-35a4eb1a0ef0/.

6   Warner, *My Hundred Years in Hollywood*, 216; Stephen Talbot, "On with the Show."

7   Jacobson, "The Warner Brothers Prove Their Patriotism."

8   Warner, *My Hundred Years in Hollywood*, 216; Jacobson, "The Warner Brothers Prove Their Patriotism"; Talbot, "On with the Show."

9   Burton W. Peretti, *The Leading Man: Hollywood and the Presidential Image* (New Brunswick, New Jersey: Rutgers University Press, 2012), http://www.jstor.org/stable/j.ctt5hjdtx; Troy, *What Jefferson Read, Ike Watched, and Obama Tweeted,* 120; Stephen Vaughn, "Spies, National Security, and the 'Inertia Projector': The Secret Service Films of Ronald Reagan," *American Quarterly* 39, no. 3 (1987): 355–80, doi:10.2307/2712884.

10   Daseler, "The Fall of the House of Warner"; Peretti, *The Leading Man,* 123–24.

11   Brinkley, *The Publisher,* 225; Gibbs, "Time . . . Fortune . . . Life . . . Luce."

12   Gibbs, "Time . . . Fortune . . . Life . . . Luce."; David Nasaw, *The Patriarch: The Remarkable Life and Turbulent Times of Joseph P. Kennedy* (New York: Penguin, 2012); Derek Leebaert, *Unlikely Heroes: Franklin Roosevelt, His Four Lieutenants, and the World They Made* (New York: St. Martin's Press, 2023), 91.

13   Alan Brinkley, interview by Jill Lepore, "Henry Luce and the American Century," June 14, 2010, transcript, Kennedy Library Forum, John F. Kennedy Presidential Library and Museum, https://www.jfklibrary.org/events-and-awards/forums/past-forums/transcripts/henry-luce-and-the-american-century.

14   Swanberg, *Luce and His Empire,* 194; James L. Baughman, *Henry R. Luce and the Rise of the American News Media* (Boston: Twayne, 1987), 106.

15   Anne Applebaum, *Red Famine: Stalin's War on Ukraine* (New York: Anchor Books, 2017), 380.

16   Brinkley, *The Publisher,* 237.

17   Swanberg, *Luce and his Empire,* 196.

18   Ibid.; Lance Morrow, "Historical Laughter," *Smithsonian Magazine,* November 2009, https://www.smithsonianmag.com/arts-culture/historical-laughter-145487035.

19   Lance Morrow, "When Time's 'Man of the Year' Meant Something," *Wall Street Journal,* December 2, 2022, https://www.wsj.com/articles/time-magazine-man-of-the-year-meant-leaders-cover-story-figure-zelensky-journalism-subject-media-11669994698.

20   Morrow, "Historical Laughter."

21   Swanberg, *Luce and his Empire,* 197.

22   "May 10, 1939." Franklin Roosevelt Day by Day, Franklin D. Roosevelt Presidential Library, http://www.fdrlibrary.marist.edu/daybyday/daylog/may-10th-1939; Graham J. White, *FDR and the Press* (Chicago: University of Chicago Press, 1979), 52; Robert E. Herzstein, *Henry R. Luce: A Political Portrait of the Man Who Created the American Century* (New York: Scribner, 1994), 30.

23   Baughman, *Henry R. Luce and the Rise of the American News Media,* 107–8; Herzstein, *Henry Luce,* 32.

24   Brinkley, *The Publisher,* 234–35.

25   White, *FDR and the Press,* 52; Swanberg, *Luce and his Empire,* 278–79.

26   Franklin D. Roosevelt, Campaign Address on the Federal Budget at Pittsburgh, Pennsylvania, October 19, 1932. Interestingly, Roosevelt liked Ford cars, driving a Model A in the late 1920s at a time when they were difficult to purchase. These much-hyped high performance and affordable "Baby Lincoln" Model As were in high demand and short supply, even as celebrities like Douglas Fairbanks, Mary Pickford—and FDR—managed to get them. FDR's was a gift from Edsel, who always

would have warmer relations with Roosevelt than his father would. Roosevelt would also drive both a 1936 and then a 1938 Ford Phaeton convertible with hand controls to allow him to control the vehicle. The latter had Ford's innovative V-8 engine; cf. Curcio, *Henry Ford*, 204; "FDR And His Automobiles," The Little White House Newsletter, Roosevelt's Little White House, Fall 2016, https://gastateparks.org/sites /default/files/parks/pdf/littlewhitehouse/LittleWhiteHouse_NewsletterFall2016 .pdf; Watts, *The People's Tycoon*, 641–42.

27 Watts, *The People's Tycoon*, 546–47.

28 John Cunningham Wood and Michael C. Wood, eds., *Henry Ford: Critical Evaluations in Business and Management* (Oxfordshire: Routledge, 2003), 204–5.

29 Wood and Wood, eds., *Henry Ford*, 204–5.

30 Watts, *The People's Tycoon*, 546–47; Wood and Wood, eds., *Henry Ford*, 204–5.

31 Watts, *The People's Tycoon*, 547–52.

32 Ibid. Jonah Goldberg, author of *Liberal Fascism*, has called Johnson "one of the most fascistic government officials in American history."

33 Watts, *The People's Tycoon*, 547–52.

34 Wood and Wood, eds., *Henry Ford*, 204–5.

35 Ibid.

36 Ibid.

37 Watts, *The People's Tycoon*, 547–52.

38 Ibid.; Martin Halpern, *Unions, Radicals, and Democratic Presidents: Seeking Social Change in the Twentieth Century* (Westport: Praeger, 2003), 48.

39 David Pietrusza, *Roosevelt Sweeps Nation: FDR's 1936 Landslide and the Triumph of the Liberal Idea* (New York: Diversion Books, 2022), 45, 306, 393.

40 "Roosevelt Invites Ford to Luncheon to Talk Recovery," *New York Times*, April 22, 1938, https://timesmachine.nytimes.com/timesmachine/1938/04/22/98124522 .pdf?pdf_redirect=true&ip=0; cf., Martin Halpern, *Unions, Radicals, and Democratic Presidents*, 44–56.

41 Mark Jones, "Mr. Ford Goes to Washington," Boundary Stones, WETA, January 29, 2013, https://boundarystones.weta.org/2013/01/30/mr-ford-goes-washington; Watts, *The People's Tycoon*, 547–52. Here's the full "exchange" between the two men:

> *President: Henry, what I want to know is what you would do if you were in my shoes.*
>
> *Henry: Shoes wouldn't make any difference; we're in a situation now where we are swimming, not hiking.*
>
> *President: You know what I mean; if you were President what would you do?*
>
> *Henry: Well, for one thing, I wouldn't run the car without having the brakes adjusted.*
>
> *President: My brakes are alright.*
>
> *Henry: Do they hold?*
>
> *President: No; that's what makes the ride so exciting!*
>
> *Henry: Speed is a great thing and I emphasize it in the sales talks, but there are other things just as important.*
>
> *President: What?*
>
> *Henry: For one thing, you've got to have good headlights.*

President: Now, Henry, you're no fellow to talk about headlights. I never saw a Ford with both headlights working except once.

Henry: Where was that? I heard there was one, but I've never been able to trace it.

President: Getting down to cases, I can't understand why you aren't with me heart and soul. You were a pioneer in giving labor higher pay and a better break.

Henry: I'm glad to know somebody remembers that. My point, Mr. President, is that I think an employer is also entitled to a break.

President: Where did you get that idea?

Henry: I think it must have been in a book.

President: Don't tell me you have read a book, Henry!

Henry: Why not? There's not much else an auto manufacturer can do these days.

President: Are you against Government in business?

Henry: Yes. I hate to think what would have happened to Lizzie if I'd had to raise her under Federal supervision.

President: You believe in spending vast sums if necessary, don't you?

Henry: Yes, but you never can convince me that when the car has broken down all you've got to do to make it work again is to keep doubling the orders for oil, gas, new tires, and expensive varnish.

President: You're like all industrialists; you criticize without making any helpful suggestions. Why don't you tell me what I ought to do?

Henry: How do I know you'd listen?

President: I listen to everybody.

Henry: That's the trouble!

President: And they told me all the knocks had been taken from the Fords!

Henry: Well, we don't seem to be getting anywhere in this chat. But it's nice seeing you, just the same.

President: What was the crack you made about coming here to show me a man who didn't want anything?

Henry: Oh, I said something like that to a reporter. And I mean it. I ain't asking a thing. There's nothing I want from the Government.

President: Up in the attic I found some of the finest antiques last week. There's a fiddle up there that must be 200 years old and a . . .

Henry: Oh, well, that's different.

(This last bit was a reference to Henry Ford's wildly popular auto show fiddle contests of the 1920s.)

42 "Roosevelt Invites Ford to Luncheon to Talk Recovery," *New York Times*.
43 "Ford Starts to Capital," *New York Times*, April 27, 1938, https://timesmachine.nytimes.com/timesmachine/1938/04/27/98127311.pdf?pdf_redirect=true&ip=0.
44 Jones, "Mr. Ford Goes to Washington"; Watts, *The People's Tycoon*, 547–52; Halpern, *Unions, Radicals, and Democratic Presidents*, 53.
45 Leebaert, *Unlikely Heroes*, 365.
46 Chernow, *Titan*, xx.

Chapter 5: Corporations and the Great War

1 Baime, *The Arsenal of Democracy*, 42, 60–61.

2   Ibid., 60–61.
3   Ibid.
4   Ibid., 78–80; Watts, *The People's Tycoon*, 641–42.
5   Baime, *The Arsenal of Democracy*, 45, 53, 86, 99; Leebaert, *Unlikely Heroes,* 142. Ford had fans as well, but they were unsavory ones: 400 German-American Nazis cheered at the prospect of Ford running for president at a 1938 Bund rally in Yorkville, New York.
6   Watts, 641–42.
7   "Willow Run," Encyclopedia of Detroit, Detroit Historical Society, https://detroit historical.org/learn/encyclopedia-of-detroit/willow-run.
8   Watts, *The People's Tycoon*, 634–35; Snow, *I Invented the Modern Age*, 286.
9   Baime, *The Aresenal of Democracy*, 179.
10   Watts, *The People's Tycoon*, 634–35; Baime, *The Arsenal of Democracy*, 179.
11   Curcio, *Henry Ford*, 95, 156.
12   Ibid., 267–68; Harry Truman, "Remarks in the Enlisted Men's Mess Hall, Aberdeen, Md., Proving Ground," transcript of speech delivered at Aberdeen Proving Ground, Aberdeen, Maryland, February 17, 1951, Harry S. Truman Library and Museum, https://www.trumanlibrary.gov/library/public-papers/38/remarks-enlisted -mens-mess-hall-aberdeen-md-proving-ground.
13   Stephen Vaughn, "Ronald Reagan, Warner Bros., and Military Preparedness, 1937–1945," *Film Historia* 3, no. 1–2 (1993), https://revistes.ub.edu/index.php/film-historia/article/view/12186.
14   Ibid.; Peretti, *The Leading Man*, 187–88.
15   Brinkley, *The Publisher*, 279; White, *FDR and the Press*, 52.
16   White, *FDR and the Press*, 52.
17   Brinkley, *The Publisher*, 302.
18   Ibid., 381–82.
19   Thomas Griffith, *Harry and Teddy: The Turbulent Friendship of Press Lord Henry R. Luce and His Favorite Reporter, Theodore H. White.* (New York: Random House, 1995), 66.
20   Brinkley, *The Publisher*, 397–401.
21   Griffith, *Harry and Teddy,* 66; Brinkley Lepore interview.

Chapter 6: The Postwar Boom

1   Brinkley, *The Publisher*, 413–14.
2   Herzstein, *Henry Luce*, 9; Brinkley, *The Publisher*, 415.
3   Thomas G. Paterson, *Meeting the Communist Threat: Truman to Reagan* (Oxford: Oxford University Press, 1988), 56; Brinkley, *The Publisher*, 351.
4   Brinkley, *The Publisher*, 478–80; Joseph Epstein, "Henry Luce: Missionary among His Own People," *Essays in Biography* (Mount Jackson: Axios, 2012), 113.
5   Brinkley, *The Publisher*, 478–80.
6   James David Barber, *The Pulse of Politics: Electing Presidents in the Media Age* (New York: Norton, 1980), 267–68.
7   Herzstein, *Henry Luce*, 160–61.
8   Ibid.

9   Barber, *The Pulse of Politics,* 267–68; Herzstein, *Henry Luce,* 160–61.

10   Herzstein, *Henry Luce,* 162–63.

11   Ibid.

12   Joan Cook, "John K. Jessup, 72, Chief Editorial Writer for Life," *New York Times,* October 27, 1979, p. 24, https://www.nytimes.com/1979/10/27/archives/john-k-jessup-72-chief-editorial-writer-for-life.html.

13   Barber, *The Pulse of Politics,* 267–68.

14   Brinkley, *The Publisher,* 481–82.

15   Ibid., 482–83; Griffith, *Harry and Teddy,* 66.

16   Sylvia Jukes Morris, "Clare, in Love and War," *Vanity Fair,* July 1, 2014, https://archive.vanityfair.com/article/2014/7/clare-in-love-and-war.

17   Brinkley, *The Publisher,* 506.

18   Herzstein, *Henry Luce,* 163; Brinkley, *The Publisher,* 481–89.

19   William H. Honan, "Thomas Griffith, 86, Former Time Editor, Dies," *New York Times,* March 17, 2002, https://www.nytimes.com/2002/03/17/nyregion/thomas-griffith-86-former-time-editor-dies.html; Brinkley Lepore interview; Brinkley, *The Publisher,* 481–87.

20   Herzstein, *Henry Luce,* 163; Brinkley Lepore interview; Joseph Epstein, "Henry Luce: Missionary among His Own People," 94–95; Alexander Nemerov, *Fierce Poise: Helen Frankenthaler and 1950s New York* (New York: Penguin Press, 2021), 149; John Lee, "Relinquishing of Editorial Control at Time, Inc., by Henry Luce Marks End of Era; MAGAZINE EMPIRE STARTED IN 1923; 41-Year Publishing Career Has Stirred Controversy and Reaped Profits," *New York Times,* April 17, 1964, https://www.nytimes.com/1964/04/17/archives/relinquishing-of-editorial-control-at-time-inc-by-henry-luce-marks.html.

21   Nemerov, *Fierce Poise,* 149; Brinkley, *The Publisher,* 481–87; Nicholas Wapshott, *Samuelson Friedman: The Battle Over the Free Market* (New York: Norton, 2021), 75.

22   Monali Gupta, "Hollywood Film Industry Statistics & Facts 2023," *New Vision* (blog), March 17, 2023. https://www.newvisiontheatres.com/hollywood-film-industry-statistics.

23   Rick Lyman, "Ideas & Trends: Movie Moguls; The Two Faces of Lew: Last of the Old and First of the New," *New York Times,* June 9, 2002, https://www.nytimes.com/2002/06/09/weekinreview/ideas-trends-movie-moguls-two-faces-lew-last-old-first-new.html; Paul Farhi, "The Man Who Remade Hollywood," *Washington Post,* July 23, 1995, https://www.washingtonpost.com/archive/lifestyle/style/1995/07/23/the-man-who-remade-hollywood/cd26c0b3-8afa-48f5-87b9-5b83dfa0618f/.

24   Richard Natale, "Lew Wasserman Dies: Hollywood Mourns the Last of Its Moguls," *Variety,* June 3, 2002, https://variety.com/2002/scene/news/h-wood-mourns-last-of-its-moguls-1117867926/; "A New Kind of King," *TIME,* January 1, 1965, 50–51.

25   A. O. Scott, "The Shimmer and Tarnish Around a Tinseltown Titan," *New York Times*; Kathleen Sharp, *Mr. & Mrs. Hollywood* (Blackstone Publishing, 2013), 5; Natale, "Lew Wasserman Dies."

26   Sharp, *Mr. & Mrs. Hollywood,* 7.

27   "A New Kind of King," *TIME*, January 1, 1965, 50–51; Ronald Brownstein, "The Rebirth of Hollywood's Political Clout," *Los Angeles Times*, December 2, 1990, https://www.latimes.com/archives/la-xpm-1990-12-02-ca-7768-story.html.

28   Lyman, "Movie Moguls; The Two Faces of Lew."

29   Natale, "Lew Wasserman Dies"; Walter Shapiro, "Lew Wasserman," *Slate*, June 6, 2002, https://slate.com/news-and-politics/2002/06/lew-wasserman-the-man-who -ruined-movies.html.

30   "Legendary Washington Post Chief Kay Graham Dies," CNN, July 18, 200, https: //www.cnn.com/2001/ALLPOLITICS/07/17/obit.graham/index.html; Gloria Cooper, "The Making of a Publisher," *Columbia Journalism Review*, June 1997, https://www.cjr.org/60th/the-making-of-a-publisher-katharine-graham-personal -history-washington-post-gloria-cooper.php; David Remnick, "Citizen Kay," *The New Yorker*, January 12, 1997, https://www.newyorker.com/magazine/1997/01/20 /citizen-kay.

31   Andrew Szanton, "Katharine Graham and the Rise of the Washington Post," *Medium*, February 18, 2023, https://medium.com/@andrewszanton/katherine -graham-and-the-rise-of-the-washington-post-7711b89fa052.

32   Ibid.

33   Betty Glad, "Reagan's Midlife Crisis and the Turn to the Right," *Political Psychology* 10, no. 4 (1989): 593–624, https://doi.org/10.2307/3791330; Peter Schweizer, "Reagan's War: The Epic Story of His Forty-Year Struggle and Final Triumph Over Communism," *Washington Post*, November 25, 2002, https://www.washingtonpost .com/wp-srv/style/longterm/books/chap1/reaganswar.htm.

34   Connie Bruck, "The Monopolist," *The New Yorker*, April 13, 2003, https: //www.newyorker.com/magazine/2003/04/21/the-monopolist; Richard Natale, "Lew Wasserman Dies."; Christopher Silvester, "Lew Wasserman," Christopher Silvester, June 5, 2002, https://www.christophersilvester.com/lew-wasserman.

35   Brownstein, "The Rebirth of Hollywood's Political Clout."

36   Frank Rose, "Twilight of the Last Mogul," *Los Angeles Times*, May 21, 1995, https: //www.latimes.com/archives/la-xpm-1995-05-21-tm-4113-story.html; Brownstein, "The Rebirth of Hollywood's Political Clout."

37   Rose, "Twilight of the Last Mogul."

38   Ronald Brownstein, *The Power and the Glitter: The Hollywood-Washington Connection* (New York: Pantheon Books, 1990), 186; Christopher Silvester, "Lew Wasserman"; Tim Gray, "Lew Wasserman: Still Remembered as Hollywood's Ultimate Mover and Shaker," *Variety*, March 22, 2016, https://variety.com/2016/biz /news/lew-wasserman-birthday-mover-shaker-1201721984/.

39   Brownstein, "The Rebirth of Hollywood's Political Clout."

40   Gray, "Lew Wasserman." $1,000 in 1963 is the equivalent of almost $10,000 today.

41   Richard Natale, "Lew Wasserman Dies."

42   Brownstein, "The Rebirth of Hollywood's Political Clout"; Brownstein, *The Power and the Glitter*, 184; Matt Novak, "Hollywood's Secret Republicans of the 1950s," *Gizmodo*, January 17, 2017, https://gizmodo.com/hollywoods-secret-republicans -of-the-1950s-1791281253.

43 Connie Bruck, *When Hollywood Had a King: The Reign of Lew Wasserman, Who Leveraged Talent into Power and Influence* (New York: Random House, 2004), 214–15.

44 Ibid., 216–17.

45 Sharp, *Mr. & Mrs. Hollywood,* 145.

46 Farhi, "The Man Who Remade Hollywood"; Sharp, *Mr. & Mrs. Hollywood,* 143–45; Rose, "Twilight of the Last Mogul."

47 Griffith, *Harry and Teddy,* 255; Brinkley, *The Publisher,* 556–62.

48 Brinkley, *The Publisher,* 556–62; Lee, "Relinquishing of Editorial Control at Time"; Mark K. Updegrove, *Incomparable Grace: JFK in the Presidency* (New York: Dutton, 2022), 124.

Chapter 7: Stagflation and War

1 Katharine Graham, *Personal History* (New York: Alfred A. Knopf, 1997), 354, 400–401; Robin Gerber, *Katharine Graham* (New York: Penguin Group, 2005), 68–69.

2 Carol Felsenthal, *Power, Privilege, and the Post* (New York: G. P. Putnam's Son, 1993), 259; Graham, *Personal History,* 400–401; Diane K. Shah, "Katharine Graham Was Not To Be Fucked With," *Deadspin,* April 18, 2018, https://deadspin.com/katharine-graham-was-not-to-be-fucked-with-1825300673; Gerber, *Katharine Graham,* 109.

3 Remnick, "Citizen Kay," *The New Yorker*; Gerber, *Katharine Graham,* 68–69; Graham, *Personal History,* 400–401; Shah, "Katharine Graham Was Not To Be Fucked With."

4 Bruck, *When Hollywood Had a King,* 216–17.

5 Frank Rose, "Twilight of the Last Mogul," *Los Angeles Time Magazine,* May 21, 1995, https://www.frankrose.com/reporting/twilight-of-the-last-mogul/.

6 Ibid.; Brownstein, "The Rebirth of Hollywood's Political Clout."

7 Natale, "Lew Wasserman Dies."

8 Bruck, *When Hollywood Had a King,* 216–17; Lew Wasserman, "Oral History Transcript, Interview with Joe B. Frantz, December 21, 1973," Lyndon B. Johnson Library Oral Histories, Lyndon B. Johnson Presidential Library, https://www.discoverlbj.org/item/oh-wassermanl-19731221-1-80–16.

9 Natale, "Lew Wasserman Dies"; Lyman, "Movie Moguls; The Two Faces of Lew"; Lew Wasserman, Oral History Transcript.

10 Lew Wasserman, Oral History Transcript.

11 Ibid.

12 Ibid.

13 Ibid.

14 Ibid.

15 Ibid.

16 Ibid.; "A New Kind of King," *TIME,* January 1, 1965, 50–51.

17 Lew Wasserman, Oral History Transcript; Robert Dallek, "Character Above All: Lyndon B. Johnson," PBS NewsHour, https://www.pbs.org/newshour/spc/character/essays/johnson.html; "The Man and His Humor Are Recalled," *New York Times,*

January 26, 1973, https://www.nytimes.com/1973/01/26/archives/the-man-and-his -humor-are-recalled.html.

18   Lew Wasserman, Oral History Transcript.

19   "A New Kind of King," *TIME*, January 1, 1965, 50–51; Lew Wasserman, Oral History Transcript.

20   Brownstein, "The Rebirth of Hollywood's Political Clout"; Bruck, *When Hollywood Had a King*, 216–17.

21   "Lyndon Johnson, Robert Kennedy, and Jacqueline Kennedy on 20 June 1964," Tape WH6406.12, Citation #3800, *Presidential Recordings Digital Edition* [Mississippi Burning and the Passage of the Civil Rights Act, vol. 7, ed. Guian A. McKee] (Charlottesville: University of Virginia Press, 2014–), http://prde.upress.virginia. edu/conversations/9070149. Accessed June 14, 2023; Lew Wasserman, Oral History Transcript. In his oral history interview description of the incident, the Jewish Wasserman referred to the competing event as a "Jewish bar mitzvah." The Ambassador Hotel, which is no longer in existence, was also the location of the assassination of Johnson and Wasserman nemesis Bobby Kennedy, on June 4, 1968.

22   Farhi, "The Man Who Remade Hollywood."

23   Bruck, *When Hollywood Had a King*, 228–29; Lew Wasserman, Oral History Transcript.

24   Brownstein, "The Rebirth of Hollywood's Political Clout."

25   Ibid.; Bruck, *When Hollywood Had a King*, 228–29; Lew Wasserman, Oral History Transcript.

26   Bruck, *When Hollywood Had a King*, 231–32.

27   Lew Wasserman, Oral History Transcript; Bruck, *When Hollywood Had a King*, 235–36.

28   Bruck, *When Hollywood Had a King*, 223.

29   Farhi, "The Man Who Remade Hollywood."

30   Epstein, "Henry Luce: Missionary among His Own People," 97; Lee, "Relinquishing of Editorial Control at Time, Inc., by Henry Luce Marks End of Era."

31   "Nation: Henry R. Luce: End of a Pilgrimage," *TIME*, March 10, 1967, http://content .time.com/time/subscriber/article/0,33009,836722,00.html.

32   Morrow, "Historical Laughter."

33   Robert D. McFadden, "Lee Iacocca, Visionary Automaker Who Led Both Ford and Chrysler, Is Dead at 94," *New York Times*, July 2, 2019, https://www .nytimes.com/2019/07/02/obituaries/lee-iacocca-dead.html; Lee Iacocca and William Novak, *Iacocca: An Autobiography* (Toronto: Bantam Books, 1984), 337; Lee Iacocca and Catherine Whitney, *Where Have All the Leaders Gone?* (New York: Scribner, 2007), 63–64.

34   McFadden, "Lee Iacocca, Visionary Automaker Who Led Both Ford and Chrysler, Is Dead at 94"; Iacocca and Novak, *Iacocca: An Autobiography*, 61.

35   Iacocca and Novak, *Iacocca: An Autobiography*, 95; McFadden, "Lee Iacocca, Visionary Automaker Who Led Both Ford and Chrysler, Is Dead at 94."

36   "Presidential Daily Diary, November 16–30, 1969," Richard Nixon Presidential Library & Museum, www.nixonlibrary.gov/sites/default/files/virtuallibrary /documents/PDD/1969/018 November 16-30 1969.pdf.

37   McFadden, "Lee Iacocca, Visionary Automaker Who Led Both Ford and Chrysler, Is Dead at 94"; "Nixon & Detroit: Inside the Oval Office," PBS Frontline, February 21, 2002, https://www.pbs.org/wgbh/pages/frontline/shows/rollover/nixon.

38   "Nixon & Detroit: Inside the Oval Office."

39   William D. Smith, "Iacocca Urges Backing for Nixon Plans," *New York Times*, September 11, 1971, https://www.nytimes.com/1971/09/11/archives/iacocca-urges -backing-for-nixon-plans-ford-president-praises-tax.html.

40   Felsenthal, *Power, Privilege, and the Post*, 272. Graham would later say that Haldeman "made my blood run cold, and I felt sure the feeling was reciprocated." Graham, *Personal History*, 442–43.

41   Felsenthal, *Power, Privilege, and the Post*, 272.

42   Graham, *Personal History*, 442–43.

43   Remnick, "Citizen Kay"; Shah, "Katharine Graham Was Not To Be Fucked With."

44   Graham, *Personal History*, 456–57; Dylan Byers and Hadas Gold, "'Charisma and Courage,'" *POLITICO*, October 21, 2014, https://www.politico.com/story/2014/10 /ben-bradlee-dies-112094.

45   Graham, *Personal History*, 400–401; Shah, "Katharine Graham Was Not to Be Fucked With."

46   David Crumpler, "Trump's Threats against NBC Recall a 1970's Incident Involving Jacksonville TV Station," *Florida Times-Union*, October 11, 2017, https://www .jacksonville.com/story/news/2017/10/11/trump-s-threats-against-nbc-recall-1970-s -incident-involving-jacksonville-tv/15776208007. Graham was disappointed that she did not have a larger presence in the movie version of *All the President's Men*, referencing the Mitchell threat in complaining to actor Robert Redford that, "Christ, the only thing of mine in the whole movie are my tits."

47   Jack Shafer, "Lee Iacocca: The Businessman President Who Wasn't," *POLITICO*, December 29, 2019, https://www.politico.com/news/magazine/2019/12/29/lee -iacocca-the-businessman-president-who-wasnt-089596.

48   Iacocca and Novak, *Iacocca: An Autobiography*, 225.

49   Ibid.; Jimmy Carter, "Remarks on Signing Into Law the Chrysler Corporation Loan Guarantee Act of 1979," January 7, 1980, The American Presidency Project, https: //www.presidency.ucsb.edu/documents/remarks-signing-into-law-the-chrysler -corporation-loan-guarantee-act-1979.

50   Peter Behr, "Iacocca: Carter, Hill Timid on Automaker Aid," *The Washington Post*, July 18, 1980, https://login.proxy.lib.duke.edu/login?url=https://www.pro quest.com/historical-newspapers/iacocca-carter-hill-timid-on-automaker-aid /docview/147061129/se-2.

51   Mark Davis, "Murdoch Spiked Story That Might Have Beat Menzies," *Sydney Morning Herald*, November 6, 2010, https://www.smh.com.au/national /murdoch-spiked-story-that-might-have-beat-menzies-20101105-17hlk.html.

52   William H. Meyers, "Murdoch's Global Power Play," *New York Times*, June 12, 1988, https://www.nytimes.com/1988/06/12/magazine/murdoch-s-global-power-play .html.

53   Ibid.; Jonathan Mahler and Jim Rutenberg, "How Rupert Murdoch's Empire of Influence Remade the World," *New York Times*, April 3, 2019, https://www.nytimes.com/interactive/2019/04/03/magazine/rupert-murdoch-fox-news-trump.html.

54   Mahler and Rutenberg, "How Rupert Murdoch's Empire of Influence Remade the World"; Meyers, "Murdoch's Global Power Play"; John F Berry, "Ex-Im Chief Pushed Loan for Murdoch," *Washington Post*, March 19, 1980, https://www.washingtonpost.com/archive/business/1980/03/19/ex-im-chief-pushed-loan-for-murdoch/e3abfd09-ec6f-428b-812b-c232081c050e/.

55   Bruck, *When Hollywood Had a King*, 289.

56   Leonard Sloane, "Westinghouse and MCA Drop Merger Plan After Trust Talks," *New York Times*, April 25, 1969, https://timesmachine.nytimes.com/timesmachine/1969/04/25/90095640.html?pageNumber=65; Bruck, *When Hollywood Had a King*, 253–54.

57   Bruck, *When Hollywood Had a King*, 280.

58   Ibid., 289–90.

59   Katherine Clarke, "Hollywood Scion Asks $125 Million for L.A. Mansion," *Wall Street Journal*, October 18, 2018, https://www.wsj.com/articles/hollywood-scion-asks-record-125-million-for-l-a-mansion-1539873135; Bruck, *When Hollywood Had a King*, 269–70.

60   James Warren, "Introducing Leonid Brezhnev to 'True Grit," *Chicago Tribune*, January 21, 2005, https://www.chicagotribune.com/news/ct-xpm-2005-01-21-0501210003-story.html. When Yablans called, Kissinger said, "How nice of you to call me. I have a problem which is probably insolvable. We have Brezhnev in Camp David over the weekend and he's a nut on cowboy movies and I've got some cowboy movies but now I've found out he doesn't speak a word of English." Yablans's humorous response was, "How about Hebrew?" to which Kissinger retorted, "Hebrew, I think he would love, particularly given the Russian fondness with Jews."

61   Bruck, *When Hollywood Had a King*, 269–70.

62   Warren, "Introducing Leonid Brezhnev to 'True Grit'"; "Memorandum of Conversation, Ford, Kissinger," The White House, January 27, 1976, Gerald R. Ford Library, https://www.fordlibrarymuseum.gov/library/document/0314/1553350.pdf.

63   Gerald Ford, "Remarks of the President at the Katharine Graham Dinner for Carroll Kilpatrick," September 15, 1975, Gerald R. Ford Presidential Library, The President's Speeches and Statements, Box 16, https://www.fordlibrarymuseum.gov/library/document/0122/1252504.pdf; Douglas B. Feaver, "Carroll Kilpatrick Dies," *Washington Post*, March 25, 1984, https://www.washingtonpost.com/archive/local/1984/03/25/carroll-kilpatrick-dies/0e82eaea-2f05-4d77-96ad-c583e7f63e2e/; Ben Bradlee, *A Good Life: Newspapering and Other Adventures* (New York: Simon & Schuster, 1995) 403; Felsenthal, *Power, Privilege, and the Post*, 375.

64   Gerber, *Katharine Graham*, 192.

65   "Press: Brzezinski's Zipper Was Up," *TIME*, December 31, 1979, https://content.time.com/time/subscriber/article/0,33009,912611,00.html.

66   Sharp, *Mr. & Mrs. Hollywood*, 268–69.

67   "Mr. Hollywood," *The Washington Post*, June 5, 2002, https://www.washing tonpost.com/archive/lifestyle/2002/06/05/mr-hollywood/bfd249e9-dec9–4dc1 –929f-273e44a607ff/.

68   Gary Susman, "Hollywood Power Broker Lew Wasserman Dies at 89," EW.com, June 4, 2002, https://ew.com/article/2002/06/04/hollywood-power-broker-lew -wasserman-dies-89/; Geraldine Fabrikant, "A Movie Giant's Unfinished Script," *New York Times*, October 20, 1985, https://www.nytimes.com/1985/10/20 /business/a-movie-giant-s-unfinished-script.html; Sharp, *Mr. & Mrs. Hollywood*, 317–18.

Chapter 8: The Reagan Boom

1   Ronald Reagan, "The President's News Conference," Transcript of Speech delivered in Washington D.C., August 12, 1986, https://www.reaganfoundation.org/ronald -reagan/reagan-quotes-speeches/news-conference-1/.

2   The American Presidency Project, University of California Santa Barbara, https: //www.presidency.ucsb.edu/.

3   Iacocca and Whitney, *Where Have All the Leaders Gone?*, 64–65; Earl W. Foell, "Lee Iacocca: The Man Who Wouldn't Be President," *Christian Science Monitor*, January 24, 1984, https://www.csmonitor.com/1984/0124/012422.html; Ronald Reagan, *The Reagan Diaries*, ed. Douglas Brinkley (New York: HarperCollins, 2007), entry for January 16, 1983; Shafer, "Lee Iacocca: The Businessman President Who Wasn't."

4   Thomas J. Healey, "Coming Face to Face with Lee Iacocca," Harvard Kennedy School: Mossavar-Rahmani Center for Business and Government, July 17, 2019, https://www.hks.harvard.edu/centers/mrcbg/news-events/healey; Iacocca and Novak, *Iacocca: An Autobiography*, 284–85.

5   Iacocca and Novak, *Iacocca: An Autobiography*, 227, 293–94.

6   Iacocca and Whitney, *Where Have All the Leaders Gone?*, 95; "Reagan Relies on 'Stooges'-Iacocca," *Los Angeles Times*, May 23, 1988, https://login.proxy.lib.duke .edu/login?url=https://www.proquest.com/newspapers/reagan-relies-on-stooges -iacocca/docview/292917663/se-2.

7   Daniel Rowe, "Lee Iacocca Was Known for His Business Skills. Why We Need to Remember His Politics, Too.," *Washington Post*, July 6, 2019, https://www.washing-tonpost.com/outlook/2019/07/08/lee-iacocca-was-known-his-business-skills-why-we-need-remember-his-politics-too; Shafer, "Lee Iacocca: The Businessman President Who Wasn't"; Fox Butterfield, "Trump Hints of Dreams Beyond Building," *New York Times*, October 5, 1987, section B, page 1, https://www.nytimes. com/1987/10/05/nyregion/trump-hints-of-dreams-beyond-building.html. The *Miami Vice* cameo came about in part because Iacocca was part of a running joke on the show. The comic relief character of Izzy Moreno, played by Martin Ferrero with an exaggerated Cuban accent, regularly cited Iacocca's autobiography, often inaccurately; cf. Steffan Piper, "Miami Vice: When Art Changed the World and a City was Powerless to Resist," Medium, April 24, 2020, https://steffanpiper.medium .com/miami-vice-when-art-changed-the-world-and-a-city-was-powerless-to -resist-85cf9ba97c46.

8   Iacocca and Whitney, *Where Have All the Leaders Gone?*, 56.

9 Rowe, "Lee Iacocca Was Known for His Business Skills. Why We Need to Remember His Politics, Too"; Iacocca and Whitney, *Where Have All the Leaders Gone?*, 104–105.

10 Ilan Ben-Meir, "That Time In 1988 Trump Told Oprah What Was Wrong With America's Foreign Policy," BuzzFeed News, July 15, 2015, https://www.buzzfeed news.com/article/ilanbenmeir/that-time-in-1988-trump-told-oprah-what-was -wrong-with-ameri.

11 Elahe Izadi, "Oprah for President in 2020? Here's Everything You Need to Know," *Washington Post*, December 3, 2021, https://www.washingtonpost.com/news/arts -and-entertainment/wp/2018/01/08/oprah-for-president-in-2020-heres-everything -you-need-to-know/.

12 Bill Clinton, "Remarks on Signing the National Child Protection Act of 1993," December 20, 1993, The American Presidency Project, https://www.presidency.ucsb .edu/documents/remarks-signing-the-national-child-protection-act-1993.

13 David Gelles, *The Man Who Broke Capitalism* (New York: Simon & Schuster, 2022), 27–29, 40–42; note: the neutron bomb is a weapon designed to kill people while leaving nearby buildings and infrastructure intact.

14 Matthew J. Belvedere, "Jack Welch on Why He's Voting for Trump," CNBC, September 20, 2016, https://www.cnbc.com/2016/09/20/jack-welch-on-why -hes-voting-for-trump.html; Reagan, *The Reagan Diaries*, 423.

15 Gelles, *The Man Who Broke Capitalism*, 48–52; David A. Vise, "GE to Buy RCA for $6.2 Billion," *Washington Post*, December 12, 1985, https://www.washingtonpost .com/archive/politics/1985/12/12/ge-to-buy-rca-for-62-billion/9d2145e1–3621-466e -93d0–592055310652/.

16 Chuck Conconi, "PERSONALITIES," *Washington Post*, February 1, 1989, https: //login.proxy.lib.duke.edu/login?url=https://www.proquest.com/newspapers /personalities/docview/307139542/se-2; Jerry Knight, "Clinton's CEO Lunch Bunch; Over Meals, the President Seeks Corporate Advice and Consent," *Washington Post*, June 30, 1993, https://login.proxy.lib.duke.edu/login?url=https://www.proquest .com/newspapers/clintons-ceo-lunch-bunch-over-meals-president/docview /307642255/se-2; Robert Slater, *Jack Welch & The G.E. Way: Management Insights and Leadership Secrets of the Legendary CEO* (McGraw Hill, 1999), 1–3, EBSCOhost, search.ebscohost.com/login.aspx?direct=true&db=nlebk&AN=6945&site=eh ost-live&scope=site.

17 John Markoff, "Steven P. Jobs, 1955–2011: Apple's Visionary Redefined Digital Age." *The New York* Times, October 11, 2011. Web. https://www.nytimes.com/2011/10/06 /business/steve-jobs-of-apple-dies-at-56.html. Accessed July 14, 2023.

18 Walter Isaacson, *Steve Jobs* (New York: Simon & Schuster, 2011), 192–93.

19 Ibid., 209; Hayley Tsukayama, "What Was in Steve Jobs's FBI File," *Washington Post*, February 10, 2012, https://login.proxy.lib.duke.edu/login?url=https://www.proquest .com/newspapers/what-was-steve-jobss-fbi-file/docview/920745740/se-2.

20 Graham, *Personal History*, 611.

21 Ibid., 612.

22 Leonard Downie Jr., *All About the Story: News, Power, Politics, and the Washington Post* (New York: Hachette Book Group, 2020), 18; Remnick, "Citizen Kay."

23 Felsenthal, *Power, Privilege, and the Post,* 412; Hedrick Smith, *The Power Game: How Washington Works* (New York: Ballantine Books, 1988), 102–103; Nancy Reagan, *My Turn: The Memoirs of Nancy Reagan* (New York: Random House, 1989), 115.

24 Graham, *Personal History,* 611.

25 Brownstein, *The Power and the Glitter,* 219–20; Natale, "Lew Wasserman Dies."

26 Sharp, *Mr. & Mrs. Hollywood,* 209; Rose, "Twilight of the Last Mogul."

27 Sharp, *Mr. & Mrs. Hollywood,* 317–18; Brownstein, *The Power and the Glitter,* 220–21.

28 Sharp, *Mr. & Mrs. Hollywood,* 252, 266; "Films Viewed by President and Mrs. Reagan," The Ronald Reagan Presidential Library and Museum, https://www .reaganlibrary.gov/reagans/reagan-administration/films-viewed-president-and -mrs-reagan; Ronald Reagan, "Address Before a Joint Session of Congress on the State of the Union," February 4, 1986, The American Presidency Project, https: //www.presidency.ucsb.edu/documents/address-before-joint-session-congress-the -state-the-union. The Reagans watched *E.T.* on June 27, 1982; *Back to the Future* on July 26, 1985; *The Secret of My Success* on April 25, 1987; and *Dragnet* on July 18, 1987.

29 Sally Bedell Smith, "Issue and Debate; Rules on TV Networks' Syndication of Shows," *New York Times,* October 8, 1983, https://www.nytimes.com/1983/10/08/arts/issue -and-debate-rules-on-tv-networks-syndication-of-shows.html.

30 Tom Shales, "Prime-Time Power Plays," *Washington Post,* March 23, 1983. Web. https://www.washingtonpost.com/archive/lifestyle/1983/03/23/prime-time-power -plays/11de762f-332e-4908–89d2-ce5f53c80935/.

31 John Lippman, "The Man in the Spotlight," *Wall Street Journal,* June 22, 2007. Web. https://www.wsj.com/articles/SB118247306490644251.

32 Bruck, *When Hollywood Had a King,* 408.

33 Connie Bruck, "The Personal Touch," *The New Yorker,* August 13, 2001, https: //www.newyorker.com/magazine/2001/08/13/the-personal-touch-3.

34 Merrill Brown, "FCC Chief Called to Oval Office," *Washington Post,* October 4, 1983, https://www.washingtonpost.com/archive/business/1983/10/04/fcc-chief -called-to-oval-office/7d54cc2f-7ff0–433f-b4c5-bff280f02e26/.

35 Bruck, "The Personal Touch."

36 Brownstein, *The Power and the Glitter,* 221; Geraldine Fabrikant, "A Movie Giant's Unfinished Script," *New York Times,* October 20, 1985, https://www.nytimes .com/1985/10/20/business/a-movie-giant-s-unfinished-script.html; Ronald Brownstein, "A Trusted Ally of Politicians," *Los Angeles Times,* June 4, 2002, https: //www.latimes.com/archives/la-xpm-2002-jun-04-me-politics4-story.html.

37 Mark Weinberg, *Movie Nights with the Reagans* (New York: Simon & Schuster, 2018), 203.

38 Shapiro, "Lew Wasserman"; "A New Kind of King," *TIME,* January 1, 1965, 50–51.

39 Walter Isaacson, "In Search of the Real Bill Gates," *TIME,* January 13, 1997, https: //content.time.com/time/magazine/article/0,9171,1120657–1,00.html.

40 Ibid.

41   James Wallace, *Hard Drive: Bill Gates and the Making of the Microsoft Empire* (New York, Wiley, 1992), 41.

42   Matt Stoller, "How Reagan, Clinton, and Bill Gates Paved the Way for the Rise of Big Tech," Open Markets, November 1, 2019, https://www.openmarketsinstitute .org/publications/reagan-clinton-bill-gates-paved-way-rise-big-tech; William F. Shughart II, "Barbarians at Bill Gates," *The Freeman*, April 1, 2000, https://www .independent.org/publications/article.asp?id=155; Adam Cohen, "A Tale of Two Bills," *TIME* January 25, 1999, https://content.time.com/time/magazine/article /0,9171,18746,00.html.

43   Wendy Goldman, "'Oh No, Mr. Bill!': The Inside Story of the Antitrust Case Against Microsoft," *Wired*, April, 1994, https://www.wired.com/1994/04/gates-6.

44   "P. M. BRIEFING: Administration Vows Tougher Enforcement of Antitrust Laws," *Los Angeles Times*, November 3, 1989, https://www.latimes.com/archives/la-xpm -1989-11-03-fi-430-story.html.

45   John Burgess, "FTC Deadlocks Again in Microsoft Investigation," *Washington Post*, July 22, 1993, https://www.washingtonpost.com/archive/business/1993/07/22/ftc -deadlocks-again-in-microsoft-investigation/dd8ce8ed-1d66-4c32-b5af-6334 f422e364/.

46   Paul Freiberger, "Bugs in Radio Shack TRS-80 Model III: How Bad Are They?," InfoWorld, Special Section: "Tandy/Radio Shack: Past, Present, Future," InfoWorld Media Group, Inc, p. 50; Jennifer Edstrom and Marlin Eller, *Barbarians Led by Bill Gates* (New York: Henry Holt, 1998), 31.

47   Goldman, "Oh No, Mr. Bill!"; Stuart Taylor, "What to Do with the Microsoft Monster?," *The American Lawyer*, November 1, 1993, https://www.stuarttaylorjr .com/content-what-do-microsoft-monster/.

48   Evelyn Richards and Mark Potts, "FTC Expands Microsoft Probe," *Washington Post*, April 13, 1991, https://www.washingtonpost.com/archive/business /1991/04/13/ftc-expands-microsoft-probe/ee95b8b7-a794-43b5-982d-748bc4 c75f91/; John Markoff, "Justice Department Considers Inquiry on Microsoft," *New York Times*, August 1, 1993, https://www.nytimes.com/1993/08/01/us/justice -department-considers-inquiry-on-microsoft.html; Philip Elmer-Dewitt, "Tripping Up the Titan: A Judge Rejects Bill Gates' Antitrust Decree," *TIME*, February 27, 1995, https://content.time.com/time/subscriber/article/0,33009,982571,00.html; Taylor, "What to Do with the Microsoft Monster?"

49   Theron Mohamed, "Warren Buffett Has Repeatedly Defended His Right to Be Political, Yet He Still Hasn't Endorsed Joe Biden," *Business Insider*, November 2, 2020, https://markets.businessinsider.com/news/stocks/warren-buffett-defended -political-rights-not-endorsed-joe-biden-2020-11.

50   Alice Schroeder, *The Snowball: Warren Buffett and the Business of Life* (United Kingdom: Bantam Books, 2009), 27-29, 31-32, 46.

51   Ibid., 185-88; David M. Rubenstein, *How to Lead: Wisdom from the World's Greatest CEOS, Founders, and Game Changers* (New York: Simon & Schuster, 2020), 84; Roger Lowenstein, *Buffett: The Making of an American Capitalist* (New York: Random House, 2008), 165.

52   Pat Borzi, "Warren Buffett Meets a Relative Whose Biggest Asset Is His Pitching Arm," *New York Times*, June 22, 2016, https://www.nytimes.com/2016/06/22/sports /baseball/oklahoma-state-tyler-buffett-warren-buffett-cws.html.

53   Bruce Page and Elaine Potter, *The Murdoch Archipelago* (London: Simon & Schuster, 2011), eBook; David McKnight, *Murdoch's Politics: How One Man's Thirst for Wealth and Power Shapes Our World* (London: Pluto Press, 2003), ProQuest Ebook Central.

54   Kevin M. Kruse and Julian Zelizer, "Perspective: How Policy Decisions Spawned Today's Hyperpolarized Media," *Washington Post*, January 17, 2019, https://www .washingtonpost.com/outlook/2019/01/17/how-policy-decisions-spawned-todays -hyperpolarized-media/.

55   Mahler and Rutenberg, "How Rupert Murdoch's Empire of Influence Remade the World."

Chapter 9: After the Cold War

1   "Steve Jobs Files Held by the Clinton Library," Internet Archive, October 23, 2017, archive.org/details/SteveJobsMergedFiles/page/n13/mode/2up.

2   Matt Novak, "Newly Released Files Show Steve Jobs Gave President Clinton Unsolicited Cabinet Recommendations," Gizmodo, October 23, 2017, gizmodo.com /newly-released-files-show-steve-jobs-gave-president-cli-1818576482.

3   Ibid.; Ted Mann, "Steve Jobs Advised Bill Clinton about a Sensitive Issue," *The Atlantic*, October 30, 2013, www.theatlantic.com/national/archive/2011/10 /steve-jobs-advised-bill-clinton-about-sensitive-issue/336430/.

4   Isaacson, *Steve Jobs*, 277–78.

5   Isaacson, *Steve Jobs*, 323; Novak, "Newly Released Files Show Steve Jobs Gave President Clinton Unsolicited Cabinet Recommendations." For the record, the clue to the crossword puzzle in question was itself fitting to their relationship: "Jobs, to friends."

6   John Carney, "Steve Jobs Heroically Resisted Politics," CNBC, October 6, 2011, www .cnbc.com/id/44801531; Mann, "Steve Jobs Advised Bill Clinton about a Sensitive Issue."

7   James Wallace, *Overdrive: Bill Gates and the Race to Cyberspace* (New York: John Wiley and Sons, 1997), 73; author interview with Clinton Chief of Staff Thomas "Mack" McLarty, May 15, 2023.

8   James V. Grimaldi, "Trustbusters Put on a Stern Face; Clinton Team Tougher Than Predecessors, but New President May Shift Path," *Washington Post*, June 29, 2000, https://www.washingtonpost.com/archive/business/2000/06/29/trustbusters -put-on-a-stern-face/46d955d9-d108–4912-91b1-c9d1722cf2cd/.

9   Wendy Goldman Rohm, *The Microsoft File: The Secret Case Against Bill Gates* (New York: Crown, 1998), 130; Mike Mills, "The Competitive Nature of Anne K. Bingaman," *Washington Post*, November 17, 1997, https://www.washingtonpost .com/archive/business/1997/11/17/the-competitive-nature-of-anne-k-bingaman /edc1be2b-d028–4d76–8f7e-3d92ea6244e4/; Wallace, *Overdrive: Bill Gates and the Race to Cyberspace*, 69–70.

10   Shughart, "Barbarians at Bill Gates"; Goldman, "Oh No, Mr. Bill!"

11   Stoller, "How Reagan, Clinton, and Bill Gates Paved the Way for the Rise of Big Tech."

12   Goldman, "Oh No, Mr. Bill!"

13   Burgess, "FTC Deadlocks Again in Microsoft Investigation"; Tripp Mickle, *After Steve: How Apple Became a Trillion-Dollar Company and Lost Its Soul* (New York: Harper Collins, 2022), 157; Max Fisher, *The Chaos Machine: The Inside Story of How Social Media Rewired Our Minds and Our World* (New York, Little Brown, 2022), 25.

14   Stoller, "How Reagan, Clinton, and Bill Gates Paved the Way for the Rise of Big Tech."

15   Kruse and Zelizer, "Perspective: How Policy Decisions Spawned Today's Hyperpolarized Media."

16   Philip Elmer-Dewitt, "Mine, All Mine," *TIME*, June 24, 2001, https://content.time.com/time/magazine/article/0,9171,134241,00.html; Elizabeth Corcoran, "Appeals Panel Backs Justice, Microsoft Deal," *Washington Post*, June 17, 1995, https://www.washingtonpost.com/wp-srv/business/longterm/microsoft/stories/1995/rebuff061795.htm.

17   Elmer-Dewitt, "Mine, All Mine."

18   Gil Troy, *The Age of Clinton: America in the 1990s* (New York: St Martin's, 2015), 260; Elizabeth Wasserman, "Gates Deposition Makes Judge Laugh in Court," CNN, November 17, 1998, https://edition.cnn.com/TECH/computing/9811/17/judgelaugh.ms.idg/.

19   Steven Levy, "Breaking Windows," *Newsweek*, November 2, 1997, https://www.newsweek.com/breaking-windows-171218.

20   Adam Cohen, "Demonizing Gates," *TIME*, November 2, 1998, https://content.time.com/time/subscriber/article/0,33009,989451-1,00.html; Conversation with former DOJ official Larry Frankel, May 24, 2023.

21   Cohen, "Demonizing Gates."

22   Grimaldi, "Trustbusters Put on a Stern Face."

23   Ibid.

24   "Janet Reno Oral History," The Miller Center, September 27, 2004, https://millercenter.org/the-presidency/presidential-oral-histories/janet-reno-oral-history.

25   William Jefferson Clinton, "The President's News Conference with European Union Leaders in London, United Kingdom," May 18, 1998, The American Presidency Project, https://www.presidency.ucsb.edu/documents/the-presidents-news-conference-with-european-union-leaders-london-united-kingdom.

26   Ibid.

27   Troy, *The Age of Clinton,* 257.

28   Edstrom and Eller, *Barbarians Led by Bill Gates,* 182; Grimaldi, "Trustbusters Put on a Stern Face."

29   Matt Rosoff, "Microsoft's Stock Just Hit the Highest Point Since a Judge Ruled It Broke Antitrust Law Back in 2000," *Business Insider*, October 22, 2015, https://www.businessinsider.com/microsoft-stock-recovers-from-antitrust-hit-2015-10;

Robby Soave, *Tech Panic: Why We Shouldn't Fear Facebook and the Future* (New York: Threshold, 2021), 12–13; Fisher, *The Chaos Machine*, 225.

30   David Bank, "Gates Steps Aside as Microsoft's CEO; Ballmer to Take Over Daily Operations," *Wall Street Journal*, January 14, 2000, https://www.wsj.com /articles/SB947799478575341462; Noam Scheiber, "Why Microsoft Has Accepted Unions, Unlike Its Rivals," *New York Times*, February 25, 2024, https://www .nytimes.com/2024/02/25/business/economy/microsoft-corporate-progressive -labor.html?searchResultPosition=2.

31   Bank, "Gates Steps Aside as Microsoft's CEO."

32   Bill Clinton, "Interview with Ron Insana of CNBC's 'Business Center' in New York City," January 13, 2000, The American Presidency Project, https://www.presidency .ucsb.edu/documents/interview-with-ron-insana-cnbcs-business-center-new -york-city.

33   Wallace, *Overdrive*, 190.

34   Don van Natta Jr., "Presidential Mulligans; Taking Second Chances: Par for Clinton's Course," *New York Times*, August 29, 1999, https://www.nytimes.com/1999/08/29/ weekinreview/ideas-trends-presidential-mulligans-taking-second-chances -par-for-clinton-s.html.

35   "Clinton Golfs with Gates, Buffet," United Press International, August 27, 1994, https://www.upi.com/Archives/1994/08/27/Clinton-golfs-with-Gates -Buffet/6677777960000/; van Natta, "Presidential Mulligans; Taking Second Chances."

36   Cohen, "A Tale of Two Bills."

37   Bill Clinton, "Remarks at the National Teacher of the Year Award Ceremony," April 23, 1996 in *Public Papers of the Presidents of the United States, Book 1* (Washington, D.C.: U.S. Government Publishing Office, 1996), 619–21, https://www.govinfo.gov/ content/pkg/PPP-1996-book1/html/PPP-1996-book1-doc-pg619.htm; Bill Clinton, "Remarks at a Democratic National Committee Reception in Palo Alto, California," October 9, 1999, The American Presidency Project, https://www.presidency.ucsb .edu/documents/remarks-democratic-national-committee-reception-san -francisco-0.

38   Bill Clinton, "Remarks to the Community in Shoreline," February 24, 1996, The American Presidency Project, https://www.presidency.ucsb.edu/documents /remarks-the-community-shoreline.

39   "Closing the Digital Divide." White House-CEO panel. C-SPAN, April 5, 2000, https://www.c-span.org/video/?156362–1/closing-digital-divide.

40   Ibid.

41   "Press Briefing by Jake Siewert, Gene Sperling and P.J. Crowley," April 4, 2000, The American Presidency Project, University of California, Santa Barbara.

42   Ibid.

43   Ibid.

44   James V. Grimaldi, "Clinton's Aides Get Briefing on Microsoft," *Washington Post*, April 26, 2000, https://www.washingtonpost.com/archive/business/2000/04/26 /clintons-aides-get-briefing-on-microsoft/f2ed1083-f526–4834-92af -9052b2e9b821/; Patrick Martin, "Two Days after Antitrust Ruling, White House,

Congress Hail Microsoft Billionaire," World Socialist Web Site, April 8, 2000, https://www.wsws.org/en/articles/2000/04/mic-a08.html.

45   Felsenthal, *Power, Privilege, and the Post,* 450; Graham, *Personal History,* 611; Robin Gerber, *Katharine Graham* (New York: Penguin Group, 2005), 206.

46   George W. Bush, "Remarks on Presenting the Presidential Medal of Freedom," The American Presidency Project, July 9, 2002, https://www.presidency.ucsb.edu /documents/remarks-presenting-the-presidential-medal-freedom-5.

47   Brownstein, "A Trusted Ally of Politicians."

48   Ibid.; Bruck, *When Hollywood Had a King,* 471.

49   Sharp, *Mr. & Mrs. Hollywood,* 412–13; Bruck, *When Hollywood Had a King,* 471.

50   Bruck, *When Hollywood Had a King,* 473; Brownstein, "The Rebirth of Hollywood's Political Clout."

51   Bruck, *When Hollywood Had a King,* 473; Sharp, *Mr. & Mrs. Hollywood,* 412–13; Brownstein, "The Rebirth of Hollywood's Political Clout."

52   Sharp, *Mr. & Mrs. Hollywood,* 412–13; Bernard Weinraub, "Among Hollywood Democrats, President Is Supported as One of Their Own," *New York Times,* September 29, 1998, https://www.nytimes.com/1998/09/29/us/among-hollywood -democrats-president-is-supported-as-one-of-their-own.html.

53   "Freedom Fighters," *Washington Post,* December 1, 2001, https://www .washingtonpost.com/archive/lifestyle/1993/12/01/the-reliable-source/e2891526 -4eb0-486b-b6d1-b109da374445/; "Lew Wasserman to Be Awarded Presidential Medal of Freedom," *Los Angeles Times,* September 15, 1995, https://www.latimes .com/archives/la-xpm-1995-09-15-fi-46271-story.html.

54   Sharp, *Mr. & Mrs. Hollywood,* 418.

55   John Schmidt, "How We Created the WTO: A Memoir," *Wilson Quarterly,* Summer 2015, https://www.wilsonquarterly.com/quarterly/_/a-world-of-hopes-and-a-world -of-fears-how-we-created-the-wto; Mickey Kantor, "Michael 'Mickey' Kantor Oral History," The Miller Center, June 28, 2002, https://millercenter.org/the-presidency /presidential-oral-histories/michael-mickey-kantor-oral-history.

56   "'Mickey' Kantor Oral History."

57   Bruck, *When Hollywood Had a King,* 464–65.

58   Schroeder, *The Snowball,* 328–29; Lowenstein, *Buffett,* 391; Pat Borzi, "Warren Buffett Meets a Relative Whose Biggest Asset Is His Pitching Arm," *New York Times,* June 22, 2016, https://www.nytimes.com/2016/06/22/sports/baseball/oklahoma -state-tyler-buffett-warren-buffett-cws.html; Andrew Kilpatrick, *Of Permanent Value: The Story of Warren Buffett* (New York: McGraw-Hill, 2001), 130–31, 805–6.

59   Schroeder, *The Snowball,* 453–55; "Buffett Notes Bush Policies Favor Rich," *The Salina Journal,* March 7, 2004, page 29, https://newscomwc.newspapers.com/ image/5096298/?terms=%22Warren%20Buffett%22%20AND%20%22George%20 Bush%22&pqsid=8B1IQ8F6a_asW6JKwEz5tQ%3A631395%3A304258290&ma tch=1.

60   Warren Buffett, "Buy American. I Am," *New York Times,* October 17, 2008, https: //www.nytimes.com/2008/10/17/opinion/17buffett.html; Joe Weisenthal, "Warren Buffett: During the Financial Crisis, George W. Bush Made the Greatest Economic

Statement of All Time," Reuters, December 9, 2013, https://finance.yahoo.com/news/warren-buffett-during-financial-crisis-012500223.html.

61 Joyce Millman, "The Road to the White House Goes through Oprah," *Salon*, September 25, 2000, https://www.salon.com/2000/09/25/oprah_10/.

62 Ibid.

63 Ibid. Bush initially said that Buddy Holly sang "Wake Up, Little Susie" before correcting himself and saying it was The Everly Brothers.

64 Gelles, *The Man Who Broke Capitalism*, 142–43, 48–52.

65 Lisa Marsh, "You Don't Know Jack—GE's Welch: I Did It My Way," *New York Post*, August 29, 2001, https://nypost.com/2001/08/29/you-dont-know-jack-ges-welch-i-did-it-my-way/; Daniel McGinn, "Anne Mulcahy, Jack Welch, and CEOs as Presidential Advisors," *Harvard Business Review*, September 10, 2010, https://hbr.org/2010/09/do-former-ceo-make-good.

66 Aarthi Swaminathan, "Jack Welch, Legendary Former GE CEO, Dead at Age 84," Yahoo Finance, March 2, 2020, https://finance.yahoo.com/news/jack-welch-legendary-former-ge-ceo-dead-at-age-84–134324399.html.

67 McFadden, "Lee Iacocca, Visionary Automaker Who Led Both Ford and Chrysler, Is Dead at 94"; "Remarks at the NAFTA Jobs and Products Day Trade Fair," The American Presidency Project, https://www.presidency.ucsb.edu/documents/remarks-the-nafta-jobs-and-products-day-trade-fair.

68 Justin Hyde, "Iacocca on Attack in New Book: U.S. Auto Industry, Bush White House Are 2 of His Targets; Up Close," *The Sun*, April 13, 2007, https://login.proxy.lib.duke.edu/login?url=https://www.proquest.com/newspapers/iacocca-on-attack-new-book-u-s-auto-industry-bush/docview/406152864/se-2.

69 Iacocca and Whitney, *Where Have All the Leaders Gone?*, 49–53.

70 Roger Lowenstein, "Jamie Dimon: America's Least-Hated Banker," *New York Times*, December 1, 2010, https://www.nytimes.com/2010/12/05/magazine/05Dimon-t.html.

71 Lowenstein, "Jamie Dimon."

72 Mark H. Rose, *Market Rules: Bankers, Presidents, and the Origins of the Great Recession* (Philadelphia, Pennsylvania: University of Pennsylvania Press, 2019), 135.

73 Andrew Clark, "Bear Stearns Saved by Rock-Bottom JP Morgan Bid," *The Guardian*, March 16, 2008, https://www.theguardian.com/business/2008/mar/16/creditcrunch.useconomy3.

74 Gerald P. Dwyer. "Stock Prices in the Financial Crisis," Federal Reserve Bank of Atlanta, September 2009, https://www.atlantafed.org/cenfis/publications/notes-fromthevault/0909; "Bear Stearns Collapses, Sold to J.P. Morgan Chase," HISTORY, January 19, 2018, https://www.history.com/this-day-in-history/bear-stearns-sold-to-j-p-morgan-chase; James B. Stewart, "Eight Days," *The New Yorker*, September 14, 2009. Web. https://www.newyorker.com/magazine/2009/09/21/eight-days; Robert Rich, "The Great Recession, December 2007–June 2009," Federal Reserve Bank of Cleveland, November 22, 2013, https://www.federalreservehistory.org/essays/great-recession-of-200709.

75   Jo Becker, Sheryl Gay Stolbeg, and Stephen Labaton, "White House Philosophy Stoked Mortgage Bonfire," *The New York Times*, December 20, 2008, https://www .nytimes.com/2008/12/21/business/21admin.html.

76   Ibid.

77   Duff McDonald, *Last Man Standing: The Ascent of Jamie Dimon and JPMorgan Chase* (New York: Simon & Schuster, 2009), 317.

78   Rose, *Market Rules,* 155–56.

79   Lowenstein, "Jamie Dimon"; Henry M. Paulson, *On the Brink: Inside the Race to Stop the Collapse of the Global Financial System* (New York: Business Plus, 2010), 362.

80   Paulson, *On the Brink,* 368; Hoyt kept his promise and threw out the number. Email exchange with author, August 28, 2023.

81   "President Bush Discusses the Economy," The White House President George W. Bush Archive, October 17, 2008, https://georgewbush-whitehouse.archives.gov /news/releases/2008/10/20081017–4.html.

82   Lowenstein, "Jamie Dimon."

83   Danielle Douglas, "JPMorgan Remorse on Bear Stearns Prompts Question: Were Crisis Mergers Worth It?," *Washington Post*, October 28, 2012, https://www.washing tonpost.com/business/economy/jpmorgan-remorse-on-bear-stearns-prompts -question-were-crisis-mergers-worth-it/2012/10/26/02cda37c-1936–11e2-b97b -3ae53cdeaf69_story.html.

84   John Cassidy, "Mark Zuckerberg and the Making of Facebook," *The New Yorker,* May 8, 2006, https://www.newyorker.com/magazine/2006/05/15/me-media.

85   Cassidy, "Mark Zuckerberg and the Making of Facebook'; Ben Mezrich, *The Accidental Billionaires: The Founding of Facebook: A Tale of Sex, Money, Genius and Betrayal* (New York: Anchor Books, 2009), eBook.

86   Cassidy, "Mark Zuckerberg and the Making of Facebook."

87   Mezrich, *The Accidental Billionaires.*

88   Ibid.

89   Ibid.; Max Chafkin, *The Contrarian: Peter Thiel and Silicon Valley's Pursuit of Power* (New York: Penguin, 2021), 109.

90   Jann S. Wenner, *Like a Rolling Stone* (New York: Little, Brown and Company, 2022), eBook.

91   Cassidy, "Mark Zuckerberg and the Making of Facebook."

92   Jose Antonio Vargas, "The Face of Facebook," *The New Yorker*, September 13, 2010, https://www.newyorker.com/magazine/2010/09/20/the-face-of-facebook; Chafkin, *The Contrarian,* 294.

93   Wenner, *Like a Rolling Stone*; Jose Antonio Vargas, "The Face of Facebook."

94   Max Fisher, *The Chaos Machine: The Inside Story of How Social Media Rewired Our Minds and Our World* (Little, Brown and Company, 2022), 235–36, Adobe Digital Editions.

95   Sheera Frenkel and Cecilia Kang, "Mark Zuckerberg and Sheryl Sandberg's Partnership Did Not Survive Trump," *New York Times*, July 8, 2021, https://www .nytimes.com/2021/07/08/business/mark-zuckerberg-sheryl-sandberg-facebook .html.

96 Ibid.; Kai Strittmatter, *We Have Been Harmonized: Life in China's Surveillance State* (London: Old Street, 2019), 79, ProQuest Ebook Central.

97 Frenkel and Kang, "Mark Zuckerberg and Sheryl Sandberg's Partnership Did Not Survive Trump"; Benjamin Wofford, "The Infinite Reach of Joel Kaplan, Facebook's Man in Washington," *Wired*, March 10, 2022, https://www.wired.com/story /facebook-joel-kaplan-washington-political-influence/.

Chapter 10: Big Tech Domination

1 Isaacson, *Steve Jobs*, 543–46.

2 Doug Gross, "Photo Shows Obama at Dinner with Steve Jobs, Mark Zuckerberg," CNN, February 18, 2011, www.cnn.com/2011/TECH/innovation/02/18/steve.jobs. obama/index.html; Drake Baer, "Steve Jobs and President Obama Had a Dinner Together in 2011 That May Have Changed the Course of US History," *Business Insider*, January 8, 2015, www.businessinsider.com/when-steves-jobs-and -barack-obama-dined-2015-1.

3 Io Dodds, "From Self-Proclaimed 'Socialist' to Team Trump and DeSantis: Elon Musk's Curious Politics Revealed," *The Independent*, May 24, 2023, https: //www.independent.co.uk/news/world/americas/us-politics/elon-musk-twitter-deal -politics-b2345301.html.

4 Ashlee Vance, *Elon Musk: Tesla, SpaceX, and the Quest for a Fantastic Future* (HarperCollins, 2015). 27–28, 36–39.

5 Ibid., 47–59, 19–22; Max Chafkin, *The Contrarian: Peter Thiel and Silicon Valley's Pursuit of Power* (New York: Penguin, 2021), 72.

6 Vance, *Elon Musk: Tesla, SpaceX, and the Quest for a Fantastic Future*, 54.

7 Ibid., 19–20; Chafkin, *The Contrarian: Peter Thiel and Silicon Valley's Pursuit of Power*, 66.

8 "SpaceX Boss Reveals He Mistook President Obama for Cold-Calling Salesman When He Phoned to Congratulate Him on Successful Rocket Launch," *Daily Mail*, May 24, 2012, https://www.dailymail.co.uk/news/article-2149507/SpaceX-boss -reveals-mistook-President-Obama-cold-calling-salesman-phoned-congratulate -successful-rocket-launch.html.

9 Vance, *Elon Musk: Tesla, SpaceX, and the Quest for a Fantastic Future*, 268–69; Ananya Gairola, "Elon Musk Reveals What He Talked in His Only Meeting with Barack Obama: I Didn't 'Promote Tesla or SpaceX . . . ,'" Benzinga, April 17, 2023, https://www.benzinga.com/news/23/04/31823421/elon-musk-reveals -what-he-talked-in-his-only-meeting-with-barack-obama-i-didnt-promote-tesla -or-spac; Tariq Malik, "President Barack Obama Hails SpaceX's Rocket Landing Success at Sea," Space.com, April 9, 2016, https://www.space.com/32525-president -obama-hails-spacex-rocket-landing.html.

10 Vance, *Elon Musk: Tesla, SpaceX, and the Quest for a Fantastic Future*, 138; Tim Higgins, *Power Play: Tesla, Elon Musk, and the Bet of the Century* (Knopf Doubleday Publishing Group, 2021), 131–36; David R. Baker, "Efficient Vehicles Get a Big Push," *San Francisco Chronicle*, June 24, 2009, NewsBank, https://infoweb-newsbank-com .proxy.lib.duke.edu/apps/news/document-view?p=WORLDNEWS&docref=news /129073A3B661F388.

11   David R. Baker, "Much Riding on Success of Tesla Sedan," *San Francisco Chronicle*, June 19, 2012, NewsBank, https://infoweb-newsbank-com.proxy.lib.duke.edu/apps/news/document-view?p=WORLDNEWS&docref=news/13F8055228F5A820; Mitt Romney, "We Need an Environment for Jobs," *Orange County Register*, October 24, 2011, https://www.ocregister.com/2011/10/24/mitt-romney-we-need-an-environment-for-jobs/; Kara Swisher, "In Debate, Romney Lists Tesla with 'Losers,'" *Wall Street Journal*, October 4. 2012, https://www.wsj.com/articles/BL-DSB-9553.

12   David R. Baker, "Tesla Boosts U.S. Loan Program," *San Francisco Chronicle*, May 23, 2013, NewsBank, https://infoweb-newsbank-com.proxy.lib.duke.edu/apps/news/document-view?p=WORLDNEWS&docref=news/1467569FA6FC4920.

13   Barack Obama, "Remarks on Presenting the Presidential Medal of Freedom," February 15, 2011, The American Presidency Project, University of California, Santa Barbara; Barack Obama, "Remarks in El Paso, Texas," May 10, 2011, The American Presidency Project, University of California, Santa Barbara.

14   Barack Obama, "Remarks at an Obama Victory Fund 2012 Fundraiser in Medina, Washington," February 17, 2012, The American Presidency Project, University of California, Santa Barbara; Barack Obama, "Remarks at an Obama Victory Fund 2012 Fundraiser in Studio City, California," May 10, 2012. The American Presidency Project, University of California, Santa Barbara.

15   Barack Obama, "Remarks at the Mandela Washington Fellowship for Young African Leaders Presidential Summit Town Hall and a Question-and-Answer Session," July 28, 2014, The American Presidency Project, University of California, Santa Barbara.

16   Barack Obama, "Remarks at a Town Hall Meeting and a Question-and-Answer Session at Millennium Steel Service, LLC, in Princeton, Indiana," October 3, 2014, The American Presidency Project, University of California, Santa Barbara.

17   Barack Obama, "The President's News Conference in Issy-les-Moulineaux, France," December 1, 2015, The American Presidency Project, University of California, Santa Barbara; Barack Obama, "The President's Weekly Address," February 6, 2016, The American Presidency Project, University of California, Santa Barbara; Barack Obama, "Remarks and a Question-and-Answer Session at a Young Southeast Asian Leaders Initiative Town Hall Meeting in Ho Chi Minh City, Vietnam," May 25, 2016, The American Presidency Project, University of California, Santa Barbara.

18   Barack Obama, "Remarks on Presenting the Presidential Medal of Freedom," November 22, 2016," The American Presidency Project, University of California, Santa Barbara.

19   The Associated Press, "A NATION CHALLENGED: Briefly Noted; WINFREY WON'T TOUR FOR BUSH," *New York Times*, March 30, 2002, https://www.nytimes.com/2002/03/30/us/a-nation-challenged-briefly-noted-winfrey-won-t-tour-for-bush.html.

20   The Associated Press, "WINFREY WON'T TOUR FOR BUSH"; Izadi, "Oprah for President in 2020? Here's Everything You Need to Know."

21   Jeff Zeleny, "Oprah Endorses Obama," *New York Times*, The Caucus, May 2, 2007, https://archive.nytimes.com/thecaucus.blogs.nytimes.com/2007/05/03/oprah-endorses-obama-2/; "Obama Campaign Press Release Oprah Winfrey to Tour Early States with Barack Obama." The American Presidency Project, November

26, 2007, https://www.presidency.ucsb.edu/documents/obama-campaign-press -release-oprah-winfrey-tour-early-states-with-barack-obama.

22 "Oprah Talks to the Obamas," Oprah.com, https://www.oprah.com/world /oprah-interviews-the-obamas-obama-interview-in-o-magazine; Caitlin McDevitt, "Obama Honors Oprah at the White House," POLITICO, November 20, 2013, https://www.politico.com/blogs/click/2013/11/obama-honors-oprah-at-the-white -house-177969; David Wright, "Oprah Endorses: 'I'm with Her,'" CNN, June 16, 2016, https://www.cnn.com/2016/06/16/politics/oprah-clinton-endorsement/index .html.

23 "Jack Welch Blasts White House," *Daily Beast,* September 23, 2010, https: //www.thedailybeast.com/jack-welch-blasts-white-house.

24 Gelles, *The Man Who Broke Capitalism,* 143–46.

25 Ibid., 56–57, 85.

26 Ibid., 176–82; Matthew J. Belvedere, "Welch: Two Presidents Asked—If Trump Calls I'd Turn Down His Cabinet Offer, Too," CNBC, June 2, 2016, https://www.cnbc .com/2016/06/02/welch-two-presidents-asked-if-trump-calls-id-turn-down-his -cabinet-offer-too.html; Matthew J. Belvedere, "Jack Welch on Why He's Voting for Trump," CNBC, September 20, 2016, https://www.cnbc.com/2016/09/20/jack-welch -on-why-hes-voting-for-trump.html.

27 Tim Levin and Lloyd Lee, "Elon Musk and Donald Trump Now Own Rival Social Networks. Here's a Timeline of Their Rocky Relationship," *Business Insider,* November 15, 2022, https://www.businessinsider.com/elon-musk-donald-trump -feud-relationship-timeline-2022–7.

28 Levin and Lee, "Elon Musk and Donald Trump Now Own Rival Social Networks"; Higgins, *Power Play,* 284; Danielle Muoio, "Elon Musk and Other Executives Are at The White House to Meet with President Trump," *Business Insider,* January 23, 2017, https://www.businessinsider.com/teslas-elon-musk-meets-trump-in-white- house-2017–1; Carolyn Lochhead, "Trump Spurns Climate Accord," *San Francisco Chronicle,* June 2, 2017, NewsBank, https://infoweb-newsbank-com.proxy .lib.duke.edu/apps/news/document-view?p=WORLDNEWS&docref=news/164C4 DD4E7E9B278; David R. Baker, "New Tariffs Put Squeeze on Firms," *San Francisco Chronicle,* March 9, 2018, NewsBank, https://infoweb-newsbank-com.proxy.lib .duke.edu/apps/news/document-view?p=WORLDNEWS&docref=news/16A89A5 44F2F2948.

29 Jena McGregor, "Elon Musk, the Say-Anything CEO," *Washington Post,* December 16, 2018, https://login.proxy.lib.duke.edu/login?url=https://www .proquest.com/newspapers/elon-musk-say-anything-ceo/docview/2156723810/se-2; Higgins, *Power Play,* 362–63; Levin and Lee, "Elon Musk and Donald Trump Now Own Rival Social Networks."

30 Vance, *Elon Musk.* 80–82.

31 Levin and Lee, "Elon Musk and Donald Trump Now Own Rival Social Networks."

32 Isaacson, "In Search of the Real Bill Gates"; Abby Johnston, "Melinda Gates 'Still Discussing' If She and Bill Gates Will Endorse a Presidential Candidate," The 19th, May 4, 2021, https://19thnews.org/2020/08/melinda-gates-still-discussing -if-she-and-bill-gates-will-endorse-a-presidential-candidate/.

33   Lisa Hagen, "Bill Gates meets with Trump," *The Hill*, December 13, 2016. https://thehill.com/homenews/administration/310151-bill-gates-to-meet-with-trump/.

34   Sean Spicer, "Press Briefing by Press Secretary Sean Spicer," March 20, 2017, The American Presidency Project, University of California, Santa Barbara.

35   Joe McCarthy, "The 2 Things Bill Gates Told Trump during Their Meeting," *Global Citizen*, March 16, 2018, https://www.globalcitizen.org/es/content/bill-gates-meeting-with-donald-trump-foreign-aid/; "Bill Gates Draws Laughs at Trump's EXPENSE, Says US PRESIDENT Confused HIV with HPV," *The Straits Times*, May 18, 2018, https://www.straitstimes.com/world/united-states/bill-gates-draws-laughs-at-trumps-expense-says-us-president-confused-hiv-with.

36   Eli Blumenthal, "Bill Gates in the White House? Trump Offered Him a Job As White House Science Advisor, He Says," *USA Today*, April 30, 2018, https://www.usatoday.com/story/tech/science/2018/04/30/bill-gates-white-house-trump-offered-him-job-white-house-science-advisor-he-says/566386002; Marco della Cava, "Bill Gates Hasn't Directly Criticized Trump. And He Has Stuck to That (Mostly)," *USA Today*, February 12, 2019, https://www.usatoday.com/story/news/nation/2019/02/12/bill-gates-congress-pushing-back-against-donald-trump/2814093002/.

37   Stuart Emmrich, "Bill Gates Warned of a Global PANDEMIC Five Years Ago. Why Isn't He Running THE Coronavirus Task Force?," *Vogue*, April 15, 2020, https://www.vogue.com/article/bill-gates-trump-who-coronavirus-task-force. Gates was not alone in his concerns. This author wrote in his 2016 book *Shall We Wake the President?* that we were unprepared for coronaviruses and had no countermeasures in the Strategic National Stockpile to deal with them, prompting *National Review*'s Jim Geraghty to write on March 17, 2020, that "Tevi Troy is a farshtunken oracle and everyone should read everything he writes. While Gates was indeed prescient, there were many reasons to be concerned about the prospect of a pandemic, and Gates was far from the only one aware of the danger.

38   Timothy Bella, "Bill Gates, in Rebuke of Trump, Calls WHO Funding Cut During Pandemic 'As Dangerous As It Sounds," *Washington Post*, April 15, 2020, https://www.washingtonpost.com/nation/2020/04/15/who-bill-gates-coronavirus-trump/.

39   Betsy McKay, "Bill Gates Has Regrets," *Wall Street Journal*, May 11, 2020, https://www.wsj.com/articles/bill-gates-coronavirus-vaccine-covid-19-11589207803?mod=tech_lead_pos2; Isobel Asher Hamilton, "Bill Gates Dismisses Trump's Claim That COVID-19 Cases Are Rising Only Because of Increased Testing As 'Completely False,'" *Business Insider*, June 26, 2020, https://www.businessinsider.com/bill-gates-donald-trump-coronavirus-testing-increased-cases-completely-false-2020-6; Inyoung Choi, "Bill Gates Called Microsoft's Potential TikTok Deal a 'Poison Chalice' and Said 'Who Knows What's Going to Happen,'" *Business Insider*, August 8, 2020, https://www.businessinsider.com/bill-gates-calls-microsofts-potential-tiktok-deal-a-poison-chalice-2020–8.

40   Bill Gates, "'We Are Running the Worst Testing System' of Any Country," *Meet The Press*, October 7, 2020, https://www.nbcnews.com/meet-the-press/video/bill-gates-we-are-running-the-worst-testing-system-of-any-country-93555269803; Matthew J. Belvedere, "Bill Gates Slams U.S. on Covid: Most Governments Listen

to Their Scientists, Not Attack Them," CNBC, October 14 2020, https://www.cnbc
.com/2020/10/14/bill-gates-slams-us-on-covid-most-governments-listen-to
-scientists.html; Max Zahn and Andy Serwer, Bill Gates Slams Trump's COVID-19
Adviser As 'Pseudo-Expert' Who's 'Off-The-Rails,'" Yahoo Finance, October 26,
2020, https://finance.yahoo.com/news/bill-gates-slams-trump-covid-adviser-scott
-atlas-143302816.html.

41 Daisuke Wakabayashi, Davey Alba, and Marc Tracy, "Bill Gates, at Odds with
Trump on Virus, Becomes a Right-Wing Target," *New York Times*, April 17, 2020,
https://www.nytimes.com/2020/04/17/technology/bill-gates-virus-conspiracy
-theories.html; Bill Gates (@BillGates), "I look forward to working with the new
administration and leaders on both sides . . ." Twitter, November 7, 2020, 1:09 p.m.,
https://x.com/BillGates/status/1325138315964682246.

42 Gael Fashingbauer Cooper and Marguerite Reardon, "Bill Gates Says He's Ready to
Work with President Biden on COVID, Climate," CNET, January 20, 2021, https:
//www.cnet.com/news/politics/bill-gates-says-hes-ready-to-work-with
-president-biden-on-covid-climate/; Thomas Catenacci, "Biden's Energy Secretary
Took Meeting with Bill Gates Immediately after Senate Confirmation," Fox News,
November 23, 2022, https://www.foxnews.com/politics/bidens-energy-secretary
-took-meeting-bill-gates-immediately-senate-confirmation.

43 Jeff Mason, "Bill Gates, Dozens of World Leaders to Attend Biden Climate Summit
-Source," Thomson Reuters, April 20, 2021, https://www.reuters.com/business
/sustainable-business/bill-gates-dozens-world-leaders-attend-biden-climate-summit
-source-2021–04-20/; Bill Gates, "My White House Remarks on COVID,"
GatesNotes, May 12, 2022, https://www.gatesnotes.com/White-House-Global
-COVID-Summit; James Freeman, "When Bill Gates Dines with Politicians . . .
taxpayers beware!," *Wall Street Journal*, August 17, 2022, https://www.wsj.com
/articles/when-bill-gates-dines-with-politicians-11660760504.

44 Ben Mezrich, *The Accidental Billionaires: The Founding of Facebook: A Tale of Sex,
Money, Genius and Betrayal* (New York: Doubleday, 2009), 248; Benjamin Mullin
and Nicole Sperling, "Netflix's Reed Hastings Will Cede Co-Chief Executive Role,"
New York Times, January 19, 2023, https://www.nytimes.com/2023/01/19/business
/media/netflix-reed-hastings.html?smid=nytcore-ios-share&referringSource
=articleShare.

45 John McCormick, "Buffett Is Obama Meal Ticket," *Chicago Tribune*, August 16,
2007, https://www.chicagotribune.com/chi-obama_thuaug16-story.html; Carol
Loomis and Nina Easton, "What Obama Means for Business," in *Tap Dancing to
Work: Warren Buffett on Practically Everything, 1966–2012,* (New York: Portfolio
Penguin, 2012), 285; Sewell Chan, "Obama Meets with Warren Buffett," *New York
Times*, July 14, 2010, archive.nytimes.com/thecaucus.blogs.nytimes.com/2010/07/14
/obama-meets-with-warren-buffett/?searchResultPosition=1.

46 Carrie Budoff Brown and Jennifer Epstein, "The Obama Paradox," POLITICO, June
1, 2014, https://www.politico.com/story/2014/06/the-obama-paradox-107304;
Warren E. Buffett, "A Minimum Tax for the Wealthy," *New York Times*, November
25, 2012, www.nytimes.com/2012/11/26/opinion/buffett-a-minimum-tax-for-the
-wealthy.html?searchResultPosition=1.

47   Paul R. La Monica, "Warren Buffett on President-Elect Trump: 'He Deserves Everybody's Respect,'" CNN Business, November 11, 2016, money.cnn .com/2016/11/11/investing/warren-buffett-donald-trump-stock/; Thomas Franck, "Trump Says Warren Buffett Has Been Right 'His Whole Life,' but Made a Mistake Selling Airlines," CNBC, June 5, 2020, https://www.cnbc.com/2020/06/05/trump -says-warren-buffetts-airline-stock-sale-was-a-mistake.html; Trip Gabriel, "US Election: Warren Buffett Takes Aim at Donald Trump," *New York Times*, August 2, 2016, https://www.smh.com.au/business/us-election-warren-buffett-calls-donald -trump-afraid-20160802-gqiykf.html; "Warren Buffett Dares Donald Trump to Release their Tax Returns Together," *ProQuest*, August 1, 2016, https: //login.proxy.lib.duke.edu/login?url=https://www.proquest.com/blogs-podcasts -websites/warren-buffett-dares-donald-trump-release-their/docview/1808885366 /se-2; Matthew J. Belvedere, "Warren Buffett: Here's Why I Haven't Been Criticizing Donald Trump," CNBC, August 30, 2017, https://www.cnbc.com/2017/08/30 /warren-buffett-heres-why-i-havent-been-criticizing-donald-trump.html; Jude Joffe-Block, "Warren Buffett Did Not Donate to Biden Presidential Campaign," *AP News*, January 28, 2021, apnews.com/article/fact-checking-afs:Content:9930768811.

48   Belvedere, "Warren Buffett: Here's Why I Haven't Been Criticizing Donald Trump"; La Monica, "Warren Buffett on President-Elect Trump: 'He Deserves Everybody's Respect.'"

49   Wright, "Oprah Endorses: 'I'm with Her'"; Nick Maslow, "Trump Once Wanted Oprah Winfrey to Be His Vice President," *Entertainment Weekly*, January 8, 2018, https://ew.com/tv/2018/01/08/donald-trump-oprah-winfrey-vice-president-larry -king-live/.

50   Maslow, "Trump Once Wanted Oprah Winfrey to Be His Vice President." Mike Allen, "Exclusive: Trump Publishing Private Letters from Oprah, Other Celebrities in New Book," Axios, March 9, 2023, https://www.axios.com/2023/03/09/trump -book-oprah-private-letters-celebrities.

51   Izadi, "Oprah for President in 2020? Here's Everything You Need to Know."

52   Scott Bixby, "How Oprah Helped Joe Biden Speak to the Nation After 9/11," *The Daily Beast*, September 10, 2021, https://www.thedailybeast.com/how-oprah -helped-joe-biden-speak-to-the-nation-after-911.

53   "Oprah Reacts to Biden and Harris's Election: 'The Soul of America Gets a Reset,'" Oprah.com. https://www.oprah.com/inspiration/oprahs-reaction-to-the-2020 -presidential-election-outcome.

54   Paul Bond, "Murdoch Says Media Too Rough on Bush," Reuters, April 25, 2007, www.reuters.com/article/industry-media-murdoch-dc/murdoch-says-media-too- rough-on-bush-idUSN2519316620070425; Brian Stelter, "Fox's Volley with Obama Intensifying," *New York Times*, October 12, 2009. www.nytimes.com/2009/10/12 /business/media/12fox.html.

55   Peter Baker and Susan Glasser, *The Divider: Trump in the White House, 2017–2021* (New York: Doubleday, 2022), eBook; Stelter, "Fox's Volley with Obama Intensifying"; "White House Advisers Say Fox News Is Not News," *St. Augustine Record*, October 20, 2009, https://www.staugustine.com/story/news/2009/10/20/white-house -advisers-say-fox-news-not-news/16220556007/.

56   Stelter, "Fox's Volley with Obama Intensifying"; Jeff Greenfield, "President Obama's Feud with Fox News," CBS News, October 24, 2009, https://www.cbsnews.com/news/president-obamas-feud-with-fox-news/.

57   Stelter, "Fox's Volley with Obama Intensifying"; "White House Advisers Say Fox News Is Not News."

58   Lowenstein, "Jamie Dimon"; Rachel Weiner, "Jamie Dimon, Democrat?," *Washington Post* (blog), June 14, 2012, https://www.washingtonpost.com/blogs/the-fix/post/jamie-dimon-democrat/2012/06/14/gJQAEEnicV_blog.html; Jackie Calmes and Louise Story, "In Washington, One Bank Chief Still Holds Sway," *New York Times*, July 18, 2009, https://www.nytimes.com/2009/07/19/business/19dimon.html; Danielle Douglas and Steven Mufson, "JPMorgan Chase CEO Jamie Dimon's Complicated Relationship with Washington," *Washington Post*, November 1, 2013, https://www.washingtonpost.com/business/economy/jpmorgan-chase-ceo-jamie-dimons-complicated-relationship-with-washington/2013/11/01/6806f9d4-3c3d-11e3-b6a9-da62c264f40e_story.html.

59   Calmes and Story, "In Washington, One Bank Chief Still Holds Sway"; Noam Scheiber, "The Breakup," *The New Republic*, June 17, 2010, https://newrepublic.com/article/75614/the-breakup; Patricia Crisafulli, *The House of Dimon: How JPMorgan's Jamie Dimon Rose to the Top of the Financial World* (Hoboken, New Jersey: Wiley, 2009), 8.

60   Calmes and Story, "In Washington, One Bank Chief Still Holds Sway."

61   Ibid;

62   Eamon Javers and Carol E. Lee, "Bank Execs Miss Obama's Tough Talk," *POLITICO*, December 14, 2009, https://www.politico.com/story/2009/12/bank-execs-miss-obamas-tough-talk-030568.

63   Ibid.; Brian Montopoli, "Obama Versus the 'Fat Cats,'" CBS News, December 13, 2009; https://www.cbsnews.com/news/obama-versus-the-fat-cats/.

64   Javers and Lee, "Bank Execs Miss Obama's Tough Talk."

65   Scheiber, "The Breakup"; Javers and Lee, "Bank Execs Miss Obama's Tough Talk."

66   Douglas and Mufson, "JPMorgan Chase CEO Jamie Dimon's Complicated Relationship with Washington."

67   Victoria McGrane, "Left Rips Obama Bonus Comments," *POLITICO*, February 10, 2010, https://www.politico.com/story/2010/02/left-rips-obama-bonus-comments-032795.

68   Ibid.

69   Ibid.

70   "Press Briefing by Press Secretary Robert Gibbs," The American Presidency Project, January 26, 2010, https://www.presidency.ucsb.edu/documents/press-briefing-press-secretary-robert-gibbs-68.

71   Douglas and Mufson, "JPMorgan Chase CEO Jamie Dimon's Complicated Relationship with Washington."

72   Ibid.

73   "JPMorgan's Dimon Hits Back at Government over Bear Stearns Suit," Reuters, October 11, 2012, https://www.reuters.com/article/us-jpmorgan-dimon-bearstearns-idUSBRE8991CE20121011.

74   Calmes and Story, "In Washington, One Bank Chief Still Holds Sway."

75   "Occupy Wall Street Protesters Target JPMorgan Chase CEO Jamie Dimon—Who Is Overseas," CBS News, October 12, 2011, https://www.cbsnews.com/newy ork/news/occupy-wall-street-protesters-plan-to-demonstrate-outside-jpmorgan chase-hq/.

76   Neil Irwin, "Sorry, Warren Buffett, Jamie Dimon Probably Wouldn't Make a Great Treasury Secretary," *Washington Post*, November 28, 2012, https://www .washingtonpost.com/news/wonk/wp/2012/11/28/sorry-warren-buffett-jamie -dimon-probably-wouldnt-make-a-great-treasury-secretary/.

77   Jeanne Cummings, "Rove's Patented Strategies Will Endure," *POLITICO*, August 13, 2007, https://www.politico.com/story/2007/08/roves-patented-strategies-will -endure-005375.

78   Chafkin, *The Contrarian*, 135; Robby Soave, *Tech Panic: Why We Shouldn't Fear Facebook and the Future.* (New York: Threshold, 2021), 16–18.

79   Randi Zuckerberg, *Dot Complicated: Untangling Our Wired Lives* (New York: Harper One, 2013), 31, Adobe Digital Editions.

80   Ibid., 33.

81   Ibid., 39.

82   Barack Obama, "Remarks by the President at Global Entrepreneurship Summit and Conversation with Mark Zuckerberg and Entrepreneurs," June 25, 2016, https: //obamawhitehouse.archives.gov/the-press-office/2016/06/25/remarks-president -global-entrepreneurship-summit-and-conversation-mark.

83   Obama, "Remarks by the President at Global Entrepreneurship Summit and Conversation with Mark Zuckerberg and Entrepreneurs"; Tevi Troy, *What Jefferson Read, Ike Watched, and Obama Tweeted: 200 Years of Popular Culture in the White House* (Washington, D.C.: Regnery History, 2013), 148.

84   Mark Milian, "Obama Targets Youth, Tech Crowd at Facebook Town Hall," CNN, April 20, 2011, http://www.cnn.com/2011/POLITICS/04/20/obama.facebook /index.html; Tevi Troy, *What Jefferson Read, Ike Watched, and Obama Tweeted: 200 Years of Popular Culture in the White House* (Washington, D.C.: Regnery History, 2013), 232.

85   Maury Litwack, "What Did Zuckerberg Accomplish With That Bush Meeting?," *Business Insider*, December 6, 2010, https://www.businessinsider.com/what-was -zuckerberg-trying-to-accomplish-with-that-bush-meeting-2010–12.

86   Ibid.

87   Zuckerberg, *Dot Complicated*, 8.

88   Barack Obama and Mark Zuckerberg, "Remarks by the President at a Facebook Town Hall," April 20, 2011, https://obamawhitehouse.archives.gov/the-press -office/2011/04/20/remarks-president-facebook-town-hall; Jamie Weil, *Mark Zuckerberg: Creator of Facebook* (North Mankato, Minnesota: Abdo Publishing, 2015), 5–7, eBook.

89   Obama and Zuckerberg, "Remarks by the President at a Facebook Town Hall"; Milian, "Obama Targets Youth, Tech Crowd at Facebook Town Hall."

90   Zuckerberg, *Dot Complicated*, 12; Milian "Obama Targets Youth, Tech Crowd at Facebook Town Hall."

91   Lis Smith, *Any Given Tuesday: A Political Love Story* (New York: Harper Collins, 2022), 155, eBook.

92   Joshua Green, "Google's Eric Schmidt Invests in Obama's Big Data Brains," *Bloomberg*, May 31, 2013, https://www.bloomberg.com/news/articles/2013–05-30/googles-eric-schmidt-invests-in-obamas-big-data-brains#xj4y7vzkg; "Eric Schmidt: Obama's Chief Corporate Ally," *Tech Transparency Report*, April 26, 2016, https://www.techtransparencyproject.org/articles/eric-schmidt-obamas-chief-corporate-ally; David Dayen, "THE ANDROID ADMINISTRATION," *The Intercept*, April 22 2016, https://theintercept.com/2016/04/22/googles-remarkably-close-relationship-with-the-obama-white-house-in-two-charts/.

93   Hannah Parry and Chris Spargo, "'They Were on Our Side': Obama Campaign Director Reveals Facebook ALLOWED Them To Mine American Users' Profiles in 2012 Because They Were Supportive of the Democrats," *Daily Mail*, March 19, 2018, https://www.dailymail.co.uk/news/article-5520303/Obama-campaign-director-reveals-Facebook-ALLOWED-data.html; Alexis C. Madrigal, "What Facebook Did to American Democracy," *The Atlantic*, October 12, 2017, https://www.theatlantic.com/technology/archive/2017/10/what-facebook-did/542502/.

94   Tony Romm, "Zuckerberg, Tech Execs Meet Obama," *POLITICO*, March 21, 2014, https://www.politico.com/story/2014/03/mark-zuckerberg-barack-obama-tech-ceos-nsa-104907.

95   Ibid.

96   Adam Entous, Elizabeth Dwoskin, and Craig Timberg, "Obama Tried to Give Zuckerberg a Wake-up Call over Fake News on Facebook," *Washington Post*, September 24, 2017, https://www.washingtonpost.com/business/economy/obama-tried-to-give-zuckerberg-a-wake-up-call-over-fake-news-on-facebook/2017/09/24/15d19b12-ddac-4ad5-ac6e-ef909e1c1284_story.html.

97   Everett Rosenfeld, "Jamie Dimon Hints at Prediction That Hillary Clinton Will Win," CNBC, October 17, 2016, https://www.cnbc.com/2016/10/17/jamie-dimon-hints-at-prediction-that-hillary-clinton-will-win.html.

98   Jacob Pramuk, "Jamie Dimon: Heavy Business Presence in Trump's White House Is a 'Good Reset,'" CNBC, December 23, 2016, https://www.cnbc.com/2016/12/23/jamie-dimon-heavy-business-presence-in-trumps-white-house-is-a-good-reset.html.

99   Henry Blodget, "At a Private Lunch in Davos, Jamie Dimon Was Asked about the Elephant in the Room," *Business Insider*, https://www.businessinsider.com/jame-dimon-trump-davos-2017-1.

100   Emily Stewart, "Donald Trump vs. JPMorgan CEO Jamie Dimon, Explained," *Vox*, September 16, 2018, https://www.vox.com/policy-and-politics/2018/9/16/17866670/jamie-dimon-comments-trump-tweet-jpmorgan; "Remarks at a Meeting of the President's Strategic and Policy Forum," The American Presidency Project, February 3, 2017, https://www.presidency.ucsb.edu/documents/remarks-meeting-the-presidents-strategic-and-policy-forum.

101   "Remarks at a Meeting of the President's Strategic and Policy Forum," The American Presidency Project, February 3, 2017.

102 Mark H. Rose, *Market Rules: Bankers, Presidents, and the Origins of the Great Recession* (Philadelphia, Pennsylvania: University of Pennsylvania Press, 2019), 191–192; Bess Levin, "The Trump-Dimon Love Affair Is Getting Messy," *Vanity Fair*, May 16, 2017, https://www.vanityfair.com/news/2017/05/the-trump -dimon-love-affair-is-getting-messy.

103 "Jamie Dimon Says He Won't Leave Trump's Strategic and Policy Forum," Fox Business, May 16. 2017, https://www.foxbusiness.com/markets/jamie-dimon-says -he-wont-leave-trumps-strategic-and-policy-forum.

104 Saheli Roy Choudhury, "JPMorgan's Dimon Says Disagrees with Trump Decision to Quit Climate Deal, but 'We Have a Responsibility to Engage Our Elected Officials,'" CNBC, June 2, 2017, https://www.cnbc.com/2017/06/02/jpmorgan-ceo -dimon-disagrees-with-trumps-decision-to-withdraw-from-climate-deal.html.

105 Lucinda Shen, "Jamie Dimon on Why He Parted Ways with Trump: 'Racism, Intolerance and Violence Are Always Wrong,'" Yahoo Finance, August 16, 2017, https://finance.yahoo.com/news/jamie-dimon-why-parted-ways-191201501.html.

106 Shen, "Jamie Dimon on Why He Parted Ways With Trump.'"

107 Liz Moyer, "Dimon, Other CEOs Talk Jobs and Economic Growth at Private White House Dinner with Trump," CNBC, February 23, 2018, https://www.cnbc .com/2018/02/23/dimon-other-ceos-talk-jobs-and-economic-growth-at-private -white-house-dinner-with-trump.html.

108 Stewart, "Donald Trump vs. JPMorgan CEO Jamie Dimon, Explained."

109 Ibid.; Donald J. Trump (@realDonaldTrump), "The problem with banker Jamie Dimon running for President . . . ," September 13, 2018, 7:22 a.m., https://twitter .com/realdonaldtrump/status/1040198906842427392.

110 "Holding Megabanks Accountable: A Review of Global Systemically Important Banks 10 Years after the Financial Crisis," Hearing before the Committee on Financial Services, U.S. House of Representatives, One Hundred Sixteenth Congress, First Session, April 10, 2019, Washington: U.S. Government Publishing Office, 2020, p. 1.

111 "Remarks on the Public Debt Limit," The American Presidency Project, October 6, 2021, https://www.presidency.ucsb.edu/documents/remarks-the-public-debt-limit; Chase Williams, "JPMorgan CEO after Overseas Visit: China 'Not a 10-Foot Giant,'" Fox Business, June 6, 2023, https://www.foxbusiness.com/politics /jpmorgan-ceo-china-visit; Erin Clark, "These Four CEOs Got the Most Face Time With Biden in 2021," *Report Door*, December 30, 2021, https://www.reportdoor.com /these-four-ceos-got-the-most-face-time-with-biden-in-2021/. The other three were Ford CEO Jim Farley, General Motors CEO Mary Barra, and Walmart CEO Doug McMillon.

112 Cheryl Teh, "JPMorgan CEO Dimon Declined to Answer Question on Second Trump Term," *Business Insider*, April 7, 2023, https://www.businessinsider.com /jpmorgan-ceo-dimon-declined-answer-question-second-trump-term-2023–4.

113 Leander Kahney, *Tim Cook: The Genius Who Took Apple to the Next Level* (New York: Penguin Publishing Group,: 2019), 25.

114 Ibid.,

115 Kelly Hodgkins, "President Obama Meets with Tim Cook, Others," Engadget, November 19, 2012, https://www.engadget.com/2012–11-19-president-obama -meets-with-tim-cook-others.html; Neil Hughes, "President Obama Calls Apple CEO Tim Cook to Discuss Fiscal Cliff," Apple Insider, November 19, 2012, https: //appleinsider.com/articles/12/11/19/president-obama-calls-apple-ceo-tim -cook-to-discuss-fiscal-cliff.

116 Tony Romm, "Obama, Tech Execs Talk Surveillance," *POLITICO*, August 8, 2013, www.politico.com/story/2013/08/tim-cook-barack-obama-technology-095362; Dominic Rushe, "Apple CEO Tim Cook Challenges Obama with Impassioned Stand on Privacy," *The Guardian*, February 13, 2015, www.theguardian.com/technology /2015/feb/13/apple-ceo-tim-cook-challenges-obama-privacy.

117 Jenna McLaughlin, "Apple's Tim Cook Lashes out at White House Officials for Being Wishy-Washy on Encryption," *The Intercept*, January 12, 2016, theintercept. com/2016/01/12/apples-tim-cook-lashes-out-at-white-house-officials-for-being -wishy-washy-on-encryption; Seung Lee, "Apple CEO Wished for More Dialogue with Government," *Newsweek*, February 24, 2016, www.newsweek.com/watch-apple -ceo-tim-cook-says-hes-disappointed-obama-administrations-approach-430096.

118 Ben Smith, "The Facebook Election," Buzzfeed, November 9, 2014. https://www .buzzfeednews.com/article/bensmith/the-facebook-election.

119 Ibid.

120 Robinson Meyer, "Here's How Facebook Could Tilt the 2016 Election," *The Atlantic*, April 18, 2016, https://www.theatlantic.com/technology/archive/2016/04/how -facebook-could-tilt-the-2016-election-donald-trump/478764/.

121 Kahney, *Tim Cook,* 177–78.

122 Russell Brandom, "Why Tim Cook Made Friends with Donald Trump," The Verge, November 20, 2019, www.theverge.com/2019/11/20/20973991/trump-tim-cook -apple-friendship-tax-cuts-china-tariffs-manufacturing-jobs.

123 Austin Carr and Mark Gurman, "Tim Cook's $2.3 Trillion Fortress," *Bloomberg Businessweek*, no. 4689, February, 2021, pp. 40–45, *EBSCOhost*, search.ebsco host.com/login.aspx?direct=true&db=bth&AN=148641744&site=ehost -live&scope=site; Tripp Mickle, "How Tim Cook Won Donald Trump's Ear," *Wall Street Journal*, October 5, 2019, https://www.wsj.com/articles/how-tim-cook-won -donald-trumps-ear-11570248040.

124 Andrew O'Hara, "Tim Cook and Lisa Jackson Attend President Trump's First State Dinner," Apple Insider, April 25, 2018, https://appleinsider.com/articles /18/04/25/tim-cook-and-lisa-jackson-attend-president-trumps-first-state-dinner; Mikey Campbell, "Apple CEO Tim Cook Cites GOP Tax Reform as Driver in $350B US Investment," Apple Insider, January 18, 2018, https://appleinsider.com/articles /18/01/17/apple-ceo-tim-cook-cites-gop-tax-reform-as-driver-in-350b-us -investment.

125 Maegan Vazquez, "How Apple's Tim Cook Built a Relationship with Trump." CNN, November 20, 2019, www.cnn.com/2019/11/20/politics/tim-cook-donald -trump-apple-tour-austin-texas/index.html. This was not the only time that Trump called a CEO by the company name. He once called Lockheed Martin's Marilyn Hewson "Marilyn Lockheed."

126 Mickle, "How Tim Cook Won Donald Trump's Ear."
127 Carr and Gurman, "Tim Cook's $2.3 Trillion Fortress"; Annabelle Williams, "Tim Cook Says Apple's Strategy for Dealing with Biden Will be the Same as Dealing with Trump," *Business Insider,* April 5, 2021, https://login.proxy.lib.duke.edu/login?url=https://www.proquest.com/newspapers/tim-cook-says-apples-strategy-dealing-with-biden/docview/2508705599/se-2; "Chips Built in the U.S. at Arizona Factory," CNBC, December 6, 2022, https://www.cnbc.com/2022/12/06/tim-cook-says-apple-will-use-chips-built-in-the-us-at-arizona-factory.html.
128 Jonathan Mahler and Jim Rutenberg, "How Rupert Murdoch's Empire of Influence Remade the World," *The New York Times.*
129 Ibid.; Peter Baker and Susan Glasser, *The Divider*; Kruse and Zelizer, "Perspective: How Policy Decisions Spawned Today's Hyperpolarized Media."
130 Baker and Glasser, *The Divider.*
131 "Highlights from New Fox News Documents Released in Dominion Lawsuit," *Washington Post*, March 7, 2023, www.washingtonpost.com/media/2023/03/07/fox-news-lawsuit; Dominick Mastrangelo, "How Murdoch's Media Empire Turned on Trump in 2022," *The Hill*, December 28, 2022, https://thehill.com/homenews/media/3783998-how-murdochs-media-empire-turned-on-trump-in-2022/.
132 Brian Stelter, "Biden Called Murdoch the 'Most Dangerous Man in the World,' New Book Alleges," CNN Business, April 3, 2022, https://amp.cnn.com/cnn/2022/04/03/media/reliable-sources-biden-murdoch-fox-news/index.html.
133 Robinson Meyer, "Here's How Facebook Could Tilt the 2016 Election," *The Atlantic.*
134 Michael Nunez, "Facebook Employees Asked Mark Zuckerberg If They Should Try to Stop a Donald Trump Presidency," Gizmodo, April 15, 2016, https://gizmodo.com/facebook-employees-asked-mark-zuckerberg-if-they-should-1771012990.
135 Jim Tankersley, "Why Donald Trump's 1980s-Style Campaign is Struggling in 2016," *Washington Post*, August 20, 2016, https://www.washingtonpost.com/news/wonk/wp/2016/08/20/why-donald-trumps-1980s-style-campaign-is-struggling-in-2016; Alexis Madrigal, "What Facebook Did to American Democracy," *The Atlantic.*
136 Joshua Green and Sasha Issenberg, "Inside the Trump Bunker, With 12 Days to Go," *Bloomberg*, October 27, 2016, https://www.bloomberg.com/news/articles/2016-10-27/inside-the-trump-bunker-with-12-days-to-go; Dareh Gregorian and Frank Thorp V, "Trump, Mark Zuckerberg Hold Surprise White House Meeting," NBC News, September 19, 2019, https://www.nbcnews.com/politics/donald-trump/trump-mark-zuckerberg-hold-surprise-white-house-meeting-n1056721; Ben Smith, "What's Facebook's Deal With Donald Trump?," *New York Times*, June 22, 2020, https://www.nytimes.com/2020/06/21/business/media/facebook-donald-trump-mark-zuckerberg.html.
137 Joshua Green and Sasha Issenberg, "Inside the Trump Bunker, with 12 Days to Go," *Bloomberg*; Alexis Madrigal, "What Facebook Did to American Democracy," *The Atlantic.*
138 Entous, Dwoskin, and Timberg, "Obama Tried to Give Zuckerberg a Wake-up Call over Fake News on Facebook," *Washington Post.*

139 Mollie Hemingway, *Rigged: How the Media, Big Tech, and the Democrats Seized Our Elections* (Washington D.C.: Regnery Publishing, 2021), 5; Frenkel and Kang, "Mark Zuckerberg and Sheryl Sandberg's Partnership Did Not Survive Trump," *New York Times.*

140 Hemingway, *Rigged*, 5; Entous, Dwoskin, and Timberg, "Obama Tried to Give Zuckerberg a Wake-up Call over Fake News on Facebook"; Max Read, "Does Even Mark Zuckerberg Know What Facebook Is?," *New York Magazine*, December 1, 2017, https://nymag.com/intelligencer/2017/10/does-even-mark-zuckerberg-know-what-facebook-is.html.

141 Frenkel and Kang, "Mark Zuckerberg and Sheryl Sandberg's Partnership Did Not Survive Trump."

142 Sheera Frenkel and Cecilia Kang, *An Ugly Truth: Inside Facebook's Battle for Domination* (New York: Harper Collins, 2021), 146–48.

143 Chafkin, *The Contrarian*, 245.

144 Ibid., viii.

145 Gregorian and Thorp, "Trump, Mark Zuckerberg Hold Surprise White House Meeting."

146 Frenkel and Kang, *An Ugly Truth: Inside Facebook's Battle for Domination*, 13; William P. Barr, *One Damn Thing After Another: Memoirs of an Attorney General* (New York: Harper Collins, 2022), eBook.

147 Chafkin, *The Contrarian*, ix, 304; Ben Smith, "What's Facebook's Deal With Donald Trump?," *New York Times.*

148 Chafkin, *The Contrarian*, ix, 304; Ben Gilbert, "Mark Zuckerberg Said Trump Is 'Exactly the Same in Person as You'd Expect Him to Be from the Stuff That He Says Publicly,'" *Business Insider*, September 9, 2020, https://www.businessinsider.com/zuckerberg-says-trump-is-exactly-who-you-expect-2020–9; Smith, "What's Facebook's Deal With Donald Trump?"

149 Ben Gilbert, "President Trump Says Mark Zuckerberg Running for President 'Wouldn't Be Too Frightening,'" *Business Insider*, January 23, 2020, https://www.businessinsider.com/president-donald-trump-facebook-mark-zuckerberg-running-for-president-2020–1.

150 Donald Trump (@realDonaldTrump), "Great honor, I think?" February 14, 2020, 6:38 p.m., https://twitter.com/realDonaldTrump/status/1228463577335554049.

151 Donald Trump, "Remarks at a 'Make America Great Again' Rally in Colorado Springs, Colorado," February 20, 2020), The American Presidency Project, University of California Santa Barbara, https://www.presidency.ucsb.edu/documents/remarks-make-america-great-again-rally-colorado-springs-colorado.

152 Ibid.

153 Frenkel and Kang, *An Ugly Truth: Inside Facebook's Battle for Domination*, 227; Benjamin Wofford, "The Infinite Reach of Joel Kaplan, Facebook's Man in Washington," *Wired.*

154 Wofford, "The Infinite Reach of Joel Kaplan, Facebook's Man in Washington."

155 Donie O'Sullivan and Jason Hoffman, "Trump and Zuckerberg Spoke on the Phone Friday," CNN, May 31, 2020, https://www.cnn.com/2020/05/31/media/trump-zuckerberg-phone-call/index.html.

156 Ibid.; Wofford, "The Infinite Reach of Joel Kaplan, Facebook's Man in Washington."

157 Frenkel and Kang, *An Ugly Truth: Inside Facebook's Battle for Domination*, 229–30; Max Fisher, *The Chaos Machine*, 237.

158 Irina Ivanova, "Mark Zuckerberg Slams Trump Administration Response to COVID-19," CBS MONEYWATCH, July 17, 2020, https://www.cbsnews.com /news/mark-zuckerberg-facebook-trump-administration-response-coronavirus -pandemic; Queenie Wong, "Facebook Built a New Center to Direct People to Accurate Coronavirus Information," CNET, March 18, 2020, https://www.cnet.com /tech/tech-industry/facebook-built-a-new-center-to-direct-people-to-accurate -coronavirus-information/.

159 Robby Soave, *Tech Panic*, 37; Wofford, "The Infinite Reach of Joel Kaplan, Facebook's Man in Washington."

160 Editorial, "Washington Post, New York Times Finally Admit Hunter's Laptop Is Real—But Only to Protect Joe Biden Some More," *New York Post*, April 1, 2022, https://nypost.com/2022/04/01/new-york-times-finally-admit-hunters-laptop -is-real-but-only-to-protect-joe-biden/.

161 Derek Saul, "Elon Musk Spreads Misleading Claim About Mark Zuckerberg Donating Millions to Get Biden in Office," *Forbes*, April 18, 2023, https://www .forbes.com/sites/dereksaul/2023/04/18/elon-musk-spreads-misleading-claim-about -mark-zuckerberg-donating-millions-to-get-biden-in-office/.

162 Parker Thayer and Hayden Ludwig, "BREAKING: New IRS Disclosures Confirm Flood of Private Money to Elections Offices from Zuckerberg Grantee," Capital Research Center December 16, 2021, https://capitalresearch.org/article/breaking -new-irs-disclosures-confirm-flood-of-private-money-to-elections-offices-from -zuckerberg-grantee/.

163 Hemingway, *Rigged*, 90–91; Saul, "Elon Musk Spreads Misleading Claim About Mark Zuckerberg Donating Millions to Get Biden in Office"; Thayer and Ludwig, "New IRS Disclosures Confirm Flood of Private Money to Elections Offices from Zuckerberg Grantee."

164 Saul, "Elon Musk Spreads Misleading Claim About Mark Zuckerberg Donating Millions to Get Biden in Office"; Associated Press, "Zuckerberg Money Won't Be in Next Round of Aid for Elections," April 11, 2022, https://ktar.com/story/5001978 /zuckerberg-money-wont-be-in-next-round-of-aid-for-elections/.

165 Shannon Bond, "Meta Allows Donald Trump Back on Facebook and Instagram," *National Public Radio*, January 25, 2023, https://www.npr.org/2023/01/25/1146961818 /trump-meta-facebook-instagram-ban-ends.

166 Grace Kay, "Elon Musk Has Called Biden a 'Damp Sock Puppet,' and Feuded with the President for Months, but Biden Shared Some Rare Praise for the Billionaire Earlier This Month," *Business Insider*, February 25, 2023, https://www .businessinsider.com/joe-biden-elon-musk-feud-tesla-union-republican-06–2022.

167 Ibid.

168 Vishwam Sankaran, "Elon Musk Changes Twitter algorithm So His Tweets Get Seen by '1000 times' More People than Normal, Report Claims," Yahoo News, February 15, 2023, https://news.yahoo.com/elon-musk-threatened-fire-twitter-061729161. html; Faiz Siddiqui, "How Auto Regulators Played Mind Games with Elon Musk,"

Washington Post, March 28, 2022, https://login.proxy.lib.duke.edu/login?url=https://www.proquest.com/newspapers/how-auto-regulators-played-mind-games-with-elon/docview/2643851931/se-2; "The Harassment of Elon Musk," *Wall Street Journal*, September 22, 2023, https://www.wsj.com/articles/elon-musk-biden-administration-justice-department-investigations-accdd84a.

169 Zachary Basu, "The Republicanization of Elon Musk," Axios, December 1, 2022, https://www.axios.com/2022/12/01/elon-musk-twitter-republican-conservative-politics.

170 Charlotte Klein, "Mark Zuckerberg Is Already Sucking Up to a Biden Administration," *Vanity Fair*, November 23, 2020, https://www.vanityfair.com/news/2020/11/mark-zuckerberg-facebook-joe-biden-administration.

171 Ibid.

172 Max Fisher, *The Chaos Machine*, 299.

173 Soave, *Tech Panic*, 65

174 The Dispatch Staff, "The Morning Dispatch: Biden and Tech," *The Dispatch*, March 11, 2021, https://thedispatch.com/newsletter/morning/the-morning-dispatch-biden-and-tech/.

175 Katherine Tangalakis-Lippert, "Despite Being Out of Office For a Year And a Half, Donald Trump Said 'Weirdo' Mark Zuckerberg Joined Him at the White House for Dinner 'Last Week,'" *Business Insider*, September 3, 2022, https://www.businessinsider.com/trump-weirdo-mark-zuckerberg-white-house-last-week-rally-pennsylvania-2022–9.

176 Wofford, "The Infinite Reach of Joel Kaplan, Facebook's Man in Washington"; Soave, *Tech Panic*, 18.

177 Soave, *Tech Panic*, 4–6; Alexandra Marquez, "Barack Obama Is Popular, Mark Zuckerberg Is Not: NBC News Poll," NBC News, November 7, 2022, https://www.nbcnews.com/meet-the-press/meetthepressblog/barack-obama-popular-mark-zuckerberg-not-nbc-news-poll-rcna55994.

Conclusion

1 William P. Barr, *One Damn Thing After Another: Memoirs of an Attorney General* (New York: William Morrow, 2022), eBook.

2 Thomas C. "Mack" McLarty, email interview with the author, August 7, 2023,

3 Mack McLarty interview; Tim Carney, email interview with the author, July 25, 2023.

4 Ibid.

5 Mack McLarty interview; The Dispatch Staff, "The Morning Dispatch: Biden and Tech," *The Dispatch*, March 11, 2021, https://thedispatch.com/newsletter/morning/the-morning-dispatch-biden-and-tech/.

6 Mack McLarty interview.

7 Tim Carney interview.

8 See Appendix 2.

Appendix 1: CEO Models of Engagement

1   William P. Barr, *One Damn Thing After Another: Memoirs of an Attorney General* (New York: William Morrow, 2022), eBook.

Appendix 2: The Development of Federal Tools for Influencing Private Sector Activity

1   Federal Register, "Federal Register Pages Published, 1936—2018," https://www .federalregister.gov/uploads/2019/04/stats2018Fedreg.pdf; Mark Febrizio and Melinda Warren, "Regulators' Budget: Overall Spending and Staffing Remain," George Washington University Regulatory Studies Center, July, 2020, https: //regulatorystudies.columbian.gwu.edu/regulators-budget-overall-spending-and -staffing-remain-stable. Done in consultation with Baron Public Affairs.

Appendix 3: CEO Joke Files

1   Mark Twain, *The $30,000 Bequest, and Other Stories,* Urbana, Illinois: Project Gutenberg, https://www.gutenberg.org/cache/epub/142/pg142-images.html.

INDEX